LINCOLN CHRISTIAN COLLEGE AND SEMINARY
P9-CML-996

TRENCH'S SYNONYMS OF THE NEW TESTAMENT

TRENCH'S SYNONYMS OF THE NEW TESTAMENT

R. C. Trench

Trench's Synonyms of the New Testament
Hendrickson Publishers, Inc.
P.O. Box 3473
Peabody, Massachusetts 01961-3473

Printed in the United States of America
ISBN 1-56563-559-0

Originally published under the title

Synonyms of the New Testament
by Baker Books,
a division of Baker Book House Company
Grand Rapids, Michigan 49516, U.S.A.

Hendrickson Publishers' edition reprinted by arrangement with Baker Book House Company.

First Printing — March 2000

Contents

Editor's Preface

Trench's *Synonyms of the New Testament* has been a popular and informative work since it first was published in 1876. This revised edition of Trench includes the following improvements:

1. Greek and Hebrew words that appear in the Bible have been coded according to *The New Strong's Exhaustive Concordance of the Bible* (Nashville: Thomas Nelson, 1984). Other Greek words are cited according to their meaning and pagination in Liddell-Scott's *A Greek-English Lexicon* (Oxford: Clarendon Press).
2. All quotations from foreign languages have been translated into English.
3. Foreign language titles to works by classical and ecclesiastical authors have been spelled out.
4. The entire book has been completely rewritten by John J. Hughes and Claire M. Hughes to modernize and simplify the English style, spelling, punctuation, and sentence structure.
5. Unless specified to the contrary, the New King James Version is the version cited.

Robert G. Hoerber

Author's Preface

This volume grew out of a course of lectures on New Testament synonyms delivered in fulfillment of my duties as professor of divinity at King's College, London. Apart from those higher and more solemn lessons that only God imparts, I have never doubted that there are few things a theological teacher should have more at heart than awakening in his students an enthusiasm for grammatical and lexical studies. We shall have done much for our students if we can persuade them to have grammars and lexicons continually in their hands and if we can make them believe that with these, and out of these, they may learn much that is real and lasting and that will remain with them forever. Grammatical and lexical studies will nourish the mind and spirit and help prepare students for their future work more effectively than reading many a volume of divinity.

As these lectures now will reach a larger audience, I would like to make a few observations on the value of studying synonyms in general and New Testament synonyms in particular. Additionally, I will mention helps for studying synonyms and include a few remarks suggested by my own experience.

Studying synonyms trains the mind by developing precise and accurate habits of thought, and it provides a wealth of knowledge. This has been implicitly recognized by most great writers, many of whom have, from time to time, studied synonyms. Studying Greek synonyms is even more rewarding, since the Greeks were a people of the subtlest intellect who saw distinctions where others saw none and who cultivated the study and use of synonyms. Thus the characteristic excellencies of the Greek language invite us to investigate the likenesses and differences between words.

There are additional reasons for studying New Testament synonyms. Because the words of the New Testament are God's words, it is important that we understand every delicate variation in an author's meaning. Increasing our intellectual riches through the study of New Testament synonyms will increase our spiritual wealth as well. And because the words of the New Testament bring eternal life to those who receive them in faith, it is important that we fathom their exact force and their intricate relationships. Failure to receive the words of the New Testament as the living and powerful words of God breeds all manner of corruptions and heresies, as the history of the church plainly shows.

The words of the New Testament are eminently the *stoicheia* ("elements," "basic principles") of Christian theology. He who will not begin his theological investigations with a patient study of these words will never make secure or significant theological advances. As is true in all other fields of study, the whole may not be possessed without embracing all of its parts. Studying synonyms necessarily compels a patient and accurate investigation of the words of the text.

I am only too aware of the deficiencies of this present work. Even if the present material were better, I have left an immense number of New Testament synonyms untouched, among which are some of the most interesting and instructive (see appendix). I can only hope and pray that despite its shortcomings, this volume may not wholly miss its aim, which is to lead its readers into a closer and more accurate investigation of the Word of God, in whom "all riches of wisdom and knowledge are contained."

Before concluding, I wish to discuss a few of the rules and principles that should guide the proper study of synonyms. These principles mainly concern the proper selection of passages.

When we say that two or more words are synonyms, we implicitly affirm two things: there are many passages where either word could be suitably used, and there are some passages where only one of the words may properly be used or where one word is more suitable than the other. The latter type of passage is the most important for the study of synonyms, and students of synonyms must be able to recognize these passages. Although identifying these passages is more an art than a science, a few hints may help.

First, find good writers who make careful distinctions between words, especially authoritative authors whose writings contain extended discussions of lexical issues. Distinguishing synonyms comes naturally to great writers. Second, locate passages in which words are used antithetically. Third, discover passages where words are used climactically, that is, where each successive word is stronger than the previous ones. These passages show the relative strength of words in a group of synonyms. Fourth, find passages where great writers alternate one synonym with another. These passages reveal the propriety of using one synonym in one context and another synonym in a different context. Fifth, observe the words with which each synonym is used. These passages disclose the synonym's domain of meaning and show if the synonym habitually is associated with one or more words. Relationships between synonyms and other words may reveal similarities and differences of meaning. Sixth, study equivalent synonyms in cognate and other languages. Seventh, when studying ethical terms, try to learn all the names by which virtues and vices have been called, especially the vocabulary used to ridicule virtues and to honor vices. Such deceitfully misused terms may reveal much about the true meaning of the nomenclature for virtues and vices.

Finally, it requires great skill to match the proper pairs or sets of synonyms. The more similar the words, the more likely they are to be confused. No words can be too near in meaning to one another, since the closer they are in meaning, the more they need to be distinguished. In such cases, the student needs to be very careful in discriminating between them. The more dissimilar the words, the more unlikely it is that they are synonyms. For example, *scarlet* and *crimson* are so similar that they may be confused, but *scarlet* and *green* are so dissimilar that one does not need to explain the difference between them. It may be helpful to distinguish *pride* and *arrogance*, but who needs to distinguish *pride* and *covetousness*?

1

ekklēsia (1577) *synagōgē* (4864) *panēgyris* (3831) — Church Synagogue Assembly Congregation

There are words whose etymology it is interesting to watch as they are transformed and consecrated by the Christian church—words that the church did not invent but has employed in a loftier sense than the world has ever used them. The very word by which the church is named is a key example of this type of transformation.[1] For we have *ekklēsia* in three distinct stages of meaning—the secular, the Jewish, and the Christian. As a secular term, *hē ekklēsia* (= *ekklētoi*)[2] was the lawful assembly of free Greek citizens met to

1. In his interesting lecture, *Profangräcität und Biblischer Sprachgeist* ([*Secular Greek and Biblical Linguistics Genius*] Leipzig, 1859), p. 5, Zezschwitz correctly noted: "Christianity would not have emerged victorious over Greek and Roman culture, as it did, had it succeeded in speaking (or had it let itself be coerced into speaking) in terms of the basic concepts of Greek ideology, of the Greek worldview. Only by means of *refashioning the language*—by eliminating what was vulgar, by stressing what Greek thinking had tended too long to ignore, and finally by transforming that by which Hellenism, so ethically oriented from a genuinely human perspective from its very beginning, had attained as a preliminary stage of divine truth—only in a Greek thus adapted and its basic concepts *Christianized* could Christ's apostles transmit the language of the Spirit, who spoke through them, to a world at the time so thoroughly Greek in its orientation and outlook."

2. L-S 509, selected to judge or to arbitrate, a committee of citizens chosen to report; Euripides, *Orestes* 939.

transact public affairs. That they were *summoned* is expressed in the latter part of the word; the first syllable indicates that they were summoned *out of* the whole population as a select portion that included neither the populace, strangers, nor those who had forfeited their civic rights. Both the *calling* (the *klēsis* [*2821*]; Phil. 3:14; 2 Tim. 1:9) and the calling *out* (the *eklogē* [*1589*]; Rom. 11:7; 2 Pet. 1:10) are the distinctives that make the word well adapted for its new Christian usage.[3] It is interesting to observe how the word returns to this earlier significance on one occasion in the New Testament (Acts 19:32, 39, 41).

Before more fully considering *ekklēsia*, however, it is necessary to review the earlier history of *synagōgē*. Although *synagōgē* occurs two or three times in Plato,[4] it is by no means an old word in classical Greek. It completely lacks the technical signification that it began to receive in the Septuagint, and even more plainly in the Apocrypha, and that it has fully acquired in the New Testament. But *synagōgē*, while evolving in this direction, did not lose the meaning it had in classical Greek; it often denotes any gathering or bringing together of persons or things.[5] Between the closing of the Old Testament canon and the opening of the New, *synagōgē* acquired the technical meaning that it possesses when the gospel history begins. It designates the places set apart for purposes of worship and the reading and expounding of the Word of God, the "synagogues." Although numerous, they were the necessary complement of the temple, which by divine intention was unique.

Ekklēsia did not pass immediately from the heathen world to the Christian church; the Septuagint supplied the point of transition. When the Alexandrian translators undertook the rendering of the Hebrew Scriptures, they found two constantly recurring words: *ʿēdāh* (5712) and *qāhāl* (6951). For these they employed their most adequate Greek equivalents: *synagōgē* and *ekklēsia*. This is the rule they seem to have followed: to render *ʿēdāh* for the most part by *synagōgē*[6] and never by *ekklēsia*. We may wish that they had shown the same consistency with respect to *qāhāl*, but they did not. Although

3. Both of these points are well made by Flacius Illyricus in his *Clavis Scriptura* under the word *payecclēsia*: "Because the word *church* comes from the word *to call*, this fact should be noted first. For this reason the conversion of people is termed a 'calling,' not only because God calls through himself and his Word, as if with a shout, but also because as a master summons from a crowd of slaves some specific ones for some particular deeds, so also God calls at times his entire people to his worship [Hos. 11:1], and at times he calls also individual persons to specific and particular functions [Acts 13:2]. Since, however, God's people are called not only to the worship of God but also are called out of the rest of the crowd or the mass of the human race, therefore they are given the name *church*, as you might say, divinely summoned out of the remaining dregs of the impious to the worship and praising of God and to everlasting happiness." Cf. Witsius, *In symbolis*, pp. 394–97.

4. *Theaetetus* 150a.

5. See *synagōgē ethnōn* (*1484*, gathering of people; Gen. 48:4); *synagōgē hudaton* (*5204*, gathering of water; Isa. 19:6); *synagōgē chrēmatōn* (*5536*, gathering of goods; Ecclus. 31:3); and other examples.

6. Exod. 12:3; Lev. 4:13; Num. 1:2; altogether more than a hundred times.

ekklēsia is the more frequent rendering of *qāhāl*,[7] *synagōgē* is also used,[8] thus breaking down for the Greek reader the distinction that undoubtedly exists between the words. Our Authorized Version shows the same lack of consistency in its use of "congregation" and "assembly." Instead of constantly assigning one English word to the same Hebrew word, it renders *'ēdāh* now by "congregation" (Lev. 10:17; Num. 1:16; Josh. 9:27) and now by "assembly" (Lev. 4:13). *Qāhāl* is sometimes translated "assembly" (Judg. 21:8; 2 Chron. 30:23) but much more often "congregation" (Judg. 21:5; Josh. 8:35).

Vitringa has an interesting discussion on the distinction between these two Hebrew synonyms.

> *Qāhāl*, strictly speaking, denotes an entire multitude of some people united by the bonds of society and making up a republic or a certain state, while the word *'ēdāh*, from the nature and force of its emphasis, speaks of only any assembly and gathering of people, whether small or large.[9]

Later in the same discussion, he says:

> *Synagōgē*, as also *'ēdāh*, always signifies an assembly joined and gathered together, although bound by no strong bond; but *hē ekklēsia* [= *qāhāl*] designates some multitude which makes up a people joined together by laws and bonds, although frequently they may happen not to be assembled or are not able to be assembled.[10]

This distinction resulted in the choice of *ekklēsia* by Christ (Matt. 16:18; 18:17) and his apostles as the more noble of the two words. It designated the new society of which Jesus was the founder, being as it was a society knit together by the closest spiritual bonds and altogether independent of space.

The title *ekklēsia*, however, is not wholly withdrawn from the Jewish congregation; that too was "the *church* in the wilderness" (Acts 7:38), for the Christian and Jewish congregations differed only in degree and not in kind. *Synagōgē* is not wholly renounced by the church; the only Christian use of it in the New Testament is by James (2:2), the apostle who maintained unbroken to the latest possible moment the outward bonds connecting the synagogue and the church. *Episynagōgē* (1997), I may add, on two occasions is honorably used but in a more general sense (2 Thess. 2:1; Heb. 10:25).[11] Still, there were causes at work that led the faithful to use *synagōgē* less and less of themselves and in the end to leave it to those whom the Lord had characterized for their fierce opposition to the truth as "the *synagogue* of Satan" (Rev. 3:9; cf. John 8:4). In addition, the use of *ekklēsia* became more widespread as

7. Deut. 18:16; Judg. 20:2; 1 Kings 8:14; in all some seventy times.

8. Lev. 4:13; Num. 10:3; Deut. 5:22; in all some twenty-five times.

9. *De synagoga vetere*, p. 80.

10. Ibid., p. 88.

11. Occasionally in the early church fathers, we find *synagōgē* still employed as an honorable designation of the church or of her places of assembly. See Ignatius, *Epistula ad Polycratem* 4. For other examples, see Suicer, *Thesaurus*, under this word.

the church rooted itself more predominantly in the soil of the secular world, breaking away from its Jewish stock and stem. The use of *synagōgē* declined because it was permanently associated with Jewish worship, while the use of *ekklēsia* increased, not only because it was already familiar but also because it had an honorable meaning in Greek culture. It is interesting that the Ebionites (in reality a Jewish sect, though temporarily part of the Christian church) acknowledged the appropriateness of this distribution of terms. Epiphanius reports of the Ebionites: "These people call their own congregation an assembly and not a church."[12]

Given these conclusions, Augustine, by a piece of good fortune, was only half in the wrong when he transferred his Latin etymologies to the Greek and Hebrew without pausing to enquire whether they would hold good there. He finds the reason for attributing *synagōgē* to the Jewish church and *ekklēsia* to the Christian church in the fact that *convocatio* (= *ekklēsia*) is a nobler term than *congregatio* (= *synagōgē*). *Convocatio* is the *calling* together of *men*, while the second term is the *gathering* together (*congregatio*, from *congrego* [gather together], and that from *grex* [herd, flock]) of *cattle.*[13]

The *panēgyris* differs from the *ekklēsia*. In the *ekklēsia* there is the sense of an assembly coming together for the transaction of business, while the *panēgyris* was a solemn assembly whose purpose was festal rejoicing.[14] Business might grow out of the fact that such multitudes were assembled (and many for various reasons would be glad to avail themselves of the gathering) but only in the same way as a "fair" grew out of a "feria" and a "holiday" out of a "holy-day." Strabo notes the businesslike aspect that the *panēgyreis* commonly assumed[15] and that was to such an extent their prominent feature that the Latins rendered *panēgyris* by *mercatus* (festive assembly), even when the Olympic games were intended.[16] These, with the other solemn games, were eminently, though not exclusively, the *panēgyreis* of the Greek nation.[17] Keeping this festal character of the *panēgyris* in mind, we shall find a peculiar fitness in the word's employment in Hebrews 12:23, the only place in the

12. *Adversus haereses* 30.18.

13. *Enarratio in Psalma* 82:1: "In a synagogue we receive the people of Israel, because their assembly is correctly accustomed to be called a synagogue, although it might also have been called a church. We [Christians] have never called a church a synagogue but always a church, either for the purpose of differentiation or because there should be a distinction between a gathering together (whence *synagogue*) and a calling together (whence the church has received its name), since, naturally, even cattle are accustomed *to be gathered together* (and we correctly speak also of their *herds*); but *to be called together* is rather a characteristic of those who use reason, as do human beings." So also the author of a *Commentary on the Book of Proverbs*, which was formerly ascribed to Jerome (*Opera*, 5:533); and by Vitringa (*De synagoga vetere*, p. 91) cited as his. Also see Field, *On the Church* 1.5.

14. Consequently, it was joined with *heortē* (*1859*, festival). See Philo, *De vita Mosis* 2.7; Ezek. 46:11; cf. Hos. 2:11; 9:5; and Isa. 66:10, where *panēgyrizein* (L-S 1297, to celebrate or to attend a public festival) is equal to *heortazein* (*1858*, to observe a festival). The word has given us "panegyric," which is a set discourse pronounced at one of these great festal gatherings.

15. "The festive assembly is some commercial affair" (10.5); cf. Pausanias, 10.32.9.

16. Cicero, *Tusculanae disputationes* 5.3; Justin, 13.5.

17. Thucydides, 1.25; Isocrates, *Panegyricus* 1.

New Testament where it occurs. The apostle sets forth the communion of the church militant on earth with the church triumphant in heaven—of the church toiling and suffering here with that church from which all weariness and toil have forever passed away (Rev. 21:4). How could he better describe this last state than as a *panēgyris*, the glad and festal assembly of heaven? Very beautifully Delitzsch says:

> *Panēgyris* is an assembly that is at full count (or has a large attendance) and is exceedingly festive in mood and indulges itself in a revelry of delights. At the mention of *panēgyris*, one thinks of festive song, festive frolicking, festive games; and, indeed, life in the presence of God is a truly unending festive celebration.[18]

18. *In loc.*

2

theiotēs (2305) *theotēs (2320)*

Godhead Divinity Deity

Neither of these words occurs more than once in the New Testament; *theiotēs* occurs only in Romans 1:20 (and once in the Apocrypha—Wisd. of Sol. 18:9), and *theotēs* is found in Colossians 2:9. We have rendered both by "Godhead"; yet the words must not be regarded as identical in meaning or even as two different forms of the same word that have over time acquired different shades of significance. On the contrary, there is a real distinction between them that is grounded in their different derivations. *Theotēs* comes from *theos (2316)*, and *theiotēs* from the adjective *theios (2304)*.

In comparing the two passages, the appropriateness of using one word in one text and one in the other is apparent. In the first (Rom. 1:20), Paul is declaring how much of God may be known from his revelation in nature, from those vestiges of himself that men may everywhere trace in the world around them. Yet it is not the personal God whom any man may learn to know by these aids (God can be known only by the revelation of himself in his Son) but only his divine attributes, his majesty and glory.[1] Paul uses this more abstract and less personal word precisely because he wishes to affirm that men may know God's power and majesty, his *theia dynamis* (*1411*, divine power;

1. See Theophylact on Rom. 1:20, where he gives *megaleiotēs* (*3618*, majesty) as equivalent to *theiotēs*.

2 Pet. 1:3), from his works. But Paul would *not* imply that they may know God personally from anything short of the revelation of his eternal Word, Jesus Christ.[2] Similar motives induce Paul to use *to theion*, rather than *ho theos*, in addressing the Athenians on Mars' Hill (Acts 17:29).

In the second passage (Col. 2:9), Paul is declaring that all the fullness of absolute Godhead dwells in the Son. No mere rays of divine glory gilded him, lighting up his person for a season and with a splendor not his own; but he was and is absolute and perfect God. The apostle uses *theotēs* to express this essential and personal Godhead of the Son. Thus according to Augustine, in this verse *theotēs* refers to "the being of him who is God."[3] And Beza rightly states: "He does not say '*tēn theiotēta*,' that is, 'divinity,' but '*tēn theotēta*,' that is, 'deity,' in order to speak even more distinctly. . . . *Hē theiotēs* seems to signify attributes more than his very nature." And Bengel says that *theotēs* refers "not only [to] divine virtues but [to] divine nature itself." De Wette has sought to express this distinction in his German translation, rendering *theiotēs* by divinity (*Göttlichkeit*) and *theotēs* by deity (*Gottheit*).

There have been those who have denied that any such distinction was intended by Paul. Such persons base their denial on the assumption that it is not possible to satisfactorily prove that there is an important difference of meaning between the two words. But even supposing that such a difference could not be shown in classical Greek, this of itself would not be decisive. The gospel of Christ might give words new shades of meaning and evolve latent distinctions, which those who previously employed the words may not have required but that had now become necessary. The distinction between *deity* (*theotēs*) and *divinity* (*theiotēs*) is one that would be strongly felt and expressed in Christian theology. Hence Latin Christian writers were not satisfied with *divinitas*, which they found in the writings of Cicero and others and which they sometimes used.[4] Instead, they coined *deitas* as the only adequate Latin representative of the Greek *theotēs*. We have Augustine's express testimony to this fact: "This *divinity* or, as I might say, *deity*—for we are no longer reluctant to use this word to translate from Greek more clearly what they call *theotēta* [deity]."[5] In addition to this statement and the different etymologies of the words,[6] various examples support this distinction. Both *theotēs* and *theiotēs*, as is generally true of abstract words in every language, are of late introduction; and one of them, *theotēs*, is extremely rare. Indeed, only two examples of it from classical Greek are known—one from Lucian (*Icaromenippus* 9), the other from Plutarch.

2. Cicero notes (*Tusculanae disputationes* 1.13): "Many have perverse ideas *about the Gods*; nevertheless, all believe that there is *a divine force and nature*."

3. *De civitate Dei* 7.1.

4. See Piper, *Theologische Studien und Kritiken* (1875), pp. 79ff.

5. *De civitate Dei* 7.1; cf. 10.1, 2.

6. One comes from *to einai tina theon* (someone being God), the other from *to einai tina* [or *ti*] *theion* (someone [or something] being divine), clearly pointing to this difference in meaning.

> Thus from human beings to heroes and from heroes to demons the superior souls assume change. Of demons few, having been wholly purified through virtue over a long period of time, have partaken of deity.[7]

To these a third example, also from Plutarch (*De Iside et Osiride* 22), may be added. In all of these examples, *theotēs* expresses (in agreement with my view) Godhead in the absolute sense, or at all events in as absolute a sense as the pagan could conceive it. *Theiotēs* is a much more frequent word, and its usage everywhere supports this distinction. It always shows a manifestation of the divine or of some divine attributes but never absolute, essential deity. Thus Lucian attributes *theiotēs* to Hephaestion, when after his death Alexander would have raised him to the rank of a god.[8] Plutarch speaks of the "divinity [*theiotēs*] of the soul."[9]

In conclusion, whether this distinction was intended (as I am fully convinced that it was) by Paul or not, it established itself firmly in the later theological language of the church. The Greek fathers never used *theiotēs* but always *theotēs* as the only word to adequately express the essential Godhead of the three separate persons in the Holy Trinity.

7. *De defectu oraculorum* 10.

8. *Calumniae non temere credendum* 17.

9. *Placita philosophorum* 5.1; cf. *De Iside et Osiride* 2; *Sulla* 6; and various other passages to the same effect.

3

hieron (2411) *naos* (3485) — *Temple*

Both *hieron* and *naos* are translated "temple" in our English versions. Although it is difficult to say how they could have been distinguished, translating them by different words would have clarified the sacred narrative and made it more precise.[1] *Hieron*[2] refers to the whole sacred enclosure, the *temenos*,[3] including the outer courts, porches, porticoes, and other related buildings.[4] *Naos*[5] refers to the temple itself, the proper *habitation* of God (Acts 7:48; 17:24; 1 Cor. 6:19), the *oikos* [3624] *tou Theou* (house of God),[6] the heart and center of the whole. *Hagiasma* is used to refer to the Holy Place and to the Holy of Holies (1 Macc. 1:37; 3:45; cf. vv. 37–42). This distinction between *hieron* and *naos* is found in secular Greek references to heathen temples and in sacred Greek references to the temple of the true God.[7]

When referring to the temple in Jerusalem, Josephus, Philo, the Septuagint, and the New Testament always distinguish *hieron* from *naos*. Often the

1. See Fuller, *A Pisgah Sight of Palestine*, p. 427.
2. The Latin equivalent is *templum*.
3. L-S 1774, a piece of land marked off and dedicated to a god.
4. See *hai oikodomai* (3619) *tou hierou* (the buildings of the temple, Matt. 24:1).
5. *Naos*, which is equivalent to the Latin *aedes* (building), comes from *naiō* (dwell), which is synonymous with the Latin *habito* (dwell).
6. Matt. 12:4; cf. Exod. 23:19; and the Latin *domus* (house).
7. See Herodotus, 1.181, 183; Thucydides, 4.90: "They were digging a ditch in a circle around the sacred enclosure and the temple" (cf. 5.18); and Acts 29:24, 27.

distinction is explicit. After describing the building of the *naos* by Solomon, for example, Josephus wrote: "Outside the temple [*naou*] he constructed a sacred enclosure [*hieron*] in the form of a square."[8] In another passage where Josephus describes how the Samaritans sought permission from the Jews to help rebuild God's house, he used the phrase "to join in the building of the temple [*naon*]."[9] Although the Samaritans' request was denied (see Ezra 4:2), they were permitted to "come into the sacred enclosure [*hieron*] to worship God," something forbidden under the penalty of death to mere Gentiles, who were not to pass beyond their own exterior court.[10]

The distinction between *hieron* and *naos* helps us better understand several New Testament passages. When Zacharias entered into "the *temple* of the Lord" to burn incense, the people who awaited his return and who stood "outside" (Luke 1:10) also were in the temple—the *hieron*—though Zacharias alone entered the *naos*, the "temple" in its narrower sense. We often read of Christ teaching "in the temple" (Matt. 26:55; Luke 21:37; John 8:20), and we might wonder how long conversations could have been maintained there without interrupting the service of God. But this "temple" is always the *hieron*, the porches and porticoes of the temple that were intended for such purposes. Christ never entered the *naos* during his earthly ministry, since that right was reserved for the priests. Jesus drove the money-changers and the buyers and sellers with their sheep and oxen from the *hieron*, not from the *naos*. Even those profane men had not dared to establish themselves in the temple in its strictest sense (Matt. 21:12; John 2:14).

Keeping in mind the distinction between *hieron* and *naos* helps us understand how the prophet Zacharias could be slain "between the temple and the altar" (Matt. 23:35). Here the word translated "temple" is *naos*, which helps to answer the questions: "Was not the altar *in* the temple? And if so, how could any locality be described as *between* the two?" The brazen altar alluded to in Matthew 23:35 was located in the *hieron*, not in the *naos*. It was situated "*in the court* of the house of the Lord,"[11] where the sacred historian (2 Chron. 24:21) lays the scene of this murder, not in the *naos*.

Finally, Judas vividly portrayed his defiance and despair by entering into the *naos* itself (Matt. 27:5)—which was reserved for the priests alone—and casting down before the priests the accursed blood money! Expositors who affirm that *naos* here stands for *hieron* should adduce some other passage where the one is used for the other.

8. *Antiquitates Judaicae* 8.3.9.
9. Ibid. 11.4.3.
10. Acts 21:29–30; Philo, *Legatio ad Gaium* 31.
11. Cf. Josephus, *Antiquitates Judaica* 8.4.1.

4

epitimaō (2008) — *Rebuke*, *Charge*

elenchō (1651) — *Convict*, *Convince*

aitia (156) — *Accusation*

elenchos (1650) — *Reproof*

One may "rebuke" a person without convicting that person of any fault. In such a case either there *is* no fault (and so the rebuke is unnecessary or unjust), or although there is fault, the rebuke does not cause the offender to admit it. Thus the distinction between *epitimaō* and *elenchō* lies in the possibility of "rebuking" for sin without "convincing" of sin.

Epitimaō connotes rebuking and can be used to refer to the unjust checking or blaming of another. In this sense Peter "began to rebuke" his Lord (*ērxato epitiman*, Matt. 16:22; cf. 19:13; Luke 18:39). *Epitimaō* also may refer to ineffectual blame—when the person rebuked fails to see his sin—as in the case of the penitent robber who "rebuked" (*epetimōn*) his fellow malefactor (Luke 23:40; cf. Mark 9:25).

Elenchō, however, is a much more pregnant word. It means to rebuke another with the truth so that the person confesses, or at least is convicted, of his sin (Job 5:17; Prov. 19:25).[1]

1. This is also the case in juristic Greek, where *elenchō* is not merely to reply to but to refute an opponent.

epitimaō

elenchō

aitia
elenchos

The difference between *epitimaō* and *elenchō* can shed a great deal of light on many New Testament passages and give them a deeper meaning. Thus our Lord could demand, "Which of you *convicts* [*elenchei*] Me of sin?" (John 8:46). Many "rebuked" him and charged him with sin (Matt. 9:3; John 9:16), but none convinced or convicted him that he was sinful. This meaning of *elenchein* also illuminates John 3:20; 8:9; 1 Corinthians 14:24–25; and Hebrews 12:5. Perhaps the most important passage to consider, however, is John 16:8: "When He [the Comforter] has come, He will *convict* the world of sin, and of righteousness, and of judgment." To translate *elenchei* here as "approve" (KJV), following the Latin *arguet*, fails to express the depth and full meaning of the Holy Spirit's work.[2] John 16:8 may properly be paraphrased as follows: "He who shall come in my place shall so bring home to the world its own 'sin,' my perfect 'righteousness,' God's coming 'judgment,' and shall so 'convince' the world of these that it shall be obliged itself to acknowledge them, and in this acknowledgment may find [shall be in the right way to find] its own blessedness and salvation."[3]

There is a similar difference in meaning between *aitia* and *elenchos*.[4] *Aitia* refers to an accusation that may be true or false. It is a term that was used in an accusation made against the Lord of glory himself (Matt. 27:37). *Elenchos*, however, refers to an accusation that is true, and often implies an inward or outward acknowledgment of that truthfulness on the part of the accused. Thus *elenchos* represents the glorious prerogative of the truth in its highest operation, not merely to silence its adversary but to convince him of his error. Therefore Job said of God: *Alētheia (225) kai elenchos par' autou* ("Truth and proof are from Him," 23:7).[5] Demosthenes[6] said: "Very often both reproach and accusation are distinguished from refutation; for it is accusation when one employs a mere statement without furnishing credence in what he says; it is refutation when one at the same time demonstrates the truth of what he says."[7]

The distinction we have drawn between "convict" and "convince" differentiates between the judicial and the moral uses of *elenchos*. But these two uses will be one in the last day when every condemned sinner will be both "convicted" and "convinced," as the phrase "he was speechless"—a reference to the guest whom the king found without a marriage garment—implies (Matt. 22:12; cf. Rom. 3:4).

2. Lampe correctly comments that this use of *elenchei* depicts "the business of a teacher who points out the truth that so far has not been recognized for the persuasion even of the person repressing it, so that he is compelled to surrender." For an admirable discussion of the word, especially as it is used here, see Archdeacon Hare's *Mission of the Comforter*, 1st ed., pp. 528–44.

3. For more on *elenchō*, see Pott's *Wurzel-Wörterbuch*, 3:720.

4. *Elenchos* occurs only twice in the New Testament: 2 Tim. 3:16; Heb. 11:1.

5. Therefore Milton could say (*Paradise Lost* 10.84): "*Conviction* to the serpent none belongs." This was a grace reserved for Adam and Eve, as only they were capable of it.

6. *Adversus Androtionem* p. 600.

7. Cf. Aristotle (*Rhetorica ad Alexandrum* 13): "Refutation is what cannot be otherwise but just as we say."

5

anathēma (334) — Gift, Donation, Object Devoted to God

anathema (331) — Accursed Object

Many interpreters understand *anathēma* and *anathema* simply as different spellings of the same word that may be used interchangeably. If that were true, there would be no point in including these words in a book of synonyms. Like *heurēma* and *heurema*[1] and *epithēma* and *epithema*,[2] *anathēma* and *anathema* probably were once no more than different pronunciations of the same word that eventually came to be spelled in two different ways. And in such cases it is not unusual for words with slightly different spellings to develop different meanings and so to become independent.[3] For example, one member in each of the following pairs of words began as a variant spelling of the other: the Greek *thrasos*[4] and *tharsos*,[5] the Latin *Thrax* (Thracian) and *threx* (a gladiator), the German *rechtlich* (just) and *redlich* (upright), the French *harnais* (armor) and *harnois* (harness), and the English *fray* and *frey*, *allay* and *alloy*,

1. L-S 729, invention, discovery.

2. L-S 634 and 633, lid, cover.

3. I have given numerous examples of this in my *English Past and Present*, 10th ed., pp. 157–64.

4. L-S 804, rashness, audacity.

5. 2291, boldness, courage. As Gregory Nazianzene (*Carmina moralia* 2.34, 35) stated: "Rashness [*thrasos*] is boldness [*tharsos*] toward what should not be undertaken."

anathēma and *mettle* and *metal*. *Anathēma* and *anathema* share that same type of derivation.

anathema Earnest debate about the different meanings of *anathēma* and *anathema* occurred even among the early Hellenists. Salmasius, for example, was among those who argued that the words had distinct meanings, at least as they were used in Hellenistic Greek; Beza was among those who denied such a distinction. Perhaps the truth lies somewhere in between, though nearer to one side than to the other. After weighing all the evidence, the most reasonable conclusion is that *anathēma* and *anathema* have distinct meanings that were recognized and observed by many but not by all.

In classical Greek *anathēma* is the predominant form and the only one that Attic writers permitted.[6] It was the technical word for costly offerings that were presented to the gods and then *suspended*[7] or otherwise displayed in their temples.[8] These offerings were separated from all common and profane uses and were openly dedicated to the honor of the deity to whom they were originally presented.[9]

When the Hebrew Scriptures were translated into Greek, however, a new meaning was needed for *anathēma*, because the Scriptures spoke of two ways in which objects might be holy, that is, set apart for God and devoted to him. The children of Israel were devoted to God, and he was glorified *in* them; the wicked Canaanites were devoted to God, and he was glorified *on* them. Persons and things might be *ḥērem*[10]—they might be devoted to God for good or for evil. There was such a thing as being "accursed *to the Lord*."[11] Part of the spoil of a city might be consecrated to the Lord in his treasury and a part utterly destroyed, though each part was dedicated to him.[12] These distinct concepts were expressed by using *anathēma* and *anathema*. Those who believe that separation *from* God is the central idea of *anathema*[13] are not able to trace a common meaning between it and *anathēma*, which plainly refers to separation *to* God, or to show the point at which these words diverge. Those who believe that separation *to* God is implied in both cases face no such difficulty.[14]

6. Lobeck, *Phrynichus*, pp. 249, 445; *Paralipomena*, p. 391.

7. Cf. *ana* (303), up; *tithēmi* (5087), put, place.

8. The Romans termed these *donaria* (votive offerings), and included among them tripods, crowns, vases of silver or gold, and so forth.

9. Xenophon, *Anabasis* 5.3.5; Pausanias, 10.9.

10. 2764; Lev. 27:28–29.

11. Josh. 6:17–18; cf. Num. 21:1–3; Deut. 13:16.

12. Josh. 6:19, 21. Or "sacred and devote," as Milton has it.

13. Theodoret, for example, commenting on Rom. 9:3, said: "*Anathema* has a double meaning, for that which is consecrated to God is called an offering [*anathēma*], and that which is different from this has the same name."

14. Flacius Illyricus (*Clavis Scripturae*, under *anathema*) explains how the two apparently opposed meanings developed from a single root: "Anathema, therefore, is a thing or a person pledged or assigned to God, either because of being dedicated to him by people on account of piety or because the justice of God has removed people guilty of some particular sins to their own prisons and punishments, as it were, with the sentiment of people approving and corroborating it. . . . For there is a twofold reason that God wishes to have something—either as pleasing and

In the Septuagint and Apocrypha *anathēma* and *anathema* were used in distinct ways. Because of the variety of readings in the various editions, however, it is difficult to determine if the distinction between them was universally observed or to know how consistently the distinction between them was observed. In Tischendorf's critical edition of the Septuagint (1850), however, the distinction between the two words is maintained in many passages,[15] though that is not the case in some earlier editions of the Septuagint.

Gift
Donation
Object Devoted to God
Accursed Object

In the New Testament *anathēma* is always used to express the *sacrum* (sacred thing) that is pleasing to God, while *anathema* is used to refer to things that deserve God's wrath. These words are not used frequently enough in the New Testament, however, to convince an opponent of this view. *Anathēma* occurs only once: "Then, as some spoke of the temple, how it was adorned with beautiful stones and *donations* [*anathēmasi*]" (Luke 21:5).[16] *Anathema* occurs no more than six times (Acts 23:14; Rom. 9:3; 1 Cor. 12:3; 16:22; Gal. 1:8–9), and its use in these passages confirms the distinction made above.

Some of the Greek fathers neglected this distinction. Others, however, observed it implicitly,[17] and some explicitly recognized the distinction and accurately and precisely traced its development.[18]

Let us summarize our findings. Based on similar phenomena in all languages, it is probable that *anathēma* and *anathema* gradually developed distinct meanings. In Scripture the two ways that persons and things may be dedicated to God—for good or for evil—are described by using these two slightly different forms of the same word. Every New Testament use of these words maintains this distinction. The later ecclesiastical books also maintain this distinction, though not perfectly. I conclude, therefore, that the sacred writers of the New Testament deliberately used *anathēma* and *anathema* in different senses. Luke used *anathēma* (21:5) because he intended to express that which was dedicated to God for its own honor as well as for God's glory. Paul used *anathema* in the sense of that which is devoted to God's honor (as were the Canaanites of old) but to its own destruction. And in the end, every intelligent being who is capable of knowing and loving God and who has been called to this knowledge must be either *anathēma* or *anathema* to him.[19]

acceptable and consecrated to himself or as detestable to him and his wrath and as owed and subject to punishment."

15. For example, Lev. 27:28–29; Jth. 16:19; 2 Macc. 2:13.

16. Even here Codd. A and D and Lachmann read *anathemasi*.

17. As does Clement of Alexandria (*Cohortatio ad Gentiles* 4: *anathēma gegonamen tō Theō [2316] hyper Christou [5545]*. Here the context plainly shows the meaning to be "we have become *a costly offering* to God").

18. For example, see Chrysostom, *Homilia 16 in Romans*, as quoted by Suicer (*Thesaurus*, under *anathema*).

19. See Witsius, *Miscellanea sacramenta*, 2:54ff.; Deyling, *Obsessiones sacrae*, 2:495ff.; Fritzsche on Rom. 9:3; Hengstenberg, *Christologie*, 2d ed., 3:655; Cremer, *Biblisch-theologisches Wörterbuch*, 2d ed., p. 550.

prophēteuō (4395) *manteuomai* (3132) — *Prophesy* *Tell Fortunes*

Although *prophēteuō* is used frequently in the New Testament, *manteuomai* is used only in Acts 16:16, where a girl possessed with a "spirit of divination" or "spirit of Apollo" is said to have "brought her masters much profit *by fortune-telling* [*manteuomenē*]." The absence of *manteuomai* elsewhere in the New Testament and its use here are noteworthy.

The inspired writers abstained from using words that would tend to destroy the distinction between heathenism and revealed religion. Thus *eudaimonia*,[1] though a religious word from a heathen point of view,[2] is never used to express Christian blessedness.[3] Similarly, *aretē* (703), the predominant word in heathen ethics for "virtue," is very rare in the New Testament. It is used only once by Paul (Phil. 4:8). In the epistles of Peter, it is used in quite a different sense than it is used in Aristotle.[4] In the same way, *ēthē* (2239), from which we derive *ethics*, occurs only in a quotation from a heathen poet (1 Cor. 15:33), indicating that its absence elsewhere in the New Testament is not accidental.

1. L-S 708, good fortune, happiness.
2. It ascribed happiness to the favor of some deity.
3. Its use would not have been fitting since its root, *daimōn* (1142), involves polytheistic error.
4. To account for its infrequent use in the New Testament, Beza called it "an exceedingly insignificant word in comparison with the gifts of the Holy Spirit."

prophēteuō
manteuomai

In keeping with this same principle, *prophēteuein* was consistently used in the New Testament to express prophesying by the Spirit of God. When the sacred writers referred to the lying art of heathen divination, they employed *manteuesthai* (cf. Deut. 18:10; 1 Sam. 28:8). What is the essential difference between "prophesying" and "soothsaying,"[5] and why was it necessary to distinguish them by using different terms (*prophēteuō* and *manteuomai*)? The answers to these questions may be found after we have investigated the etymology of one of the words.

Before doing that, however, we will deal with what used to be a very common error (especially among the fathers),[6] which was to understand the *pro* (4253) in *prophēteuein* and in *prophētēs* in a temporal sense.[7] That way of interpreting *prophētēs* results in understanding its primary meaning as "he who declares things *before* they come to pass." Although such *fore*telling or *fore*announcing may have characterized the office of prophet, it was not the essence of that office, either in sacred or in classical Greek. The *prophētēs* is the *out*speaker, the one who speaks *out* the counsel of God with the clearness, energy, and authority that spring from the consciousness of speaking in God's name and of having received a direct message from him to deliver. This appeared in a less distinct form in classical Greek, since the word only came to its full expression when used of the prophets of the true God. But there too the *prophētēs* is the *interpres deorum* (interpreter of the gods).[8] The meaning of the word, however, diminished from referring to the interpreter *of the gods* or *of God* to referring to no more than an interpreter in a general sense, though still an interpreter of the good and true.[9] *Prophētēs* is used in the Old and New Testaments primarily to refer to one who had been taught by God and who spoke out God's will (Deut. 18:18; Isa. 1; Jer. 1; Ezek. 2; 1 Cor. 14:3). Foretelling the future was concomitant to that.

Manteuomai introduces us to a different sphere. *Manteuomai* is related to *mantis*[10] and through that word (as Plato taught) to *mania* (3130) and *mainomai* (3105). Consequently, *manteuomai* refers to the tumult of the mind, to the *fury* or temporary *madness* of those who were supposedly possessed by the god during the time that they delivered their oracles. This mantic fury was displayed by rolling eyes, foaming lips, and flying hair, as well as by other

5. *Weissagen* ("foretelling" in German, derived from *wizan* [= *wissen*] to know) and *Wahrsagen* (fortune telling) are a similar pair of terms.

6. See Suicer, *Thesaurus*, under *prophētēs* (4396).

7. The *pro* in *prophēteuein* and in *prophētēs* is no more temporal than is the *pro* in *prophasis* (4392).

8. Thus Euripides (*Ion*, 372, 413; *Bacchae*, 211) stated: "Since you do not see this light, Teiresias, I shall be for you an interpreter [*prophētēs*] of the message." Pindar said (*Fragmenta* 15): "You, Muse, give an oracle [*manteuēo*], I shall interpret [*prophateusō*]." Philo (*Quis rerum divinarum heres sit* 52) defined the *prophētēs* as *ermēneus Theou* (an interpreter of God) and said: "He is a resounding [musical] instrument of God, being struck and plucked invisibly by him."

9. Cf. Plato, *Phaedrus* 262d; and the fine answer that Lucian puts into Diogenes' mouth when he is asked what trade he followed (*Vitarum auctio* 8d).

10. L-S 1080, seer.

signs of a more than natural agitation.[11] Perhaps these symptoms were sometimes produced (and no doubt often aggravated) in seers like Pythonesses, Sibyls, and others by inhaling earth vapors or by other artificial stimulants.[12] Everyone who believes that real spiritual forces underlie all forms of idolatry also will acknowledge that often there was more than mere trickery or fraud in these manifestations. Anyone with insight into the awful mystery of the world's false religions will see in these symptoms the result of an actual relation to a spiritual world—a spiritual world that lies not above but beneath.

Scripture speaks of such mantic fury only to condemn it. "The spirits of the prophets are subject to the prophets" (1 Cor. 14:32).[13] The true prophet did not speak on his own authority: "For a prophet does not speak anything of himself, but all that he utters belongs to others, as if another one is prompting."[14] The prophet was transported out of himself. He was said to be *en pneumati* (in the Spirit, Rev. 1:10), *en ekstasei* (in a trance, Acts 11:5), and *hypo pneumatos hagiou pheromenoi* (carried along by the Holy Spirit, 2 Pet. 1:21).[15] The prophet was *lifted above*, not *set beside*, his everyday self. It was not discord and disorder but a divine harmony and order that were introduced into his soul. He was not overcome in his lower life by forces stronger than his own, by an insurrection from beneath; but his spirit was lifted out of that region into a clearer, divine atmosphere. All that he previously had still remained his, but it was purged, exalted, and quickened by a power higher than, yet not alien to, his own. Man is most truly man when he is most filled with the fullness of God.[16]

And even within heathenism, the superior dignity of the *prophētēs* to the *mantis* was recognized on these very grounds. Plato's *Timaeus* (71e–72b), for example, depicts the *mantis* as one in whom all reason is suspended, as one who more or less *rages*. Plato draws the line broadly and distinctly between the *mantis* and the *prophētēs*, subordinating the former to the latter. The

11. Cicero loved to extol the superiorities of the Latin language over the Greek and claimed such a superiority in this case. Latin had *divinatio*, a word that refers to the *divine* character of prophecy and that stresses that prophecy was a *gift of the gods*, but Greek had only *mantikē* (L-S 1080, faculty of prophesy), which set forth only one of the external signs that accompanied the giving of prophecy. Cicero stated (*De divinatione* 1.1): "As we [Romans] have done many other things better than the Greeks, so we are superior in giving to this most remarkable practice a name derived from *divis* [*gods*], while the Greeks, as Plato recognizes, derived a name from *furore* ["frenzy"; Greek *mania*, *3130*]."

12. Plutarch, *De defectu oraculorum* 48.

13. Cf. Chrysostom, *In Epistulam I ad Corinthios Homilia* 29, at the beginning.

14. Philo, *Quis rerum divinarum heres sit* 52d; cf. Plutarch, *Amatorius* 16.

15. "Carried along by the Holy Spirit" is much stronger than the NKJV's "moved by the Holy Spirit." De Wette rightly uses the German *getrieben* (driven). Cf. Knapp, *Scriptores variorum argumentorum*, p. 33. The prophet was *theolēptos* (L-S 790, possessed, inspired; Cyril of Alexandria). We must not go so far in our opposition to heathen and Montanist error as to deny this, as some have done, especially Jerome and others engaged in controversy with the Montanists. Also see the masterly discussion of this subject in Hengstenberg's *Christologie*, 2d ed., vol. 3, pt. 2, pp. 158–88.

16. See John Smith, the Cambridge Platonist, *On Prophecy*, chap. 4, "The Difference of the True Prophetical Spirit from All Enthusiastical Imposture."

utterances of the *mantis* were allowed to pass only after they had received the approval of the *prophētēs*.

> It is customary to appoint the class of interpreters [*prophētōn*] as judges of those divinely inspired. Some call them prophets [*manteis*], not knowing at all that they are expositors of dark sayings and visions and are not prophets [*manteis*], but they might very fittingly be called interpreters [*prophētai*] of prophecy.

The truth that Plato glimpsed was permanently embodied in the Christian church. The church kept and used *prophēteuō* but relegated *manteuomai* to the heathenism it was about to displace and overthrow.

7

timōria (5098) *kolasis* (2851)

Punishment Torment

Timōria occurs once in the New Testament (Heb. 10:29; cf. Acts 22:5; 26:11), and *kolasis* occurs twice (Matt. 25:46; 1 John 4:18). The verb *timōrein* (5097) appears twice (Acts 22:5; 26:11), as does *kolazein* (2849) (Acts 4:21; 2 Pet. 2:9). The classical use of *timōria* emphasizes the *vindictive* character of punishment.[1] It was punishment that satisfied the inflicter's sense of outraged justice and that defended his own honor or that of the violated law. The meaning of *timōria*, then, agrees with its etymology.[2]

Kolasis refers to punishment that is designed to correct and better the offender.[3] Thus Plato[4] uses *kolaseis* and *nouthetēseis*[5] together. Several times in one passage in the *Protagoras*, Plato's use illustrates the distinction we have drawn.

1. In *De inventione rhetorica* 2.22, Cicero explained the Latin *vindicatio* as that act "by which we defensively and with vengeance repel from ourselves and our friends violence and insult and by which we punish crimes."

2. *Timōria* derives from *timē* (5092), and *ouros* (L-S 1274, watcher, guardian) and *horaō* (3708), and thus means the guardianship or protectorate of honor. German uses *Ehrenstrafe* (the penalty for offended honor) or, better, *Ehrenrettung*, a "safeguarding of honor" that is achieved when due satisfaction is demanded for an offense against some aspect of the code of honor (Delitzsch).

3. See Philo, *Legatio ad Gaium* 1; Josephus, *Antiquitates Judaicae* 2.6.8. The Latin *castigatio* usually has a milder sense than *timōria*.

4. *Protagoras* 324a, b.

5. L-S 1183, admonition, warning.

> For nobody punishes wrongdoers ... because one has done wrong in the past (unless he is taking blind vengeance like a beast) ... but for the sake of the future, in order that one may not do wrong again.

Plato's use of the terms may be compared with Clement of Alexandria's,[6] who defined *kolaseis* as "particular instructions" and *timōria* as "retaliation for evil." Aristotle[7] distinguished the terms this way: "*Timōria* [vengeance] and *kolasis* [corrective punishment] differ, for corrective punishment is on account of the one suffering wrong, but vengeance is on account of the one doing wrong, that there may be satisfaction."[8] Aulus Gellius referred to these and similar definitions.

> It has been thought that there should be three reasons for punishing wrongs. One reason is what in Greek is called *nouthesia* [3559, rebuke] or *kolasis* [punishment] or *parainesis* [L-S 1310, admonition]. It is punishment applied for the sake of correcting or reforming in order that one who has erred accidentally may become more attentive and improved. Another reason is what those who have differentiated these words more exactly call *timōria* [vengeance]. This is the reason for punishing when the dignity and prestige of the person wronged must be protected in order that an omission of punishment may not make him despised and diminish his honor. For that reason people think that this word was derived from the preservation of honor [*timē*, 5092].[9]

It would be quite erroneous, however, to transfer that distinction in its entirety to the New Testament use of *timōria* and *kolasis*. The *kolasis aiōnios* (everlasting punishment) of Matthew 25:46 is not merely corrective and therefore temporary discipline but rather the *athanatos timōria* (eternal vengeance),[10] the *aidioi timōriai* (everlasting vengeance)[11] with which the Lord elsewhere threatens finally impenitent men (Mark 9:43–48).[12]

Part of Aristotle's distinction is reflected in the scriptural usage of the words. In *kolasis* the relation of the punishment to the punished is predominant, while in *timōria* the punisher is emphasized.

6. *Stromata* 4.24; 7.16.

7. *Rhetorica* 1.10.

8. See also *Ethica Nicomachea* 4.5: "Vengeance puts an end to anger, producing pleasure in the place of grief."

9. *Noctes Atticae* 6.14. There is a profound commentary on these words in Göschel's *Zerstreute Blätter*, 2:343–60. Also see the instructive note in Wyttenbach's *Animadversiones in Plutarchum*, 12:776.

10. Josephus, *De bello Judaico* 2.8.11; cf. *Antiquitates Judaicae* 18.1.3, *eirgmos aidios* (everlasting imprisonment).

11. Plato, *Axiochus* 372a.

12. There are numerous passages in Hellenistic Greek that show that *kolasis* with *kolazesthai* (2849) had acquired this severe sense and simply meant "punishment" or "torment," with no reference to its correctional value. Cf. Josephus, *Antiquitates Judaicae* 15.2.2; Philo, *De agricultura* 9; 2 Macc. 4:38; Wisd. of Sol. 19:4; and the words of Peter himself (2 Pet. 2:9).

alēthēs (227) *alēthinos* (228) — *True*

The Latin *verax* (speaking truly, veracious) and *verus* (true, real, genuine) respectively represent the Greek *alēthēs* and *alēthinos* and reproduce the distinction between them. The Vulgate uses the two Latin words to indicate which of the two Greek terms stands in the original. However, because *very*[1] is no longer used in English as an adjective but only as an adverb, we use *true* to translate both Greek terms, thereby obliterating the difference between them.[2] One exception to this is the Nicene Creed's "*very* God of *very* God," which preserves the distinction.[3] Although the distinction has faded in common English usage, it would have been worth making an attempt to preserve it because the differences that *true* covers up are quite real.

God is both *alēthēs* and *alēthinos*, and each word represents very different attributes. Because he cannot lie, God is *alēthēs*;[4] he is *apseudēs*,[5] the truth-

1. French *vrai* (true, real, genuine; veracious, truthful).

2. This is not the fault of our translators, unless they have erred in not recovering the older meaning of *very*. Although Wycliffe's translation preserves that meaning and commonly translates *verus* in this way (cf. John 15:1, "I am the *verri* vine"), it would have been difficult to preserve that meaning (though some English translations use it in Gen. 27:21, 24). It would not be impossible to resurrect that meaning today.

3. *Theon alēthinon ek Theou alēthinou.*

4. John 3:33; Rom. 3:4; = *verax* (truthful).

5. 893, Titus 1:2.

speaking and the truth-loving God.[6] But God also is *alēthinos*,[7] *very* God as distinguished from idols and from all other false gods. Idols are the dreams of people's diseased fancy; they have no substantial existence in the real world.[8]

> The adjectives in =*i-nos* express the material out of which anything is made, or rather they imply a mixed relation, of quality and origin, to the object denoted by the substantive from which they are derived. Thus *xul-i-nos* means "of wood," "wooden"; [*ostrak-i-nos*, "of earth," "earthen"; *hual-i-nos*, "of glass," "glassen";] and *alēth-i-nos* signifies "genuine," made up of that which is true [that which, in chemical language, has truth for its stuff and base]. This last adjective is particularly applied to express that which is all that it pretends to be; for instance, pure gold as opposed to adulterated metal.[9]

It does not necessarily follow from the preceding remarks that whatever is contrasted with the *alēthinos* has no substantial existence or is completely fraudulent. Subordinate realizations or partial and imperfect anticipations of the truth may be set over against the truth in its highest and most complete form, to which alone *alēthinos* applies. As Kahnis noted:

> *Alēthēs* lays bare what is not true and not real; *alēthinos* lays bare what is incongruous with the concept in question. The standard applied by *alēthēs* is reality; by *alēthinos* it is the concept. In *alēthēs* the concept is congruous with the matter at hand; in *alēthinos* the matter at hand is congruous with the concept.[10]

Thus Xenophon[11] affirmed that Cyrus commanded *alēthinon strateuma* (4753), an army that deserved the name, though Xenophon also used *army* to refer to inferior hosts. Plato[12] referred to the sea beyond the Straits of Hercules as "virtually high sea, genuine [*alēthinos*] open sea," implying that it alone realized *to the full extent* the idea of the great ocean deep.[13]

If we consistently interpret *alēthinos* to mean the *true* as opposed to the *false*, we shall miss the exact force of the word and find ourselves entangled in serious embarrassments. Frequently, in fact, *alēthinos* refers to the substantial as opposed to the indistinct or, as Origen[14] put it, to the "genuine [*alēthinos*] as distinguished from shadow and copy and image." Thus in Hebrews 8:2 we read of the "real [*alēthinē*] tabernacle" into which our great High Priest entered. This does not imply that the tabernacle in the wilderness was not also pitched at God's bidding and according to the pattern that he gave (Exod. 25). Rather the tabernacle and its contents were weak earthly copies of heav-

6. Cf. Euripides, *Ion* 1554.

7. Isa. 65:16; John 17:3; 1 Thess. 1:9; = *verus* (genuine).

8. Cf. Athenaeus, 6.62, who records how the Athenians received Demetrius with divine honors: "As if he alone were very god, but the others are asleep or absent or do not exist."

9. Donaldson, *New Cratylus*, p. 426.

10. *Abendmahl*, p. 119.

11. *Anabasis* 1.9.17.

12. *Timaeus* 25a.

13. Cf. *Republic* 1.347d, "the truly genuine [*alēthinos*] ruler," and 6.499c, "the genuine [*alēthinos*] love of genuine [*alēthinēs*] philosophy."

14. *Commentarii in evangelium Joannis* 2, sec. 4.

enly realities—"types of the genuine [*alēthinōn*]." The entry of the Jewish high priest into the Holy of Holies, along with everything pertaining to the worldly sanctuary, was but the "shadow of the good things to come." The "substance"—the filling of these outlines so that they were no longer shadows—was of Christ (Col. 2:17).[15]

In John the Baptist's statement "the law was given by Moses, but grace and *truth* by Jesus Christ" (John 1:17), the antithesis is not between the false and the true but between the imperfect and the perfect, between the shadowy and the substantial. The Eternal Word also is declared to be "the genuine [*alēthinon*] Light" (John 1:9), but that does not preclude John from being called "a burning and a shining lamp" (John 5:35) or the faithful from being called "lights in the world" (Matt. 5:14; Phil. 2:15). Rather it means that Jesus is greater than all; he is "the Light which gives light to every man who comes into the world" (John 1:9).[16] Christ's proclamation that he is "the genuine [*alēthinos*] Bread" (John 6:32) does not imply that the bread Moses gave was not the "bread of heaven" (Ps. 105:40). It was bread but in a secondary sense. It was not food in the highest sense because it did not grant eternal life to those who ate it (John 6:49). To call Jesus "the genuine [*alēthinē*] Vine" (John 15:1) does not preclude Israel's being God's vine (Ps. 80:8; Jer. 2:21); it affirms that Christ alone is the full embodiment of this name (Deut. 32:32; Hos. 10:1).[17] Other illustrations could be given, but these examples (drawn chiefly from John) should suffice.[18]

Thus to refer to Jesus Christ as *alēthēs* affirms that he fulfills his promises. To refer to him as *alēthinos* affirms that he fulfills the wider promise of his name—all that his name implies when taken in its highest, deepest, and widest sense. Because that is true of things, as well as of persons, *pistoi* (*4103*, trustworthy) and *alēthinoi* (*228*, genuine) are both properly used together in Revelation 21:5.

15. F. Spanheim (*Dubia Evangelica*, p. 106) notes: "*Alētheia* [*225*, truth] in Sacred Scripture at times is employed morally and is opposed to falsehood and a lie. At times it is used symbolically and is set against copies and images as a corresponding statue. This truth also in another way is called by the Holy Spirit substance as distinct from its shadow." Cf. Deyling, *Obsessiones sacrae*, 3:317; 4:548, 627; and Delitzsch: "It is a term that corresponds in the fullest, deepest, unrestricted sense of the word to what its name and concept express, to the thing mentioned not only relatively but absolutely, not only materially but intellectually and spiritually, not only temporarily but eternally, not only figuratively (i.e., as a model, a copy, a replica) but antitypically and archetypically."

16. According to Lampe (*in loc.*): "Here therefore is a contrast—now of luminaries in nature, such as were the light of creation, the light of the Israelites in Egypt, the light of the pillar in the wilderness, the light of the jewels in the breastplate, which were mere copies of this genuine Light—now of those who falsely boast that they are the light of human beings, such as individually were the sun and the moon of the Judaic church, which must be darkened by the rising of this Light (Joel 2:31)—now finally also of true lights, but in a smaller degree, which borrow all their light from this Light, such as are all saints, teachers, and angels of light, and at last John the Baptist himself."

17. According to Lampe: "Christ is the genuine Vine . . . and as much he may be *placed at the head of* (nay, even be set against) all the others depicted under this figure in the prophetic writings."

18. That John used *alēthinos* twenty-two times, versus five times in the rest of the New Testament, is not an accident.

9

therapōn (2324)	*Servant*
doulos (1401)	*Slave*
oiketēs (3610)	
diakonos (1249)	*Minister*
	Deacon
hypēretēs (5257)	*Officer*

Hebrews 3:5 is the only passage in the New Testament where *therapōn* is used: "And Moses indeed was faithful in all his house *as a servant* [*hōs therapōn*]." This is clearly an allusion to Numbers 12:7, where the Septuagint has *therapōn* for the Hebrew *'ēber*.[1] The Septuagint, however, also uses *doulos* for *'ēber*, thus giving rise to its use in Revelation 15:3: "Moses, the servant [*ho doulos*] of God."

This does not imply that there is no difference between *doulos* and *therapōn* or that there may not be occasions where one word would be more fitting than the other. It only implies that there are many occasions that do not require highlighting the difference between them.

There are genuine differences between *doulos* and *therapōn*. The *doulos*, as opposed to the *eleutheros*,[2] has *despotēs*[3] or (more commonly in the New Tes-

1. *5650*; cf. Exod. 4:10; Deut. 3:24; Josh. 1:2.
2. *1658*; 1 Cor. 12:13; Rev. 13:16; 19:18; Plato, *Gorgias* 502d.
3. *1203*; Titus 2:9.

therapōn
doulos
oiketēs
diakonos

hypēretēs

tament) *kurios*[4] as its antithesis. The *doulos* was properly the "bond-man,"[5] one who was in a permanent relation of servitude to another, one whose will was completely subject to the will of the other.[6] One was a *doulos* apart from any service he rendered at any given moment. The *therapōn*, however, was one who served without regard to his state as a freeman or as a slave and without regard to whether he was bound by duty or impelled by love. Therefore the services of the *therapōn* are implied to have been more tender, noble, and free than those of the *doulos*. Thus Achilles referred to Patroclus as his *therapōn*,[7] one whose service was not compelled but who ministered out of love.[8] The verb *therapeuein*,[9] as distinguished from *douleuein*,[10] underscores even more strongly the noble and tender character of the service. *Therapeuein* may be used of the physician's watchful tending of the sick or a person's service to God. It was beautifully applied by Xenophon[11] to refer to the care that the gods have of men.

The author of the Epistle to the Hebrews called Moses a *therapōn* in the house of God (3:5), implying that Moses occupied a more confidential position, offered a freer service, and possessed a higher dignity than a *doulos*. Moses' service more closely resembled the service of an *oikonomos* (*3623*, overseer) in God's house. Numbers 12:6–8, which ascribes exceptional dignity to Moses and elevates him above other *douloi* of God, confirms this view.[12] Similarly, only Moses is given the title "attendant [*therapōn*] of the Lord" (Wisd. of Sol. 10:16) in a chapter of the Wisdom of Solomon that mentions other prominent people of the old covenant.[13] It would have been helpful if our translators had discerned a way to indicate the exceptional and honorable title given to Moses (who "was faithful in all God's house").[14]

4. *2962*; Luke 12:46.

5. From *deō* (*1210*); Latin *ligo* (bind).

6. As Xenophon noted (*Cyropaedia* 8.1.4): "The slaves [*douloi*] unwillingly serve their masters."

7. Homer, *Iliad* 16.244.

8. This is very much like the service of the squire or page of the Middle Ages. Meriones was *therapōn* to Idomeneus (23.113), Sthenelus to Diomed, and all the Greeks were "attendants [*therapontes*] of Ares" (2.110 and often; cf. Nägelsbach, *Homerische Theologie*, p. 280). Hesiod also claimed to be "an attendant [*therapōn*] of the Muses." Similarly, in Plato (*Symposium* 203c) Eros was called the "follower and attendant [*therapōn*] of Aphrodite"; cf. Pindar, *Pythia* 4.287, where the *therapōn* is contrasted with the *drastēs* (L-S 449, slave). This agrees with the definition of Hesychius ("the friends of a lower rank"), Ammonius ("the attending friends"), and Eustathius ("the more active of one's friends").

9. *2323*, to wait upon; Latin *curare* (to care for).

10. *1398*, to be a slave. It is also connected with the Latin *faveo* (to favor) and *foveo* (to cherish), and the Greek *thalpō* (*2282*, cherish).

11. *Memorabilia* 4.3.9.

12. Augustine called Moses "an outstanding servant of your faith" (*Confessions* 12.23); cf. Deut. 34:5, where Moses is called "the servant [*oiketēs*] of the Lord."

13. In Wis. of Sol. 18:21, *therapōn* also is applied to Aaron.

14. The Vulgate attempted to do so by using *famulus* (attendant); Cicero wrote of the "*handmaidens* (*famulae*) of the Idean mother." Tyndale and Cranmer attempted to do so by using *minister*, perhaps as adequate a word as the English language affords.

The distinction between *diakonos* and *doulos* also should be maintained in English versions of the New Testament, but that is not difficult to do. *Diakonos* does not derive from *dia* and *konis*—one who in haste runs *through the dust*[15]—but probably comes from the same root that has given us *diōkō* (*1377*), "to hasten after" or "pursue," and indeed still means "a runner."[16]

The difference between *diakonos* on the one hand and *doulos* and *therapōn* on the other is that *diakonos* represents the servant in his activity *for the work*,[17] not in his relation *to a person*—either as a slave (*doulos*) or as a freeman (*therapōn*). Regardless of their condition as freemen or slaves, for example, the attendants at a feast were *diakonoi*.[18] The importance of preserving the distinction between *doulos* and *diakonos* may be illustrated from the parable of the marriage supper (Matt. 27:2–14). In the Authorized Version, the king's "servants" bring in the invited guests (vv. 3, 4, 8, 10), and his "servants" are bidden to cast out that guest who was without a wedding garment (v. 13). In Greek, the *douloi* bring in the guests, and the *diakonoi* fulfill the king's sentence. This distinction is a real one and essential to the parable. The *douloi* are *men*, the ambassadors of Christ who invite their fellow men into his kingdom now. The *diakonoi* are the *angels* who execute the Lord's will in all the acts of judgment at the end of the world. The parable certainly does not turn on this distinction, but these words should not be confused any more than *douloi* and *theristai* (*2327*, reapers) should be in Matthew 13:27, 30 (cf. Luke 19:24).

Oiketēs is often used as a synonym for *doulos*. This is certainly the case in 1 Peter 2:18 and in its three other New Testament occurrences (Luke 16:13; Acts 10:7; Rom. 14:4). Neither the Septuagint[19] nor the Apocrypha[20] distinguished these terms. At the same time, *oiketēs*[21] does not emphasize the servile relation as strongly as does *doulos*. Instead, the relation is viewed in a way that tends to mitigate its extreme severity. The *oiketēs* was one of the household, one of the "family" in the older sense of this word, but not necessarily one born in the house.[22] In its best uses, *oiketēs* included the wife and children, as in Herodotus;[23] in Sophocles[24] only the children of Deianira are included as *oiketai*.[25]

15. This fanciful derivation is precluded by the quantity of the antepenultima in *diakonos*.

16. So Buttmann, *Lexikon* 1.219; but see Döderlein, *Lateinische Synonyme*, 5:135.

17. *Diakonein ti*, Eph. 3:7; *diakonos tou euangeliou* (2098), Col. 1:23; 2 Cor. 3:6.

18. Matt. 22:13; John 2:5; cf. John 12:2.

19. Exod. 21:27; Deut. 6:21; Prov. 17:2.

20. Ecclus. 10:25.

21. This is equivalent to the Latin *domesticus* (household servant).

22. *Oikogenēs* (L-S 1203) is the word for this in the Septuagint (Gen. 14:14; Eccles. 2:7) as *verna* is in Latin; cf. the Gothic *baim* and the Spanish *criado*. As Athenaeus (6.93) noted: "An *oiketēs* is one who generally spends his time in the house, even if he is a free person."

23. 8.106; and often.

24. *Trachiniae* 894

25. On the different names given to slaves and servants of various classes and degrees, see Athenaeus, as quoted above.

therapōn
doulos
oiketēs
diakonos

hypēretēs

Hypēretēs is a military term that originally referred to someone who rowed on a war galley,[26] as distinguished from the soldiers on board. Later the term was used to refer to anyone who performed strong and hard labor and later still to subordinate officials who waited to carry out the orders of their superiors, as in the case of an orderly who attends a commander in war.[27] *Hypēretēs* also refers to the herald who carried solemn messages.[28] Undoubtedly Prometheus intended a taunt when he characterized Hermes as *Theōn hypēretēs*,[29] one who runs the errands of the other gods. Mark was the *hypēretēs* of Paul and Barnabas (Acts 13:5); he was an inferior minister who performed certain defined functions. Indeed, *hypēretēs* is predominantly used in the New Testament in the official sense of the Latin *lictor* and *apparitor*.[30] John's use of *douloi* and *hypēretai* together (18:18) indicates that he also observed a distinction between these terms. Thus the one who struck the Lord on the face (John 18:22) could not be the same person whose ear the Lord had just healed (Luke 22:51); the latter was a *doulos*, but the profane and petulant striker was a *hypēretēs* of the high priest. The meanings of *diakonos* and *hypēretēs* are closer, and there are innumerable occasions where the words might be used indiscriminately. They are distinguished by the more *official* character and functions of the *hypēretēs*.[31]

26. From *eressō* (L-S 685, to row); the Latin is *remigo*.
27. Xenophon, *Cyropaedia* 6.2, 13.
28. Euripides, *Hecuba* 503.
29. Aeschylus, *Prometheus vinctus* 990.
30. Matt. 5:25; Luke 4:20; John 7:32; 18:18; Acts 5:22.
31. See Vitringa, *De synagoga vetere*, pp. 916–19; and the *Dictionary of the Bible* under *Minister*.

10

deilia (*1167*) *eulabeia* (*2124*) *phobos* (*5401*)

Fear *Terror*

Deilia is always used in a bad sense, *eulabeia* predominantly in a good sense (though sometimes in an evil sense), and *phobos* is used both ways.

Deilia[1] (cowardice) is only used once in the New Testament (2 Tim. 1:7).[2] *Deiliaō* (*1168*) is used in John 14:27, and *deilos* (*1169*) is used in Matthew 8:26; Mark 4:40; and Revelation 21:8.[3] *Deilia* is associated with *anandreia* (L-S 113, unmanliness; Plato, *Phaedrus* 254c; *Leges* 2.659a), *leipotaxia* (L-S 1053, desertion; Lysias, *In Alcibiadem*, p. 140), *psychrotēs* (L-S 2028, sluggishness; Plutarch, *Fabius Maximus* 17), and *eklysis* (L-S 513, faintness; 2 Macc. 3:24). Josephus applied it to the spies who brought an ill report of the Promised Land.[4] It is constantly contrasted with *andreia*,[5] and *deilos* is contrasted with

1. *Deilia* is equivalent to the Latin *timor* (timidity), and has *thrasutēs* (foolhardiness) for its opposite (Plato, *Timaeus* 87a).

2. According to Bengel: "It is timidity of which the cause is in the mind more than from without."

3. In the last passage, the *deiloi* are those who have denied the faith in times of persecution because they fear suffering (cf. Eusebius, *Historia ecclesiastica* 8.3).

4. *Antiquitates Judaica* 3.15.1.

5. L-S 128, manliness.

deilia
eulabeia
phobos

andreios (manly).[6] *Deilia* seeks to shelter its timidity under the more honorable title of *ulabeia*[7] and pleads that it is indeed *asphaleia*.[8]

Phobos, often used with *tromos*,[9] is a middle term that is sometimes used in a bad but more often in a good sense in the New Testament.[10] Plato[11] added *aischros* (*150*) to it when he wanted to indicate an unmanly timidity.[12]

Eulabeia only occurs twice in the New Testament (Heb. 5:7;[13] 12:28), and on each occasion it means piety contemplated as a *fear* of God. This usage is based on the image of the careful handling (*eu lambanesthai*) of some precious yet fragile vessel that might easily be broken if treated less delicately and meticulously.[14] Such caution in conducting affairs[15] springs partially from a fear of failure that easily exposes it to the charge of timidity.[16] It is not surprising, then, that fear came to be regarded as an essential element of *eulabeia* and sometimes as its only sense.[17] For the most part, it is not dishonorable fear that is intended[18] but the fear that a wise and good man might maintain. Cicero[19] stated: "Turning away from evil, if it should occur with reason, would be called *caution* and would be perceived to reside in wisdom alone; however, should it be without reason and with slight and faint fright, it would be termed *fear*." Cicero probably had the definition of the Stoics in mind. They denied *phobos* was a *pathos* (*3806*), but they affirmed *eulabeia* was a virtue.[20] By using these distinctions, the Stoics tried to escape the embarrass-

6. For example, see the long discussion on valor and cowardice in Plato's *Protagoras* 360d. Also see the lively description of the *deilos* in the *Characters* (27) of Theophrastus.

7. L-S 720, caution; Philo, *De providentia* 739; cf. Dryden: "And calls that *providence*, which we call *flight*."

8. 803; Plutarch, *Animine an corporis affectiones sint peiores* 3; Philo, *Quod deterius potiori insidiari soleat* 11.

9. L-S 1826, trembling. See Gen. 9:2; Exod. 15:6; Deut. 11:25; 1 Cor. 2:3; Phil. 2:12. It is equivalent to the Latin *metus* (fear).

10. It is used in a bad sense in Rom. 8:15; 1 John 4:18; cf. Wisd. of Sol. 17:11. It is used in a good sense in Acts 9:31; Rom. 3:18; Eph. 6:5; Phil. 2:12; 1 Pet. 1:17.

11. *Protagoras* 360d.

12. On the distinction between *timor* (timidity), *metus* (fear), and *formido* (terror), see Donaldson, *Complete Latin Grammar*, p. 489.

13. See Bleek.

14. "For caution preserves everything," Aristophanes noted (*Aves* 377). Also see Balde's sublime funeral hymn on the young German empress: "Whom with hands of bone it touches, / As a crystal plate it crushes; / O absurd and awkward death, / O the fleeting fate of youth!"

15. The word is joined to *pronoia* (*4307*) by Plutarch (*Marcellus* 9); Euripides (*Phoenissae* 794) declared it *chrēsimōtatē* (*5539*) *Theōn*.

16. Thus Demosthenes (517), who contrasted *eulabeia* with *thrasos* (L-S 804, rashness), claimed that he was only *eulabēs* (*2126*), but his enemies charged him with being *deilos* and *atolmos* (L-S 271, cowardly). In Plutarch (*Fabius Maximus* 17), *eulabēs* and *dyselpistos* (L-S 455, despondent) are joined together.

17. Josephus, *Antiquitates Judaica* 11.6.9.

18. Wis. of Sol. 17:8 is a remarkable exception.

19. *Tusculanae disputationes* 4.6.

20. They defined it as "avoidance with reason" (Clement of Alexandria, *Stromata* 2.18). Thus Diogenes Laertius wrote (7.1.116): "People say that caution [*tēn eulabeian*] is the opposite of fear, being a reasonable avoidance; for, as they claim, a wise person never fears but is cau-

ments of their ethical position, which led them to admit that the wise man might feel "even certain indications of the passions of anger" but not the "passions" themselves.[21] Nevertheless, these distinctions did not conceal the Stoics' virtual abandonment of their position. They were, in fact, really only fighting about words; they were "name-calling," as a Peripatetic adversary charged.[22]

The more distinctly religious aspect of *eulabeia* will be covered in section 48.

---

tious." Plutarch (*De Stoicorum repugnantiis* 11) quoted their maxim: "To be cautious is characteristic of the wise."

21. Seneca, *De ira* 1.16; cf. Plutarch, *De virtute morali* 9.

22. On this matter, see the full discussion in Clement of Alexandria, *Stromata* 2.7–9; and cf. Augustine, *De civitate Dei* 9.4.

11

kakia (2549) *kakoētheia* (2550)

Evil(-mindedness) Wickedness Malice Malignity

Although classical authors often use *kakia* in a way that embraces the whole complex of moral evil, that is not the way the word is used in the New Testament. In classical literature, *aretē* (703) and *kakia* refer to virtue and vice,[1] respectively, though Cicero[2] refused to translate *kakia* by *malitia* (malice) and coined *vitiositas* (vice) instead. Cicero justified this by saying: "For malice [*malitia*] is the name of a particular fault; vice [*vitiositas*] includes all." In Cicero's estimation, *kakia* is not the name of one vice but of the viciousness out of which all vices spring. In the New Testament, however, *kakia* is not so much viciousness as a special form of vice. If *kakia* referred to viciousness, other evil habits of the mind would be subordinated to it (as a larger term includes the lesser), but in fact they are coordinated with it.[3] We must find a more suitable definition.

Kakia refers to a more evil mind set, to the *malitia* (malice) that Cicero refused to use, and *ponēria* (4189) refers to the active result of that evil habit of

1. Plato, *Republic* 444d. *Aretai* (703) *kai kakia* are virtues and vices (Aristotle, *Rhetorica* 2.12; *Ethica Nicomachea* 7.1; Plutarch, *Conjugalia praecepta* 25; and often).

2. *Tusculanae disputationes* 4.15.

3. Rom. 1:29; Col. 3:8; 1 Pet. 2:1.

mind.[4] Elsewhere Cicero explained *malitia* as "the shrewd and deceitful calculation of doing harm."[5] And, indeed, our English translators often have rendered *kakia* by "malice,"[6] showing that they regarded it in this way.[7]

Although *kakia* occurs several times in the New Testament, *kakoētheia* occurs just once in Paul's long and terrible catalogue of the wickedness that filled the heathen world (Rom. 1:29).[8] In that passage, *kakoētheia* has been translated by "malignity." When understood in this broader sense (which it often has),[9] *kakoētheia* corresponds exactly to the term *ill-nature* that was used by our early divines.[10] When used in that sense, however, it is difficult to assign *kakoētheia* to any domain not already occupied by *kakia* or *ponēria*. Therefore I prefer to understand Paul's use of *kakoētheia* in its more restricted sense, as it is so understood in the Geneva Version and by Aristotle.[11] Indeed, *kakoētheia* is Pliny's "ill-will of interpreters" (*Letters* 5.7)[12] and is exactly opposed to what Seneca[13] so happily called the "kind evaluation of things."[14]

Aristotle cited the unfavorable interpretation of all the words and actions of others as one of the vices of old people[15]—they are *kakoētheis* (L-S 861, malicious) and *kachypoptoi* (L-S 933, suspicious). We can assume that *kakoētheia* in Romans 1:29 has this narrower meaning. Its position in that dread cata-

4. Calvin said of *kakia* (Eph. 4:31): "The apostle indicates by this word *a depravity of the soul* that is set against humaneness and fairness and is generally termed malice." Cicero defined *malevolentia* (ill-will) as "the pleasure arising from harm to another without one's own gain" (*Tusculanae disputationes* 4.9).

5. *De deorum natura* 3.30; *De finibus* 3.11 toward the end.

6. Eph. 4:31; 1 Cor. 5:8; 14:20; 1 Pet. 2:1.

7. Theodoret, whose explanation of Rom. 1 agrees with this view, said: "He calls *kakian* the inclination of the soul toward the baser things and the calculation for the harm of one's neighbor." In nearly the same way, the Second Epistle of Clement (which is no longer regarded as an epistle at all) warned that *kakia* is the forerunner (*proodoiporos*) of all other sins (par. 10). See *Bosheit* in Herzog's *Real-Encyclopädie*.

8. *Kakoētheia* occurs four or five times in the Books of the Maccabees (3 Macc. 3:22; 7:3; 4 Macc. 1:4; 3:4). *Kakoēthēs* (L-S 861, ill-disposed, malicious) appears there as well (4 Macc. 1:25; 2:16) but never in the Septuagint.

9. Plato, *Republic* 1.384d; Xenophon, *On Hunting* 13.16. It appears in an even broader sense in Basil the Great: "*Kakoētheia* is, as I conclude, the very basic and hidden vice of character" (*Prologus 3: prooemium in regulas brevius tractatas* 77).

10. See my *Select Glossary* under this word. In the same way, the author of 3 Maccabees (3:22) spoke of some "who have rejected the noble through innate maliciousness [*kakoētheia*] and continuously turn to evil."

11. See the Geneva Version's periphrastic translation: "taking all things in the evil part," which is precisely Aristotle's definition of the word, to whose ethical terminology *kakoētheia* belongs. According to Aristotle, "*kakoētheia* is the interpreting of everything for the worse" (*Rhetoric* 2.13). Jeremy Taylor called *kakoētheia* "a baseness of nature by which we take things by the wrong handle and expound things always in the worst sense." Grotius described *kakoētheia* as "when we take in a worse meaning what we are able to interpret in a good sense, contrary to what the courtesy of love requires."

12. The use of *interpretor* as in "to interpret *awry*" is striking in Tacitus (who was not free of this vice), Pliny, and the other writers of their age.

13. *On Anger* 2.24.

14. For precisely such a use of *kakoēthōs* (maliciously), see Josephus, *Antiquitates Judaica* 7.6; cf. 2 Sam. 10:3.

15. *Rhetoric* 2.13 is a mournful but most instructive passage for Christians.

logue of sins entirely justifies our treating it as a peculiar form of evil. It manifests itself in a malignant interpretation of the actions of others, attributing to them the worst imaginable motives.

We should note the deep psychological truth that the secondary meaning of *kakoētheia* brings out: the evil that we find in ourselves makes us ready to suspect and believe that evil exists in others. The *kakoēthēs* (malicious person), himself being of an evil moral habit, sees himself in those around him.[16] Contrast that with Schiller's description of the kind of love that "delightedly believes Divinities, *being itself divine*." In the same way one who is thoroughly evil finds it impossible to believe anything but evil about others (Job 1:9–11; 2:4–5). At the very time when they are plotting to take the life of Telemachus, the suitors in the *Odyssey* are persuaded that he intends to kill them at a banquet by mingling poison with their wine.[17] And Iago[18] apparently believed that the world was peopled only with other Iagoes; he could not conceive of any other type of humanity. Socrates[19] wanted to show that physicians benefit from their association with the sick but that teachers and rulers do not benefit from an association with the bad. He explained how young men, as yet uncorrupted, are *euētheis* (good-hearted) rather than *kakoētheis* (malicious), "inasmuch as they do not possess patterns of feeling similar to the wicked."

16. Our English proverb states "ill doers are ill deemers," or, as it runs in the monkish line, "The scoundrel asserts of me what he knows is in himself."

17. *Odyssey* 2.329, 330.

18. In Shakespeare's *Othello*.

19. Plato, *Republic* 3.409a, b.

12

agapaō (25) *phileō* (5368) — *Love*

Although no attempt has been made in our Authorized Version to discriminate between *agapaō* and *phileō*, the frequently noteworthy difference between them should have been reproduced. Because this difference is nearly equivalent to the one between the Latin *diligo* (esteem) and *amo* (love), understanding the exact distinction between these Latin verbs will help us understand the difference between the two Greek verbs.

Cicero frequently opposed *diligo* and *amo* in an instructive manner. In a letter about his affection for another friend he said: "In order that you might know that he is not only *esteemed* [*diligi*] by me but also *loved* [*amari*]."[1] From these and similar passages[2] we might conclude that *amare* corresponds to *philein* (5368) and is stronger than *diligere*, which corresponds to *agapan*. This is true, but it is not the whole truth. Ernesti correctly noted the different meanings of the Latin verbs: "To *esteem* [*diligere*] pertains more to judgment; to *love* [*amare*], however, extends to the innermost feeling of the soul." Cicero (in the passage first quoted) really was saying: "I do not *esteem* the man merely, but I *love* him; there is something of the passionate warmth of affection in the feeling with which I regard him."

1. *Letters to Friends* 13.47. Also see *Letters to Brutus* 1: "L. Clodius strongly *esteems* [*diligit*] me or (to speak more forcibly) strongly *loves* [*amat*] me."

2. There is an ample collection of them in Döderlein's *Lateinische Synonyme*, 4:98ff.

Although a friend may desire "to be loved" rather than "to be esteemed" by his friend, "being esteemed" is more than "being loved"; the *agapasthai* is more than the *phileisthai*. The first term expresses an intellectual attachment of choice and selection ("diligere" = "deligere" = "to choose"). Esteem may spring from a sense of obligation (as in the case of a benefactor) or a regard for worthy qualities in an object or person. The second term refers to a relation that is more emotional and that implies more passion, though it is not necessarily an unreasoning attachment.[3]

There are two passages in Xenophon[4] that illuminate the relation between *agapaō* and *phileō*. These passages show how the notions of respect and reverence are always implied in *agapan*, though not in *philein* (though *philein* does not exclude them). In the second passage Xenophon stated: "The women were loving [*ephiloun*] him as one who cares; he was esteeming [*ēgapa*] them as beneficial." This helps to explain why people are commanded *agapan ton Theon* (*2316*)[5] and good men do;[6] but people are never commanded *philein ton Theon*. The Father, however, does both in relation to his Son.[7]

Unlike the Authorized Version, by using *diligo* (esteem) and *amo* (love), the Vulgate has preserved a distinction between *agapaō* and *phileō* in almost all of the New Testament passages. It is especially unfortunate that the Authorized Version did not preserve the important and instructive distinction between *agapaō* and *phileō* in John 21:15–17. In this passage Christ asked Peter three times: "Do you love Me?" Christ's first question, "*Agapas me?*," seems a cold way for him to address the penitent Peter, who was overflowing with love for his Lord, since it fails to express the warmth of Peter's affection toward him. Although any form of the question would have been painful (v. 17), the use of *agapas* was even more distressing.[8] In his answers, Peter twice substituted *philō se* (v. 15)—the more personal word for love—for Christ's *agapas*. Christ's third formulation of the question, which uses *phileis* not *agapas*, shows that Peter has triumphed. But all of this subtle play of feeling disappears in a translation that either does not care or that is not able to reproduce the original variation of words.

Erōs, *eran*, and *erastēs*[9] never occur in the New Testament, though *eran* and *erastēs* occasionally occur in the Septuagint.[10] Their absence, which is

3. Thus Antonius in Caesar's funeral discourse addressed the Roman people: "You loved [*ephilēsate*] him as a father, and you esteemed [*ēgapēsate*] him as a benefactor" (Dion Cassius 44.48).

4. *Memorabilia* 2.7.9.12.

5. Matt. 22:37; Luke 10:27; 1 Cor. 8:3.

6. Rom. 8:28; 1 Pet. 1:8; 1 John 4:21.

7. *Agapa ton Huion* (*5207*; John 3:35; cf. Matt. 3:17) and also *philei ton Huion* (John 5:20; cf. Prov. 8:22, 30; John 1:18).

8. Bengel generally has the honor "of having pin-pointed the matter"; but here he has really missed the point. "*Agapan* (*amare*) comes from need and desire; *philein* (*diligere*) is the result of judgment."

9. L-S 695 and 681, love, to love, lover (respectively)—referring to sexual passion.

10. Thus *eran* appears in Esther 2:17; Prov. 4:6; *erastēs* is generally used in a dishonorable sense such as "paramour" (Ezek. 16:33; Hos. 2:5). Once or twice, however, it has a more honorable meaning (as in Wisd. of Sol. 8:2).

significant, is partially explained by the way that the world had corrupted their meanings. These words had become so associated with the idea of sensual passion and carried such an aura of unholiness about them[11] that they were not used in Scripture. Rather than employing one of them, the writers of Scripture created the new word *agapē* (26), which occurs in the Septuagint[12] and in the Apocrypha[13] but not in any heathen writings.[14]

But there may have been a more important reason to avoid using *erōs*, which, like other words, could have received a new consecration despite the degradation of its past history.[15] And, indeed, there were tendencies among Platonists to use *erōs* to refer to the longing after unseen but eternal Beauty, whose faint vestiges appear everywhere.[16] In this sense Philo called *erōs* "heavenly love."[17] Because *erōs* expressed this yearning desire[18] and longing after the unpossessed,[19] it was unsuitable to express Christian love.[20] Christian love is not merely a sense of need, emptiness, and poverty and a longing after fullness and an unattainable Beauty. Christian love is a love to God and to man that is the result of God's love shed abroad in the hearts of his people. Since the incarnation, mere longing and yearning (*erōs* at its best) have given place to a love that not merely desires but that also possesses the one loved.

11. See Origen, *Prologus in canticum canticorum*, 3:28, 30.

12. 2 Sam. 13:15; Song of Sol. 2:4; Jer. 2:2.

13. Wisd. of Sol. 3:9.

14. Although Philo and Josephus use *philanthrōpia* (L-S 1932, benevolence) and *philadelphia* (L-S 1931, brotherly love), the last word is used only to refer to the love between blood brothers (cf. Cremer, *Wörterbuch des Neues Testamentes Gräcität*, p. 12).

15. On the attempt which some Christian writers had made to distinguish between *amor* and *dilectio* or *caritas*, see Augustine, *De civitate Dei*, 14.7: "Some believe that esteem [*dilectionem*] or affection [*caritatem*] are different from love [*amorem*]. For they say that 'esteem' must be taken in a good sense and 'love' in an evil one." Augustine showed the impossibility of maintaining this distinction by pointing out many examples where *dilectio* and *diligo* are used in a bad sense in the Vulgate and where *amor* and *amo* are used in a good sense.

16. I cannot regard as an evidence of such reconsecration the celebrated words of Ignatius, *Ad Romanos* 7: *ho emos erōs estaurōtai*. It is far more consistent with the genius of these Ignatian Epistles to take *erōs subjectively* here, "My love of the world is crucified," i.e., with Christ, rather than *objectively*, "Christ, the object of my love, is crucified."

17. *De vita contempliva* 2; *De vita* Mosis 1.

18. "The dreadful yearning" in Sophocles, *Trachiniae* 476. Cf. Euripides, *Ion* 67; *Alcestis* 1101.

19. In Plato's exquisite myth in *Symposium* 203b, *Erōs* is the offspring of *Penia*, the goddess Poverty.

20. Gregory of Nazianzene best expressed that *erōs* is no more than desire: "Yearning is desire for either the noble or ignoble; *Erōs* is a yearning warm and hard to restrain," *Carmina* 2.34, 150, 151.

13

thalassa (2281) *pelagos* (3989) — Sea

Curtius[1] and Pott[2] connect the noun *thalassa* with the verb *tarassein* (5015) and consequently define the former as "agitated" or "disturbed." Schmidt dissented[3] and urged that the sea's predominant impression on the beholder is not one of unrest and agitation but of rest and quietude. According to Schmidt, *thalassa* refers to "the sea as a huge body of saltwater in view of its natural consistency and in view of its meaning; it is not any different from the brine [*hals*] mentioned in poetic literature." Schmidt also called the sea "the great salt flood." Without further discussion of this point, suffice it to say that like the Latin *mare* (sea), *thalassa* is the sea as contrasted with the land[4] or, more strictly, with the shore.[5]

Pelagos[6] is the vast uninterrupted expanse of open water—the *altum mare* (high sea)[7]—as distinguished from a sea broken by islands and shut in by

1. P. 596.
2. *Etymologische Forschungen*, 2:56.
3. 1:642.
4. Gen. 1:10; Matt. 23:15; Acts 4:24.
5. See Hayman's *Odyssey*, 1:33. *Appendix*.
6. *Pelagos* is closely related to *plax* (4109) and to *platys* (4116, plat, plot, flat).
7. It has the same meaning in Latin: "As rafts held to the open sea [*pelagus*], nor any more did any Land meet them, salt waters everywhere and everywhere sky" (Virgil, *Aeneid* 5.8).

coasts and headlands.[8] *Pelagos* primarily suggests the breadth of the open sea and not its depth, except as a secondary notion. Thus Sophocles said: "The open sea [*pelagos*] here is large and not navigable."[9] The murmuring Israelites[10] likened *pelagos* to the illimitable sand-flats of the desert. In Herodotus (2.92) the Nile that overflows Egypt is said "to keep flooding [*pelagizein*] the plains," though it covered them in water only a few feet deep (cf. 2.97). Plato[11] recognized this distinction between breadth and depth and refused to call the Mediterranean Sea *pelagos*, because he saw it as a harbor with the narrow entrance between the Pillars of Hercules as its mouth. Only the great Atlantic Ocean can be acknowledged as "a genuine sea, truly an open sea [*pelagos*]."[12]

In Matthew 18:6, however, one of only two New Testament uses of *pelagos*, that distinction may seem invalid. Matthew 18:6 says: "It would be better for him if a millstone were hung around his neck, *and he were drowned in the depth of the sea*."[13] But the sense of depth that the passage requires is found in *katapontisthē* (he were drowned), not in *pelagos*.[14] *Katapontisthē* implies the sea in its *perpendicular* depth, just as *pelagos* is the sea in its *horizontal* dimensions and extent.[15]

8. Thucydides, 6.104; 7.49; Plutarch, *Timoleon* 8. Hippias in the *Protagoras* of Plato (338a) charged the eloquent sophist with "fleeing into an open sea [*pelagos*] of words, having lost sight of land." This last idiom reappears in the French *noyer la terre* (to drown the land), applied to a ship sailing out of sight of land, as indeed in Virgil's "we leave behind the citadels of the Phaeacians" (*Aeneid* 3.291).

9. *Oedipus Coloneus* 659.

10. Philo, *De vita Mosis* 35.

11. *Timaeus* 25a, b.

12. Cf. Aristotle, *De mundo* 3. In *Meteorologica* 2.1 Aristotle states: "The sea [*hē thalatta*—another spelling of *hē thalassa*] appears to flow at the Straits of Gibraltar, if anywhere the open sea [*pelagos*] is contrasted from large to small on account of the encircling land."

13. *Kai katapontisthē en tō pelagei tēs thalassēs*.

14. *Katapontisthē* comes from *pontos* (not in the New Testament), which is related to *bathos* (L-S 301, depth), *bythos* (L-S 333, depth; Exod. 15:5), and the poetic *benthos* (L-S 313, depth).

15. This is equivalent to the Latin *aequor maris* (the even surface of the sea in its calm state). Cf. Döderlein, *Lateinische Synonyme*, 4:75.

14

sklēros (4642) — Hard
austēros (840) — Austere

In the parable of the talents in Matthew 25, the slothful servant charges his master with being *sklēros* (a *hard* man, v. 24), but in the corresponding parable in Luke 19 he accuses him of being *austēros* (an *austere* man, v. 21). The words are similar but not identical in meaning.

Sklēros[1] is correctly applied to something that is hard and dry (and therefore rough and disagreeable to the touch) because of a lack of moisture.[2] More frequently, *sklēros* is used as an ethical term that expresses roughness, harshness, and intractability in a person's moral nature. Thus Nabal (1 Sam. 25:3) is described as *sklēros*, a fitting epithet for this churlish man.[3]

1. *Sklēros* is derived from *skellō*, 2 aor. *sklēnai* (L-S 1606, dry up). It is equivalent to the Latin *arefacio* (make dry).

2. More than this, *sklēros* may refer to something that is warped and intractable and may combine the concepts of *asper* (rough) and *durus* (hard).

3. *Sklēros* also is associated with *auchmēros* (850; Plato, *Symposium* 195d), *antitypos* (499; *Theaetetus* 155a; Plutarch, *De Pythiae oraculis* 26), *ametastrophos* (L-S 82, unalterable; Plato, *Cratylus* 407d), *agrios* (66; Aristotle, *Ethica Nicomachea* 4.8; Plutarch, *Consolatio ad Apollonium* 3), *anēdyntos* (L-S 137, unpleasant; *Praecepta gerendae reipublicae* 3), *apēnēs* (L-S 188, rough; *De vitioso pudore*), *anerastos* (L-S 134, loveless; *De adulatore et amico* 19), *trachys* (5138; *De liberis educandis* 18), *apaideutos* (521; *De Alexandri magni fortuna aut virtute* 1.5), *atreptos* (L-S 272, unchangeable; Diogenes Laërtius, 7.1.64, 117), *aphēniastēs* (L-S 289, rebellious; Philo, *De septem orbis spectaculis* 1), *authadēs* (829; Gen. 44:3), *ponēros* (4190; 1 Sam. 25:3), and *pikros* (4089). *Sklēros* is contrasted with *euēthikos* (L-S 713, good-natured; Plato, *Charmides* 175c), *malakos* (3120; *Protagoras* 331d), and *malthakos* (L-S 1077, soft; *Symposium* 195d; Sophocles, *Oedipus Coloneus* 771).

Austēros is used only once in the New Testament (Luke 19:21) and never in the Septuagint. *Austēros* primarily refers to something that contracts the tongue and that is harsh and *stringent* to the palate, something like unaged wine or unripe fruit.[4] Just as we use *strict*[5] as an ethical term, so the Greeks used *austēros* in the realm of ethics, borrowing an image from the concept of taste, just as *sklēros* is borrowed from the concept of touch. The person described as *austēros* is neither amiable nor attractive.[6]

None of the words associated with *austēros* imply the kind of deep moral perversity that is indicated by many of the words that are associated with *sklēros*. Moreover, *austēros* often occurs in more honorable company, and so is frequently used with *sōphrōn*,[7] *mousikos*,[8] and *sōphronikos*.[9] An otherwise noble and great person[10] is called *austēros* when he does not sacrifice to the Graces.[11] The Stoics claimed that all good men were austere.[12]

In Latin, *austerus* is predominantly an honorable word[13] that describes an earnest and severe person who is opposed to all levity. It describes a person who may need to guard against harshness, rigor, or moroseness,[14] though he is not yet guilty of these traits.

We may distinguish *sklēros* and *austēros* in this way. On the one hand, *sklēros* always conveys a serious reproach and indicates a harsh, inhuman, and (in the earlier sense of that word) uncivil character.[15] On the other hand, *austēros* does not necessarily convey a reproach at all.[16] And even where it does, it conveys a far less opprobrious reproach than the one implied by *sklēros*. *Austēros* is the exaggeration of a virtue pushed too far rather than an absolute vice.

4. Cowper, describing himself as a boy gathering "sloes *austere*" from the hedgerows, used "austere" in an exact sense.

5. *Strict* comes from the Latin *stringo* (draw tight).

6. *Austēros* also is associated with *aēdēs* (L-S 30, unpleasant; Plato, *Republic* 3.398a), *akratos* (194), *anēdyntos* (L-S 137, unpleasant; Plutarch, *Conjugalia praecepta* 29), *anēdystos* (*Phocion* 5), and *authekastos* (L-S 275, blunt; *De adulatore et amico* 14. Plutarch used this word in a negative sense to mean "self-willed" and joined it to *atenktos* [L-S 268, not to be softened], which means "not to be molded and fashioned like moist clay in the hands of another." The German equivalent is *eigensinnig* [self-willed, stubborn]. There are words in all languages that begin with a positive sense [Aristotle, *Ethica Nicomachea* 4.7] but end with a negative one.), *pikros* (4089; *De adulatore et amico* 2), *agelastos* (L-S 8, gloomy), *anenteuktos* (L-S 133, unsociable; *De cupiditate divitiarum* 7), and *auchmēros* (850; Philo, *De praemiis et poenis* 5). Aristotle (*Ethica eudemia* 7.5) contrasted the *austēros* with the *eutrapelos* (L-S 735, witty), using the latter word in a good sense.

7. 4998; Plutarch, *Conjugalia praecepta* 7, 29; *Quaestiones convivales* 40.

8. 3451; *Septem sapientium convivium* 5.2.

9. L-S 1751, self-controlled; Clement of Alexandria, *Paedagogus* 2.4.

10. *Gennaios* [L-S 344, noble] *kai megas* [3173].

11. Plutarch, *Amatorius* 23.

12. Diogenes Laërtius, 7.1.64, 117: "They say that all good men are austere [*austērous*] by not busying themselves with pleasure nor expecting from others what relates to pleasure." Cf. Plutarch, *Conjugalia praecepta* 27.

13. Döderlein, *Lateinische Synonyme*, 3:232.

14. "Let his austerity not be sad nor his affability licentious" (Quintilian, 2.2.5).

15. In the words of Hesiod (*Opera et dies* 147), "having a dauntless spirit of steel."

16. Just as the German *streng* (strict), which is very different from *hart* (harsh), does not necessarily convey the notion of a reproach.

15

eikōn (1504) *homoiōsis* (3669) *homoiōma* (3667) — *Image Likeness Similitude*

The distinction between *eikōn* and *homoiōsis* and *homoiōma* is interesting for two reasons. First, these terms were debated in the Arian controversy. In that context the question was: Are these words suitable to represent the relation of the Son to the Father? Second, as used in Genesis 1:26 (LXX) these terms raise the question:[1] Does this passage draw a distinction between the "image" (*eikōn*) of God *in which* and the "likeness" (*homoiōsis*) of God *after which* man was created, and if so, what exactly is the distinction?

During the course of the long Arian debate, a very definite distinction was drawn between *eikōn* and *homoiōsis* and *homoiōma*.[2] Apart from the Arian controversy, *eikōn*[3] and *homoiōma* frequently were used as synonyms. For example, *homoiōmata* and *eikones* were used interchangeably by Plato[4] to describe the earthly copies and representations of the heavenly archetypes. But when the church needed to defend itself against Arian error and equivocation, it

1. It seems at first sight removed from any controversy, but it has insinuated itself into more than one question.

2. See Lightfoot's note on Col. 1:15 in his *Commentary on the Colossians*, especially his discussion of the words *eikōn tou Theou* (2316, image of God).

3. This word comes from *eikō*, *eoika* (1503).

4. *Phaedrus* 250b.

drew a sharp distinction between these two words that was not arbitrary but based on an essential difference of meaning.

Eikōn[5] always refers to a prototype that it resembles and from which it is drawn—a *paradeigma*.[6] Thus Gregory Nazianzene stated: "For this is the nature of an image [*eikonos*]: to be an imitation of an archetype."[7] The monarch's head on a coin is an *eikōn* (Matt. 22:20); the reflection of the sun in the water is an *eikōn*;[8] and the statue in stone or other material also is an *eikōn* (Rev. 13:14). The illustration that comes closest to fully revealing the meaning of *eikōn* is that of the relation of a child to his parents, for a child is "a living image" (*empsychos eikōn*) of his parents.

Although *homoiōma*, or *homoiōsis*, implies that one thing resembles another, the resemblance is not necessarily acquired in the same way as is the resemblance of an *eikōn* to that which it resembles. Unlike an *eikōn*, in the case of *homoiōma* and *homoiōsis*, the resemblance is not a *derived* resemblance but may be an accidental one, as when one egg is like another or when two unrelated men resemble one another. According to Augustine,[9] the *imago* (image = *eikōn*) includes and involves the *similitudo* (likeness), but the *similitudo* (= *homoiōsis*) does not involve the *imago*. This explains why the New Testament uses *eikōn* to describe the Son's relation to the Father[10] but does not use any of the *homoios* (3664) words to do so. In fact, as soon as the church saw that the *homoios* word family was not used in good faith, it condemned the use of these words to describe Christ.[11]

Although *eikōn* expresses the truth about Christ's relation to the Father, this term is inadequate to express the whole truth about a matter that transcends the limits of human thought.[12] *Eikōn* denotes an image that has been derived from an archetype. But because no derived image has the same worth and dignity as its prototype, the use of *eikōn* to describe Christ's relation to the Father must be compensated for. Because *homoiotēs*,[13] *homoiōsis*, and related words express mere *similarity*, they do not suitably describe Christ's relation to the Father.[14] The church, guided by exactly the same considerations,

5. It is equivalent to the Latin *imago* (image), and *imitago* (representation), and the Greek *apeikonisma* (L-S 182, copy) and is used in the same way as *Logos* is used by Philo (*Legum allegoriarum libri* 3.31).

6. L-S 1307, model; Philo, ibid. It is the German *Abbild* (likeness) that always presumes a *Vorbild* (model).

7. *Oratio* 36.

8. Plato, *Phaedo*, 99d.

9. *Questiones* 83.74.

10. 2 Cor. 4:4; Col. 1:15; cf. Wisd. of Sol. 7:26.

11. Thus Hilary, addressing an Arian, said, "I may use them to exclude Sabellian error, but I will not suffer you to do so, whose intention is altogether different" (*Contra Constantinum Imperatorem* 17–21).

12. As are its closest theological allies *charaktēr* (5481) and *apaugasma* (5481; Heb. 1:3) and words even more removed in meaning, like *esoptron* (2072), *atmis* (822), *aporroia* (640; Wisd. of Sol. 5:2, 26), and *skia* (4639; Philo, *Legum allegoriarum libri* 3.31; but not Heb. 10:1).

13. L-S 1225, resemblance.

14. If these words did not actually imply error, they might suggest it by seeming to justify error with no compensating advantage.

allowed the verb *gennan* (1080) but not the verb *ktizein* (2936) to be used to describe the Son's relation to the Father.[15]

The exegetical issue surrounding the use of *eikōn* and *homoiōsis* has to do with the nature of man. In the great fiat announcing man's original constitution, "Let Us make man in Our *image*,[16] according to Our *likeness*,"[17] is anything different intended by the second phrase than by the first? Or is the second phrase simply the result of the first—"in Our image" and therefore "after Our likeness"? The New Testament claims that man is both the *eikōn* (1 Cor. 11:7) and the *homoiōsis* (James 3:9). This whole subject is discussed at length by Gregory of Nyssa,[18] who, with many of the fathers and schoolmen, saw a real distinction between *eikōn* and *homoiōsis*. Thus the great Alexandrian theologians taught that the *eikōn* was something *in* which men were created that was common to all men both before and after the fall (Gen. 9:6) and that the *homoiōsis* was something *toward* which man was created, something for him to strive after. As Origen stated: "He received the dignity of the image [*imaginis*] in the first circumstance, but the perfecting of the likeness [*similitudinis*] has been preserved for the consummation."[19]

The influence of Platonic ideas on Alexandrian theologians is evident in that distinction. It is well known that Plato presented the "becoming like God [*homoiousthai*] according to one's ability"[20] as the highest scope of man's life.[21] The schoolmen also drew a distinction, though not the same one, between "these two divine stamps upon man." Thus in Anselm, "image [*imago*] is according to the knowledge of truth; likeness [*similitudo*] is according to the love of virtue."[22] The first word specifies the intellectual and the second the moral preeminence in which man was created.

Without justification, many interpreters have refused to acknowledge these or any other distinctions between the two declarations in Genesis 1:26.[23] The Alexandrians were very near the truth, even if they did not completely grasp it. The words of Jerome (originally applied to the Book of Revelation) may aptly be applied to other passages of Scripture: "as many terms, so

15. Those who are interested in the great controversy that arose over the relation of these words to one another—especially the questions of the exact force of *eikōn* as applied to the Son—will find Petavius's *De Trinitate* 2.11; 4.6; 6.5, 6 helpful. Gfrörer (*Philo*, 1:261ff.) has an interesting but wholly inadequate treatment of the Alexandrian theosophists on the same subject.

16. *Kat' eikona* (LXX), *ṣelem* (6755) in Hebrew.

17. *Kath' homoiōsin* (LXX), *dmût* (1823) in Hebrew.

18. *De creatione hominis sermo primus et sermo alter*, ed. Hörner, pp. 2–72. This treatise is devoted exclusively to this question, mainly in its bearing on controversies of his own day.

19. *De principiis* 3.6. Cf. *Commentarii in evangelium Joannis*, 20:20; Irenaeus, 5.16.2; Tertullian, *De baptismo* 5.

20. *Theaetetus* 176a.

21. Clement (*Stromata* 2.22) brings this same passage of Plato to bear upon this very discussion.

22. *Meditationes* I^{ma}; Peter Lombard, *Sententiae* 2. dist. 16; H. de S. Victore, *De anima*, 2.25; *De sacris* 1.6.2.

23. Baxter, in his interesting reply to the inquiries of Elliott, the Indian missionary, rejected all distinctions among these terms as groundless conceits, though he himself in general was only too anxious for distinction and division (*Life and Times, by Sylvester*, 2:296).

eikōn
homoiōsis
homoiōma

many mysteries." A passage like Genesis 1–3, which is the important history of man's creation and his fall, is one where we might expect to find mysteries—prophetic intimations of truths that might require ages to develop.

Without attempting to draw a very strict distinction between *eikōn* and *homoiōsis* or their Hebrew counterparts, we may say that the *whole* history of man—not only in his original creation but later in his restoration and reconstitution in the Son—is significantly wrapped up in the double statement of Genesis 1:26. Perhaps the reason for this double statement was because God did not stop at the contemplation of man as he was originally created, but looked forward to him as "*renewed* in knowledge according to the image of him who created him."[24] Only as a partaker of this double benefit would man attain the true end for which he was ordained.

24. Col. 3:10, on which see Lightfoot *in loco*.

16

asōtia (810)

aselgeia (766)

Dissipation
Riotous Excess
Licentiousness
Wantonness
Lasciviousness
Lewdness

Although *asōtia* and *aselgeia* are not synonyms, it is unlikely that one who is *asōtos*[1] would not also be *aselgēs*.[2] *Asōtia* and *aselgeia* express different aspects of the same sin or at least depict it from different perspectives.

Asōtia[3] occurs three times in the New Testament (Eph. 5:18; Titus 1:6; 1 Pet. 4:4), once in the Septuagint (Prov. 28:7), and once in the Apocrypha (2 Macc. 6:4), where it is joined with *kōmoi* (*2970*). The adverb *asōtōs* (*811*) occurs in Luke 15:13, and *asōtos* occurs once in the Septuagint (Prov. 7:11). In the Authorized Version, *asōtia* is translated "dissipation." In medieval Latin, the Vulgate's use of *luxuria* and *luxuriose* implied a loose and profligate life-style. This is far from our present use of *luxury* and *luxuriously* (see my *Select Glossary*). *Asōtos* is sometimes taken in a passive sense as equivalent to

1. L-S 267, profligate.
2. L-S 255, licentious.
3. This word had greater ramifications in heathen ethics than they intended or knew.

asōstos[4] or as referring to one who cannot be saved[5] or as equivalent to *perditus* (hopeless).[6] Grotius states: "The race of humans is so immersed in vices that their salvation has been regarded as lost." *Asōtos* is prophetic of the doom that will come to those to whom it applies,[7] though this is a comparatively rare use. More commonly the *asōtos* is a spendthrift.[8] According to Aristotle, who used the word as part of his ethical terminology, *asōtia* is the extravagant squandering of means.[9] Aristotle argued that the *eleutherios* (the truly liberal man) keeps the golden mean between the two extremities, namely, the *asōtia*[10] on the one hand and the *aneleutheria*[11] on the other. When Plato[12] named the various catachrestic terms that men use to describe vices by the names of the virtues they caricature, he described *asōtia* as *megaloprepeia*.[13]

It is easy to see how one who is *asōtos* (spending more than his means warrant) easily falls under the fatal influence of flatterers. In the end the temptations with which he has surrounded himself lead him to spend his resources *on his own lusts and appetites*, for the gratification of his own sensual desires. Thus *asōtia* indicates not only expensive habits but even more a dissolute, debauched, and profligate manner of living.[14]

Asōtia is used that way in the New Testament.[15] Because *asōtia*'s two meanings—"dissipation" and "riotous excess"—often blend into one another, it is not possible to keep them strictly separated. Thus the examples of *asōtos* and *asōtia* given by Athenaeus (4.59–67) sometimes have one meaning and sometimes the other. One who wastes his goods often wastes everything else, including his own time, faculties, and powers. Uniting the active and passive

4. Plutarch, *Alcibiades* 3.

5. *Sōzesthai mē dynamenos*, as Clement of Alexandria (*Paedagogus* 2.1) explained it.

6. Horace, *Satirae* 1.2.15. It is *heillos* (unrelieved) in German, or as we used to say in English, a "losel," a "hopelost." This noticeable word is in Grimeston's *Polybius*.

7. Thus in the *Adelphi* of Terence (6.7) there is a description of a youth "ruined [*perditum*] by debauchery." According to Terence, "If *Salus* [Salvation, a Roman goddess] herself should desire, it is utterly impossible to *save* [*servare*] this household." Most likely in the original Greek there was a threefold play on *asōtos*, *sōtēria* (4991, salvation), and *sōzein* (4982, to save), but the absence of a corresponding group of words in Latin prevented Terence from preserving it.

8. Latin has *prodigus* (spendthrift) and Old English has a "scatterling," as used by Spenser.

9. *Ethica Nicomachea* 4.1.3. "*Asōtia* [profligacy] is an excess regarding money."

10. It is equivalent to the Latin *effusio* (prodigality).

11. L-S 131, ignoble stinginess. This is equivalent to the Latin *tenacitas* (niggardliness). Cf. Augustine, *Epistulae* 167.2.

12. *Republic* 8.560e.

13. L-S 1087, magnificence. Cf. Quintilian (*Institutiones oratiorae* 8.36): "It is called generosity instead of extravagance." At this point in the development of the meaning of the word, Plutarch joined it with *polyteleia* (L-S 1444, costliness; *Apophthegmata Laconica* 1), and Menander joined *asōtos* with *polytelēs* (4185; Meineke, *Fragmenta Comoeda Graeca*, p. 994).

14. This is equivalent to the German *liederlich* (dissolute). Aristotle noted: "Wherefore most of the prodigal people [*tōn asōtōn*] are also self-indulgent, for they spend easily and waste money on their indulgences, and they incline toward pleasures since they do not live for what is noble" (*Ethica Nicomachea* 4.1.36). Earlier, Aristotle had said: "Those lacking self-control and spending money on self-indulgence we call prodigal."

15. Elsewhere we find *asōtiai* and *kraipalai* (2897) joined together (Herodian, 2.5).

meanings of *asōtia*, we may say of such a person that he will be laid waste; he at once loses himself and is lost.[16]

The etymology of *aselgeia* is obscure. Some have seen it as a reference to Selge, a city of Pisidia whose inhabitants were infamous for their vices; others believe that it comes from *thelgein*.[17] *Aselgeia* occurs more frequently in the New Testament than *asōtia* and is generally translated "lasciviousness" in our Authorized Version,[18] though sometimes it is translated "wantonness."[19] In the Vulgate *aselgeia* is translated by *impudicitia* (lewdness) and *luxuria* (wantonness).[20] If our English or Latin translators only had impurities and lusts of the flesh in mind, their translations are certainly too narrow. *Aselgeia*[21] is best described as wanton, lawless insolence. It is a somewhat stronger term than the Latin *protervitas* (impudence)—though of the same quality—and more closely resembles the Latin *petulantia* (wantonness). Chrysostom[22] correlated *aselgeia* with *itamotēs*,[23] and Basil the Great[24] defined it as "a disposition of the soul not having or bearing any struggle with remorse." Passow observed that the *aselgēs*[25] is very closely allied to the *hybristikos*[26] and the *akolastos*.[27] The *akolastos* acknowledges no restraints and dares to do whatever his caprice and wanton petulance may suggest.[28] Although *aselgeia* may display itself in "lascivious" acts, which are the worst manifestations of *hybris* (5196), it primarily refers to acts that are petulant and insolent.[29] "Wantonness" is the better of the two translations used in the Authorized Version because it has the same duplicity of meaning as *aselgeia*, a term with which it has a remarkable ethical connection.

In many passages *aselgeia* does not imply lasciviousness. In classical Greek *aselgeia* is defined as "violence with abuse and rashness."[30] Thus Demosthenes[31] denounced the *aselgeia* of Philip and characterized the blow that

16. In the *Tabula* of Cebes, *Asōtia*, one of the courtesans—the temptresses of Hercules—keeps company with *Akrasia* (192, self-indulgence), *Aplēstia* (L-S 190, insatiate desire), and *Kolakeia* (2850, flattery).

17. L-S 788, enchant, bewitch. *Thelgein* probably has the same meaning as the German *schwelgen* (to carouse). See, however, Donaldson, *Cratylus*, 3d ed., p. 692.

18. Mark 7:22; 2 Cor. 12:21; Gal. 5:19; Eph. 4:29; 1 Pet. 4:3; Jude 4.

19. Rom. 13:13; 2 Pet. 2:18.

20. It is defined in the *Etymologicon magnum* as "readiness for every pleasure."

21. It is noteworthy that *aselgeia* is not grouped in the catalogue of sins in Mark 7:21–22.

22. *Homilia 37 in Matthaeum*.

23. L-S 844, effrontery.

24. *Prologus 3: prooemium in regulas brevius tractatas* 67.

25. L-S 255, licentious, wanton.

26. L-S 1841, wanton.

27. L-S 52, incontinent.

28. Thus Witsius observed: "*Aselgeia* can be termed *every* impudence, wantonness, and licentiousness, as much of one's innate disposition as of one's behavior, which Aeschines sets against moderation and prudence" (*Meleteum Leiden*, p. 465). Also see Cocceius's long note (par. 136) on *aselgeia* in his comments on Gal. 5.

29. *Aselgeia* is linked by Polybius (5.111) with *bia* (970).

30. Bekker, *Anecdota*, p. 451.

31. *First Philippic* 42.

asōtia

aselgeia

Meidias had given him as characteristic of the *aselgeia* of the man.[32] Plutarch characterized a similar outrage that Alcibiades had committed against an honorable citizen of Athens as *aselgeia*.[33] Indeed, he painted Alcibiades in the full-length portrait of an *aselgēs*. Aristotle spoke of "the wantonness [*aselgeian*] of demagogues" as a frequent cause of revolutions.[34] Josephus ascribed *aselgeia* and *mavia* (*3130*, madness) to Jezebel because she dared to build a temple of Baal in the holy city itself.[35] Josephus also ascribed these traits to a Roman soldier who by a grossly indecent act committed while on guard at the temple during the Passover provoked a riot that resulted in the loss of many lives.[36]

Thus *aselgeia* and *asōtia* are clearly distinguishable. *Asōtia* refers to wastefulness and riotous excess; *aselgeia* refers to lawless insolence and wanton caprice.

32. Demosthenes joined *aselgeia* with *hybris* (*Contra Meidiam* 514). He also joined *aselgōs* and *despotikōs* (L-S 381, despotically; *Oratio* 17.21) and *aselgōs* and *propetōs* (L-S 1494, recklessly; *Oratio* 59.46).

33. *Alcibiades* 8.

34. *Politica* 5.4.

35. *Antiquitates Judaicae* 8.13.1.

36. 20.5.3. Other passages that help define *aselgeia* include 3 Macc. 2:26; Polybius, 8.14.1; and Eusebius, *Historia ecclesiastica* 5.1.26 (see the quotations in Wetstein, 1:588).

17

thinganō (2345) *haptomai* (680) *psēlaphaō* (5584)

Touch *Handle* *Feel (for)* *Grope for*

An accurate distinction among synonyms sometimes may cause us to reject an interpretation of Scripture we might otherwise find acceptable. Thus many interpreters have explained Hebrews 12:18 ("for you have not come to the mount *that may be touched*"[1]) by the use of Ps. 104:32 ("he *touches* the hills, and they smoke"), coupled with a reference to the giving of the Law at Mount Sinai, which "was completely in smoke, because the Lord descended upon it" (Exod. 19:18). This interpretation, however, is not possible because *psēlaphaō* never refers to handling an object in order to mold or modify it but either to feeling an object's surface (Luke 24:39; 1 John 1:1) perhaps to learn its composition (Gen. 27:12, 21, 22) or to feeling *for* or *after* an object without actually touching it. *Psēlaphaō* frequently expresses a groping in the dark (Job 5:14) or the groping of the blind (Gen. 27:12; Deut. 28:29; Judg. 16:26; Isa. 59:10).[2] This is plainly the meaning of Hebrews 12:18.[3] "You have not

1. *Psēlaphōmenō orei.*

2. It is sometimes used figuratively (Acts 17:27). Cf. Plato (*Phaedo* 99b): "groping [*psēlaphōntes*] as in darkness"; Aristophanes, *Pax* 691; *Ecclesiazusae* 315; and Philo, *Quis rerum divinarum heres sit* 51.

3. The Vulgate uses *mons palpabilis* (mountain that can be touched or felt) and *tractabilis* (that can be touched or handled).

thinganō
haptomai
psēlaphaō

come," the apostle would say, "to any *material* mountain, like Sinai, capable of being touched and handled; not, in this sense, to the mountain that might be *felt* but to the heavenly Jerusalem, to a mountain grasped by the mind [*noēton*], not by the senses [*aisthēton*]."[4]

Haptesthai[5] and *thinganein* are the verbs that would be used to refer to handling any object in order to modify it.[6] Although these words sometimes are used interchangeably (Exod. 19:12),[7] the first usually has a stronger sense than the second.[8] It is appropriate to use *haptomai* but not *thinganein* to refer to the sculptor's shaping of his materials;[9] the self-conscious effort that sometimes is present in *haptomai* is never found in *thinganein*. Our Authorized Version has exactly reversed the true order of the words in Colossians 2:21, where it reads: "*Touch* not, taste not, *handle* not."[10] The first and last prohibitions should be transposed, and the passage should read: "*Handle* not, taste not, *touch* not."[11] This translation would more vividly describe the ever-ascending scale of superstitious prohibition among the false teachers at Colossae. To abstain from "handling" was not sufficient; they forbade Christians to "taste" and, lastly, even to "touch" things that might have been considered unclean. As Beza has noted: "The verb *thigein* must be distinguished from the verb *haptesthai* so that as the sentence always diminishes the superstition may be understood to increase." The verb *psauein*[12] does not occur in the New Testament or in the Septuagint.[13]

4. Thus Knapp asserted: "Clearly what is felt [*to psēlaphōmenon*] is what is perceived or anything observed or discovered in any way by a sense, as plainly stated by Tacitus 'to come into contact with the eyes' (*Annales* 3.12), and in a similar manner by Cicero 'to come in contact with the mind' (*Tusculanae disputationes* 3.15). Indeed also Mount Sinai, for that reason, is called 'perceived,' since it is set against Zion, on which mountain are not seen what occurs to the senses but only those things that can be perceived by the mind and reason—mental, spiritual, moral things. In a similar vein Chrysostomus said: 'Accordingly at that time all things were perceived—both sights and sounds; not everything is comprehensible—even invisible things' (*Homilia 32 in epistulam ad Hebraeos*)" (*Scriptores variorum argumentorum*, p. 264).

5. The Septuagint of Psalm 104:32 reads: *Ho haptomenos tōn oreōn kai kapnizontai*.

6. See the French *manier* (to handle), as distinguished from *toucher* (to touch), and the German *betasten* (to feel), as differentiated from *berühren* (to touch).

7. Cf. Aristotle, *De generatione et corruptione* 1.8, quoted by Lightfoot with other passages in his comments on Col. 2:21.

8. *Haptesthai* (equal to the Latin *contrectare* [to come into contact with]) is stronger than *thinganein* (Ps. 104:15; 1 John 5:18). This is apparent in a passage of Xenophon where the child Cyrus, rebuking his grandfather's delicacies, says: "I see that whenever you handle [*hapsē*] the bread you wipe your hand for no reason, but whenever you touch [*thigēs*] any of these [delicacies] you clean your hand at once in the napkins, as if being vexed" (*Cyropaedia* 1.3.5).

9. Plutarch, *Maxime cum principibus philosopho esse disserendum* 1.

10. *Mē hapsē, mēde geusē, mēde thigēs*.

11. Similarly, in the Latin versions *tangere*, which now stands for *haptesthai*, and *attaminare* or *contrectare*, which stand for *thigein*, should not be transposed.

12. L-S 2018, touch.

13. There is a very careful study on this group of words in Schmidt's *Synonymik*, 1:224–43.

18

palingenesia (3824) *anakainōsis* (342)

Regeneration Renewing

Palingenesia is one of the many words that the gospel found and then glorified by expanding its meaning and lifting it to new heights to express deeper truths. Although *palingenesia* was used before the birth of Christ, it could be used to refer to the *Christian* new birth only after Christ's death. Men could not experience new birth until Christ was born (John 1:12), and their regeneration could only follow his generation.

Although *palingenesia* could not be used in its highest and most mysterious sense until the birth of the Son of God, it is quite interesting to trace its subordinate and preparatory uses. In some instances it means nothing more than revivification.[1] In the Pythagorean doctrine of the transmigration of souls, their reappearance in new bodies was called their *palingenesia*.[2] For the Stoics, *palingenesia* referred to the periodic renovation of the earth, to that time when the earth awakened in the blossoming of springtime from its winter sleep and *revived* from its winter death.[3] Philo often used *palingenesia* to refer to the phoenixlike resurrection of the material world out of fire, a doctrine

1. E.g., Lucian, *Muscae encomium* 7.

2. Plutarch, *De esu carnium* 1.7; 2.6; *De Iside et Osiride* 35: "the deaths and rebirths [*palingenesiai*]" of Osiris; *De Eiapud Delphos* 9: "deaths and rebirths [*palingenesiai*]"; *De defectu oraculorum* 51: "transitions and rebirths [*palingenesiai*]."

3. Marcus Antoninus called this revival "the periodical rebirth [*palingenesian*] of the universe" (2.1).

that also was taught by the Stoics,[4] and Philo described Noah and his companions in the ark with these words: "They became leaders of a restoration [*palingenesias*] and chiefs of a second cycle."[5] Basil the Great spoke thusly of some heretics who brought old heathen speculations into the Christian church: "They introduce infinite destructions and rebirths [*palingenesias*] of the world."[6] Cicero called his restoration to dignity and honor after his return from exile "this rebirth [*palingenesian*] of ours."[7] Josephus characterized the restoration of the Jewish nation after the Babylonian captivity as "the recovery and restoration [*palingenesia*] of the fatherland."[8] Olympiodorus, a later Platonist, styled recollection or reminiscence (which must carefully be distinguished from memory)[9] as the *palingenesia* of knowledge: "Recollection is a restoration [*palingenesia*] of knowledge."[10]

Thus the pre-Christian usage of *palingenesia* refers to a recovery, a restoration, or a revival, but not to the type of new birth referred to in the New Testament. *Palingenesia* is not used in the Old Testament[11] and appears only twice in the New Testament (Matt. 19:28; Titus 3:5). In each case it has a different meaning. Our Lord's own words evidently refer to the new birth of the whole creation, the *apokatastasis pantōn* (the restoration of all things, Acts 3:21), that will occur when the Son of Man comes in his glory. Paul, however, used "the washing of regeneration" to refer to the new birth of human souls, not to the birth of the new creation. Is there a common denominator to the two New Testament uses of *palingenesia*? Certainly, otherwise all the laws of language would be violated. *Palingenesia* is used in a wider sense by Christ and in a narrower sense by Paul. There are two concentric circles of meaning with a common center. The *palingenesia* of Scripture begins with the microcosm of single souls but does not end until it has embraced the whole macrocosm of the universe. As seen in the Pauline reference, the primary seat of the *palingenesia* is man's soul. Having established its center there, the *palingenesia* extends in ever-widening circles, first embracing man's body, for

4. *De aeternitate mundi* 17, 21; *De opificio* 15.

5. *De vita Mosis* 2.12.

6. *Homiliae in hexaemeron* 3.

7. *Epistulae ad Atticum* 6.6. Cf. Philo, *Legatio ad Gaium* 41.

8. *Antiquitates Judaicae* 11.3.9. In that instance, *palingenesia* is synonymous with *zōopoiēsin* (L-S 760, revival; Ezra 9:8, 9).

9. The purpose of this passage was to bring out the old Aristotelian and Platonic distinction between "memory" (*mnēmē*, *Gedächtniss*) and "recollection," or "reminiscence" (*anamnēsis* [364]; Heb. 10:3; *Wiedererinnerung*). Memory is instinctive and is commonly possessed by beasts and men; recollection refers to the act of *reviving* faded impressions by a distinct act of the will (Plato, *Philebus* 34b; *Leges* 5.732b: "Recollection is an influx of knowledge after it has departed"; cf. Philo, *De congressu eruditionis gratia* 8). As such, recollection belongs only to mankind (Aristotle, *Historia animalium* 1.1.15; Brandis, *Aristoteles*, pp. 1148–53). Only Olympiodorus could describe recollection as "a restoration [*palingenesia*] of knowledge."

10. *Journal des Savans*, 1834, p. 488.

11. But *palin* (3825) *ginesthai* (1096) (to become again) occurs in Job 14:14; cf. Josephus, *Contra Apionem* 2.30.

which the day of resurrection is its *palingenesia*.[12] Jesus' words in Matthew 19:28 certainly imply (or presuppose) the resurrection, but they involve much more. Beyond the day of resurrection, or contemporaneous with it, will come a day when all nature will put off its soiled, worn garments and clothe itself in holy attire. This will be "the times of restoration of all things" that is referred to in Acts 3:21. In an interesting intimation of this glorious truth, Plutarch refers to the "new arrangement,"[13] and frequently the Bible mentions "the new heaven and the new earth."[14] According to Paul, the day of the *palingenesia* of the whole creation is one day in the labor-pangs of which all creation is groaning and travailing until now (Rom. 8:21–23).[15] Man is presently the subject of the *palingenesia* and the wondrous changes it implies, but in that day the *palingenesia* will include the whole world.

The uses of *palingenesia* in Matthew 19:28 and Titus 3:5 may be reconciled as follows. In Titus 3:5 *palingenesia* refers to the single soul; in Matthew 19:28 it refers to the whole redeemed creation. Each use refers to a different stage of the same event. As Delitzsch so concisely said: "*Palingenesia* is a brief term expressing rebirth or transfiguration of human bodily existence and of the entire non-human nature."[16]

Anagennēsis,[17] a word commonly found in the Greek fathers,[18] does not occur in the New Testament.[19] If it were in the New Testament, it would constitute a closer synonym to *palingenesia* than does *anakainōsis*. Were it used in the New Testament, *anagennēsis*[20] would refer to the active operation of Christ, the author of the new birth, and *palingenesia*[21] to the new birth itself. Without further discussion, we will examine *anakainōsis*[22] and its relation to *palingenesia*.

12. Thus, there is some justification for those fathers who made *palingenesia* equivalent to *anastasis* (386, resurrection) in Matt. 19:28 and who continually used the words as synonyms. See Eusebius, *Historia ecclesiastica* 5.1.58; 3.23. Euthymius explains: "By restoration [*palingenesian*] he means the resurrection [*anastasin*] from the dead, as a revival [*palinzōian*]." Also see Suicer, *Thesaurus*, under this word.

13. *De facie in orbe lunae*, 13.

14. Isa. 65:17; 66:22; 2 Pet. 3:13; Rev. 21:1.

15. Parallels from heathen writers are often deceptive, especially the ones found in Seneca. On this see Lightfoot (*Appendix* to his commentary on Paul's *Epistle to the Galatians*, pp. 268ff.) and Aubertin (*Sur les Rapports supposés entre Sénèque et S. Paul.*) Even so, the following quotation must be acknowledged as remarkable (*Epistulae* 102): "As the mother's womb keeps us for nine months and prepares us not for itself but for that place into which we are, so to speak, let out, now ready to draw breath and to endure in the open, so after the period of time that lasts from infancy to old age we are taken into another birth of nature, and *another beginning and another circumstance of the universe awaits us*."

16. *Apologetik*, p. 213. Cf. Engelhardt, *Weltverklärung und Welterneuerung* in the *Zeitschrift für Lutherische Theologie*, 1871, pp. 48ff.

17. L-S 100, regeneration.

18. See Suicer, under this word.

19. Although the verb *anagennaō* (*313*) appears twice (1 Pet. 1:3, 23).

20. *Anagennēsis* is equivalent to the Latin *regeneratio*.

21. *Palingenesia* is equivalent to the Latin *renascentia*.

22. *Anakainōsis* is equivalent to the Latin *renovatio*.

palingenesia
anakainōsis

Although *palingenesia* is drawn from the realm of nature, *anakainōsis* is derived from the world of art. *Anakainōsis* is found only in the Greek New Testament, where it occurs twice—once in connection with *palingenesia* (Titus 3:5) and in Romans 12:2. The verb *anakainoō* (*341*) also occurs only in the Greek New Testament—in 2 Corinthians 4:16 and in Colossians 3:10. The more classical *anakainizō* (340) appears in Hebrews 6:6, and the nouns derived from it are *anakainismos* (L-S 107, renewal) and *anakainisis* (L-S 107, renewal).[23] *Ananeoō* (365) is used in a similar way in Ephesians 4:23.[24] The "collect" for Christmas day well expresses the relationship between the *palingenesia* and the *anakainōsis*. That prayer reads: "That we being regenerate" (in other words, having already been made the subjects of the *palingenesia*) "may daily be renewed by the Holy Spirit"—may continually know the renewal (*anakainōsis*) of the Holy Spirit. In this "collect," which contains profound theological truths in simple and accurate form, the new birth is contemplated as already past, and the "renewal," or "renovation," takes place daily. The gradual restoration of the divine image progresses in the one who through the new birth has come under the transforming[25] powers of the world to come. It is called "the renewal *of the Holy Spirit*" because he alone is the means for putting off the old man and putting on the new.

Palingenesia and *anakainōsis* are closely bound together; the second is the consequence, or consummation, of the first. The *palingenesia* is that free act of God's mercy and power by which he removes the sinner from the kingdom of darkness and places him in the kingdom of light; it is that act by which God brings him from death to life.[26] In the act itself (rather than the preparations for it), the recipient is passive, just as a child has nothing to do with his own birth. Such passivity does not characterize the *anakainōsis*, the gradual conforming of the person to the new spiritual world in which he now lives, the restoration of the divine image. In this process the person is not passive but is a fellow worker with God.[27] How many conflicts and obscurations of God's truth have arisen from confusing and separating *palingenesia* and *anakainōsis*!

23. The nouns were frequently used by the Greek fathers. Thus Gregory of Nazianzus stated: "I await a change in form of the sky, an alteration of the earth, the freedom of the planets, a renewal [*anakainisin*] of the entire universe" (*Oratio* 10).

24. More on these words will be found in section 60.

25. *Metamorphousthe tē anakainōsei tou noos* (Rom. 12:2). The striking words of Seneca, "I perceive that I not only am *improved* [*emendari*] but am *transformed* [*transfigurari*]" (*Epistulae* 6), are far too grand to express any benefits that he might have received from his books and philosophy; they reach out after blessings to be obtained, not in the schools of men, but only in the church of the living God.

26. It is the "born again/from above" of John 3:3, the "born of God" of 1 John 5:4, the "Godly-birth" of Dionysius the Areopagite and other Greek theologians; the "born of incorruptible seed" of 1 Pet. 1:23. It is the beginning fulfillment of the statement: "Behold, I make all things new" (Rev. 21:5).

27. *Palingenesia* is equivalent to the Latin *regeneratio* (regeneration); *anakainōsis* is equivalent to the Latin *renovatio* (renewal). These two words should not be separated or confused, as Gerhard (*Loci theologi* 21.7.113) has declared: "Let renewal be differentiated from regeneration strictly and specifically understood; nevertheless they are joined by an inseparable and continuous bond."

19

aischynē (152) *aidōs* (127) *entropē* (1791)

Shame Shamefacedness Reverence

At one time *aidōs* included those meanings that later were divided between it and *aischynē*. *Aidōs* had the same double meaning that is latent in the Latin *pudor* (shame) and in our own *shame*.[1] Thus Homer, who did not know *aischynē*, sometimes[2] used *aidōs* where in later Greek *aischynē* would have been preferable.[3] In a difficult passage in *Cratylus* where both words occur (1.84), some scholars believe that Thucydides used *aischynē* and *aidōs* as synonyms.[4] Similarly, in a passage in Sophocles where the two words are used, it is difficult, if not impossible, to distinguish their meanings.[5] Generally, however, *aischynē* and *aidōs* were not considered synonymous in Attic Greek. Ammonius formally distinguished them on philological grounds, while the Stoics[6] distinguished them on ethical grounds. Almost every passage in which either word occurs indicates a real difference in meaning.

1. It retained its double meaning even in later Greek (see Euripides, *Hippolytus* 387–89).

2. As in the *Iliad* 5.787.

3. Elsewhere, however, Homer employed *aidōs* in the sense that it had in later Greek (*Iliad* 13.122; cf. Hesiod, *Opera et dies* 202).

4. Donaldson, *Cratylus*, 3d ed., p. 545.

5. In this passage, *aidōs* is joined with *phobos* (5401), and *aischynē* is linked with *deos* (L-S 379, fear; *Ajax* 1049, 1052).

6. See Plutarch, *De vitiosa pudore* 2.

aischynē
aidōs
entropē

The distinction between *aidōs* and *aischynē* has not always been clearly understood. Sometimes *aidōs* has been understood as the "shame" or sense of honor that hinders one from doing an unworthy act and *aischynē* as the "disgrace"—outward or inward—that follows from the act itself (Luke 14:9). This distinction is partially but not completely accurate. It would be erroneous to assume that *aischynē* only retrospectively refers to the conscious result of unworthy actions.[7] Rather, *aischynē* refers to the feeling that leads one to shun what is unworthy out of an anticipation of dishonor. Thus in the *Definitions* ascribed to Plato (416), *aischynē* is defined as "fear of anticipated ill-repute." Aristotle included the future in his comprehensive definition: "Let there be shame [*aischynē*], a certain pain and discomfort concerning those evils—whether present, past, or future—that appear to lead to ill-repute."[8] In Ecclesiasticus 4:21, *aischynē* is used to mean "a fleeing from disgrace." Plato also uses the term.[9] And according to Xenophon, "although they feared the road and were unwilling, nevertheless the majority followed on account of shame [*aischynēn*] before one another and before Cyrus."[10]

Aidōs[11] is the more noble word and implies an innate moral repugnance to the performance of dishonorable acts. Such repugnance, however, is not implied by *aischynē*, which refers only to the outward disgrace that makes one refrain from such acts. According to Aristotle, *aischynē* is only "imagination concerning ill-repute," or, as South said, it is "the grief a man conceives from his own imperfections considered with relation to the world taking notice of them; and in one word may be defined as *grief upon the sense of disesteem*." Thus Jeremiah 2:26 says: "As the thief is ashamed [*aischynē*] when he is found out." Locke's definition of *shame* rises no higher.[12] The root of shame, as Aristotle argued, is neither a person's moral sense nor his awareness of a right that has been or that would be violated by the act but only his fear that others might discover his violation. If the apprehension of discovery is removed, the *aischynē* ceases. *Aidōs*, however, is self-motivated and implies reverence for the good as good,[13] not merely as that to which honor and reputation are attached.[14] Thus *aidōs* often is connected with *eulabeia*[15] to refer to a reverence

7. In Cicero's definition of *pudor* (shame), there is the same one-sidedness (though on the opposite side) that makes *pudor* merely prospective: "*Pudor* is a *fear* of dishonorable things and a certain innate timidity that flees from disgrace and pursues praise." But Ovid wrote: "He rushes in and publicizes our *shame* [*pudorem*] with a shout."

8. *Rhetorica* 2.6. Cf. *Ethica Nicomachea* 4.9.1.

9. *Gorgias* 492a.

10. *Anabasis* 3.1.10. Xenophon was implying that although (for several reasons) they were not inclined to join Cyrus in assailing his brother's throne, they were ashamed to refuse.

11. It is equivalent to the Latin *verecundia*, which is defined by Cicero (*De republica* 6.4) as "a certain fear of justifiable blame." In the Latin of the silver age, *verecundia* had acquired a sense of *false* shame. Thus Quintilian said: "*Verecundia* is a certain fear that turns back the mind from what ought to be done" (12.5, 2). It is on the mischiefs of the *dysōpia* (shamefacedness) that Plutarch wrote such a graceful little essay.

12. *Of Human Understanding* 2.20.

13. See Aristophanes, *Nubes* 994.

14. On this matter, see Gladstone's admirable remarks in his *Studies on Homer*, 2:431, and also in his *Primer on Homer*, p. 112.

15. *2124*; Heb. 12:28, if this reading may stand.

before God's majesty and holiness that leads one to be careful not to offend God.[16] In summary, *aidōs* would always restrain a good man from an unworthy act; *aischynē* would sometimes restrain a bad one.

Entropē occurs only twice in the New Testament (1 Cor. 6:5; 15:34) but is used elsewhere with *aischynē*[17] and *aidōs*.[18] *Entropē* also should be rendered "shame," though it connotes something not connoted by *aidōs* or by *aischynē*. *Entropē* is related to *entrepō, entrepomai* (1788) and hints at a change of conduct that results from wholesome shame. This is evident in phrases such as "learning through shame" (*entropēs*, Job 20:3), and it is this shame that Paul wished to arouse in his Corinthian converts (cf. 2 Thess. 3:14; Titus 2:8).[19] Pott traced the successive meanings of the words in this way:

> *Entrepō*, to turn about, to turn back, to turn around; the transferred meaning: to cause one to turn within oneself, to bring a person to himself, to give one occasion for introspection ... *entropē*, the act of turning about; 2. introspection, being made ashamed, a sense of shame, respect, deference, regard, as *aidōs*.[20]

16. This is similar to the German *Scheu* (reverence). See Plutarch, *Caesar* 14; *Conjugalia praecepta* 47; Philo, *Legatio ad Gaium* 44. It also appears with *deos* (Plato, *Euthydemus* 126c), *eukosmia* (L-S 719, orderly behavior; Xenophon, *Cyropaedia* 8.1.33), *eutaxia* (L-S 734, good conduct) and *kosmiotēs* (L-S 984, propriety; Plutarch, *Caesar* 4), and with *semnotēs* (4587; *Conjugalia praecepta* 26).

17. Ps. 34:26; cf. 69:3; Ezek. 35:32.

18. In Iamblichus as quoted by Rost and Palm.

19. These verses read *hina entrapē* (in order that he may be ashamed). Grotius correctly paraphrased this as "that touched by shame he may return to a better attitude."

20. *Etymologische Forschungen*, 5:138.

20

aidōs (127) — *Modesty, Propriety, Sobriety*

sōphrosynē (4997) — *Shamefacedness, Self-Control, Moderation*

Paul used both of these words[1] in 1 Timothy 2:9 to describe the truest adornment of a Christian woman. *Sōphrosynē* occurs in two other places in the New Testament: Acts 26:25 and 1 Timothy 2:15. If the distinction drawn in section *19* is correct, then Xenophon was wrong when he had Cyrus say: "He always distinguished between modesty [*aidō*] and self-control [*sōphrosynē*] in this way: The modest flee the openly shameful things, but the self-controlled also flee the things that are secretly shameful."[2] These remarks are incorrect for both words. *Aidōs* does not refer merely to the avoidance of open and manifest baseness, though *aischynē* (*152*) may do so; and in the case of *sōphrosynē*, a mere characteristic is given as its essence. The etymology of *sōphrosynē* to mean "preserving wisdom,"[3] or "the preservation of wisdom,"[4]

1. Cf. Plato, *Phaedrus* 253d.
2. *Cyropaedia* 8.1.31.
3. Aristotle, *Ethica Nicomachea* 6.5.
4. Plato, *Cratylus* 411e; cf. Philo, *De sobrietate* 3.

aidōs

sōphrosynē

must not be taken seriously. Chrysostom's account of its etymology is correct: "*Sōphrosynē* is derived from having a sound mind." It is contrasted with *akolasia*[5] and with *akrasia*,[6] and is the mean between *asōtia* (*810*) and *pheidōlia*.[7] It refers to complete control over the passions and desires, so that they are lawful and reasonable.[8] Aristotle defined it as "the virtue that causes people to behave in respect to bodily pleasures as the law commands."[9] And according to Plutarch, *sōphrosynē* refers to "a certain curtailment and regulation of passions, both removing those that are improper and excessive and also arranging those that are necessary to the proper time and in moderation."[10] In Jeremy Taylor's words:

> It is reason's girdle, and passion's bridle. . . . it is "the soul's strength," as Pythagoras calls it; "the foundation of virtue," so Socrates; "the adornment of all that is good," so Plato; "the stability of the noblest habits," so Iamblichus.[11]

Often *sōphrosynē* is joined to *kosmiotēs*,[12] *eutaxia*,[13] *karteria*,[14] and *hagneia*.[15]

No single Latin word exactly represents *sōphrosynē*, which Cicero translated by *temperantia* (temperateness), *moderatio* (moderation), and *modestia* (sobriety). According to Cicero, "a characteristic of it [*sōphrosynē*] seems to be a striving to control and calm the impulses of the mind and to preserve a firmness that opposes passion and is moderate in every respect."[16]

Sōphrosynē was a more important virtue in heathen than in Christian ethics,[17] not because Christianity attached less value to it but because the number of virtues was smaller in heathen ethics, and so each virtue received more attention. Additionally, for those who are "led by the Spirit," the condition of self-command is transformed into a higher sphere in which a man does not order and command himself but is ordered and commanded by God.

In 1 Timothy 2:9, *aidōs* refers to that "shamefastness"[18] or modesty that

5. L-S 52, intemperance; Thucydides, 3.37; Aristotle, *Rhetorica* 1.9; Philo, *De opificio mundi* 16b.

6. *192*; Xenophon, *Memorabilia* 4.5.

7. L-S 1921, thrift; Philo, *De praemiis et poenis* 918b.

8. "A mastery over passions" (4 Macc. 1:31; cf. Titus 2:12). Plato (*Symposium* 196c) stated: "For *sōphrosynē* is agreed to be the controlling of pleasures and passions." Plato's *Charmides* is entirely dedicated to the investigation of the exact force of the word.

9. *Rhetorica* 1.9.

10. *De curiositate* 14; *De virtute morali* 2; cf. Diogenes Laërtius 3.57.91; and Clement of Alexandria, *Stromata* 2.18.

11. *The House of Feasting*.

12. L-S 984, propriety; Aristophanes, *Plutus* 563, 564.

13. L-S 734, orderly behavior; 2 Macc. 4:37.

14. L-S 880, steadfastness; Philo, *De agricultura* 22.

15. *47*; Clement of Rome, 1 Cor. sec. 58.

16. *Tusculanae disputationes* 3.8; cf. 5.14.

17. Euripides called it "a most noble gift of the gods" (*Medea* 632).

18. It is a pity that *shamefast* (Ecclus. 41:16) and *shamefastness*, the Authorized translation of *sōphrosynē* in 1 Timothy 2:9, have been corrupted in modern use to *shamefaced* and *shamefacedness*. The words are properly of the same formation as *steadfast*, *steadfastness*, *soothfast*, *soothfastness*, and other Old English words now lost to us, such as *rootfast* and *rootfastness*. Similar

shrinks from exceeding the limits of womanly reserve, as well as from the dishonor that would justly attach to doing so. *Sōphrosynē* is that habitual inner self-control, with its constant rein on all the passions and desires, that hinders temptations from overcoming the checks and barriers that *aidōs* opposes.

Modesty
Propriety
Sobriety
Shamefacedness
Self-Control
Moderation

---

words include *masterfast* (engaged to a master), *footfast* (captive), *bedfast* (bedridden), *handfast* (betrothed), and *weatherfast* (weatherbound). As *rootfast* meant that which was firm and *fast* by its *root*, so *shamefast* meant that which was established and made *fast* by (an honorable) *shame*. To change *shamefast* to *shamefaced* devalues the former and leaves us with an ethically weaker word. It is inexcusable that all modern reprints of the Authorized Version should have given in to this corruption. As long as a word's spelling does not affect its meaning, we should use the modern spelling. We do not want to use the spellings "sonne" and "marveile," when everyone now uses "son" and "marvel." But when the meaning of a word is changed by changing its spelling, the edition of 1611 should be exactly adhered to and considered authoritative and exemplary for all subsequent editions.

21

syrō (4951) *helkyō* (1670) — *Drag Draw*

The difference between *syrō* and *helkyō* is theologically important and is best expressed in English by translating *syrein* as "to drag" and *helkyein* as "to draw." The notion of force is always present in *syrein*. Thus Plutarch spoke of the headlong course of a river "as dragging [*syrōn*] and carrying along everything."[1] Consequently, where persons and not things are in question, *syrein* involves the notion of violence.[2] Although the notion of force or violence may be present in *helkyein*,[3] it is not necessarily so,[4] any more than the English *draw*, when used to refer to mental and moral attraction, necessarily implies the use of force.[5]

Only by keeping these differences in mind can we correct the erroneous interpretation of two doctrinally important passages in the Gospel of John. The first is John 12:32: "I, if I am lifted up from the earth, *will draw* all peoples [*pantas helkysō*] to myself." But how does a crucified and exalted Savior draw all people to himself? Certainly not by force, for the will is incapable of force, but by the divine attractions of his love. In John 6:44 Jesus said: "No one can

1. *De liberis educandis* 8.

2. Acts 8:3; 14:19; 17:6; cf. *katasyrein*, 2694, Luke 12:58.

3. Acts 16:19; 21:30; James 2:6; cf. Homer, *Iliad* 11.258; 24.52, 417; Aristophanes, *Equites* 710; Euripides, *Troiades* 70: "Ajax was dragging Cassandra by force."

4. Thus Plato (*Republic* 6.494e) stated: "If ever he is drawn [*helkētai*] to philosophy"; cf. 7.538d.

5. Cf. the use of the Latin *traho* in the phrase "one's own pleasure draws [*trahit*] each one."

come to Me, unless the Father who sent Me *draws* him [*helkysē auton*]." Those who deny theories of "irresistible grace" that portray men as machines that are dragged to God[6] must assert that *helkysē* refers only to the drawing power of love, to the Father's attracting men to the Son.[7] Had *syrein* been used in either of these Johannine texts, then those who believe that "irresistible grace" means forcing someone to believe against his or her will might argue that Jesus' declarations leave no room for any other interpretation than theirs. But *syrein* was not used in these passages.

More specifically, *helkyein* predominantly refers to drawing someone or something to a certain point; *syrein* refers to dragging something after oneself. Thus Lucian, in comparing a man to a fish that has been hooked and dragged through the water, described him as "being dragged [*syromenon*] and led by necessity."[8] Frequently, *syrein* refers to something that is dragged or trailed on the ground,[9] quite apart from its own will, such as a dead body.[10] To confirm this, compare John 21:6, 11 with verse 8 of the same chapter. In verses 6 and 11, *helkyein* refers to drawing the net full of fish to a certain point on the ship and to drawing the net to the land. But in verse 8, where the disciples drag the net full of fish behind them through the water, *syrein*, not *helkyein*, is used. The Authorized Version maintains this distinction, as does De Wette's German translation.[11] Neither the Vulgate nor Beza, however, distinguish the two words, which they translate by *traho* (draw).

6. Augustine, who is sometimes thought to have held such a view, said about this passage: "No one comes to me unless the Father has drawn him. Do not think that you are drawn against your will; the soul is drawn even by love. Nor ought we fear that by human beings who ponder words and have been far removed from comprehending matters particularly divine, perhaps we may be rebuked on this word of good news in holy Scriptures and we may be asked, 'How do I believe willingly if I am drawn?' I say: 'Indeed you are drawn willingly, even with delight.' Furthermore, if a poet may say, 'One's own pleasure draws each one'—not necessity but pleasure, not obligation but delight—how much more ought we to say that a person is drawn to Christ when he delights in truth, delights in beauty, delights in justice, delights in eternal life—all of which is Christ" (*In evangelium Johannis tractatus* 26.4).

7. Cf. Jer. 31:3, "With lovingkindness *I have drawn you* [*heilkysa se*]," and the Song of Sol. 1:3–4.

8. *De mercede conductis potentium familiaribus* 3.

9. Cf. *syrma*, *syrdēn*, and Isa. 3:16.

10. Philo, *In flaccum* 21.

11. De Wette used *ziehen* (to pull) for *helkyein* and *nachschleppen* (to drag along) for *syrein*.

22

holoklēros (3648)

teleios (5046)
artios (739)

Perfect
Whole
Complete
Entire

Holoklēros and *teleios*—"perfect and complete"—are used together in the reverse order in James 1:4.[1] *Holoklēros* is used only one other time in the New Testament (1 Thess. 5:23), and *holoklēria* (3647) occurs once (Acts 3:16; cf. Isa. 1:6), and then in a physical, not ethical, sense. As is apparent from its etymology, *holoklēros* primarily refers to that which retains all that was initially allotted to it (Ezek. 15:5); it implies completion and wholeness in all of its parts. Thus Darius would not have cared about taking Babylon if Zopyrus, who had maimed himself in the process of conquering the city, were still *holoklēros*.[2] Unhewn stones are called *holoklēroi* because they have not lost anything in the shaping and polishing process (Deut. 27:6; 1 Macc. 4:47). Perfect weeks are said to be *ebdomades holoklēroi* (Lev. 23:15), and a man is said to be *en holoklērō dermati* ("in a *whole* skin").[3] *Holoklēros* also can be used to refer to a body that has no deficiency (cf. Lev. 21:17–23), to the type of body that Levitical priests were required to have to minister at the altar and

1. Cf. Philo, *De sacrificiis Abelis et Caini* 33: "full and complete [*holoklēra*] and perfect [*teleia*]"; and Dio Chrysostom, *Oratio* 12, p. 203.

2. Plutarch, *Regum et imperatorum apophthegmata*.

3. Lucian, *Philopseudes sive incredulus* 8.

holoklēros

teleios
artios

to the type of body that sacrifices were required to have. Josephus used *holoklēros* in both of these senses,[4] as did Philo, who consistently used the term to refer to the wholeness of body required of Levitical priests and of sacrifices and who saw a mystical significance in the word.[5] Homer used *teleios* in the same sense.[6]

Holoklēros and *holoklēria*,[7] which originally referred to the wholeness or completeness of the body, came to refer to mental and moral completeness.[8] The only reference of this type in the Apocrypha is Wisdom of Solomon 15:3: "complete [*holoklēros*] righteousness." In an important passage in Plato,[9] however, *holoklēros* refers to the perfection of man before the fall,[10] when men, who still were "complete [*holoklēroi*] and unaffected by evil," were granted "complete [*holoklēra*] images." Plato contrasted this with the weak and partial glimpses of Eternal Beauty granted to most people after the fall. According to Plato, then, the person or thing that is *holoklēros* is "complete in all categories" (*omnibus numeris absolutus*). And according to James 1:4, such a person is "lacking nothing" (*en mēdeni leipomenos*).

All of the various uses of *teleios* refer to the *telos* (5056), which is its goal. In a natural sense the *teleioi* are adults who have attained their full stature, strength, and mental powers; they have attained their *telos*. Such adults are distinguished from the *neoi* (3501) or *paides* (3816)—young men or boys.[11] This image of full and complete growth—as contrasted with that of infancy and childhood—is the ground of Paul's ethical use of *teleioi*, which he contrasts with *nēpioi* (3516) *en Christō*.[12] Similarly, the *teleioi* correspond to the *pateres* (3962) of 1 John 2:13–14, who are contrasted with the *neaniskoi* (3495) and the *paidia* (3813).

The ethical use of *teleios* is not confined to Scripture. The Stoics distinguished the one who was *teleios* in philosophy from the one who was progressing in philosophy, just as in 1 Chronicles 25:8 the *teleioi* are contrasted with those who still are learning. In heathen circles, the *teleioi* were those who had been initiated into the latest and most important mysteries.[13]

The English word *perfect* has the same ambiguous meaning as the Greek *teleios*. Both are used in a relative and in an absolute sense. Thus Christ said: "Therefore you shall be *perfect* [*teleioi*], just as your Father in heaven is *perfect* [*teleios*]" (Matt. 5:48; cf. 19:21). Christians are commanded to be "perfect"

4. *Antiquitates Judaicae* 3.12.2.

5. *De agricultura* 29; *De cherubim* 28; cf. Plato, *Leges* 6.759c.

6. *Iliad* 1.66.

7. Like the Latin *integer* (whole) and *integritas* (completeness).

8. Suetonius, *Claudius* 4.

9. *Phaedrus* 250c; cf. *Timaeus* 44c.

10. That is, to the fall as Plato understood it.

11. Plato, *Leges* 11.929c; Xenophon, *Cyropaedia* 8.7.6; Polybius, 5.29.2.

12. 1 Cor. 2:6; 14:20; Eph. 4:13–14; Phil. 3:15; Heb. 5:14; cf. Philo, *De agricultura* 2.

13. Just as the Lord's Supper was called *to teleion* (Bingham, *Christian Antiquities* 1.4.3) because it was the highest privilege the Christian could enter.

but not, however, in the sense of a doctrine of "perfectionism."[14] The faithful Christian is to be "perfect" in the sense of striving by God's grace to be fully furnished and firmly established in the knowledge and practice of the things of God.[15] Such "perfection" refers to spiritual and moral maturity and is to be contrasted with the moral and spiritual condition of those who are babes in Christ. Those who are "perfect" in this sense are "not always employed in the elements and infant propositions and practices of religion but [in] doing noble actions, well skilled in the deepest mysteries of faith and holiness."[16] In this sense Paul claimed to be *teleios*, not *teteleiōmenos* (5048, Phil. 3:12, 15).

The distinction between *holoklēros* and *teleios* is clear. The former word refers to one who has preserved, or regained, his *completeness*; the latter to one who has attained the moral *end* for which he was intended, namely, to be a man in Christ. And as men reach this point, other and higher ends will open before them, so that Christ is increasingly formed in them.[17] In the one who is *holoklēros*, no Christian grace is deficient. In the the one who is *teleios*, no grace is in its weak or imperfect beginning stages; each grace has reached a certain ripeness and maturity.

Holotelēs (3651) occurs once in the New Testament (1 Thess. 5:23).[18] Because it derives from *holoklēros* and from *teleios*, it conceptually and etymologically joins these two terms.

Artios occurs only once in the New Testament (2 Tim. 3:17) and is explained more fully as *exērtismenos (1822)*. It is closer in meaning to *holoklēros*[19] than to *teleios*. Calvin explained *artios* as that "in which nothing is maimed."[20] *Artios* is contrasted with *chōlos*,[21] *kolobos*,[22] and *anapēros*.[23] Lucian describes Vulcan as "not perfect [*artios*] in respect to his feet."[24] *Artios* refers not only to the presence of all the parts that are necessary for completeness but also to the further adaptation and aptitude of these parts for their designed purpose. Paul says that the man of God should be furnished with all that is necessary to carry out his appointed work (2 Tim. 3:17).

14. Sects that teach "perfectionism" either mean nothing by *perfection* that could not be expressed by some word that is less likely to be misunderstood, or they mean something that no man in this life can ever attain—moral and spiritual perfection in the here and now—something that if someone claimed to have attained it would amount to no more than gross self-deception.

15. Col. 4:12; James 3:2: "perfect [*teleioi*] and complete."

16. See Jeremy Taylor (from whom this quotation is drawn) for a full discussion of the sense in which "perfection" is demanded of Christians (*Doctrine and Practice of Repentance*, 1.3.40–56).

17. Seneca (*Epistulae* 120) said of someone: "He had an excellent mind, developed to his highest potential."

18. Cf. Plutarch, *Placita philosophorum* 5.21.

19. Philo also joined it with this word (*De plantatione* 29).

20. See the quotation from Theodoret in Suicer, under this word.

21. *5560*; Chrysostom.

22. L-S 973, mutilated; Olympiodorus.

23. *376*; Theodoret.

24. *De sacrificiis* 6.

23

stephanos (4735) *diadēma* (1238) — Crown

We must not confuse these two words, which are both translated "crown." In classical literature *stephanos* does not denote the kingly or imperial crown. Instead, it refers to the crown that symbolized victory in the games, civic worth, military valor, nuptial joy, and festal gladness. A *stephanos* was woven of oak, ivy, parsley, myrtle, olive, or gold leaves, which imitated these plants, and of flowers such as violets or roses.[1] A *stephanos* was a "wreath" or "garland"[2] but never the emblem or sign of royalty.[3]

A *diadēma* was a "token of kingdom,"[4] a white linen band or fillet[5] that encircled the brow. The phrase *peritithenai diadēma* ("to put on a crown") commonly indicated the assumption of royal dignity.[6] In Latin only the "diadema" is the "mark of kings."[7] Selden's comments on the distinction between "crowns" and "diadems" also agree with this.

1. See Athenaeus, 15.9–33.

2. *Stephanos* is equivalent to the German *Kranz* (wreath) as distinguished from *Krone* (crown).

3. Just as the Latin *corona* (garland) was not a sign of royalty.

4. As Lucian called it (*Revivescentes sive piscator* 35; cf. Xenophon, *Cyropaedia* 8.3.13; Plutarch, *De fraterno amore* 18).

5. A *taenia* (ribbon) or *fascia* (band); Curtius, 3.3.

6. Polybius, 5.57.4; 1 Macc. 1:9; 11:13; 13:32; Josephus, *Antiquitates Judaicae* 12.10.1.

7. Tacitus, *Annales* 15.29.

stephanos
diadēma

> However those names have been from ancient time confounded, yet the diadem strictly was a very different thing from what a crown now is or was; and it was no other than only a fillet of silk, linen, or some such thing. Nor appears it that any other kind of crown was used for a royal ensign, except only in some kingdoms of Asia, but this kind of fillet, until the beginning of Christianity in the Roman Empire.[8]

Another passage in Plutarch confirms this distinction. The kingly crown offered by Antonius to Caesar is described as "a crown [*diadēma*] woven with a wreath [*stephanō*] of laurel."[9] Here *stephanos* refers to the garland or laureate wreath that is woven into the diadem proper. Indeed, according to Cicero, Caesar was already *coronatus* (that is, wreathed, which is equivalent to *estephanōmenos*) as a consul when the offer was made.[10] This distinction helps to explain Suetonius's version of the same incident.[11] Someone placed "a laurel wreath [*coronam*] bound with white bands" on Caesar's statue.[12] The tribunes did not command the removal of the *corona* (wreath) but of the *fascia*, or diadem, which alone suggested Caesar's traitorous claim to kingship.[13]

The accuracy of the distinction made in the Septuagint and Apocrypha between *diadēma* and *stephanos* may be seen by comparing the passages in 1 Maccabees where *diadēma* is employed[14] and those where *stephanos* appears.[15] Compare these with Isaiah 62:3, where Israel shall be "a crown [*stephanos*] of glory" and "a royal diadem [*diadēma*]."

In the New Testament, Paul always used *stephanos* to refer to the conqueror's, not the king's, crown.[16] Although 1 Peter 5:4 does not necessarily allude directly to the Greek games, it still contrasts the wreaths of heaven that never fade[17] with the garlands of earth that quickly lose their beauty and freshness. It is unlikely that other New Testament passages that use *stephanos*[18] refer to the Greek games, for there was a long-standing Jewish antipathy to them as idolatrous and profane.[19] To have used imagery that referred to the prizes awarded at these games would have repelled, not attracted, the Jewish members of the church. In those passages the *stephanos*, or the "crown [*stephanos*] of life," is not the emblem of royalty but of highest joy

8. *Titles of Honour*, chap. 8, sec. 2.
9. Plutarch, *Caesar* 61.
10. *Orationes Philippicae* 2.34.
11. *Caesar* 79.
12. Plutarch informs us that his statues were "bound with royal crowns [*diadēmasin*]."
13. Cf. Diodorus Siculus (20.24), who says: "He did not choose to have a crown [*diadēma*], for he always wore a wreath [*stephanon*]."
14. 1 Macc. 1:9; 6:15; 8:14; 11:13, 54; 12:39; 13:32.
15. 1 Macc. 4:57; 10:29; 11:35; 13:39; cf. 2 Macc. 14:4.
16. 1 Cor. 9:24–26; 2 Tim. 2:5. This is also true in the supposed Second Epistle of Clement, sec. 7.
17. The *amarantinos stephanos tēs doxēs*.
18. James 1:12; Rev. 2:10; 3:11; 4:4.
19. Josephus, *Antiquitates Judaica* 15.8.1–4; 1 Macc. 1:14; 2 Macc. 4:9, 12.

and gladness[20] and of glory and immortality. On the three occasions where John referred to *kingly* crowns, he employed *diadēma*.[21] Revelation 19:12 depicts Christ, the King of kings and Lord of lords, with the words "on his head were *many crowns*."[22] This phrase would be difficult to understand if the crowns were similar to those worn by present monarchs, but the meaning is immediately apparent if they are "diadems," the narrow fillets that encircle the brow. The "many diadems" will be the tokens of Christ's many kingdoms—earth, heaven, and hell (Phil. 2:10). Satan, the usurper of these kingdoms and of their honors, has his own seven diadems (13:1), but Christ will rightfully assume his lordship. This may be illustrated by the earthly example of Ptolemy, king of Egypt. When he entered Antioch in triumph, he set two "crowns," or rather "diadems" (*diadēmata*), on his head, the "diadem" of Asia and the "diadem" of Egypt (1 Macc. 11:13). In Diodorus Siculus (1.47) we read of a queen "having three kingdoms on her head." The context plainly shows that these are three diadems, the symbols of a triple royalty.

The only occasion where *stephanos* may refer to a kingly crown is Matthew 27:29 (cf. Mark 15:17; John 19:2). The soldiers mocked Jesus' royalty by placing a crown of thorns (*stephanos akanthinos*) on his head. The nature of the woven materials, perhaps the *Juncus marinus* (rush from the sea) or the *Lycium spinosum* (a prickly thorn bush) would make the word *diadēma* inappropriate, though this word was fit for the purpose the soldiers had in mind.[23]

20. Cf. *stephanos agalliamatos* (cf. 20), Ecclus. 6:31.

21. Rev. 12:3; 13:1; cf. 17:9–10: "the seven heads . . . are seven kings"; 19:12.

22. *Diadēmata polla*.

23. On the whole subject of this section, see the *Dictionary of the Bible* under the words *crown* and *diadem* and the article on "Coronation" in the *Dictionary of Christian Antiquities*, p. 464.

24

pleonexia (4124) / *philargyria* (5365)

Covetousness / Greediness / Love of Money

The same distinction exists between *pleonexia* and *philargyria* as between *covetousness* and *avarice*.[1] *Pleonexia*[2] is the more active sin, *philargyria* the more passive. *Pleonexia* refers to having more and (more usually) to the desire to have more, to seeking to posses what is not possessed. *Philargyria* refers to seeking to retain what is possessed and, through accumulation, to multiplying what is possessed. *Pleonexia* often implies bold and aggressive methods of acquisition; it frequently refers to behavior that is as free in scattering and squandering as it was eager and unscrupulous in acquiring. The *pleonektēs* (4123) is often *rapti largitor*, "a squanderer of what he has seized."[3] Theodoret defined this sin as "the desire for more and the seizure of what does not belong to a person."[4] *Philargyria* refers to miserly behavior that frequently is also

1. This same distinction is also found in the German *Habsucht* (greed) and *Geiz* (stinginess).

2. I.e., the *amor sceleratus habendi* (the wicked love of *having*).

3. This was the case with Catiline, of whom Cicero said: "Who is more covetous in greediness? Who is more lavish in prodigality?" (*Pro M. Caelis* 6). The same idea is present in Sir Giles Overreach of Massinger. *Pleonektēs* is used with *arpax* (727, 1 Cor. 5:10); *pleonexia* is used with *barytēs* (L-S 308, arrogance; Plutarch, *Aristides* 3); and *pleonexiai* is used with *klopai* (2829, Mark 7:22), *adikiai* (93; Strabo, 7.4.6), and *philoneikiai* (5397; Plato, *Leges* 3.677b).

4. *Epistula ad Romanos* 1.30. Also see the definition of *avaritia* (greediness) as "an unjust grasping after what belongs to others" (*Ad Herennium* 4.25). Cf. Bengel's note (on Mark 7:22):

pleonexia

philargyria

cautious and timid, not necessarily having cast off an outward show of righteousness.[5] The Pharisees, for example, are described as *philargyroi* (5366, Luke 16:14), and this is not irreconcilable with the maintenance of a religious profession, as would have been the case with *pleonexia*.

Cowley drew this distinction quite well:

> There are two sorts of avarice; the one is but of a bastard kind, and that is the rapacious appetite for gain; not for its own sake, but for the pleasure of refunding it immediately through all the channels of pride and luxury; the other is the true kind, and properly so called, which is a restless and unsatiable desire of riches, not for any further end or use, but only to hoard and preserve, and perpetually increase them. The covetous man of the first kind is like a greedy ostrich, which devours any metal, but it is with an intent to feed upon it, and, in effect, it makes a shift to digest and excern it. The second is like the foolish chough, which loves to steal money only to hide it.[6]

Another way of looking at the two terms is to see *pleonexia* as the genus and *philargyria* as the species. Looked at in this way, *philargyria* refers to the love of money and *pleonexia* to the sinner's drawing and snatching to himself of the creature in every form and kind.[7] Bengel observed that Paul's lists of sins often associate *pleonexia* with sins of the flesh (1 Cor. 5:11; Eph. 5:3, 5; Col. 3:5). Bengel stated: "It is customary, however, to link covetousness [*pleonexian*] with impurity, for a person without God seeks nourishment for the material body either through pleasure or through greed; he takes for himself another's good." The connection between these two provinces of sin is deeper and more intimate than Bengel realized. Not only is *pleonexia*, which signifies covetousness, used to refer to sins of impurity, but the word is sometimes used to designate these sins themselves as the root from which they grow.[8] *Pleonexia* refers to the ever-increasing desire of the person who has forsaken God to fill himself with the lower objects of sense. The Roman emperors were monsters of lust as well as covetousness.[9] In this respect, *pleonexia* has a much wider and deeper sense than *philargyria*. Plato, in his commentary on this word,[10] likened the desire of man to the sieve or pierced

---

"*Pleonexia*, involving a comparison, designates a certain mean between theft and robbery, whereby through various devices it happens that another person by himself, but to his own loss, unknowingly or unwillingly, offers, yields, and grants what you receive unworthily." It is therefore fitly used with *aischrokerdeia* (cf. 146; Polybius, 6.46.3).

5. It is used with *mikrologia* (L-S 1133, stinginess; Plutarch, *Quomodo adulator ab amico internoscatur* 36).

6. *Essay 7, Of Avarice*. Earlier, in his *Persones Tale* and in his descriptions of Covetise and Avarice in *The Romaunt of the Rose* (pp. 183–246), Chaucer made the same distinction.

7. It is the *indigentia* (insatiable desire) of Cicero: "Insatiable desire is a passion that cannot be filled" (*Tusculanae disputationes* 4.9.21). Cf. Dio Chrysostom, *De avaritia oratio* 17; Augustine, *Enarratio in Psalma* 118.35, 36.

8. Eph. 5:3. See Jerome, *in loc.*; and often by the Greek fathers (see Suicer, *Thesaurus* under this word; and Hammond's excellent note on Rom. 1:29).

9. Suetonius, *Caligula* 38–41.

10. *Gorgias* 493.

vessel of the Danaids, which they were ever filling but might never fill.[11] Plato's definition summed up that ever-defeated longing of the prodigal son who despised the children's bread but was forced to satisfy his hunger with the husks of the swine.

11. It is evident that the same comparison had occurred to Shakespeare: "The cloyed will, / That satiate yet unsatisfied desire, / *That tub both filled and running.*" *Cymbeline*, act 1. sc. 7.

25

boskō (1006)

poimainō (4165)

Feed
Tend
Shepherd
Rule

Boskein and *poimainein* are often used in a figurative and spiritual sense in the Old Testament (1 Chron. 11:2; Ps. 77:72; Jer. 23:2; Ezek. 34:3). *Poimainein* also is used this way in the New Testament, but *boskein* is only used in this sense in John 21:15, 17. Christ, while giving Peter his commission to feed his "lambs" (v. 15), his "sheep" (v. 16), and again his "sheep" (v. 17), first used *boske*, then *poimaine*, and finally *boske*. This return to *boske* in the third repetition of the charge has been interpreted as indicating that *boskein* and *poimainein* are used synonymously in this passage. Those who argue this way urge that Christ could not have had progressive aspects of the pastoral work in mind here, since he returned to the word that he began with. But the variations in these words cannot be accidental any more than the other changes found in these same verses: *agapan* (25) to *philein* (5368, see sec. 12) and *arnia* (721) to *probata* (4263). The Authorized Version renders *boske* and *poimaine* by "feed," and the Vulgate translates both words by *pasce* (feed). Due to the limitations of language, neither translation has attempted to follow the changes of the original text. "Tend" for *poimaine* is the best suggestion that I can make.[1]

1. The German *weiden* (to feed) is equivalent to *boskein*, and *hüten* (to feed) is equivalent to *poimainein*, but De Wette uses *weiden* throughout.

boskō

poimainō

There is a real distinction between *boskein* and *poimainein*. *Boskein* and the Latin *pascere* simply mean "to feed"; but *poimainein* indicates much more. It refers to the whole office of the shepherd, to the guiding, guarding, and folding of the flock, as well as providing pasture.[2] The more extensive meaning of *poimainein* is seen in Revelation 2:27 and 19:15, where it would be impossible to substitute *boskein* for it.[3]

The shepherd's work fittingly illustrates man's highest ministry in which he seeks the well-being of his fellow man. The phrase *shepherds of their people* has frequently been transferred to those who are, or who should be, the faithful guides and guardians of others. Thus in Homer kings are called "shepherds of the people."[4] In Scripture God himself is referred to as a shepherd (Ps. 23; Isa. 40:11; Ezek. 34:11–31), and Christ refers to himself as "the good shepherd" (John 10:11). Jesus is called the "Chief Shepherd" (1 Pet. 5:4) and "the great Shepherd of the sheep" (Heb. 13:20) and as such fulfills the prophecy of Micah 5:4.[5]

If *poimainein* is the more comprehensive word and was added to *boske* in Jesus' instruction to Peter in John 21:15ff., how do we account for Jesus' return to *boske* and his concluding with the narrower and weaker admonition? Dean Stanley[6] suggested the answer, and his suggestion is a most important lesson that the church and all who rule her need diligently to apply. Feeding the flock and finding them spiritual food is paramount and should not be superseded by any other concerns. Often in false ecclesiastical systems the preaching of the Word loses its preeminence, and the *boskein* recedes into the background and is swallowed up in the *poimainein*. In such situations, the *poimainein* is not a true *poimainein*, because it is not a *boskein* as well, but is the sort of "shepherding" that is denounced by Ezekiel.[7]

2. Lampe stated: "This symbol includes the entire guidance of the church." Bengel noted: "Feeding [*boskein*] is a part of tending [*poimainein*]."

3. Cf. Philo, *Quod deterius potiori insidiari soleat* 8.

4. Cf. 2 Sam. 5:2; 7:7; Ps. 78:71, 72.

5. Cf. the following sublime passage in Philo with the preceding three paragraphs: "Tending [*to poimainein*] is so admirable that perfect things are dedicated rightly not only to kings and wise men and souls purified but also to God, the ruler of all" (*De agricultura* 12).

6. *Sermons and Essays on the Apostolic Age*, p. 138.

7. Ezek. 34:2, 3, 8, 10; cf. Zech. 11:15–17; Matt. 23.

26

zēlos (2205) — *Zeal*, *Emulation*

phthonos (5355) — *Envy*, *Jealousy*

Although these words are frequently joined by Paul (Gal. 5:20–21), Clement of Rome (*Epistula i ad Corinthios* 3, 4, 5), Cyprian (*De zelo et livore*), and classical writers as well,[1] there are differences between them. First, *zēlos* is a middle term and sometimes is used in Scripture in a good sense[2] but more frequently in an evil one.[3] *Phthonos*, however, never has a good meaning; it is always used in an evil sense. When used in a good sense, *zēlos* refers to honorable emulation[4] and the consequent imitation of that which is excellent.[5]

1. See Plato, *Philebus* 47e; *Leges* 3.679c; *Menexenus* 242a; Plutarch, *Marcius Coriolanus* 19; and others.

2. John 2:17; Rom. 10:2; 2 Cor. 9:2.

3. Acts 5:17; Rom. 13:13; Gal. 5:20. In James 3:14, to make it quite clear what *zēlos* means, the term is qualified by the addition of *pikros* (4089) and is joined to *eritheia* (2052).

4. *Eris* (2054) is often found in the *Odyssey* and in later Greek, though not in the *Iliad*. It closely resembled *zēlos* in referring to emulation and was capable of a nobler application. Basil the Great defines it in this way: "It is *eris* whenever a person is eager to do something in order not to appear inferior to another" (*Regulae morales* 66).

5. "Zeal [*zēlos*] for the best" (Lucian, *Adversus indoctum et libros multos ementem* 17); "zeal [*zelos*] for the better" (Philo, *De praemiis et poenis* 3); "love of honor and emulation [*zēlos*]" (Plutarch, *De Alexandri magni fortuna aut virtute* 2.6; *An seni respublica gerenda sit* 25); "emulation [*zēlos*] and imitation" (Herodian, 2.4); "emulator [*zēlōtēs*] and imitator" (6.8). It is the Latin

zēlos

phthonos

The verb *aemulor* (emulate), which expresses the difference between worthy and unworthy emulation, governs an accusative in cases where the first sense is intended and a dative when the second sense is meant. South noted:

> We ought by all means to note the difference between envy and emulation; which latter is a brave and noble thing, and quite of another nature, as consisting only in a generous imitation of something excellent; and that such an imitation as scorns to fall short of its copy, but strives, if possible, to outdo it. The emulator is impatient of a superior, not by depressing or maligning another, but by perfecting himself. So that while that sottish thing envy sometimes fills the whole soul, as a great dull fog does the air; this, on the contrary, inspires it with a new life and vigour, whets and stirs up all the powers of it to action. And surely that which does so (if we also abstract it from those heats and sharpnesses that sometimes by accident may attend it), must needs be in the same degree lawful and laudable too, that it is for a man to make himself as useful and accomplished as he can.[6]

Aristotle employed *zēlos* exclusively in the nobler sense of an active emulation that grieves over the good it lacks, not over another who possesses the good. When used in this way, *zēlos* refers to one who seeks to supply his own deficiencies. In this sense, Aristotle contrasted *zēlos* with envy: "Emulation [*zēlos*] is a certain distress over the apparent presence of honorable good things . . . not because they belong to another but because they do not also belong to oneself. Thus emulation [*zēlos*] is both proper and concerns proper things, but envying [*to phthonein*] is both contemptible and concerns contemptible things."[7] The church fathers followed in Aristotle's footsteps. Jerome stated: "Emulation [*zēlos*] may be taken also in a good sense when someone endeavors to emulate that which is good. Envy, in truth, is tormented by another's good fortune."[8] In another place Jerome said: "They emulate properly who, when they see graces, gifts, and virtues in others, desire that they themselves be such persons."[9] Oecumenius said: "Emulation [*zēlos*] is a striving of an ecstatic soul toward something with a certain similarity to that which is termed zeal."[10] Compare the words of our English poet: "*Envy*, to which the ignoble mind's a slave, is *emulation* in the learned and brave."

It is all too easy for zeal and honorable rivalry to degenerate into meaner passions. The Latin *simultas* (rivalry) is not related[11] to *simulare* (to imitate) but to *simul* (together) and points out that those who *together* aim at the same object (i.e., competitors) are in danger of being enemies as well, just as *hamilla*

---

aemulatio (emulation), which does not necessarily include envy, though our *emulation* may. It is like the German *Nacheiferung* (zealous emulation) as distinguished from *Eifersucht* (jealousy).

6. *Works*, London, 1737, 5:403; and cf. Bishop Butler, *Works*, 1836, 1:15.

7. *Rhetorica* 2.11.

8. *Expositio in Galatios* 5.20.

9. Ibid. 4.17.

10. Cf. Plutarch, *Pericles* 2.

11. See Döderlein, *Lateinische Synonyme*, 3:72.

(contest)[12] is related to *hama* (at the same time) and as *rivales* (competitors) at first referred to the occupants of the banks of the same river.[13] These degeneracies, which closely follow emulation, sometimes cause *emulation* to be used for that into which it degenerates, as in the phrase *pale and bloodless emulation* (Shakespeare). There are two types of degenerate forms of emulation: (1) a desire to make war upon the good it beholds in another—and so to trouble that good and make it less[14]—and (2) a desire (but not the power) to diminish the good, accompanied by petty complaining and fault finding.[15]

Zēlos relates to *phthonos*[16] in this way: the latter is essentially passive, and the former is active and vigorous. Although *phthonos* is not used in the comprehensive catalogue of sins in Mark 7:21–22, the idea of envy[17] is implied by the circumlocution: *an evil eye* (cf. Ecclus. 14:8, 10).[18] Also see Matthew 20:15 and 1 Samuel 18:9: "Saul *eyed* [i.e., envied] David." The "burning eyes" of Persius[19] and the "evil eye" of the Italians must receive the same explanation.

Phthonos, the meaner of the two sins,[20] refers to displeasure at another's good.[21] The Stoics defined it as "distress at others' good fortunes."[22] It is the desire that the good of another might diminish, quite apart from any corresponding gain.[23] It is not surprising that long ago Solomon described it as "rottenness to the bones" (Prov. 14:30). It is not a desire to be raised to the

12. The word has kept its more honorable use. Cf. Plutarch, *Animine an corporis affectiones sint peiores* 3.

13. Pott, *Etymologische Forschungen* 2.2.191.

14. *Zēlos* and *eris* are frequently used together (Rom. 13:13; 2 Cor. 12:20; Gal. 5:20; Clement of Rome, *Epistula i ad Corinthios* 3, 36), and *zēlos* is joined with *philoneikia* (5379, Plutarch, *De capienda ex inimicis utilitate* 1).

15. Thus *phthonos* and *mōmos* (3470) may be used together, as in Plutarch, *Praecepta gerendae reipublicae* 27.

16. Plato (*Menexenus* 242a) has: "First emulation [*zēlos*] and from emulation [*zēlou*] envy [*phthonos*]." Aeschylus (*Agamemnon* 939) stated: "The unenvied person [*ho aphthonētos*] is not one to be emulated [*epizēlos*]."

17. Aeschylus describes it as a "malignant poison" (*Agamemnon* 755); Demosthenes as "a mark of a thoroughly evil nature" (499, 21); Euripides as "the greatest disease of all those in humans"; and Herodotus (3.80) said: "It is implanted in mankind from of old."

18. This circumlocution is related to the Latin *invidia* (envy), which is derived, as Cicero observed (*Tusculanae disputationes* 3.9), "from excessively observing the good fortune of another."

19. *Satira* 2.34.

20. Therefore the beautiful Greek proverb says, "Envy [*ho phthonos*] is outside the divine chorus."

21. Augustine's definition of *phthonos* (*Expositio in Galatios* 5.21) introduces a rare ethical element: "Envy is the pain of the soul when an *unworthy* [*indignus*] person seems to pursue even that after which you were not striving." This would be *nemesis* and *nemesan* (L-S 1167, 1166, indignation, to be indignant) in the ethical terminology of Aristotle (*Ethica Nicomachea* 2.7, 15; *Rhetorica* 2.9).

22. Diogenes Laërtius, 7.63, 111. Basil called it "distress over the success of one's neighbor" (*Homilia de invidia*). Cicero described it as "grief incurred because of another's successes, which in no way harms the one who is envious" (*Tusculanae disputationes* 4.8; cf. Xenophon, *Memorabilia* 3.9.8). Augustine styled it "hatred of someone else's good luck" (*De generibus litterarum* 11–14). Phineas Fletcher said: "Sick of a strange disease, another's health."

23. Aristotle, *Rhetorica* 2.10.

zēlos

phthonos

level of the envied but only to lower the envied to one's own level. When the victories of Miltiades would not allow the youthful Themistocles to sleep,[24] this was *zēlos* in its nobler form. This emulation prevented his rest, until he had set a Salamis of his own against the Marathon of his great predecessor. But it was *phthonos* that made that Athenian citizen weary of hearing Aristides constantly called "the Just."[25]

Baskania, a word that frequently means "envy" in later Greek, does not occur in the New Testament. *Baskainein* (940) appears only once (Gal. 3:1).

24. Plutarch, *Themistocles* 3.

25. Plutarch, *Aristides* 7. This envy contained no impulses that led him to strive after the other's justice. See the beautiful remarks of Plutarch (*De virtute et vitio* 14). On the likenesses and differences between *misos* (L-S 1138, hatred) and *phthonos*, see his subtle analysis of the human heart, *De invidia et odio*.

27

zōē (2222) *bios* (979)

Life Lifetime Livelihood Living

There is only one Latin word, *vita*, and one English word, *life*, for the two Greek terms *zōē* and *bios*. If *zōē* and *bios* were synonyms, this would not be a problem. But *zōē* and *bios* view life from different perspectives and so are not synonymous. Inevitably, by using one word to translate both Greek words, we have concealed the important differences between *zōē* and *bios*.

The antithesis of *zōē* is *thanatos*,[1] and the antithesis of *zēn* (2198) is *apothnēskein*.[2] *Zōē* is closely related to *aō*, *aēmi* (to breathe the breath of life)—a necessary condition of living—and to *pneuma* (4151) and *psychē* (5590).[3]

Although *zōē* refers to *intensive* life,[4] *bios* refers to *extensive* life,[5] the *period* or duration of life. In a secondary sense, *bios* also refers to the means by which that life is sustained. And in a tertiary sense, *bios* refers to the manner in

1. 2288; Jer. 8:3; Ecclus. 30:17; Rom. 8:38; 2 Cor. 5:4; Plato, *Leges* 12.944c.

2. 599; Luke 20:38; 1 Tim. 5:6; Rev. 1:18; cf. *Iliad* 23.70; Herodotus, 1.31; Plato, *Phaedo* 71d: "Do you not say that dying [*to tethnanai*] is opposite to living [*tō zēn*]?"

3. The Latin equivalents are *spiritus* and *anima*.

4. *Vita qua vivimus* (life by which we live).

5. *Vita quam vivimus* (the life which we live).

which that life is spent—that is, one's profession or career. The New Testament includes examples of all three senses of *bios*.

Bios as the period or duration of life is referred to as *chronos tou biou* (time of life; 1 Pet. 4:3, a variant reading).[6] *Bios* as the means of life, or "livelihood," is referred to in Mark 12:44; Luke 8:43; 15:12; and 1 John 3:17.[7] *Bios* as the manner of life, or life in its moral conduct, is referred to in the passages listed in the accompanying note.[8]

When *bios* is used to refer to a manner of life, it often has an ethical sense not found in the classical usage of *zōē*. Aristotle said that the slave is "a partner of *zōēs*" (he lives with the family) but not "a partner of *biou*" (he does not share in the career of his master).[9] According to Ammonius, Aristotle defined *bios* as "a rational life," and Ammonius argued that *bios* was never, except incorrectly, applied to the *existence* of plants or animals but only to the *lives* of men.[10] Although that distinction is made too absolutely,[11] it is a real one that is reflected in our words *zoology* and *biography* but not in *biology*, which as now used is a manifest misnomer.[12] On the one hand, we speak of "*zo*ology," for animals (*zōa*) live equally with men and may be classified according to the differences of their natural lives. On the other hand, we speak of "*bio*graphy" for human beings, not merely because they *live* but because they *lead lives* and make moral choices. They not only have "years of existence [*zōēs*]," they also have "ways of living [*biou*]" (Prov. 4:10).[13]

Thanatos and *zōē* are antonyms only when physical life is contemplated.[14] When life is regarded from a *moral* perspective as the opportunity for living nobly, *thanatos* and *bios*, not *thanatos* and *zōē*, are antonyms. Thus compare

6. Cf. *bios tou chronou* (a life of time; Job 10:20); *mēkos biou* (length of life; Prov. 3:2). Plutarch (*De liberis educandis* 17) has: "Every lifetime [*bios*] is a moment of time [*chronou*]."

7. Cf. Plato, *Gorgias* 486d; *Leges* 11.936c; Aristotle, *Historias animalium* 9.23.2; Euripides, *Ion*, 329. These means of life sometimes include a sense of largeness and abundance.

8. Its equivalents were *tropos* (*5158*), *ēthē* (*2239*), and *praxis* (*4234*); it was sometimes joined to *kosmios* (*2887*), *chrēstos* (*5543*), *sōphrōn* (*4998*), and *hēsychios* (*2272*). Cf. 1 Tim. 2:2; Plato (*Republic* 1.344e) called it the "course of life [*biou*]." Plutarch referred to "a mode of life and living [*bios*]" (*De virtute et vitio* 2) and stated (*De Iside et Osiride* 1): "If knowing and thinking were removed, immortality would not be living [*bion*] but passing time [*chronon*]." In *De liberis educandis* he spoke of "a settled life [*bios*]"; cf. Josephus, *Antiquitates Judaica* 5.10.1. Cf. Augustine (*De trinitate* 12.11): "Let each one be of this life [*vitae*], that is, *in what manner he may do temporal deeds*, which life [*vitam*] the Greeks term not *zōēn*, but *bion*."

9. *Politica* 1.13.13. Cf. *Ethica Nicomachea* 10.6.8.

10. On these two synonyms, see Vömel, *Synonymisches Wörterbuch*, pp. 168ff.; and Wyttenbach, *Animadversiones in Plutarchum*, 3:166. I do not know how Ammonius reconciled this statement with *Historia animalium* 1.1.15; 9.8.1, unless he included Aristotle in his censure.

11. See Stallbaum's note on the *Timaeus* of Plato, 44d.

12. *Biology* came to us from the French. Gottfried Reinhart Trevisanus, who died in 1837, probably invented it in his book *Biologie, ou la Philosophie de la Nature vivante*. The first volume of his work appeared in 1802. Canon Field of Norwich, in *Biology and Social Science*, has dealt well with this blunder.

13. Philo (*De caritate* 4) spoke of a period of time in Moses' life where "he began to change from mortal existence [*zōēs*] to immortal life [*bion*]."

14. Thus the Son of Sirach (30:17) stated: "Death [*thanatos*] is better than a bitter existence (*zōēn*) or chronic illness."

Xenophon: "Noble death [*thanaton*] is preferable to shameful life [*bion*]"[15] with Plato: "Striving soon for a shameful existence [*zōēn*] rather than for an honorable and blessed death [*thanaton*]."[16] In the last passage the craven soldier prefers the *present* boon of a shameful life (therefore *zōē*) to an honorable death. In the former passage Lycurgus teaches that an honorable death is to be chosen, rather than a long and shameful *existence*,[17] a *vita non vitalis* (a life not livable) because all the reasons for living are gone. Plato[18] distinguished between the words themselves, as well as their derivatives.[19]

Although *bios*, not *zōē*, is used in an ethical sense in classical Greek, in Scripture the opposite seems to be the case. In the New Testament *zōē* is the more noble word and expresses the highest and best that the saints possess in God. Thus we read of the "crown of life [*zōēs*]" (Rev. 2:10); "tree of life [*zōēs*]" (Rev. 2:7); "book of life [*zōēs*]" (Rev. 3:5); "water of life [*zōēs*]" (Rev. 21:6); "life [*zōē*] and godliness" (2 Pet. 1:3); "life [*zōē*] and immortality" (2 Tim. 1:10); "the life [*zōē*] of God" (Eph. 4:18); "eternal life [*zōē*]" (Matt. 19:16; Rom. 2:7);[20] "an endless life [*zōē*]" (Heb. 7:16); and "what is truly life [*zōēs*]" (1 Tim. 6:19). Sometimes *zōē* is used by itself (Matt. 7:14; Rom. 5:17; and often). All of these examples illustrate the highest blessedness of the creature. Contrast the preceding examples with the following uses of *bios*: "pleasure of life [*biou*]" (Luke 8:14); "affairs of this life [*biou*]" (2 Tim. 2:4); "the pride of life [*biou*] (1 John 2:16); "the livelihood [*bios*] of the world" (1 John 3:17); and "cares of this life [*biōtikai*]" (Luke 21:34). How may we explain these differences?

Only revealed religion relates death and sin as necessary correlatives (Gen. 1–3; Rom. 5:12) and consequently relates life and holiness. Only God's Word proclaims that wherever death exists, sin was there first. And wherever there is life, sin has not existed or has been expelled. Because Scripture reveals that death came into the world only through sin, life is the correlative of holiness. Against this background, *zōē* assumes profound moral significance and becomes the best way to express blessedness. Absolute *zōē* is synonymous with absolute holiness. In John 14:6 Christ affirmed: "I am . . . the life [*hē zōē*]" (cf. 1 John 1:2) and implicitly affirmed that he was absolutely holy. This is also true for the person that truly *lives*, or triumphs, over death (both spiritual and physical). Such a person has first triumphed over sin. It is not surprising that Scripture should use *zōē* to set forth the blessedness of God and the blessedness of the creature in communion with God.

Expositors who translate *apēllotriōmenoi tēs zōēs tou Theou* in Ephesians 4:18 as "alienated *from a divine life*" or as "*from a life lived according to the will*

15. *De republica Lacedaemoniorum* 9.1.

16. *Leges* 12.944d.

17. "An intolerable life [*bios*]" (*Empedocles* 326). Cf. Xenophon, *Memorabilia* 4.8.8; Meineke, *Fragmenta Comoeda Graeca* 142; "a life [*bios*] not livable" (Plato, *Apologia Socratis* 38a).

18. *Gorgias* 82, 83.

19. Cf. Herodotus, 7.46.

20. *Zōē aiōnios* occurs once in the Septuagint (Dan. 12:2; cf. *zōē aenaos* [L-S 28, everlasting] in 2 Macc. 7:36) and in Plutarch, *De Iside et Osiride* 1.

and commandments of God" are wrong.[21] Such an alienation exists, but in Ephesians 4:18 the apostle was affirming the miserable condition of those estranged from the one fountain of life,[22] those who did not possess life because they were separated from the only One who absolutely lives (John 5:26)—the living God (Matt. 16:16; 1 Tim. 3:15). Only those in fellowship with him have life. Galatians 5:25 will always seem to contain a tautology until *zōē* (and the verb *zēn* as well) receives the force claimed for it here.

21. *Remoti a vita illa quae secundum Deum est*, as Grotius has it, since *zōē* never meant that.
22. "For with you is the fountain of life [*zōēs*]," Ps. 37:9.

28

kyrios (2962) *despotēs* (1203) — *Lord* *Master*

According to the later Greek grammarians, a man was a *despotēs* in relation to his slaves[1]—and therefore an *oikodespotēs* (3617)—but a *kyrios* in relation to his wife and children.[2] Certainly there is a degree of truth to this distinction, since *kyrios* implies a limited moral authority whose wielder takes into consideration the good of those over whom it is exercised. The *despotēs*, however, exercises a more unrestricted power and domination, with no such limitations or restraints. To address another as *despota* implies an element of submission not found in the title *kyrie*. The Greeks refused the title of *despotēs* to any but the gods.[3] Our own use of the terms *despot*, *despotic*, and *despotism*, when contrasted with our use of *lord* and *lordship*, attests that these words are colored for us as well.

Nevertheless, there were influences that tended to dissolve this distinction. Slavery—the appropriating without payment of other men's toil—however legalized is so abhorrent to men's innate moral sense that they seek to mitigate its atrocity, in word at least.[4] In antiquity, wherever a more humane

1. Plato, *Leges* 6.756e.

2. When speaking about him or to him, they gave him this title of honor: "As Sara obeyed Abraham, calling him *lord*" (*kyrion auton kalousa*; 1 Pet. 3:6; cf. 1 Sam. 1:8; Plutarch, *Mulierum virtutes*, under the words *Mikka kai Megistō*).

3. Euripides, *Hippolytus* 88: "Sir, one ought to call gods 'despots' [*despotas*]."

4. No southern plantation owner in America willingly spoke of his "slaves" but preferred to use some other term.

view of slavery was present, the antithesis of *despotēs* to *doulos* (*1401*) was replaced by that of *kyrios* to *doulos*. The harsher antithesis might survive, but the milder existed along with it. Paul's writings contain examples that show that the distinction of the Greek grammarians was not observed in popular speech. In Paul's usage, masters are both *kyrioi* (Eph. 6:9; Col. 4:1) and *despotai* (1 Tim. 6:1–2; Titus 2:9; cf. 1 Pet. 2:18).[5]

Experience has shown that sinful man cannot be trusted with unrestricted power over his fellow man, for such power will certainly be abused.[6] When man regards God as the absolute Lord, Ruler, and Disposer of his life, however, it results in great benefits, since God's power is never disconnected from his wisdom and love. Just as the Greeks were willing to call the gods *despotai*, though they refused this title to any other, so in Scripture both *despotēs* and *kyrios* are applied to the true God.[7] In 2 Peter 2:1 and in Jude 4 the term is applied to Christ as God. Erasmus—perhaps because of an unconscious, latent Arianism—denied that *despotēs* in Jude 4 refers to Christ; he attributed *kyrios* to Christ and *despotēs* to the Father. But the fact that in Erasmus's Greek text *Theon* (*2316*) followed *despotēn* and was joined to it really lay at the root of his reluctance to ascribe *despotēs* to Christ. It was really not a philological but a theological difficulty for Erasmus, regardless of how he may have sought to persuade himself otherwise.

The Christian use of *despotēs* expresses a sense of God's absolute disposal of his creatures, of his autocratic power[8] more strongly than *kyrios*. Philo[9] found evidence of Abraham's *eulabeia* (*2124*) when he tempered boldness with reverence and godly fear in addressing God not as the usual *kyrie* but as *despota*. As Philo elaborated, *despotēs* is not only *kyrios* but a "frightful *kyrios*" that implies a more complete prostration of self before the might and majesty of God than does *kyrios*.

5. Cf. Philo, *Quod omnis probus liber sit* 6.

6. This moral fact is attested by our use of "despot" as a synonym for "tyrant," as well as by the history of the word *tyrant* itself.

7. For examples of this in the Septuagint, see Josh. 5:14; Prov. 29:25; Jer. 4:10; in the Apocrypha, see 2 Macc. 5:17 and elsewhere; in the New Testament, see Luke 2:29; Acts 4:24; 2 Pet. 2:1; Jude 4; Rev. 6:10.

8. "He does according to his will in the army of heaven and among the inhabitants of the earth" (Dan. 4:35).

9. *Quis rerum divinarum heres sit* 35.

29

alazōn (213) *hyperēphanos* (5244) *hybristēs* (5197)

Boastful Proud Insolent Violent

All of these words occur in Romans 1:30, though in the reverse order from the way I have listed them. They constitute an interesting subject for synonymous discrimination.

Alazōn occurs twice in the Septuagint (Job 28:8; Hab. 2:5) and twice in the New Testament (Rom. 1:30; 2 Tim. 3:2). *Alazoneia* (212) does not occur in the Septuagint but appears four times in the Apocrypha (Wisd. of Sol. 5:8; 17:7; 2 Macc. 9:8; 15:6) and twice in the New Testament (James 4:16; 1 John 2:16). *Alazoneia* is derived from *alē* (a wandering about), which at first designated the *vagabond* mountebanks,[1] conjurers, charlatans, or exorcists (Acts 19:13; 1 Tim. 5:13).[2] *Alazōn* refers to those who are full of empty and boastful professions of cures and other supposed feats they can accomplish.[3] Later the term was applied to any braggart or boaster.[4] Such a person would claim the

1. German *Marktschreier* (quack, charlatan).

2. It is joined with *goēs* (1114; Lucian, *Revivescentes sive piscator* 29); with *phenax* (L-S 1921, cheat, quack, impostor; Aristophanes); and with *kenos* (2756; Plutarch, *Quomodo quis suos in virtute sentiat profectus* 10).

3. Cf. Volpone in *The Fox* of Ben Jonson (act 2, sc. 1).

4. "*Alazōn* and overboastful" (Philo, *De congressu eruditionis gratia* 8). For other indifferent company that the word keeps, see Aristophanes, *Nubes* 445–52.

possession of skill (Wisd. of Sol. 17:7), knowledge, courage, virtue, riches, and so forth that were not truly his.[5] This kind of person is the exact antithesis of the *eirōn*,[6] who makes less of himself and his belongings than is in fact the case, in the same way that the *alazōn* makes more.[7] In the supposed *Definitions* of Plato, *alazoneia* is defined as "a habit of making pretense to good things that are not possessed."[8] In describing the *alazōn*, Xenophon said:

> The boaster [*ho alazōn*] seems to me to be a name for those who pretend to be wealthier than they really are, more courageous, and who undertake to do what is beyond their ability; it becomes apparent that they do this for the sake of gain and profit.[9]

Aristotle said: "The boaster [*ho alazōn*] is one who makes pretense to things held in high esteem, even though he does not possess them, and to greater things than he actually has."[10] As such he is likely to be a busybody and meddler, which may explain the juxtaposition of *alazoneia* and *polypragmosynē*.[11]

The essential nature of the *alazōn* is to boast beyond the truth (Wisd. of Sol. 2:16–17). Aristotle portrayed him as one who not merely boasts about what he possesses but who brags about qualities he does not possess. Aristotle contrasted him with the person who is "truthful both in manner of life and in word."[12] Although "boaster" is a fairly accurate translation of *alazōn*,[13] "ostentation" is not a good translation of *alazoneia*, since someone can only be "ostentatious" in things that he really has to "show." There is no English word (certainly not "pride," 1 John 2:16) that is as adequate a translation of *alazoneia* as is the German *Prahlerei* (bragging).[14] Such braggadocio is a vice that is sometimes ascribed to whole nations. Thus an "inborn boasting

5. Plutarch, *De laude ipsius* 4.
6. L-S 491, dissembler.
7. Aristotle, *Ethica Nicomachea* 2.7.12.
8. *Definitions* 416a.
9. *Cyropaedia* 2.2.12.
10. *Ethica Nicomachea* 4.7.2. Cf. Theodoret on Rom. 1:30: "He calls those persons boasters [*alazonas*] who have no basis for pretense to wisdom, but are puffed up in vain."
11. L-S 1442, meddlesomeness; *Epistula ad Diognetum* 4. It is also joined with *blakeia* (L-S 317, stupidity; Plutarch, *De recta ratione audiendi* 18), *typhos* (L-S 1838, delusion; Clement of Rome, *1 Epistula* 13), *agerōchia* (L-S 8, arrogance; 2 Macc. 9:7), *apaideusia* (L-S 175, lack of education, stupidity; Philo, *De Abrahamo* 24). In the passage just quoted from Xenophon, the *alazones* are distinguished from the *asteioi* (*791*) and *eucharites* (L-S 738, charming, gracious).
12. Cf. *Rhetorica* 2.6: "Claiming as one's own what belongs to another is a mark of boasting [*alazoneias*]." Cf. Xenophon, *Memorabilia* 1.7. Plato (*Republic* 8.560c) joined *pseudeis* (*5571*) with "boastful [*alazones*] words." Plutarch (*Pyrrus* 19) joined *alazōn* with *kompos* (L-S 976, boast). There is a lively description of the *alazōn* in the *Characters* (23) of Theophrastus, and in *Ad Herennium* (4.50–51) there is an even better description of his shifts and evasions.
13. Jebb suggests "swaggerer" in *Characters of Theophrastus*, p. 193.
14. On the one hand, Falstaff and Parolles, both "unscarred braggarts of the war," are excellent, though diverse, examples; so is Bessus in Beaumont's and Fletcher's *King and No King*. On the other hand, Marlowe's Tamburlaine, despite all of his boasting, is no *alazōn*, because he could sustain his "boasts of a great tongue" by a fearful display of power.

[*alazoneia*]" is ascribed to the Aetolians[15] and in modern times to the Gascons, from which we get the word *gasconade*. The Vulgate's translation of *alazones* by *elati* (exalted)[16] does not capture the word's central meaning as successfully as does Beza's *gloriosi* (bragging).[17]

Boastful Proud Insolent Violent

Sometimes a distinction has been made between the *alazōn* and the *perperos*.[18] The former is said to brag of things he does not possess, the latter of things he does (though his bragging is unbecoming). This distinction, however, cannot be maintained[19] because both the *alazōn* and the *perperos* are liars.

Habitual boasting is accompanied by contempt for the boasting of others. The *alazōn* is often *authadēs* (829) as well (Prov. 21:24). *Alazoneia* is related to *hyperopsia*,[20] with which it is almost used interchangeably.[21] Because there is only one step from *hyperopsia* to *hyperēphania*, it is not surprising to find *hyperēphanos* joined with *alazōn*.[22] A picturesque image serves as the basis for this synonymy: the *hyperēphanos*[23] is one who *shows himself above* his fellows.[24] As Deyling stated: "The word strictly speaking denotes a person projecting above others by his head, so that he is conspicuous in comparison with the rest, just as was Saul, 1 Sam. 9:2."[25]

A person is *alazōn* only in the company of others, but the proper seat of the *hyperēphania*[26] is within. The one guilty of this sin compares himself (secretly or openly) *with* others and lifts himself *above* others, in honor preferring himself. Theophrastus described this sin as "a certain contempt for others, except oneself."[27] The bearing of the *hyperēphanos* toward others is the consequence of his sin, not its essence. His "arrogance" consists in claiming honor and

15. Polybius, 4.3; cf. Livy, 33.11.

16. In the Rhemish it is translated by *haughty*.

17. We formerly used *glorious* in this sense. Thus North's *Plutarch* (p. 183) reads: "Some took this for a glorious brag; others thought he [Alcibiades] was like enough to have done it." And Milton (*The Reason of Church Government* 1.5) said: "He [Anselm] little dreamt then that the weeding hook of Reformation would, after two ages, pluck up his *glorious* poppy [prelacy] from insulting over the good corn [presbytery]."

18. L-S 1395, braggart. *Hē agapē ou perpereuetai*, 1 Cor. 13:4.

19. See Polybius, 32.6.5; 40.6.2.

20. L-S 1867, contempt.

21. Philo, *De caritate* 22–24.

22. Cf. Clement of Rome, *1 Epistula* 16. Other places where it occurs in the New Testament that have not already been mentioned are Luke 1:51; James 4:6; 1 Pet. 5:5; cf. *hyperēphania* in Mark 7:22.

23. From *hyper* (5228) and *phainomai* (5316).

24. This is the same as the Latin *superbus* (proud), which is derived from *super* (above), and as the English *stilts*, which is related to the German *stolz* (proud) and to *stout* in its earlier sense of "proud" or "lifted up."

25. *Obsessiones sacrae*, 5:219. Cf. Horace (*Carmina* 1.18.15): "And Pride [*Gloria*] raising her empty head by far too much."

26. The German *Hochmuth* (pride).

27. *Characters* 34. Therefore *alazōn* is used with *hyperopsia* (L-S 1867, disdain; Demosthenes, *Oratio* 21.247) and with *exoudenōsis* (L-S 598, contempt; Ps. 31:19), and *hyperēphanos* is used with *authadēs* (Plutarch, *Comparatio Alcibiadis et Marcii Coriolani* 4).

alazōn
hyperēphanos
hybristēs

observance for himself.[28] His indignation, and perhaps his cruelty and revenge— if these are withheld[29]—are only the results of his false self-estimate.[30] There may be the perversion of a nobler character in the *hyperēphanos* (the melancholic temperament) than in the *alazōn*, (the sanguine temperament) and in the *hybristēs* (the choleric temperament). But because this character is nobler, when it falls, it descends more deeply into sin. The *hyperēphanos* is one "who is proud in heart [*hypsēlokardios*]" (Prov. 16:5) and sets "the mind on high things" (Rom. 12:16), as opposed to being "lowly in heart" (Matt. 11:29).[31] His pride is directed not only against man but against God, and he may assail the very prerogatives of deity itself.[32] Theophylact called this sin *akropolis kakōn* (the stronghold of evils). In Scripture we are reminded three times that "God resists the proud" (*hyperēphanois antitassetai*; Prov. 3:34; James 4:6; 1 Pet. 5:5); he sets himself in battle array against them, as they do against him.

The final synonym in this group is *hybristēs*,[33] which etymologically is related to *hyperēphanos*.[34] *Hybris* denotes insolent wrongdoing for the sheer pleasure of inflicting pain on others, not out of revenge or a similar motive. Thus Aristotle said: "For wanton violence [*hybris*] is the damaging and grieving in matters that cause shame to the victim for the sole purpose of furnishing pleasure to the doer; in fact those who resist do not commit an outrage, but seek vengeance."[35] *Hybristēs* occurs only twice in the New Testament (Rom. 1:30 [violent] and 1 Tim. 1:13 [insolent]) but frequently in the Septuagint.[36] Aristotle related the words in a similar manner (*Rhetorica* 2.16). And *hybristēs* is related to other words such as *agrios* (66; Homer, *Odyssey* 6.120), *atasthalos* (L-S 268, reckless; Homer, *Odyssey* 24.282), *aithōn* (L-S 37, fiery; Sophocles, *Ajax* 1061), *anomos* (459, Sophocles, *Trachiniae* 1076), *biaios* (972; Demosthenes, *Oratio* 24.169), *paroinos* (3943), *agnōmōn* (L-S 12, hard-hearted), *pikros* (4089; Demosthenes, *Oratio* 54.1261), *adikos* (94; Plato, *Leges* 1.630b), *akolastos* (L-S 52, undisciplined; Plato, *Apologia Socratis* 26e), *aphrōn* (878; Plato, *Philebus* 45e), *hyperoptēs* (L-S 1866, disdainful; Aristotle, *Ethica Nicomachea* 4.3.21), *thrasus* (L-S 804, rash; Clement of Alexandria, *Stromata* 2.5), *phaulos* (5337; Plutarch, *De defectu oraculorum* 45), and *philogelōs*.[37] Plutarch wrote about "an insolent [*hybristēs*] man [who was] . . . full of all

28. *Hyperēphania* (5243) is used with *philodoxia* (L-S 1935, love of fame) in Esther 4:10.

29. See Esther 3:5–6; Appian, *De rebus Punicis* 8.118: "cruel and haughty [*hyperēphana*]."

30. For this reason the following terms are used together: *hyperēphanos* and *epiphthonos* (L-S 670, envious; Plutarch, *Pompeius* 24); *hyperēphanoi* and *bareis* (926, *Quaestiones convivales* 63); and *hyperēphania* and *agerōchia* (2 Macc. 9:7).

31. He is "puffed up" (1 Tim. 3:6) or "haughty" (2 Tim. 3:4), besotted with pride and far from all true wisdom (Ecclus. 15:8).

32. 1 Macc. 1:21, 24; Ecclus. 10:12–13; Wisd. of Sol. 6: "haughty giants."

33. This term is derived from *hybris* (5196), which is derived from *hyper* (according to Schneider and Pott, but Curtius, *Grundzüge*, 2d ed., p. 473, expressed doubts) and thus denotes "uppishness."

34. See Donaldson, *New Cratylus*, 3d ed., p. 552.

35. *Rhetorica* 2.2. Its harvest is described in the dread lines of Aeschylus (*Persae* 822).

36. In Job 40:11–12 and Isaiah 2:12 it is associated with *hyperēphanos* (cf. Prov. 8:13).

37. L-S 1935, fond of the ludicrous; Plutarch, *Symposium* 8.5, but here in a far milder sense.

contempt and rashness."[38] Such a person is the exact antithesis of the *sōphrōn*.[39] The *hybristēs* is insolently abusive; his contempt for others results in *acts* of wantonness and outrage. The term *hybristēs* was applied to Menelaus when he wanted to refuse the rites of burial to the body of Ajax.[40] Hanun, king of Ammon, was described as *hybris* when he cut short the garments of King David's ambassadors, shaved off half their beards, and returned them to their master (2 Sam. 10). When Paul persecuted the church, he was described as *hybristēs* (1 Tim. 1:13; cf. Acts 8:3) but was *hybristheis* (*5195*; 1 Thess. 2:2) at Philippi (see Acts 16:22–23). In prophesying the order of his passion, Christ declared that the Son of Man *hybristhēsetai* (Luke 18:32). And the blasphemous masquerade of royalty that was forced upon Christ (Matt. 27:27–30) constituted the fulfillment of this prophecy. Tacitus described the martyrdoms of the Christians under Nero's persecution as "mockeries added to those perishing."[41] The Christians died, Tacitus said, "with wanton insolence [*hybreōs*]." In Shakespeare's *Henry VI* the same may be said of York, when (before Margaret and Clifford stab him) the paper crown was placed on his head in mockery of his kingly pretensions. The Spartans were not satisfied with throwing down the Long Walls of Athens, unless they did it to the sound of music.[42] The story of mankind is full of examples of this demonic element that lies deep within the human heart—this evil for evil's sake that ever begets itself anew.

Boastful Proud Insolent Violent

The two main forms of *hybris* are cruelty and lust, which at root are not two sins but one.[43] Josephus included both concepts when he characterized the men of Sodom as being *hybristai* to men (cf. Gen. 19:5) no less than they were *asebeis* (*765*) to God.[44] And Josephus used the same language about the sons of Eli (cf. 1 Sam 2:22).[45] By using *hybris* on both occasions, Josephus intended an assault on the chastity of others.[46]

Alazōn, *hyperēphanos*, and *hybristēs* are clearly distinguishable. Each word has its own distinct sphere of meaning. These three words portray an ascending scale of guilt, respectively designating those who are boastful *in words*, those who are proud and overbearing *in thoughts*, and those who are insolent and injurious *in deeds*.

38. *Lucullus* 34.

39. 4998; Xenophon, *Apologia Socratis* 19; *Agesilaus* 10.2; cf. *prauthymos* (L-S 1461, of gentle mind; Prov. 16:19).

40. Sophocles, *Ajax* 1065.

41. *Annales* 15.44.

42. Plutarch, *Lysander* sec. 15. Another example would be prisoners in a Spanish civil war who are shot in the back.

43. The hideous records of human wickedness have often attested to this—the trial, for example, of Gilles de Retz, marshal of France, in the fifteenth century. Milton described it as "lust hard by hate."

44. *Antiquitates Judaicae* 1.11.1.

45. Ibid. 5.10.1.

46. Cf. Euripides, *Hippolytus* 1086. Critias (quoted by Aelian, *Variae historiae* 10.13) called Archilochus "lewd and insolent [*hybristēs*]." Plutarch, comparing Demetrius Poliorcetes and Antony, gave this title to both of them (*Comparatio Demetrii et Antonii* 3. Cf. *Demetrius* 24; Lucian, *Dialogi deorum* 6.1; and the article *Hybreōs dikē* in Pauly's *Encyclopädie*).

30

antichristos (500) *pseudochristos* (5580)

Antichrist False Christ

The five occurrences of *antichristos* in the New Testament are all found in the Johannine Epistles (1 John 2:18 twice; 2:22; 4:3; 2 John 7). Although only John used this word, Paul referred to the same person with terms that are identical in denotation: "the man of sin," "the son of perdition," "the lawless one" (2 Thess. 2:3, 8).[1] Paul provides the most instruction about this archenemy of Christ and God. We shall bypass many questions concerning this foe, such as whether the Antichrist is a single person, a succession of persons, or a system. We are concerned only with the force of *anti* (473) in the compound *antichristos*. Does *anti* differentiate *antichristos* from *pseudochristos*? Does *antichristos* imply one who sets himself up *against* Christ, or like *pseudochristos*, does *antichristos* refer to one who sets himself up *in the stead of* Christ? Is the *antichristos* one who proclaims that there is no Christ, or is he one who proclaims himself to be Christ?

There is no quick solution to the question of the distinguishing force of *anti* in *antichristos*, since *anti* in compound words can mean either "against" or "instead of."[2] *Anti* often expresses *substitution—antibasileus* (he who is instead of the king), *prorex* (viceroy), *anthypatos* (proconsul), *antideipnos* (one who fills the place of an absent guest), *antipsychos* (one who lays down his life for oth-

1. With the exception of Grotius, all important expositors agree with this identification. Cf. Augustine, *De civitate Dei* 20.19.2.

2. For a subtle analysis of the meanings *instead of* and *against*, see Pott, *Etymologische Forschungen*, 2d ed., p. 260.

antichristos
pseudochristos

ers),[3] *antilutron* (the ransom paid instead of a person). But it also implies *opposition*, as in *antilogia* (contradiction), *antithesis* (477), and *antikeimenos* (480). *Anti* not only expresses the fact of opposition but may also indicate what the opposition is directed against, as in *antinomia* (opposition to law),[4] *anticheir* (the thumb[5]), *antiphilosophos* (one of opposite philosophical opinions), *antikatōn* (the title of a book that Caesar wrote against Cato), and *antitheos*.[6] The jests that Antipater[7]—who sought to murder his father—was *pherōnymos*[8] would have been pointless if *anti* did not have this meaning.[9] These examples show that *anti* in compound words sometimes implies substitution and sometimes opposition. The force of these words may be different, depending on the way they are used by different authors. For example, according to Thucydides (7.86) an *antistratēgos* was the commander of the *hostile* army, but according to later Greek writers, such as Plutarch (who was involved in Roman affairs), an *antistratēgos* was the standing equivalent of a *propraetor* (a magistrate who was sent out to govern a province after he had served as praetor at Rome). Therefore it is not possible to determine the exact meaning of *antichristos* in Scripture by first determining the meaning of *anti*. The question must be settled by other considerations.[10]

I believe that John's words imply that the essential mark of the Antichrist is resistance to Christ and defiance of him, not any treacherous assumption of his character and offices (1 John 2:22; 2 John 7). In the parallel passage, 2 Thessalonians 2:4, the Antichrist is described as *ho antikeimenos* (he who opposes).[11] The Antichrist will not even acknowledge the fulfillment of God's Word in himself. Instead, he will deny all biblical truth, even hating erroneous worship simply because it is worship. He will hate everything that is called "God" (2 Thess. 2:4), and most of all he will hate the church's worship in spirit and truth (Dan. 8:11). He will seek to establish his throne on the destruction of every religion and every acknowledgment that man is governed by a power higher than his own. He will substitute his own lie for God's

3. Josephus, *De bello Judaico* 17; Ignatius, *Epistula ad Ephesios* 21.

4. See Suicer, *Thesaurus* under this word.

5. The thumb receives its name not because it is equivalent in strength to the whole hand but because it is set over against the hand.

6. Its meaning in Homer is different, where it is applied to Polyphemus (*Odyssey* 1.70) and to the Ithacan suitors (14.18; cf. Pindar, *Pythia* 3.88) and means "godlike" in strength and power. In Philo, however, *antitheos nous* (*De confusione linguarum* 19; *De somniis* 2.27) can only mean the "mind opposed to God" and is used in the same way by the Christian fathers.

7. *Anti-pater* as equal to "against father."

8. L-S 1924, well-named.

9. I will not cite *Anterōs* (L-S 152, returned love or against love), where the force of *anti* is more questionable.

10. Lücke (*Kommentar über die Briefe des Johannes*, pp. 190–94) has an excellent discussion of the word. On the whole subject of Antichrist, see Schneckenburger, *Jahrbuch für Deutsche Theologie*, 4:405ff.

11. Many of the fathers understood the word in this sense. Tertullian (*De praescriptionibus hereticorum* 4) asked: "Who are antichrists but those who rebel against Christ?" In Theophylact's language, the Antichrist is "opposed to Christ," or in Origen's words (*Contra Celsum* 6.45) "diametrically opposed to Christ." *Widerchrist* (counterchrist) is the German rendering.

truth that in Christ God is man, asserting that in him, the Antichrist, man is God.

The term *pseudochristos* appears only twice in the New Testament (Matt 24:24; Mark 13:22) in accounts of the same discourse. In form, *pseudochristos* resembles similar compound words where *pseudos* (5579) is combined with almost any other noun.[12] Ecclesiastical Greek refers to the *pseudopoimēn* (false shepherd) and *pseudolatreia* (false worship), and classical Greek mentions the *pseudangelos* (false messenger; Homer, *Iliad* 15.159), *pseudomantis* (false seer; Herodotus, 4.69), and a hundred other *pseudo* compounds. The *pseudochristos* does not deny the being of a Christ but builds on the world's expectations of such a person and appropriates them. The *pseudochristos* will blasphemously affirm that he is the foretold one, the one in whom God's promises and men's expectations will be fulfilled. Barchochab (Son of the Star) appropriated the prophecy of Numbers 24:17 and in Hadrian's reign started a Jewish insurrection that destroyed him and more than a million of his fellow countrymen. There has been a long series of blasphemous pretenders and impostors—false messiahs—who, since the rejection of the true Messiah, have in almost every age fed and betrayed the expectations of the Jews.

The distinction is plain: the *antichristos* denies that there is a Christ; the *pseudochristos* affirms himself to be the Christ. Both make war against Christ, and though under different pretenses, each would set himself on the throne of glory. Even though *antichristos* and *pseudochristos* may thus be broadly distinguished as words that represent two different manifestations of the kingdom of wickedness, there is a sense in which the final "Antichrist" will be a "Pseudochrist" as well. This will be similar to the last revelation of hell itself, in which all subordinate forms of error are combined in a last assault against the truth. The Antichrist will not call himself the Christ, because of his enmity against the name, offices, and temper of Jesus of Nazareth, the exalted King of glory. No one can resist the truth by a mere negation, so the Antichrist will offer something positive in place of the faith he will seek to abolish. We may conclude that the final Antichrist will reveal himself to the world[13] as its messiah and savior but not as the Messiah of prophecy, the Messiah of God. The Antichrist will bless those who obey him with the full enjoyment of material things in the present, not with a distant and uncertain heaven. He will abolish the troublesome distinctions between church and world, spirit and flesh, holiness and sin, and good and evil that are the source of disquietude and that deprive men of pleasure. Although he will not assume the name of Christ and so will not be a *pseudochristos*, he will usurp Christ's offices and present himself as the true center of the world's hopes. He will claim to be the satisfier of all mankind's needs and the healer of all our hurts. "The Red Christ," as his servants already call him, will take unto himself all the names and forms of blasphemy and will be both the great *pseudochristos* and *antichristos*.

12. *Pseudapostolos* (5570; 2 Cor. 11:13), *pseudadelphos* (5569; 2 Cor. 11:26), *pseudodidaskalos* (5572; 2 Pet. 2:1), *pseudoprophētēs* (5578; Matt. 7:13; cf. Jer. 33:7), *pseudomartyr* (5575; Matt. 26:60; cf. Plato).

13. For he too will have his *apokalypsis* (602; 2 Thess. 2:3, 8), his *parousia* (3552; v. 9).

31

molynō (3435) *miainō* (3392) — *Defile*

Although both of these words are translated as *defile* in the New Testament,[1] they differ in their underlying imagery. Properly speaking, *molynein* means "to besmear" or "to besmirch," as with mud or filth.[2] *Miainein* basically means "to stain" with color, not "to smear" with matter.[3]

In a secondary and ethical sense, *molynō* and *miainō* have an equally dishonorable meaning. The "filthiness [*molysmos*, *3436*] of the flesh" (2 Cor. 7:1) is the same as the "pollutions [*miasmata*, *3393*] of the world" (2 Pet. 2:20). Both words are also used to refer to the defiling of women (cf. Gen. 34:5; Zech. 14:2). But this synonymy is only true when the terms are used figuratively or ethically. In classical Greek *miainein* is the word that is most frequently used to refer to the profaning or unhallowing of anything.[4] On the

1. *Molynō* is used in 1 Cor. 8:7; Rev. 3:4; 14:4; *miainō* is used in John 18:28; Titus 1:15; Heb. 12:15; Jude 8.

2. "To befoul" is simply another form of "to defile." Aristotle (*Historia animalium* 6.17.1) spoke of swine "sullying [*molynontes*] themselves in the mud," and the context suggests that they were crusting themselves over with mud. Cf. Plato, *Republic* 7.535e; Song of Sol. 5:3; Ecclus. 13:1.

3. The first word corresponds to the Latin *inquinare* (to befoul; Horace, *Satirae* 1.8.37) and to *spurcare* (to make filthy), which is probably related to *porcus* (pig; cf. the German *besudeln*, to besmirch). The second word corresponds to the Latin *maculare* (to spot) and to the German *beflecken* (to spot).

4. Plato, *Leges* 9.868a; *Timaeus* 69d; Sophocles, *Antigone* 1031; cf. Lev. 5:3; John 18:28.

molynō
miainō

one hand, however, when *miainein* is used literally, it may have a good sense, as in the English staining of glass or ivory.[5] On the other hand, *molynein*'s literal meaning is as negative as its figurative one.[6]

5. *Iliad* 4.141; cf. Virgil, *Aeneid* 12.67. In Latin the *macula* (spot) is not necessarily the *labes* (blemish); in English the "spot" is not always a "blot."

6. The verb *spiloun* (4695), a late word that appears only twice in the New Testament (James 3:6; Jude 23), is closer in meaning to *miainein*. See Lobeck, *Phrynichus*, p. 28.

32

paideia (3809)

nouthesia (3559)

Chastening Instruction Training Nurture Admonition

Although *paideia* and *nouthesia* occur together in Ephesians 6:4, either they are not distinguished in our English translations, or they are distinguished incorrectly. Thus it is worthwhile to attempt to discriminate between these two words.

Paideia is one of those words to which Christianity gave a deeper meaning (the new wine made new even the old vessel into which it was poured). For the Greek, *paideia* simply meant "education."[1] But those who had learned that "foolishness is bound up in the heart" both "of a child" and of man and that "the rod of correction will drive it far from him" (Prov. 22:15) gave *paideia* an additional meaning. All effectual instruction for sinful mankind includes and implies chastening, or "correction," in which there must be *epanorthōsis* (*1882*), or "rectification."[2] *Epanorthōsis*, which occurs only once

1. In his many definitions of *paideia*, Plato gives no hint of the new meaning it would assume in Christian usage.

2. Greeks acknowledged this relationship to a certain extent in the secondary usage of *akolastos* (L-S 52, undisciplined), whose primary meaning was "the unchastised." For example, Menander said: "One who has not been whipped [*dareis*, *1194*] is not being trained [*paideuetai*,

paideia

nouthesia

in the New Testament, is closely related to *paideia* in 2 Timothy 3:16.

We shall compare two definitions of *paideia*: one by a great secular philosopher, the other by a great Christian theologian. On the one hand, Plato defines *paideia* this way: "Education [*paideia*] is the drawing and guiding of children toward reason as stated correctly by the law."[3] On the other hand, Basil the Great defined *paideia* thusly: "Education [*paideia*] is a guidance beneficial to the soul, frequently cleansing it painfully of its defilements from evil."[4] Basil asserted that *paideia* was not simply *eruditio* (instruction). Augustine, who noticed the new Christian use of the word, defined it as "instruction *through vexations*."[5] And this is the predominant meaning of *paideia* and *paideuein* in the Septuagint, Apocrypha, and New Testament.[6] The only occasion in the New Testament where *paideuein* occurs in the old Greek sense is Acts 7:22. In Ephesians 6:4 "discipline" might be a better word than "nurture," which is too weak a translation of *paideia*. The transgression of the laws and ordinances of the Christian household will induce the correction that *paideia* indicates.

Nouthesia[7] is more successfully translated as "admonition" in the English versions. In defining *nouthesia*, Cicero said: "Admonition is, at it were, a milder rebuke." *Nouthesia* is training by word—either of encouragement, when this is sufficient, or of remonstrance, reproof, or blame, where required. Thus *nouthesia* is distinguished from *paideia*, which is training by act and by discipline.[8] There are many examples in Greek literature that illustrate the distinctive meaning of *nouthesia* as training by the spoken word.[9] *Nouthesia* is a milder term than *paideia*.

Nouthesia's association with *paideia* teaches us that *nouthesia* is a necessary element of Christian education. Without it, the *paideia* would be incomplete. In fact, when childhood is over, *paideia* is swallowed up in *nouthesia*. Where necessary, the *nouthesia* will be earnest and severe. *Nouthesia* is much more than a feeble Eli-like remonstrance—"No, my sons! For it is not a good report that I hear" (1 Sam 2:24). With respect to these sons, Eli "did not restrain [*ouk enouthetei*] them" (3:13).[10] *Nouthetein* predominantly has the sense of

---

3811]." In other secular Greek uses of *paideuein*, there are slight hints of this. See Xenophon, *Memorabilia* 1.3.5; Polybius, *Historiae* 2.9.6.

3. *Leges* 2.659d.

4. *Homilia in principium proverbiorum* 1.

5. *Enarratio in Psalma* 119:66.

6. Lev. 26:18; Ps. 6:1; Isa. 53:5; Ecclus. 4:17; 22:6, *mastiges* (3148) *kai paideia*; 2 Macc. 6:12; Luke 23:16; Heb. 12:5, 7, 8; Rev. 3:19; and frequently.

7. In Attic Greek, *nouthetia* or *nouthetēsis* (Lobeck, *Phrynichus*, pp. 513, 520).

8. Bengel missed the exact distinction here. On *en paideia kai nouthesia* in Eph. 6:4 he has this note: "One of these remedies ignorance; the other forgetfulness and fickleness. Either one encompasses both vocal and other instruction."

9. *Paraineseis* [L-S 1810, exhortations] *kai nouthesiai* (Plutarch, *De cohibenda ira* 2), "admonishing [*nouthetikoi*] words" (Xenophon, *Memorabilia* 1.2.21), "teaching and admonition [*nouthetēsis*]" (Plato, *Republic* 3.399b), "to admonish [*nouthetein*, 3560] and to teach" (*Protagoras* 323d).

10. Plutarch united *nouthesia* with *mempsis* (L-S 1101, blame; *Conjugalia praecepta* 13) and with *psogos* (L-S 2025, censure; *De virtute morali* 12; *Quomodo adulator ab amico internoscatur* 17).

admonishing *with blame.*[11] Jerome was only partially correct when he desired to get rid of the Vulgate's *correptio* in Ephesians 6:4 and Titus 3:10. Jerome argued that *nouthesia* does not imply a rebuke or austerity, as does *correptio*, and that therefore *correptio* is not the best translation for *nouthesia.*[12] *Nouthesia*, however, does not exclude a rebuke but implies that whatever is needed to cause the admonition to be heeded, to be *taken to heart*, will be said.[13]

The predominant sense of *nouthesia* in our English versions is admonition *by word*, as distinguished from *paideia*, although both *paideia* and *nouthetein* are sometimes used to refer to correction *by deed*. The primary use of both words is the appeal to the reasonable faculties. In phrases like "admonition [*nouthetēsis*] of a rod"[14] and "to admonish [*nouthetein*] with blows,"[15] the words are used in a secondary but more emphatic sense. The same emphasis lies in the statement that Gideon "took thorns of the wilderness and briers, and with them he *taught* the men of Succoth" (Judg. 8:16). The primary idea of "to teach" is the *oral* communicating of knowledge.[16]

Philo related *nouthesia* with *sōphronismos* (4995; Lösner, *Obsessiones ad Novum Testamentum e Philone*, p. 427).

11. Plutarch, *Quomodo quis suos in virtute sentiat profectus* 11; *Conjugalia praecepta* 22.

12. Jerome said: "What we read as *reproach* [*correptionem*] in Greek it is rendered better as *admonition* [*nouthesia*] and *instruction* more than *austerity*."

13. The derivation from *nous* (3563) and *tithēmi* (5087) affirms this.

14. Plato, *Leges* 3.700c.

15. *Leges* 9.879d; cf. *Republic* 8.560a.

16. On the relations between *nouthetein* and *didaskein* (*1321*), see Lightfoot on Col. 1:28.

33

aphesis (859) — *Forgiveness, Remission*

paresis (3929) — *Passing over (of Sins)*

Aphesis is the primary word used to express forgiveness (or remission) in the New Testament.[1] In the Septuagint, however, *aphesis* is not used in that way.[2] *Aphesis* is derived from *aphienai* (863), and the underlying imagery depicts the release of a prisoner (Isa. 61:1) or the remission of a debt (Deut. 15:3). The Year of Jubilee[3] (Lev. 25:31, 40; 27:24), the year when all debts were forgiven, may have suggested the higher application of the word, a usage frequently found in the New Testament.[4] On a single occasion, however, the phrase *paresis tōn hamartēmatōn* (265) occurs (Rom. 3:25). The Authorized Version's marginal note about this variation of the apostle's phrase translates *paresis* as "remission," just as elsewhere "remission" is used to translate *aphesis*. Although many scholars have agreed with this translation, others have more correctly affirmed that Paul deliberately used *paresis* to express something that *aphesis* would not adequately express and that our translators should have reproduced Paul's change.

Cocceius and his school used Romans 3:25 as one of the main supports for their doctrine that there was no remission of sins in the fullest sense under

1. See Vitringa, *Obsessiones sacrae*, 1:909–33.
2. Gen. 4:13 is the closest example of that usage.
3. Called the *etos* (2094), *eniautos* (1763), *tēs apheseōs*, or simply *aphesis*.
4. It occurs more in Luke than in all the other books of the New Testament combined.

aphesis

paresis

the old covenant. Cocceius taught that there was no *teleiōsis* (5050, Heb. 10:1–4), no entire abolition of sin even for the faithful themselves, only a present *praetermission* (*paresis*), a temporary dissimulation by God in consideration of the sacrifice that was one day to be. Until that sacrifice the "remembrance of sins" remained. A violent controversy raged among the theologians of Holland at the end of the sixteenth and the beginning of the following century about this matter.[5] On the one hand, those who opposed the Cocceian scheme incorrectly denied that there was any distinction between *aphesis* and *paresis*.[6] On the other hand, Cocceius and his followers were undoubtedly wrong in saying that *for the faithful* under the old covenant there was only a *paresis*, not an *aphesis*, of sins and in applying *to them* what was asserted by the apostle *in respect to the world*. But Cocceius and his followers were correct in maintaining that *paresis* is not perfectly synonymous with *aphesis*. And indeed, Beza had already drawn attention to the distinction between the two words.[7]

Aphesis and *paresis* suggest different meanings. If *aphesis* means "remission,"[8] then *paresis*[9] naturally means "*praeter*mission"[10]—the "passing by [*paresis*] of sins." The *praetermission* (passing by) of sins for the present leaves the future open for God either to *remit* the sins entirely or for him adequately to punish them, as may seem good to him who has the power and right to do one or the other. Fritzsche spoke plainly on this point:

> These two words—*aphesis* and *paresis*—agree in that whether the one or the other occurs to you, no reckoning of your sins is made; they differ in that when the former is given, you *never* pay the penalty for your deeds, but when the latter is granted, you suffer no punishment for your deeds as long as he who has the right of chastising your transgressions decides to leave them unpunished.[11]

The classical usage of *parienai* and *paresis* bears out this distinction. Thus Xenophon stated: "It is not right to pass over [*parienai*] unpunished sins."[12] And Josephus related that although Herod desired to punish a certain offense, he passed it by.[13] When the Son of Sirach (Ecclus. 23:2) prayed that God *would not "pass by"* his sins, he did not use *ou mē parē* as a synonym for *ou mē aphē*

5. For a brief history of this controversy, see Deyling, *Obsessiones sacrae*, 5:209; Vitringa, *Obsessiones sacrae*, 4:3; Venema, *Dissertationes sacrae*, p. 72. A full statement of what Cocceius meant may be found in his *Commentary on the Romans, in loc.* (*Opera*, 5:62). He defended and justified this viewpoint at greater length in his treatise *Utilitas distinctionis duorum vocabulorum Scripturae, pareseōs et apheseōs* (9:121ff.).

6. See Witsius, *De oeconomico foedere* 4.12.36.

7. In his Latin Version first published in 1556, he did not note it. At a later period he acknowledged his error and said, "These two words differ from each other very much," and he translated *paresis* by *dissimulatio* (disregarding).

8. In German *Loslassung* (release).

9. From *pariēmi* [3935].

10. In German *Vorbeilassung* (a passing by).

11. *Ad Romanos*, 1:199.

12. *Hipparchicus* 7.10.

13. *Antiquitates Judaicae* 15.3.2: *parēke tēn hamartian* (266).

but asked only that he might not be without a wholesome chastisement following close on his transgressions.

Although *aphesis* and *paresis* suggest different meanings, the following passage from Dionysius of Halicarnassus has been adduced to prove that *paresis* is synonymous with *aphesis*: "They did not find complete remission [*holoscherē paresin*], but they delayed for as long as they were able."[14] It is "complete" *paresis* that is synonymous with *aphesis*, and Dionysius of Halicarnassus undoubtedly added that epithet because *paresis* alone would not have properly expressed his meaning.

Thus there is a strong prima facie probability that Paul intended something different by the sole use of *paresis hamartēmatōn* in his letters (Rom. 3:25) as contrasted with the many places where he used *aphesis*. The Authorized Version translates Romans 3:25 in this way: "Whom God hath set forth to be a propitiation through faith in his blood, to declare his righteousness *for the remission* of sins that are past, through the forbearance of God." I would translate Romans 3:25 this way: "Whom God hath set forth as a propitiation, through faith in his blood, for a manifestation of his righteousness *because of the praetermission* [*dia* (*1223*) *tēn paresin*, not *dia tēs pareseōs*], in the forbearance of God, of the sins done aforetime." I think this was Paul's exact meaning: "There needed to be a signal manifestation of the righteousness of God, on account of the long praetermission or passing over of sins, in his infinite forbearance, with no adequate expression of his wrath against them, during all those long years which preceded the coming of Christ; which manifestation of God's righteousness found place, when he set forth no other and no less than his own Son to be the propitiatory sacrifice for sin" (Heb. 9:15, 22). Prior to the incarnation, God's extreme indignation against sin and sinners had not been pronounced. During that time, God's *connivance*—the holding of his peace—was only partial, for as Paul declared, the wrath of God was revealed from heaven against all unrighteousness of men (Rom. 1:18). And in verses 24 through 32, Paul traced some ways in which God's wrath was displayed. This was the time when God "allowed all nations to walk in their own ways" (Acts 14:16); they were "the times of ignorance" that "God overlooked" (Acts 17:30), the times of the *anochē* [463] *tou Theou*.[15]

By its very nature, this position regarding sin could only be transient and provisional. Among humans the passing over (praetermission) of offenses is often identical with their remission, that is, *paresis* is synonymous with *aphesis*. This is because people forget, because they are not able to bring the distant past into judgment, and because we do not have the righteous energy to will such a judgment. But with an absolutely righteous God, the *paresis* can only be temporary, and there must be a final settlement. Forbearance is not

14. *Antiquitates Romanae* 7.37. Still more unfortunate is a passage from Philo (*Quod deterius potiori insidiari soleat* 47) that Lösner mentions in his *Obsessiones ad Novum Testamentum e Philone* (p. 249) in an attempt to prove that *paresis* is synonymous with *aphesis*. A cursory examination of the passage, however, is sufficient to show that Lösner misunderstood Philo's words.

15. This *anochē* is the correlative of *paresis*, as *charis* (5485) is of *aphesis*. The occurrence of *anochē* here confirms this view.

aphesis

paresis

acquittal; every sin must either be absolutely forgiven or adequately avenged. As the Russian proverb tells us, "God has no bad debts." And as long as these sins are passed by, the *paresis* itself might seem to call into question God's absolute righteousness. Because God held his peace, people wrongly concluded that God, like them, was morally indifferent to good and evil.[16] But now "at the fitting time" God, by the sacrifice of his Son, has rendered such an interpretation impossible. Bengel wrote:

> The object of passing by [*pareseōs*] is sin, of forbearance [*anochēs*] it is the sinner. As long as passing by and forbearance existed, God's righteousness was not apparent; for he did not seem to be angered vehemently at sin, but to be indifferent, unconcerned, and negligent with the sinner, Heb. 8:9. But through Christ's blood and propitious death God's justice has been displayed—with punishment against sin itself, that he himself might be just, and with zeal in behalf of the sinner, that he himself might be justifying.[17]

Thus the one who partakes of the *aphesis* has his sins forgiven, and unless he commits new acts of disobedience (Matt. 18:32, 34; 2 Pet. 1:9; 2:20), his sins will not be imputed to him or mentioned against him any more. The *paresis* is different from the *aphesis* and is a subordinate benefit. The *paresis* is the present passing over of sin, the suspension of its punishment, the not shutting up of all the ways of mercy against the sinner, the giving to him of space and helps for repentance.[18] If such repentance follows, then the *paresis* will lose itself in the *aphesis*; if not, then the punishment that was suspended but not averted will arrive in due time (Luke 13:9).

16. That such a supposition was the consequence of the *anochē tou Theou*, the psalmist himself declared (Ps. 50:21; cf. Job 22:13; Ps. 73:11; Mal. 2:17).

17. Cf. Hammond (*in loco*), who accurately and precisely discerned the true distinction between the words; and Godet, *Comm. sur l'Epitre aux Rom.* iii. 25, 26, who deals admirably with the whole passage.

18. Cf. Wisd. of Sol. 11:24: *paroras amartēmata anthpōpōn eis metanoian*; Rom 2:3–6.

34

mōrologia (3473) *aischrologia* (148) *eutrapelia* (2160)

Foolish Talk Filthy Language Coarse Jesting Falsely Refined Discourse

Mōrologia, *aischrologia*, and *eutrapelia* all refer to different sins of the tongue.

Mōrologia,[1] which only occurs once in the New Testament (Eph. 5:4), is aptly translated in the Vulgate by *stultiloquium* (silly talk).[2] *Mōrologia* includes the "every idle word" mentioned by Jesus (Matt. 12:36) and also the "every corrupt communication" referred to by his apostle (Eph. 4:29). Like all of our other actions as Christians, our speech needs to be seasoned with the salt of grace and is in danger of growing insipid and corrupt without it. Those who define *mōrologia* as simply "idle words" miss its full meaning. Calvin's definition—"unsuitable and empty discourses with no result"—is too weak. Even Jeremy Taylor failed to reproduce the full force of the word.

> That which is here meant by stultiloquy or foolish speaking is the *lubricum verbi*, as Ambrose calls it, the "slipping with the tongue" which prating people often

1. Although Aristotle used this term (*Historia animalium* 1.11), it was rarely used until later.

2. This word may have been coined by Plautus (*Miles gloriosus* 2.3.25) but was seldom employed in later Latin, just as *stultiloquy*, a word coined by Jeremy Taylor, was not received in English.

suffer, whose discourses betray the vanity of their spirit, and discover "the hidden man of the heart."[3]

In heathen writings *mōrologia* may very well have been used as a synonym for *adoleschia*[4] and for *mōrologein*[5] to *lērein*,[6] but Greek words that were taken up into the ethical terminology of Christianity were given new meanings. When we consider *mōrologia*, we need to remember that *fool*, *foolish*, and *folly* receive greater emphasis in Scripture than elsewhere. We need to consider both the positive and negative aspects of folly when we are weighing the meaning of *mōrologia*: it is that "talk of fools" that is both foolishness and sin.

Aischrologia, which also occurs only once in the New Testament (Col. 3:8), should not be confused with *aischrotēs* (*151*; Eph. 5:4). The Greek fathers[7] understood *aischrologia* to refer to obscene discourse, *turpiloquium* (filthy communication), that fosters wantonness, to "a vehicle of fornication," as Chrysostom explained it.[8] Certainly *aischrologia* sometimes has this sense predominantly or even exclusively.[9] But more often *aischrologia* indicates every kind of foul-mouthed abusiveness, not just the most obvious and offensive kind, including "foul language for sacred things." Thus Polybius spoke of "foul language [*aischrologia*] and abuse against the king,"[10] and the author of a supposed treatise by Plutarch[11] denounced all *aischrologia* as unbecoming to youth ingenuously brought up. In this he included *every* license of the ungoverned tongue used to abuse others, all the "wicked condiments of saucy speech."[12] Both the context and the company in which Paul used *aischrologia* show that he certainly intended to forbid such speech, and all the other sins he warned against are outbreaks of a *loveless* spirit toward our neighbor.

Paul did not use *eutrapelia*,[13] which, like its synonyms, occurs only once in the New Testament (Eph. 5:4), in its common, worldly sense of something that *turns easily*, of something that adapts itself to the shifting circumstances of the hour, to the moods and conditions of those around it.[14] In classical us-

3. *On the Good and Evil Tongue*, sermo 32, pt. 2.

4. *3473*, random talk.

5. L-S 1158, speak foolishly.

6. L-S 1045, be silly; Plutarch, *De garrulitate* 4.

7. See Suicer, *Thesaurus* under this word, followed by most expositors.

8. In a chapter of his *Paedagogus*, *peri aischrologias* (2.6), Clement of Alexandria recognized only this meaning.

9. Xenophon, *De republica Lacedaemoniorum* 5.6; Aristotle, *Politica* 7.15; see also Becker, *Charikles*, 1st ed., 2:264.

10. 8.13.8; 12.13.3; 31.10.4.

11. *De liberis educandis* 14.

12. *Hēdysmata ponēra tēs parrhēsias*.

13. *Eutrapelia* is derived from *eu* (*2095*) and from *trepesthai*. Cf. L-S 1813, to turn oneself; cf. *eutrapeloi* as "witty" in Aristotle, *Ethica Nicomachea* 4.8.4; cf. Pott, *Etymologische Forschungen*, 5:136.

14. Chrysostom, like most great teachers, here turned etymology into the materials of exhortation. To the other reasons why Christians should renounce *eutrapelia*, he added this: "Observe the very name; *eutrapelos* denotes one who is subtle, fickle, unstable, easily led, who becomes ev-

age, *eutrapelia* seldom has the evil sense that Paul gives it and that it has in the Greek fathers. The better sense of *eutrapelos*[15] is applied to Paul in Acts 26:29. In his panegyric of the Athenians that he put into the mouth of Pericles, Thucydides employed *eutrapelōs* (2.41) as a synonym for *eukinētōs* (easily moved) to characterize the "versatile nature" of his countrymen.[16] For Aristotle, also, the *eutrapelos* or *epidexios*[17] is one who keeps the happy mean between the *bōmolochos*[18] and the *agrios*,[19] *agroikos*,[20] or *sklēros*.[21] Such a person is not merely a *gelōtopoios*, or buffoon, but in all his pleasantry or banter he is still *charieis*, or refined. He always restrains himself within the limits of becoming mirth,[22] never ceasing to be the gentleman.[23]

Even classical usage—most obviously in the adjective *eutrapelos*—anticipated the unfavorable sense in which Paul used *eutrapelia*.[24] *Eutrapelia* gradually sank from a better meaning to a worse and in that respect resembles the history of the Latin *urbanitas* (elegance),[25] its best Latin equivalent and the one Erasmus used in his translation.[26] The following quotation from Cicero attests that *urbanitas* is the best translation for *eutrapelos*: "Insult, if it is hurled too impudently, is called reproach; if it is more polite, it is termed urbanity."[27] This agrees with Aristotle's striking phrase that *eutrapelia* is "trained insolence"[28] or "chastened insolence," as Sir Alexander Grant rendered it. Already in Cicero's time,[29] *urbanitas* was beginning to obtain the

---

erything; that is far from those who serve the Rock. Such a person quickly turns and changes" (*Homilia 17 in Ephesios*).

15. L-S 735, ready with an answer.

16. Plato (*Republic* 8.563a) joined *eutrapelia* with *charientismos* (L-S 1978, a wit), as did Plutarch (*Quomodo adulator ab amico internoscatur* 7) and Josephus (*Antiquitates Judaicae* 12.4.3). Isocrates (*Antidosis* 296) joined *eutrapelia* with *philologia* (L-S 1937, love of learning) and Philo (*Legatio ad Gaium* 45) with *charis* (5485).

17. L-S 629, clever; *Ethica Nicomachea* 2.7; 4.8; cf. Brandis, *Aristoteles*, p. 1415.

18. L-S 334, coarse.

19. L-S 15, harsh.

20. L-S 15, rude.

21. L-S 1612, cruel.

22. *Emmelōs paizōn*.

23. Thus P. Volumnius, the friend or acquaintance of Cicero and Atticus, bore the name *Eutrapelus* because of his festive wit and talent in society, though certainly there is nothing particularly amiable in the story that Horace (*Epistulae* 1.18.31–36) tells about him.

24. Thus see Isocrates (*Areopagiticus* 49) and Pindar (*Pythia*, 1.92; 4.104) where Jason, the model of a noble-hearted gentleman, affirms that during twenty years of fellowship in toil he has never spoken to his companions *epos eutrapelon* (a tricky word), a counterfeit, deceitful, hypocritical word. In writing about the last passage, Dissen traced the downward progress of *eutrapelos*: "First it concerns ease in movement, then it is transferred to ethics and signifies a person catering to the times, and then it refers to counterfeit, deceitful, hypocritical speech, especially with the connotation of levity, flattery, and pretense."

25. Quintilian, 6.3.17.

26. *Urbanitas* is an improvement on the *jocularitas* (jest) of Jerome and still more on the *scurrilitas* (buffoonery) of the Vulgate, which is totally unsuitable.

27. *Pro M. Caelio* 3.

28. *Rhetorica* 2.12; cf. Plutarch, *Cicero* 50.

29. *De finibus* 2.31.

questionable significance that is found more distinctly in Tacitus's[30] and in Seneca's usage of the word.[31] The history of *facetious* and *facetiousness* would supply an instructive parallel.

The fineness of the form in which evil might clothe itself did not make Paul more tolerant of the evil itself. Although a sin may lose its coarseness, it does not for that reason lose any of its malignity. The finer banter of the world, however—its "persiflage" or "badinage"—attracts many who would not be tempted to speak or to hear foul-mouthed and filthy abuse and who would find scurrile buffoonery revolting and repelling. Indeed *eutrapelia* defines a far more subtle sin than those indicated by the previous synonyms. As Bengel correctly noted: "It is more subtle than base or silly talk, *for it relies on innate talent.*" Chrysostom called it "disagreeable charm," and Jerome wrote: "It descends from a wise mind and deliberately seeks certain phrases, either clever or boorish or unseemly or humorous." In this last citation, I would only object to the word *unseemly*, which belongs to the other forms of speech. Chrysostom noted that the *eutrapelos* always "says clever things," and Cicero remarked: "These things especially are laughed at which signify and describe some shamefulness unshamefully."[32] What the *eutrapelos* deals in are "charms," albeit "charms of fools" (Ecclus. 20:13). All of his polish, refinement, knowledge of the world, presence of mind, and wit are enlisted in the service of sin, not in the service of truth. The very profligate old man of Plautus[33] prided himself (and not without reason) on his wit, elegance, and refinement—exactly those abilities that characterize the *eutrapelos*. It is interesting to note that the sole prohibition against *eutrapelia* is found in Ephesians (5:4) and that Ephesus was the town in which Plautus's old man lived, an old man who attributed his wit, elegance, and refinement to his Ephesian upbringing: "At Ephesus I was born, not at Apulia or at Animula!"[34]

Although all of these words indicate sins of the tongue, *mōrologia* refers to foolishness, *aischrologia* to foulness, and *eutrapelia* to false refinement, to discourse that is not seasoned with the salt of grace. All of these sins of speech are noted and condemned.

30. *Historia* 2.88.

31. *De ira* 1.28.

32. *De oratore* 2.58.

33. *Miles gloriosus* 3.1.42–52.

34. For a history of *eutrapelos*, see the interesting and instructive article by Matthew Arnold in the *Cornhill Magazine*, May 1879.

35

latreuō (3000) — *Serve*

leitourgeō (3008) — *Worship*, *Minister to*

Although *latreuō* and *leitourgeō* both refer to service, the former word refers to service with special limitations. *Latreuein*[1] properly means "to serve for hire" and thus does not refer to compulsory service, such as that of a slave, though this distinction between *latris* and *doulos* (*1401*) was by no means always observed. Already in classical Greek *doulos* and *latreia* (2999) are occasionally transferred from the service of men to the service of the higher powers,[2] a use that anticipates, in part, the only meaning that *doulos* has in Scripture. In the Septuagint *latreuein* refers to service either to the true God or to the false gods of heathenism.[3] Augustine was perfectly correct when he said: "*Latreia*—in the customary terminology of those who have formed for us communication to deities—either always or almost always designates service which pertains to worshiping God."[4] Again Augustine stated: "Adoration,

1. *Latreuein* is related to *latris* (a hired servant), *latron* (pay), and perhaps to *leia*, *lēis* (L-S 1034, booty; so Curtius).

2. See Plato, *Apologia Socratis* 23c: "service [*latreia*] to God"; cf. *Phaedrus* 244e; and Euripides, *Troiades* 450, where Cassandra is "the servant [*latris*] of Apollo."

3. Deut. 28:48, a seeming exception, is not such in fact.

4. *De civitate Dei* 10.1, 2.

which in Greek is called service [*latreia*], in Latin cannot be expressed by one word, since it is strictly speaking a particular ministration owed to a deity."[5]

Leitourgein has a more noble origin[6] and thus *eis to dēmosion ergazesthai* means "to serve the state in a public office or function." Like *latreuein*, *leitourgein* was occasionally transferred to the highest ministry of all, the ministry to the gods.[7] When the Christian church was forming its terminology, which it did partly by shaping new words and partly by elevating old ones to higher uses, it more readily adopted those words that previously had been employed in civil and political life than those that had been used in religious matters—even when it was searching for the adequate expression of religious truth. The same motives that induced the church to turn basilicas (buildings that had been used in civil life), rather than temples, into churches (because basilicas were less closely associated with heathenism) were at work in the church's selection of religious terminology. The principle of selecting words that were less closely associated with heathenism than other words is exemplified by the church's use of *leitourgos* (*3011*), *leitourgia* (3009), and *leitourgein* and by the prominent place these words assumed in ecclesiastical language. Additionally, by using *leitourgein* to refer to the performing of priestly or ministerial functions (Exod. 28:39; Ezek. 40:46), the Septuagint had prepared the way for its higher use in the New Testament.[8] The words of this group, however, were not entirely separated from their primary uses, as were *latreia* and *latreuein*, and occasionally were used in the Septuagint and in the New Testament to refer to the ministry *unto men* (2 Sam. 13:18; 1 Kings 10:5; 2 Kings 4:43; Rom. 15:27; Phil. 2:25, 30).

The pre-New Testament distinction that *latreuein* meant "to serve" and *leitourgein* "to serve in an office and ministry" helps to explain the distinctive uses of these words in the New Testament and in the Septuagint. To serve God is the duty of all men; *latreuein* and *latreia* are demanded of the whole people.[9] But to serve God in special offices and ministries can be the duty and privilege only of a few who are set apart for this function. Thus in the Old Testament *leitourgein* and *leitourgia* are ascribed only to the priests and the Levites who were separated to minister in holy things; they alone are called *leitourgoi*.[10] The same language reappears in the New Testament, where these words designate not only the old priesthood and ministry[11] but also the ministry of the New Testament apostles, prophets, and teachers,[12] as well as the

5. *Contra Faustum* 20.21.

6. *Leitourgein* derives from *leitos* (equivalent to *dēmosios*) and from *ergon*.

7. Diodorus Siculus, 1.21.

8. *Leitourgein* is equivalent to *šērēt* (8335).

9. Exod. 4:23; Deut. 10:12; Josh. 24:31; Matt. 4:10; Luke 1:74; Acts 7:7; Rom. 9:4; Heb. 12:28.

10. *3011*; Num. 4:24; 1 Sam. 2:11; Neh. 10:39; Ezek. 44:27.

11. Luke 1:23; Heb. 9:21; 10:11.

12. Acts 13:2; Rom. 15:16; Phil. 2:17.

great High Priest of our profession, "a Minister [*leitourgos*] of the sanctuary" (Heb. 8:2).[13]

Serve* *Worship* *Minister to

Against the distinction drawn above, it may be argued that *latreuein* and *latreia* are sometimes applied to *official* ministries, as in Hebrews 9:1, 6. And of course this is true. Where two circles have the same center, the greater will necessarily include the lesser. The notion of service is central here. In *leitourgein* it is limited service *in an office*. Thus every *leitourgia* will necessarily be a *latreia*, but not every *latreia* will be a *leitourgia*. No passage better distinguishes these two words than Ecclesiasticus 4:14: "They that *serve* her [i.e., Wisdom] shall *minister* to the Holy One."[14]

13. Occasionally, later ecclesiastical usage attempted to push the special application of *leitourgia* still further and to limit its use to those prayers and offices that stand in a more immediate relation to the Holy Eucharist. But there is no warrant in the best ages of the church for any such limitation. Thus see Suicer, *Thesaurus* under this word; Bingham, *Christian Antiquities* 13.1.8; Deyling, *Obsessiones sacrae*, 1:285; Augusti, *Christliche Archäologie*, 2:537; Scudamore, *Notitia eucharistica*, p. 11.

14. *Hoi latreuontes autē* [i.e., *tē Sophia*] *leitourgēsousin Hagiō*.

36

penēs (3993) *ptōchos* (4434) — Poor, Beggar

Both *penēs* and *ptōchos* refer to poverty in terms of this world's goods. In the Septuagint—especially in the psalms—these words always occur together and are not sharply distinguished,[1] just as the words *poor* and *needy* in the phrase *poor and needy*. Whatever distinction may have existed between the Hebrew *'ebyôn* (34) and *'ānî* (6041) was considered untranslatable or unimportant by the Alexandrian translators, who followed no fixed rule, translating both Hebrew words by *ptōchos* and *penēs*, though in some passages they did maintain a distinction and used *penēs*[2] where *ptōchos* would have been unsuitable.

Penēs occurs only once in the New Testament, in a quotation from the Old Testament (2 Cor. 9:9); *ptōchos* is used between thirty and forty times. *Penēs* is derived from *penomai*[3] and is related to *ponos* (4192), *poneomai*,[4] and to the Latin *penuria* (scarcity). Properly speaking, *penēs* refers to one who is so poor that he earns his daily bread by his labor. Hesychius called such a person *autodiakonos*, one who provides for his own necessities. *Penēs* does not indicate extreme want (or that which verges upon it), any more than the *pauper* (poor man) and *paupertas* (poverty) of the Latin, but only the *res angusta*

1. Pss. 39:18; 73:22; 81:4; cf. Ezek. 18:12; 22:29.
2. Deut. 24:16–17; 2 Sam. 12:1, 3, 4.
3. L-S 1360, to toil.
4. L-S 1447, work hard, suffer.

(scanty means) of one for whom *plousios* (*4145*, wealthy) would be inappropriate. Xenophon has provided the popular definition of a *penēs*: "I regard as poor [*penētas*] those who do not have enough to pay for necessities, and those who possess more than sufficient as wealthy [*plousious*]."[5] *Penēs* was commonly applied to Socrates, who claimed *penia*[6] several times for himself.[7] Xenophon defined *penia* as having fewer than five Attic minae worth of possessions.[8] Likewise, the *Penestai*[9] in Thessaly were a subject population, though they were not reduced to abject want but retained partial rights as serfs or cultivators of the soil.

But in Latin, though *penēs* means *pauper* (poor person), *ptōchos* means *mendicus* (beggar), one who lives not by his own labor or industry but on other men's alms (Luke 16:20–21), an individual whom Plato would not endure in his ideal State.[10] Etymologically, *prosaitēs*[11] or *epaitēs*[12] would be more equivalent to our word *beggar*; *ptōchos* generally refers to one who abjectly *crouches*[13] in the presence of his superiors. It may be safest, however, to add the words of Pott: "In case he actually was named after a timid, subservient demeanor, and not as a greedy person."[14] The derivation of *ptōchos* from *piptō* (4098), as though he were one *who had fallen* from a better estate,[15] is mere fancy.[16]

Thus *penēs* and *ptōchos* are clearly distinct. *Ptōcheia* implies a deeper destitution than does *penia*, and keeping this distinction in mind makes Paul's contrasts in 2 Corinthians 6:10 and 8:9 more vivid. The *penēs* may be so poor that he earns his bread by daily labor, but the *ptōchos* is so poor that he only obtains his living by begging. When Plato spoke of tyrannies as "ending in poverty [*penias*] and exile and finally in beggary [*ptōcheias*],"[17] he intended the last term as a climax to the former. The *penēs* has nothing extra, and the *ptōchos* has nothing at all.[18] In dealing with Jesus' words "Blessed are the poor [*hoi ptōchoi*]" (Luke 6:20), Tertullian noted this same distinction and changed *Beati pauperes* (Blessed are the *poor*)—which still is found in the Vulgate—to *Beati mendici* (Blessed are the *beggars*). Tertullian justified this change by saying: "For so demands the interpretation of the word in the Greek text."[19] In another place[20] Tertullian translated *ptōchos* by *egeni* (destitute). The two

5. *Memorabilia* 4.2.37.
6. L-S 1360, poverty.
7. Plato, *Apologia Socratis* 23c; 31c.
8. Xenophon, *Oeconomicus* 2.3.
9. L-S 1359, serfs; if, indeed, the derivation of the name is from *penesthai*.
10. *Leges* 11.936c.
11. Its cognate verb (*4319*, beg) occurs in John 9:8.
12. Its cognate verb (*1871*, beg) appears in Luke 16:3; 18:35; Mark 10:46.
13. From *ptōssō*, L-S 1550.
14. *Etymologische Forschungen*, 3:933.
15. *Ekpeptōkōs ek tōn ontōn* (Herodotus, 3.14).
16. See Didymus, *Fragmenta in Psalmos* 12:5, in Mai's *Nova patula bibliotheca*, vol. 7, pt. 2, p. 165.
17. *Republic* 10.618a.
18. See Döderlein, *Lateinische Synonyme*, 3:117.
19. *Adversus Marcionem* 4.14.
20. *De idolotria* 12.

words (*penia*[21] and *ptōcheia*[22]) may be sisters, as a character in Aristophanes said;[23] but if they are, the latter possesses fewer of the world's goods than the former. In that passage, *Penia* rejects any such close relationship. Aristophanes discriminated between the two words in this way:

Poor
Beggar

> Life of a beggar [*ptōchou*] is living without having anything; a poor person [*penētos*] lives sparingly and pays attention to his work, but he has nothing superfluous, indeed nothing left over.

21. Which is synonymous with *paupertas* (poverty); cf. Martial, 2.32: "It is not poverty [*paupertas*], Nestor, to have nothing."
22. Which is synonymous with *egestas* (destitution).
23. *Plutus* 549.

37

thymos (2372)

orgē (3709)
parorgismos (3950)

Anger
Indignation
Wrath
Revenge
Vengeance

Thymos and *orgē* occur together several times in the New Testament (Rom. 2:8; Eph. 4:31; Col. 3:8; Rev. 19:15), in the Septuagint (Ps. 77:49; Dan. 3:13; Mic. 5:15), and in secular writings.[1] These words may be juxtaposed, or one may depend on the other.[2] Although *orgē thymou* does not occur in the New Testament, it is frequently found in the Old Testament (2 Chron. 29:10; Isa. 30:27; Lam. 1:12; Hos. 11:9). On one occasion in the Septuagint, all three words occur together (Jer. 21:5).

After considerable development, *thymos* and *orgē* came to refer to the passion of anger, the strongest of all passions, impulses, and desires.[3] Although the grammarians and philologers spent some time distinguishing these words, there are a number of passages where they cannot be distinguished.[4] The

1. Plato, *Philebus* 47e; Polybius, 6.56.11; Josephus, *Antiquitates Judaicae* 20.5.3; Plutarch, *De cohibenda ira* 2.

2. Thus *thymos tēs orgēs* (Rev. 16:19; cf. Josh. 7:26; Job 3:17).

3. See Donaldson, *New Cratylus*, 3d ed., pp. 675–79; and Thompson, *Phaedrus of Plato*, p. 165.

4. Plato, *Leges* 9.867.

thymos

orgē
parorgismos

grammarians and philologers only assumed that the words were not used indifferently on every occasion and concluded that *thymos*[5] refers to turbulent commotion, the boiling agitation of the feelings.[6] Basil the Great called *thymos* "an inebriation of the soul" that will either subside and disappear[7] or else settle down into *orgē*, which is more of an abiding and settled habit of mind ("an enduring anger") that is focused on revenge.[8] Thus Plato[9] joined *echthra* (2189) with *orgē*, and Plutarch joined *dysmeneia*[10] with *orgē*.[11]

This more passionate but temporary character of *thymos*[12] may explain Xenophon's remark that *thymos* in a horse is what *orgē* is in a man.[13] The Stoics, who were often involved in definitions and distinctions, defined *thymos* as "beginning anger."[14] In his wonderful comparison of old age and youth, Aristotle characterized the angers of old men in this manner: "Their passions [*thymoi*] are keen but weak"[15]—like fire in straw, quickly blazing up and as quickly extinguished.[16] In his discussion of the two words, Origen arrived at the same conclusion: "*Thymos* differs from *orgē* in that *thymos* is anger [*orgē*] rising in vapor and burning up, while *orgē* is a yearning for revenge."[17] Jerome said: "*Thymos* is incipient anger and displeasure fermenting in the mind; *orgē* however, when *thymos* has subsided, is that which longs for re-

5. It is related to the intransitive *thuō* (2380) and derived, according to Plato, "from the raging [*thyseōs*] and boiling [*zeseōs*] of the soul" (*Cratylus* 419e). According to Tittmann it is "as a vehement exhalation." Cf. the Latin *fumus* (steam).

6. *Thymos* is commonly translated *furor* (raging) in the Vulgate. Augustine (*Enarratio in Psalma* 87:8) was dissatisfied with the application of this word to God, because *furor* (raging) is commonly attributed to the insane and in its place proposed *indignatio* (displeasure). For another distinction—one that ascribes both *ira* (anger) and *furor* to God—see Bernard, *Sermones in canticum canticorum* 69, par. 3—a remarkable passage.

7. Like the Latin *excandescentia* (nascent anger), which Cicero defined as "an anger beginning and soon ceasing" (*Tusculanae disputationes* 4.9).

8. "A desire to avenge the grief" (Seneca, *De ira* 1.5); "an impulse of the soul in pursuit of ill-treatment against one who has provoked" (Basil, *Prologus 3: prooemium in regulas brevius tractatas* 68). In *aganaktēsis* (24), Basil found that this eagerness to punish adds the offender to its scope. Certainly the one passage in the New Testament where *aganaktēsis* occurs (2 Cor. 7:11) does not refute this meaning. It is also the German *Zorn* (anger), "the indignation vented against someone or something, opposition of an indignantly aroused temperament" (Cremer).

9. *Euthyphro* 7.

10. L-S 458, enmity; *Pericles* 39.

11. Cf. *Theologische Studien und Kritiken*, 1851, pp. 99ff.

12. *Thymoi* as defined by Jeremy Taylor are "great but transient angers" (cf. Dan. 3:19; Luke 4:28). Hampole in his great poem, *The Pricke of Conscience*, does not agree. In his vigorous but unattractive picture of an old man, this is one trait—"He es lyghtly wrath, and waxes fraward, / bot to turne hym fra wrethe, it es hard."

13. *De re equestri* 9.2; cf. Wisd. of Sol. 7:20, "passions [*thymoi*] of beasts"; Plutarch, *Gryllus* 4, at the end; and *Pyrrhus* 16, *pneumatos mestos kai thymou*, "full of animosity and rage."

14. Diogenes Laërtius, 7.1.63.114. Ammonius said: "*Thymos* is temporary; *orgē* is a long-lasting memory of evil."

15. *Rhetorica* 2.11.

16. Cf. Euripides, *Andromacha* 728, 729.

17. *Selecta in Psalma* 2.5. Cf. *Commentarii in epistulam ad Romanos* 2:8, which only exists in the Latin: "As if, for the sake of argument, we would speak of *anger* [= *orgē*] in reference to a very bad wound, but its swelling and distension would be called *indignation* [= *thymos*]."

venge and desires to injure the one thought to have caused harm."[18] This agrees with the Stoic definition of *orgē*: "a desire for revenge on the person who seems to have caused injury wrongfully."[19] So Gregory Nazianzene said, "*Thymos* is the sudden boiling of the mind, / *orgē* is enduring *thymos*."[20] Where the words occur together, Theodoret noted: "Through *thymos* is revealed suddenness, and through *orgē* continuation."[21] Josephus described the Essenes as "stewards of *orgē* and controllers of *thymos*."[22] Dion Cassius noted that one of Tiberius's characteristic traits was that "he became violent [*ōrgizeto*] at what barely aroused his anger [*ethymouto*]."[23]

Mēnis[24] and *kotos* are, respectively, "anger of long standing" and "anger of very long standing,"[25] and do not occur in the New Testament.

Parorgismos is not found in classical Greek but occurs several times in the Septuagint (as in 1 Kings 15:30; 2 Kings 19:3). It is not synonymous with *orgē*, though we have translated it as "wrath." But *parorgismos* cannot properly be translated by "wrath," because the *parorgismos*[26] is absolutely forbidden—the sun shall not go down upon it—but under certain conditions *orgē* may be righteous. Scripture does not absolutely condemn anger, as did the Stoics, but teaches *metriopatheia*, a moderation, not *apatheia*, an absolute suppression, of the passions.[27] Nor does Scripture take a loveless view of other men's sins, such as is reflected in the words, "Do not trouble yourself. Does someone sin? He sins against himself."[28] Aristotle was in agreement with all the deeper ethical writers of antiquity[29] when he affirmed that anger guided by reason is a proper affection, just as Scripture not only permits but on certain occasions demands anger. And this view is held by the great teachers of the church. As Gregory of Nyssa wrote: "Anger [*thymos*] is a good beast whenever it is under the yoke of reason." And Augustine stated: "Our training does not inquire *whether* a dutiful mind is angry but *why* it is angry."[30] Furthermore, Scripture refers to the "wrath *of God*" (Matt. 3:7; Rom. 12:19; and often). God would not love good unless he hated evil; the two are inseparable. Either God must do both or neither.[31] And there is also a wrath of the

18. *In Ephesios* 4:31.

19. Diogenes Laërtius, 7.113.

20. *Carmina* 2.34.43, 44.

21. *In Psalma* 69:24.

22. *De bello Judaico* 2.8.6.

23. *Vita Tiberii*.

24. Isa. 16:6; Ecclus. 28:4; "enduring anger" in Damm's *Lexis Homerica*.

25. John of Damascus, *De fide orthodoxa* 11.16.

26. Eph. 4:26 is its only New Testament occurrence, though *parorgizein* (3949) occurs in Rom. 10:19 and in Eph. 6:4.

27. Plutarch said that passions were given to man as winds to fill the sails of his soul (*De virtute morali* 12).

28. Marcus Antoninus, 4.46.

29. Thus see Plato, *Leges* 5.731b: "Every man should be high-spirited [passionate]"; Thompson's *Phaedrus of Plato*, p. 166; and Cicero, *Tusculanae disputationes* 4.19.

30. *De civitate Dei* 9.5.

31. On the anger of God as the necessary complement of his love, see the excellent words of Lactantius: "For if God is not angered at the impious and the unjust, surely neither does he value

thymos

orgē
parorgismos

merciful Son of Man (Mark 3:5) and a wrath that righteous men not merely may but (as they are righteous) must feel. There can be no surer and sadder token of an utterly prostrate moral condition than not being able to be angry with sin—and with sinners. Fuller said: "Anger is one of the sinews of the soul; he that wants it hath a maimed mind, and with Jacob sinew-shrunk in the hollow of his thigh, must needs halt. Nor is it good to converse with such as cannot be angry."[32] "The affections," as another English divine has said, "are not, like poisonous plants, to be eradicated; but as wild, to be cultivated." Thus in Ephesians 4:26 Paul is not condescending to human infirmity and saying (as many understand him): "Your anger shall not be imputed to you as a sin if you put it away before nightfall."[33] Instead he was saying, "Be angry, yet in this anger of yours allow no sinful element to mingle; there is that which may cleave even to a righteous anger—the *parorgismos*, the irritation, the exasperation, the embitterment[34]—which must be dismissed at once in order that, being defecated of this impurer element which mingled with it, that only may remain which has a right to remain."

---

highly the just. For in opposite situations either he must be moved by each or by none" (*De ira Dei*, chap. 4).

32. *Holy State* 3.8.

33. See Suicer, *Thesaurus* under the word *orgē*.

34. *Exacerbatio* in Latin.

38

elaion (1637) *myron* (3464) (*chriō* [5548] *aleiphō* [218])

Oil *Ointment* (*Anoint*)

By arguing on the insufficient grounds that the Septuagint sometimes translates *šemen* (8081) by *myron*[1] but far more frequently by *elaion*, some scholars have denied that the Old Testament makes any distinction between *oil* and *ointment*. Often, however, a single word in one language contains two of another, especially when (as in the case of Greek compared with Hebrew) the other abounds in finer distinctions and in more subtle meanings.[2] To convey this duplicity of meaning is the responsibility of a well-skilled translator. *Myron*[3] naturally grew out of *elaion*[4] because it had oil for its base, with only the addition of spice, scent, or other aromatic ingredients. Clement of Alexandria called *elaion* "adulterated oil."[5] Because of this close relationship between *elaion* and *myron*, it was a long time before the need for different

1. Prov. 27:9; Song of Sol. 1:3; Isa. 39:2; Amos 6:6.

2. *Paroimia* (3942) and *parabolē* (3850) furnish a well-known example, since both are present in the Hebrew *māšāl* (4912).

3. *Myron* is equivalent to the Latin *unguentum* (ointment).

4. *Elaion* is equivalent to the Latin *oleum* (oil).

5. *Dedolōmenon elaion* (*Paedagogus* 2.8). Cf. what Plutarch said of Lycurgus: "He rejected ointment [*myron*] as a corruption and destruction of oil [*elaion*]" (*Apophthegmata Laconica* 16). Cf. Virgil (*Georgica* 2.466): "Nor is the use of oil spoiled by a liquid fragrance."

elaion
myron
(chriō
aleiphō)

names for these terms arose in other languages. In Greek, *myron* first appears in the writings of Archilochus.[6] Although there were ointments in Homer's time, he used "sweet-smelling oil"[7] and "roseate oil"[8] instead.

Later a clear distinction was drawn between *elaion* and *myron*. In fact, a passage in Xenophon[9] depends entirely on the suitability of *elaion* for men and of *myron* for women: women prefer men to smell of manly "oil," rather than of effeminate "ointment." According to Xenophon: "The odor of oil [*elaiou*] in gymnasiums when present is more pleasant to women than that of ointment [*myron*] and is more longed for when absent." And this distinction underlies Christ's rebuke to the discourteous Pharisee: "You did not anoint My head with *oil* [*elaiō*], but this woman has anointed My feet with *fragrant oil* [*myrō*]" (Luke 7:46). Thus in effect Christ said: "You withheld from me cheap and ordinary courtesies, while she bestowed upon me costly and rare homages." Grotius well remarked:

> There is continuous contrast. That woman employed tears for washing Christ's feet; Simon did not even furnish water. She constantly kissed the feet of Jesus; Simon received Christ without even one kiss. She poured precious ointment [*ungentum* = *myron*] on both His head and His feet; he gave not even mere oil [*merum* = *elaion*], which was the custom of perfunctory friendship.

Because some scholars have distinguished the verbs *aleiphein* and *chriein* on the basis of the difference between *myron* and *elaion*, we need to deal with this topic here. These scholars claim that *aleiphein* commonly refers to a luxurious or superfluous anointing with ointment and that *chriein* refers to a sanitary anointing with oil. Thus Casaubon stated: "To be anointed with ointment [*aleiphesthai*] is characteristic of those devoted to pleasure and a delicate life; to be anointed with oil [*chriesthai*] is suitable occasionally to temperate people and to those who live virtuously."[10] Valcknaer stated: "People *surrendered to pleasures*, who anointed their head and hands with precious *ointment*, were particularly said to be *aleiphesthai*; *chriesthai* was applied to those smearing their bodies with *oil* for the sake of *health*." No traces of this distinction appear in the New Testament (cf. Mark 6:13; James 5:14 with Mark 16:1; John 11:2), however, nor are there traces of the distinction of Salmasius: "They *smear* [*chriousi*] more solid substances; they *pour* [*aleiphousi*] liquids."[11]

The New Testament does distinguish the two verbs *aleiphein* and *chriein*, but not as they were distinguished above. In the New Testament, *aleiphein* is used as the mundane and profane term, and *chriein* is used as the sacred and religious term. *Aleiphein* is used indiscriminately of all actual anointings, whether with oil or with ointment, and *chriein*[12] is absolutely restricted to the

6. Athenaeus, 15.37.
7. *Euōdes elaion* (*Odyssey* 2.339).
8. *Rodoen elaion* (*Iliad* 23.186).
9. *Symposium* 2.3, 4.
10. *Animadversiones in Athenaeum* 15.39.
11. *Exercitia*, p. 330.
12. No doubt in its connection with *christos* (anointed).

Father's anointing of the Son with the Holy Spirit for the accomplishment of the Son's great office. In the New Testament, *chriein* is completely separated from all profane and common uses.[13] The same holds true in the Septuagint, where *chrisis, chrisma* (5545)[14] and *chriein* are frequently used to refer to all religious and symbolic anointings. *Aleiphein* occurs only twice in this sense (Exod. 40:13; Num. 3:3).

13. Thus see Luke 4:18; Acts 4:27; 10:38; 2 Cor. 1:21; Heb. 1:9. These are the only New Testament occurrences of *chriein*.

14. Cf. 1 John 2:20, 27.

39

Hebraios (1445) — Hebrew
Ioudaios (2453) — Jew
Israēlitēs (2475) — Israelite

Although all of these names are used to designate members of the elect family and chosen race, the terms may be distinguished.

Because it is the oldest term, *Hebraios* deserves to be considered first.[1] Most likely *Hebraios* is derived from *'ēber* (5676), the same word as *hyper* (5228) and the Latin *super* (beyond). *Hebraios* alludes to *the passing over* of Abraham from the other side of the Euphrates. In the language of the Phoenician tribes among whom he came to live, he was "Abram *the Hebrew*," or *ho peratēs*[2] as it appears in the Septuagint (Gen. 14:13), because he was from *beyond* (*peran*, 4008) the river. Thus Origen correctly spoke of "Hebrews, which is translated *foreigners* [*peratikoi*]."[3] Therefore *Hebraios* is not a name the chosen people adopted for themselves but one that others gave them. It is not a name they have taken but one that others have imposed on them. The use of *Hebraios* throughout the Old Testament is entirely consistent with this etymology. In every case *Hebraios* is either a title foreigners use to designate the chosen race[4] or one the chosen people use to designate

1. Josephus, *Antiquitates Judaicae* 1.6.4.
2. L-S 1365, wanderer, emigrant.
3. *In Matthaeum, tomus* 11.5.
4. Gen. 39:14, 17; 41:12; Exod. 1:16, 19; 1 Sam. 4:6; 13:19; 29:3; Jth. 12:11.

themselves to foreigners[5] or when they set themselves in tacit opposition to other nations.[6] *Hebraios* is never used without either a latent or an expressed sense of national antagonism.

Later when *Ioudaios* came into use,[7] the meaning of *Hebraios* changed. Frequently when a new term appears, a related word's meaning will contract and be more narrowly defined. This happens when new terms arise and all the various meanings of related older terms are no longer needed. At the same time, such older words lend themselves to new shades of meaning, as was the case with *Hebraios*. In the New Testament the "external perspective" on the Hebrew nation no longer existed. Not every member of the chosen family was a *Hebraios*, only those who retained Hebrew as their native language (whether they lived in Palestine or elsewhere). The true complement and antithesis to *Hebraios* is *Hellēnistēs* (*1675*), a word that first appeared in the New Testament[8] to designate a Jew of the Dispersion who spoke Greek, not Hebrew, and who read or heard the Septuagint version of the Scriptures in the synagogue.

The distinction between *Hebraios* and *Hellēnistēs* first appears in Acts 6:1 and is probably intended in the two other New Testament passages where *Hebraios* occurs (2 Cor. 11:22; Phil. 3:5), as well as in the superscription of the Epistle to the Hebrews. It is important to remember that the language one spoke, not the place where one lived, was the defining factor in being considered a "Hebrew" or a "Hellenist." As long as a person's mother tongue was Hebrew, he was considered a "Hebrew," regardless of where he lived. Thus Paul, though settled in Tarsus, a Greek city in Asia Minor, described himself as a "Hebrew" of "Hebrew" parents and as "a Hebrew of Hebrews" (Phil. 3:5; cf. Acts 23:6).[9] Although the greatest number of "Hebrews" *were* resident in Palestine, it was their language, not their place of residence, that gave them this title.

The distinction between *Hebraios* and *Hellēnistēs* is a distinction *within the nation* and not between it and other nations.[10] This distinction is exclusively a scriptural one, though it was hardly recognized by later Christian writers and not at all by Jewish and heathen ones. Thus Eusebius said of Philo, an Alexandrian Jew[11] who wrote exclusively in Greek, "By race he was a Hebrew [*Hebraios*]."[12] Clement of Alexandria[13] always made *Hellēnes* (*1672*) and *ethnē* (*1484*), not *Hellēnistai*, the antithesis to *Hebraioi*. Theodoret styled the Greek-writing historian Josephus as "a Hebrew [*Hebraios*] author."[14]

5. Gen 40:15; Exod. 2:7; 3:18; 5:3; 9:1; Jon. 1:9.
6. Gen. 43:32; Deut. 15:12; 1 Sam. 13:3; Jer. 34:9, 14.
7. The precise epoch will be discussed later.
8. See Salmasius, *De Hellenistica*, 1643, p. 12.
9. It is certainly possible that these terms were used to emphasize Paul's Judaism.
10. This is clear in Acts 6:1 and probably is intended in 2 Cor. 11:22 and in Phil. 3:5.
11. He visited Jerusalem only once in his life (cf. his own words in 2:646, Mangey's ed.).
12. *Historia ecclesiastica* 2.4. Cf. 4.16 and *Praeparatio evangelica* 7.13.21.
13. As quoted by Eusebius, *Historia ecclesiastica* 6.14.
14. *Opera*, 2:1246. Cf. Origen, *Epistula ad Africanum* 5.

No traces of the New Testament distinction between *Hebraios* and *Hellēnistēs* exist in Josephus, Philo, or in heathen writers.[15] *Hebraios,* however, though rarer than *Ioudaios,* always refers to the people *in terms of their language,* a rule observed by Jewish, heathen, and Christian writers alike. Even today we speak of the *Jewish* nation but of the *Hebrew* tongue.

The name *Ioudaios* is of much later origin. It did not originate at the birth of the chosen people, when Abram passed over the river and entered the land of inheritance, but later at a time of national disruption and decline when the Jewish tribes separated into the rival kingdoms of Israel and Judah. At that time the ten tribes[16] assumed "Israel" as their title, and the other two tribes took the name *yihûdîm* (3064), or *Ioudaioi,* from the more important of the two. Josephus's first use of *Ioudaioi* was in reference to Daniel and his young companions,[17] not in the earlier history of the Jewish people. In reference to Daniel, however, Josephus used *Ioudaioi* by anticipation[18]—namely, that it first arose *after* the return from Babylon, because the earliest colony to return was of that tribe: "They were called by this name from the day they went up out of Babylon, [taken] from the tribe of Judah as it was the first to enter those regions; both they and the land adopted this very name."[19] But Josephus's account is clearly erroneous. *Ioudaioi,* or its Hebrew equivalent, first appears in biblical books that were composed before or during the captivity as a designation of those who belonged to the smaller group of the tribes, the kingdom of Judah,[20] not first in Ezra, Nehemiah, and Esther, though the term occurs more frequently in these books (especially in Esther).

It is easy to see how *Ioudaioi* was extended to the nation as a whole. When the ten tribes were carried into Assyria and were absorbed and lost among the nations, the smaller group of Jews who remained behind came to represent the entire Jewish nation. Thus it was only natural that *Ioudaios* should refer to any member of the nation—a "Jew" in the wider sense of one who was not a Gentile—and not just to someone from the kingdom of Judah as distinguished from the kingdom of Israel. In fact *Ioudaioi* underwent a process exactly the converse of the one *Hebraios* had undergone earlier. On the one hand, *Hebraios* initially referred to the nation as a whole but later came to refer only to a part of the nation. On the other hand, *Ioudaios* initially referred only to a part of the nation and later to the nation as a whole. The later use of *Ioudaios,* like the earlier use of *Hebraios,* was employed as a national self-designation to distinguish a descendant of Abraham from other peoples (Rom. 2:9–10). Consequently the Scriptures contrast "*Jew* and Gentile" but never "*Israelite* and Gentile." Additionally, *Ioudaios* was used by others to maintain the distinction between Jews and Gentiles. Thus the wise men from the East inquired, "Where is He that is born King *of the Jews?*" (Matt. 2:2). The form

15. Plutarch, *Septem sapientium convivium* 4.6; Pausanias, 5.7.3; 10.12.5.
16. Though with less reason. See Ewald, *Geschichte des Volkes Israel,* vol. 3, pt. 1, p. 138.
17. *Antiquitates Judaicae* 10.10.1.
18. That is, if his own account of the appearance of the name is correct.
19. Ibid. 11.5.7.
20. 2 Kings 16:6; Jer. 32:12; 34:9; 38:19.

of this question implies that the wise men were Gentiles. Had they been Jews, they would have asked for the King *of Israel*. So, too, the Roman soldiers and governor gave Jesus the mocking title "King *of the Jews*" (Matt. 27:29, 37), but his own countrymen challenged him to prove by coming down from the cross that he is the "King *of Israel*" (Matt. 27:42).

Israēlitēs is the absolute name used to express the dignity and glory of a member of the theocratic nation in a unique covenant relation with God. *Israēlitēs* rarely occurs in the Septuagint but often was used by Josephus in his earlier history as a synonym for *Hebraios*.[21] In the middle period of his history, Josephus used *Israēlitēs* to refer to a member of the ten tribes[22] and toward the end of his history as a synonym for *Ioudaios*.[23] We will only consider the last meaning here. *Israēlitēs* was the Jew's special badge and title of honor. The honor of being descendants of Abraham was shared with the Ishmaelites (Gen. 16:15), and the honor of being descendants of Abraham and Isaac was shared with the Edomites (Gen. 24:25). Only the Jews, however, are descended from Jacob, a name that is declared in the title *Israelite*. The Jews did not trace their descent from Jacob as Jacob but from Jacob as Israel, who as a prince had power with God and with men and prevailed (Gen. 32:28). There is ample proof that this title was the noblest of them all. When the ten tribes cast off their allegiance to the house of David, they pridefully and pretentiously took the title "the kingdom *of Israel*," thus implying that their kingdom was heir to the promises and the true successor of the early patriarchs. Jesus could not have given a more noble title to Nathanael than to have called him "an *Israelite* indeed" (John 1:47), one in whom all that the name involved might be found. When Peter and Paul wanted to obtain a hearing from the men of their own nation, they addressed them with the name they would most welcome, *andres Israēlitai*,[24] by whose use they sought to secure their favor.

By restricting ourselves to the New Testament usage and distinctions among these three words, we may say that *Hebraios* refers to a Hebrew-speaking as contrasted with a Greek-speaking or Hellenizing Jew,[25] that *Ioudaios* refers to a Jew nationalistically in distinction from Gentiles, and that *Israēlitēs*, the most majestic title of all, refers to a Jew as a member of the theocracy and heir of the promises. The first word predominantly refers to a Jew's language, the second to his nationality,[26] and the third to his theocratic privileges and glorious vocation.

21. *Antiquitates Judaicae* 1.9.1, 2.

22. Ibid. 8.8.3; 9.14.1.

23. Ibid. 11.5.4.

24. Acts 2:22; 3:12; 13:16; cf. Rom. 9:4; Phil. 3:5; 2 Cor. 11:22.

25. In our Authorized Version this is translated by "Grecian," as distinct from *Hellēn*, a veritable "Greek" or other Gentile.

26. *Ioudaismos* (2454); Josephus, *De Maccabibus* 4; Gal. 1:13; *Ioudazein* (2450), Gal. 2:14.

40

aiteō (154)

erōtaō (2065)

Ask
Inquire
Request
Seek
Beseech

Aiteō and *erōtaō* are frequently translated as though they were synonymous. In numerous instances it is correct to translate either word by "to ask," though sometimes the translators of the Authorized Version marred the perspicuity of their work by not varying their words where the original indicates a difference. For example, obliterating the distinction between *aitein* and *erōtan* in John 16:23 might easily suggest a wrong interpretation of the verse—as though its two clauses were closely related and directly antithetical, which is not the case. Our English version reads: "In that day *you will ask* Me nothing [*eme ouk erōtēsete ouden*]. Most assuredly, I say to you, whatever *you ask* [*hora an aitēsēte*] the Father in my name He will give you." All competent scholars agree that the "*you will* ask" in the first half of the verse has nothing to do with the "*you* ask" in the second. In the first half Christ is referring back to the *ēthelon auton erōtan* of verse 19—to the questions the disciples wanted to ask him, the perplexities they wanted him to resolve if only they dared to ask. "In that day," he would say, "in the day of my seeing you again I will by the Spirit so teach you all things that you will be no longer perplexed, no longer wishing to ask me questions [cf. John 21:12], if only you might venture to do so." Thus Lampe well stated:

> It is a new promise for the fullest light of understanding, by which the situation in the New Testament must be properly illuminated. For as an inquiry presupposes ignorance, so the person who no more asks questions believes that he has been fully taught, and he agrees to a teaching as completely explained and understood.

This verse does not draw a contrast between asking *the Son*, which will cease, and asking *the Father*, which will begin. The first half of the verse closes the declaration of one blessing: from now on the Spirit will teach them so that they will have nothing further *to inquire*; the second half of the verse begins the declaration of a new blessing: whatever they *seek* from the Father in the Son's name, he will give to them. No one would say that this is the impression conveyed by the English text.

The distinction between *aiteō* and *erōtaō* is as follows. *Aiteō*[1] is the more submissive and suppliant term. It is consistently used to refer to an inferior's seeking something from a superior (Acts 12:20), of a beggar's seeking alms from a potential donor (Acts 3:2), of a child's seeking something from a parent (Lam. 4:4; Matt. 7:9; Luke 6:11), of a subject's seeking something from a ruler (Ezra 8:22), and of a man's seeking something from God.[2] In classical Greek, *erōtaō*[3] never means "to ask" but only "to interrogate," or "to inquire." Like *rogare* (inquire),[4] *erōtaō* implies an equality between the one who asks and the one who is asked—as a king with another king (Luke 14:32)—or if not equality, then a familiarity that lends authority to the request.

It is noteworthy that Jesus never used *aitein* or *aiteisthai* to refer to himself when speaking to God on behalf of his disciples,[5] for his is not the *petition* of the creature to the Creator but the *request* of the Son to the Father. Jesus' consciousness of his equal dignity and prevailing intercession appears whenever he asks (or declares that he will ask) anything of the Father, because he always uses *erōtō* or *erōtēsō*, an asking on equal terms (John 14:16; 16:26; 17:9, 15, 20), and never *aiteō* or *aitēsō*. Martha, on the contrary, by ascribing *aiteisthai* to Jesus,[6] recognized him as no more than a prophet and thus revealed her poor conception of him.[7]

1. This is the Latin *peto*.

2. 1 Kings 3:11; Matt. 7:7; James 1:5; 1 John 3:22; cf. Plato, *Euthyphro* 14: "To pray is to seek after [*aitein*] the gods."

3. This is the Latin *rogo* (inquire) or sometimes (as in John 16:23; cf. Gen. 44:19) *interrogo* (interrogate).

4. Thus Cicero said: "For neither was I *inquiring* [*rogabam*] in such a manner so that I appeared to be *seeking* [*petere*], since he was my friend" (*Oratio pro Plancio* 10.25).

5. This underscores the accurate use of these words throughout the New Testament.

6. "Whatever You ask [*aitēsē*] of God, God will give you" (John 11:22).

7. Concerning John 11:22, Bengel observed: "In speaking of himself asking, Jesus says *edeēthēn* [*1189*] (Luke 22:32) and *erōtēsō* but never *aitoumai*. Although Martha did not speak in Greek, John correctly expresses her improper term, which the Lord kindly endured, for *aiteisthai* seems to be a less dignified word." Cf. his note on 1 John 5:16.

Erōtan, the term of authority, is proper for Christ but not for his creatures to use. In fact, in the New Testament *erōtan* is never used to refer to a man's prayer to God. The only passage that seems to contradict this assertion is 1 John 5:16, a difficult verse. Whatever solution is accepted will not be a true exception to the rule, and perhaps, in the substitution of *erōtēsē* for the *aitēsei* of the earlier clause of the verse, will rather confirm it.

41

anapausis (372) *anesis* (425) — Rest Ease

Our version translates both *anapausis* and *anesis* as "rest."[1] Although this is not objectionable, on closer examination these words appear to derive from different images and to depict "rest" from different perspectives. *Anapausis*[2] refers to a pause or cessation from labor (Rev. 4:8) and is consistently used in the Septuagint to refer to the rest of the Sabbath.[3] *Anesis*[4] refers to the relaxation of chords or strings that had been taut; its exact and literal antithesis is *epitasis*.[5] Thus Plato used the phrase "in the stretching and relaxing [*anesei*] of the chords."[6] And Plutarch stated: "We relax the bows and the lyres in order to be able to stretch them."[7] According to Josephus,[8] in the year of jubilee Moses gave "rest [*anesin*] to the ground from plowing and planting." Perhaps the best illustration of *anesis* comes from *De liberis educandis* 13, a work ascribed to Plutarch:

1. *Anapausis* in Matt. 11:29; 12:43; *anesis* in 2 Cor. 2:13; 7:5; 2 Thess. 1:7.
2. From *anapauō* (373).
3. Exod. 16:23; 31:15; 35:2; and often.
4. From *aniēmi* (447).
5. L-S 664; stretching, from *epiteinō* (stretch).
6. *Republic* 1.349e.
7. *De liberis educandis* 13. He also said: "It was not a relaxing [*anesis*] but a tightening [*epitasis*] of the government" (*Lycurgus* 29).
8. *Antiquitates Judaicae* 3.12.3.

> One must give children respite from continuous toil, pondering that our entire life is divided between rest [*anesin*] and activity, and therefore there is not only wakefulness but also sleep, not only war but also peace, not only storms but also clear weather, not only energetic deeds but also festivals . . . in general the body is preserved by want and fulfillment and the soul by rest [*anesei*] and toil.

Plato distinguished *anesis* and *spoudē* in the same way,[9] and Plutarch[10] contrasted *anesis*, a dwelling at large, with *stenochōria* (4730), a narrow, straight room. Paul contrasted *anesis* with *thlipsis*;[11] he did not want some churches to have "ease" (*anesis*) while the Corinthian church suffered "affliction" (*thlipsis*) because of an excessive contribution. When used figuratively, *anesis* refers to the *relaxation* of morals.[12]

Luke's use of the phrase *echein* (*2192*) *anesin* in Acts 24:23 is an excellent one. Felix, who took a more favorable view of Paul's case, commanded the centurion in charge of Paul to *relax* the strictness of Paul's imprisonment and to keep him under honorable arrest, not in actual confinement. The partial *relaxation* of Paul's bonds is exactly what this phrase implies.[13]

The distinction, then, is obvious. When our Lord promises *anapausis* to the weary and heavy laden who come to him (Matt. 11:18, 29), his promise is that they will *cease* from their toil, no longer laboring for that which does not satisfy. When Paul expressed his confidence that the Thessalonians, though presently troubled, will find *anesis* in the day of Christ (2 Thess. 1:7), he anticipated not so much their cessation from labor as the *relaxation* of their chords of affliction that were stretched so tightly. Christ's promise and Paul's confidence are related, though they portray the blessings of Christ under different aspects and images. Each word has its appropriate context.

9. *4710*; *Leges* 4.724a.

10. *Septem sapientium convivium* 5.6.

11. *2347*; 2 Cor. 8:13.

12. Thus Athenaeus (14.13) spoke of "licentiousness and relaxation [*anesin*]" and contrasted *anesin* with *sōphrosynē* (4997). Cf. Philo, *De cherubim* 27; *De ebrietate* 6: *anesis*, *rhathymia* (L-S 1564, rashness), *tryphē* (*5172*).

13. Cf. Ecclus. 26:10; and Josephus, *Antiquitates Judaicae* 18.6.10, where *anesis* is used in a perfectly similar case.

42

tapeinophrosynē (5012) — *Humility, Lowliness*

praotēs (4236) — *Meekness*

The mission of Christ's gospel involves putting the mighty down from their seats and exalting the humble and meek. In accordance with this mission, the gospel dethroned the heathen virtue of *megalopsychia*[1] and replaced it with *tapeinophrosynē*, the despised Christian virtue. The gospel stripped the former of the honor it had unjustly assumed and delivered the latter from the unjust dishonor that previously had attached to it. One Christian writer has called *tapeinophrosynē* the treasure house that contains all the other virtues.[2] *Tapeinophrosynē* is a fruit of the gospel. No Greek writer employed it before the Christian era, and apart from the influence of Christian writers, it was not used later. In the Septuagint, *tapeinophrōn*[3] (Prov. 29:23) and *tapeinophronein* (to humble; Ps. 130:2) each occur once, and both words are used in an honorable fashion. Plutarch also employed *tapeinophrōn*,[4] though in a bad sense. The ways in which heathen writers used *tapeinos* (5011), *tapeinotēs*,[5] and other words of this family indicate how they would have employed *tapeinophrosynē*. There are few instances where *tapeinos* signifies anything other than grovel-

1. L-S 1088, highmindedness.
2. Basil, *Constitutiones ascetica* 16.
3. L-S 1757, humble.
4. *De Alexandri magni fortuna aut virtute* 2.4.
5. L-S 1757, abasement, dejection, vileness.

ling, slavish, mean-spirited behavior. *Tapeinos* is associated with *aneleutheros*,[6] *andrapodōdēs*,[7] *agennēs*,[8] *katēphēs*,[9] *adoxos*,[10] *doulikos* and *douloprepēs*,[11] and *chamaizēlos*.[12] Similarly, the German *Demuth* (humility), which originated in the heathen period of the language, originally referred to "a slavish spirit"[13] and attained its present honorable position through Christian influence.

The exceptional uses of *tapeinos*, however, are more numerous than some will admit. Plato related *tapeinos* to being "orderly,"[14] and Demosthenes spoke of "moderate and humble [*tapeinoi*] words." On more than one occasion, Xenophon contrasted the *tapeinos* with the "arrogant."[15] According to Plutarch, the purpose of divine punishment was so that the soul might become "thoughtful and humble [*tapeinē*] and fearful toward God."[16] In addition to these earlier intimations of the honor that one day would be associated with the words for humility, a passage in Aristotle vindicates the Christian use of *tapeinophrosynē*.[17] Having confessed how hard it is for a man "to be truly magnificent,"[18] Aristotle observed[19] that to think humbly of oneself, *where that humble estimate is the true one*, is not a culpable meanness of spirit but a true prudence.[20] If that is correct, then since one's humble self-estimate is true for everyone, Aristotle unconsciously vindicated *tapeinophrosynē* as a virtue that every man should possess. Even according to his standard, Aristotle confessed that "to be truly magnificent" was difficult. But the Christian, convinced by the Spirit of God and having God's perfect standard of righteousness, knows that it is not merely difficult but impossible. The Christian definition of *tapeinophrosynē* is not merely modesty or the absence of pretension that the best heathen writers referred to; it is not a self-made virtue. By characterizing pride as making ourselves small *when we are great*, Chrysostom brought pride in under the disguise of humility.[21] Bernard's definition is truer and deeper: "Virtue exists when a person through a most genuine self-evaluation deems himself worthless." *Tapeinophrosynē* involves evalu-

6. L-S 131, servile; Plato, *Leges* 4.774c.

7. L-S 128, slavish; Aristotle, *Ethica eudemia* 3.3.

8. L-S 8, low-born; Lucian, *Calumniae non temere credendum* 24.

9. L-S 927, downcast; Plutarch, *Fabius Maximus* 18.

10. L-S 24, ignoble; *De vitioso pudore* 14.

11. L-S 446, slavish and L-S 447, servile; Philo, *Quod omnis probus liber sit* 4.

12. L-S 1975, of low estate; *De specialibus legibus* 1.

13. The first syllable comes from "servant to a god [*deo* in Latin]." Cf. Grimm, *Wörterbuch* under *Demuth*.

14. *Leges* 4.716a.

15. *Agesilaus* 2.11; cf. Aeschylus, *Prometheus vinctus* 328; Luke 1:51, 52. Cf. Plutarch, *Quomodo quis suos in virtute sentiat profectus* 10.

16. *De sera numinis vindicta* 3.

17. *Ethica Nicomachea* 4.3.3; cf. Brandis, *Aristoteles*, p. 1408; Nägelsbach, *Homerische Theologie*, p. 336.

18. According to Aristotle, magnificence or great spirituality depends on goodness and moral greatness. Aristotle's magnificent person is one "who deems himself worthy of great things, as he is so worthy."

19. Aristotle could not have foreseen the extent of his words.

20. Aristotle's words are: "For he who is worthy of little and deems himself so is prudent."

21. See Suicer, *Thesaurus* under *tapeinophrosynē*.

ating ourselves as small because we are so; it requires us to think truly, and therefore humbly, of ourselves.

How is this Christian view of *tapeinophrosynē* as that which derives from a sense of unworthiness compatible with Christ's claim to this virtue, since he is sinless?[22] The answer is that *for the sinner*, *tapeinophrosynē* involves the confession of sin (because this is the sinner's true condition); but for the unfallen creature, it is not an acknowledgment of *sinfulness* (which would be untrue) but of *creatureliness*, of absolute dependence, of possessing nothing and of receiving all things from God. And thus because he is a creature, the virtue of humility belongs to the highest angel before the throne, and even—it is true—to the Lord of glory himself. In his human nature, Jesus must exemplify true humility, true creaturely dependence. It is only *as a man* that Christ claimed to be *tapeinos*, for his human life was a constant living on the fullness of his Father's love, as becomes the creature in the presence of its Creator.

The gospel of Christ did not rehabilitate *praotēs* as completely as it did *tapeinophrosynē* because *praotēs* did not need rehabilitating to the same extent. *Praotēs* did not need to be transformed from a bad sense to a good one but needed only to be lifted from a lower level of good to a higher one. Based on Aristotle's portrait of the *praos* (*4235*) and of the *praotēs*,[23] it is apparent that *praotēs* needed such an elevating. When the heathen virtue is compared with the Christian one, it is obvious that revelation has given to these words a depth, a richness, and a significance they did not previously possess. Aristotle, the great moralist of Greece, defined *praotēs* as the "mean concerning anger" between the two extremes of irascibility and the lack of irascibility. And in Aristotle's view, *praotēs* leaned more toward the latter and easily ran into this defect. Aristotle praised the virtue of *praotēs* primarily because it helps a man to retain his own equanimity and composure, rather than for any more noble reason. Plutarch associated *praotēs* with *metriopatheia*,[24] *acholia*,[25] *anexikakia*,[26] *megalopatheia*,[27] *eupeitheia*,[28] and *eukolia*.[29] Plutarch's graceful little essay, *Concerning Lack of Irascibility* (*Peri aorgēsias*), does not contain a more noble concept of *praotēs* than that found in Aristotle, though we might have looked for something higher from him. Plato contrasted *praotēs* with *agriotēs*,[30] Aristotle with *chalepotēs*,[31] and Plutarch (or some other writer using his name) with *apotomia*.[32] Apparently, all of these writers attached a somewhat superficial meaning to *praotēs*.

22. "I am gentle and *lowly in heart*"—*tapeinos tē kardia* (*2588*)—Matt. 11:29.
23. *Ethica Nicomachea* 4.5.
24. L-S 1122, restraint over the passions; cf. *3356*; *De fraterno amore* 18.
25. L-S 297, lack of anger; *Consolatio ad uxorem* 2.
26. L-S 133, patient endurance; cf. *420*; *De capienda ex inimicis utilitate* 9.
27. L-S 1087, patience; *De sera numinis vindicta* 5.
28. L-S 726, ready obedience; cf. *2138*; *Comparatio Lycurgi et Numae* 3.
29. L-S 718, contentedness; *De virtute et vitio* 1.
30. L-S 15, savageness; cf. *66*; *Symposium* 197d.
31. L-S 1972, ruggedness; cf. *5467*; *Historia animalium* 9.1; cf. Plato, *Republic* 6.472f.
32. *663*; *De liberis educandis* 18.

tapeinophrosynē

praotēs

Certain modern expositors who rule out the possibility that the New Testament writers modified the meaning of classical Greek words restrict the meaning of *praotēs* in the New Testament to the meaning it had in the best classical writings. By doing so, however, they deprive themselves (and those who accept their interpretations) of much of the deeper teaching in Scripture.[33] The Scriptural *praotēs* is manifested not only in a man's outward behavior, nor merely in his relations with others, nor in his natural disposition. It is an inwrought grace of the soul that is exercised primarily toward God (Matt. 11:29; James 1:21). It is a quality of spirit that accepts God's dealings with us as good, without disputing or resisting them. It is closely linked with *tapeinophrosynē* and follows directly upon it (Eph. 4:2; Col. 3:12; cf. Zeph. 3:12), because it is only the humble heart that is also meek, that does not fight against God or struggle with him.

This meekness exists first of all before God, but it is also to be exercised before men—even evil men—knowing that the insults and injuries they inflict are permitted and employed by God to chasten and purify his elect. This was the root of David's *praotēs* when Shimei cursed and flung stones at him. David realized that the Lord had bidden Shimei (2 Sam. 16:11) and that it was just for him to suffer these things, however unjustly Shimei might inflict them. True Christian *praotēs* must spring from similar convictions. The one who is truly meek acknowledges himself as a sinner among sinners,[34] and this knowledge of his own sin teaches him to meekly endure the provocations of others and not to withdraw from the burdens their sins may impose on him (Gal. 6:1; 2 Tim. 2:25; Titus 3:2).

Praotēs, or meekness (if more is meant than mere gentleness of manner, that is, if the Christian virtue of meekness of spirit is referred to), must rest on the deeper foundations of *tapeinophrosynē*, on which alone it can subsist. *Praotēs*, though not more precious than *tapeinophrosynē*, is a grace in advance of it and one that presupposes it and that is not able to exist without it.

33. They stop short of Fritzsche (a learned but unconsecrated modern expositor of Romans), who (on Rom. 1:7) wrote: "The phrase in the New Testament, 'grace [*charis*] to you and peace,' must be regarded as expressing nothing more than what the Greeks were accustomed to declare in their 'greeting' [*chaireis*] or 'fair well' [*eu prattein*]—that is, that a person be fortunate or in the words of Horace (*Epistulae* 1.8.1) that he 'be happy and successful."' With reference to this word there are some excellent observations by F. Spanheim (*Dubia Evangelica*, 3:398) and Rambach (*Institutio hermeneumatis sacri*, p. 169). Rambach concluded: "Hence he is worthy of censure who substitutes those meager and inadequate concepts which the pagans held concerning virtues for the terms of Christian virtues." Cf. Zezschwitz, *Profangräcität und Biblischer Sprachgeist*, previously quoted (p. 1), and the article, *Hellenistisches Idiom*, by Reuss in Herzog's *Real-Encyclopädie*.

34. Even Jesus, who was sinless, bore a sinner's doom and therefore endured the contradiction of sinners (Luke 9:35–36; John 18:22–23).

43

praotēs (4236) *epieikeia* (1932)

Meekness Gentleness Clemency Equity

Tapeinophrosynē (5012) and *epieikeia*, though related by Clement of Rome,[1] are too distinct to be synonyms. *Praotēs*, however, is a middle term that is related to both words. In the previous section we dealt with its relation to *tapeinophrosynē*, and in this section we will consider its relation to *epieikeia*.

The existence of a word like *epieikeia* shows a high degree of ethical development among the Greeks.[2] *Epieikeia* refers to the sort of moderation that recognizes that it is impossible for formal laws to anticipate and provide for all possible cases and that asserting *legal* rights can be dangerous since these rights can be pushed into *moral* wrongs, so that the highest right (*summum jus*) can in practice prove to be the greatest injustice (*summa iniuria*). By not claiming its own rights to the fullest, *epieikeia* rectifies and redresses the injustices of justice.[3] Thus *epieikeia* is more truly just than strict justice would

1. *Epistula* 1.56.

2. No Latin word exactly and adequately translates *epieikeia*. *Clementia* (clemency) represents one aspect of it, *aequitas* (equity) another, and perhaps *modestia* (moderation, the Vulgate translation in 2 Cor. 10:1) a third. No single Latin word combines all of these nuances.

3. In the words of Persius (4.11), "It discerns the right where it goes among wrongs or when a rule fails through irregular step."

have been; it is "just and superior to the just," as Aristotle said.[4] According to Brandis, "it namely is not what is legally just but what rectifies it." In Aristotle's words, *epieikeia* is "a correction of law where law falls short on account of generalities,"[5] and he contrasted the man who stands up for the last tittle of his legal rights with the *epieikēs* (*1933*). Plato defined *epieikeia* as "a lessening of legalities and advantages."[6] In a fragment of Sophocles, *epieikeia* is opposed to "pure justice." Grotius defined *epieikeia* as "a correction when law fails on account of generality." *Eugnōmosynē*[7] is similar to *epieikeia* but not as closely related to the language of ethics. *Epieikeia* always refers to drawing back from the letter of the law to preserve its spirit. Seneca emphasized this aspect of *epieikeia*: "It does not effect less than the just, as it were, but as it really is the most just."[8] Aquinas asserted: "It is the lessening of punishment when it is proper, of course, and in what respect it is fitting." Göschel, who often wrote on the relation between theology and jurisprudence, has some excellent material on this subject.[9]

The archetype and pattern of *epieikeia* is found in God. God does not strictly assert his rights against men. He gives their imperfect righteousness a value it would not have if rigorously judged. He refuses to exact extreme penalties.[10] He remembers our natures and deals with us accordingly. All of these attitudes exemplify God's *epieikeia* and require, in turn, *epieikeia* in our dealings with one another. After being restored, Peter had to strengthen his brethren (Luke 22:32). In the parable, the servant who was forgiven much (Matt. 18:23), who experienced the *epieikeia* of his lord and king, is justly expected to show the same *epieikeia* to his fellow servant. *Epieikeia* is often used with *philanthrōpia*,[11] *hēmerotēs*,[12] *makrothymia*,[13] *anexikakia*,[14] and *praotēs*.[15] Some have sought to degrade *epieikeia* by calling it *anandria*,[16] the name of the vice that is its caricature.[17]

4. *Ethica Nicomachea* 5.10.6.

5. In a poem addressed to Lord Chancellor Egerton, Daniel (a notable poet and illustrious thinker) expanded this concept. Indeed, the whole poem is written in honor of *epieikeia*, or "equity," as being "the *soul* of law, the *life* of justice, and the *spirit* of right." In Spenser's *Fairy Queen*, the Legend of Artegal is devoted to the glorifying of the Christian virtue of *epieikeia*.

6. *Definitions* 412b. Lucian (*Vitarum auctio* 10) related it to *aidōs* (*127*) and to *metriotēs* (L-S 1122, moderation).

7. L-S 708, prudence.

8. *De clementia* 2.7.

9. *Zur Philosophie und Theologie des Rechts und der Rechtgeschichte*, 1835, pp. 428–38.

10. Wisd. of Sol. 12:18; Song of Three Children 18; 2 Macc. 10:4; Ps. 86:5: "For You, Lord, are good, and ready to forgive [*epieikēs*], and abundant in mercy"; cf. Clement of Rome, *Epistula* 1.29: "forbearing [*epieikēs*] and kind Father"; Plutarch, *Marcius Coriolanus* 24; *Pericles* 39; *Caesar* 57.

11. *5363*; Polybius, 5.10.1; Philo, *De vita Mosis* 1.36; 2 Macc. 9:27.

12. L-S 771, gentleness; Philo, *De carminibus* 18; Plutarch, *De vitioso pudore* 2.

13. *3115*; Clement of Rome, *Epistula* 1.13.

14. L-S 133, patient endurance; cf. *420*; Wisd. of Sol. 2:19.

15. 2 Cor. 10:1; Plutarch, *Pericles* 39; *Caesar* 57; cf. *Pyrrhus* 23; *Quomodo quis suos in virtute sentiat profectus* 9.

16. L-S 113, unmanliness, cowardice.

17. Aristides, *De concordia* 1, p. 529.

The distinction between *praotēs* and *epieikeia* is partially explained by Estius: "*Praotēs* pertains more to the mind, *epieikeia* however more to outward conduct."[18] Bengel remarked: "*Praotēs* is rather an unrestricted virtue, *epieikeia* is applied more to others." Aquinas also has an excellent discussion on the similarities and differences of these words.[19] Among other distinctions, Aquinas emphasized two. First, *epieikeia* always refers to the condescension of a superior to an inferior, something not necessarily implied by *praotēs*.[20] Second, *praotēs* is more passive, and *epieikeia* is more active; or at least the seat of the *praotēs* is the inner spirit, and the *epieikeia* necessarily embodies itself in outward acts. According to Aquinas: "They differ from each other inasmuch as *epieikeia* is a moderation of outward punishment; *praotēs* strictly speaking diminishes the passion of anger."

Translators from Wycliffe onward have used a variety of words to reproduce *epieikeia* and *epieikēs* for English readers. *Epieikeia* occurs on two or three[21] occasions (Acts 24:4; 2 Cor. 10:1; Phil. 4:5). It has been translated "meekness," "courtesy," "clemency," "softness," "modesty," "gentleness," "patience," "patient mind," and "moderation." *Epieikēs* occurs five times in the New Testament (2 Cor. 10:1; 1 Tim. 3:3; Titus 3:2; James 3:17; 1 Pet. 2:18) and appears in the several versions of the Hexapla as "temperate," "soft," "gentle," "modest," "patient," "mild," and "courteous." Although "gentle" and "gentleness" are probably the best translations of *epieikeia*, there is no English equivalent that completely captures *epieikeia*'s meaning. This accounts for the diversity of translations, in which the sense of equity and fairness that is so strong in the Greek is more or less absent.

18. On 2 Cor. 10:1.

19. *Summa theologia* 2a 3ae, *quaestio* 157. The discussion is entitled "Whether *epieikeia* and *praotēs* are entirely the same."

20. "*Epieikeia* is the gentleness of a superior toward an inferior; *praotēs* is not only that of a superior toward an inferior but of anyone to anyone else."

21. Counting *to epieikes* as an equivalent substantive.

44

kleptēs (2812) — Thief
lēstēs (3027) — Robber

The occurrence of *kleptēs* and *lēstēs* together in John 10:1, 8 does not constitute a tautology there[1] or elsewhere or a mere rhetorical amplification.[2] The *kleptēs* and the *lēstēs* both appropriate what is not theirs, but the *kleptēs* does so by fraud and in secret;[3] the *lēstēs* does so by open violence.[4] The former is the "thief" who steals, the latter is the "robber" who plunders, as his name (from *lēis*[5] or *leia*[6]) indicates.[7] They are respectively the Latin *fur* (thief) and *latro* (robber). As Jerome said: "Thieves [*fures*] deceive craftily and by secret fraud, robbers [*latrones*] audaciously snatch away what belongs to others."[8] The French *larron*, however, has come to refer to a thief who steals secretly and through cleverness, despite *larron*'s relation to *latro* (robber). Wycliffe's translations of "night-thief" and "day-thief" are not adequate.

1. Grotius distinguished *kleptēs* and *lēstēs* this way: "A thief [*kleptēs*] in that he comes to seize what is another's; a robber [*lēstēs*] in that he comes to kill."

2. Cf. Obad. 5; Plato, *Republic* 1.351c.

3. Matt. 24:43; John 12:6; cf. Exod. 22:2; Jer. 2:26.

4. 2 Cor. 11:26; cf. Hos. 9:1; Jer. 7:11; Plutarch, *De superstitione* 3: "He who keeps the house guarded does not fear robbers [*lēstas*]."

5. L-S 1044, booty.

6. L-S 1034, booty.

7. Just as our English "robber" comes from the German *Raub* (booty).

8. *In Osee* 7.1.

kleptēs
lēstēs

Our translators have always translated *kleptēs* as "thief." Unfortunately, they were not as consistent with *lēstēs*, and translated it as "robber" and as "thief," thus abolishing the distinction between the two words. However, we cannot charge *them* with carelessness, since in their day *thief* and *robber* did not have the distinct meanings they now have.[9] With open violence, Falstaff and his company rob the king's treasure on his highway and are called "thieves" throughout Shakespeare's *Henry IV*. Nevertheless it is unfortunate that on several occasions our Authorized Version uses "thieves," not "robbers." In Matthew 21:13 we read: "My house shall be called the house of prayer, but you have made it a den of *thieves*." It is robbers and not thieves, however, that have dens or caves; the original King James correctly translated "den of robbers" in Jeremiah 7:11, the origin of the quotation. Again, Matthew 26:55 in the KJV reads: "Are ye come out as against a *thief* with swords and staves for to take Me?" But a party armed with swords and clubs would come against some bold and violent robber, not against a lurking thief.[10] The poor traveler in the parable (Luke 10:30) fell not among thieves but among robbers, who are revealed as such by their violent and bloody treatment of him.

No passage has suffered more seriously by confusing *thief* and *robber* than Luke 23:39–43. The previous moral condition of "the penitent *thief*" is obscured by the associations that cling to this name. Both malefactors crucified with Jesus (one was inflexible, the other penitent) probably belonged to the band of Barabbas who had been cast *with his fellow insurgents* into prison for murder and insurrection (Mark 15:7). Barabbas himself was a *lēstēs* (John 18:40), not a common malefactor but "a notorious prisoner."[11] The fierce enthusiasm of the Jewish populace on his behalf, combined with his imprisonment for an unsuccessful insurrection,[12] leads to the conclusion that Barabbas was one of the Zealots. The Zealots encouraged resistance against the Roman domination by flattering and feeding the futile hopes of their countrymen, who still hoped they could break Roman supremacy. When hard pressed, the Zealots would retreat to the mountains and wage petty wars against their oppressors, living by plundering their enemies when possible, or by plundering anyone within reach. The history of Dolcino's "Apostolicals," as of the Camisards in the Cevennes, illustrates their downward progress as they receive and deserve the name *robbers*. The Romans called them by this name and dealt with them accordingly.[13] In the great French Revolution, the Vendean royalists were styled "the brigands of the Loire"; perhaps in the moral perversion of this period the name of robber, like *klept* among the mod-

9. There are numerous passages in Elizabethan literature that attest to this.

10. So the NKJV more correctly reads: "Have you come out, as against a robber, with swords and clubs to take Me?"

11. *Desmios* (*1198*) *episēmos* (*1978*), Matt. 27:16.

12. We must remember the moral condition of the Jews at this period, when false Christs and false deliverers arose every day.

13. See Josephus, *Antiquitates Judaicae* 20.8, 6, toward the end.

ern Greeks, ceased to be dishonorable and would have been acceptable to them.

Thief Robber

The character of the Zealots, the men who maintained the last protest against foreign domination, probably was quite different from that of the mean and cowardly purloiners called "thieves." The bands of these *lēstai* contained some of the worst people but probably included some that originally were among the most noble spirits of the nation. The latter had mistakenly sought by the wrath of man to work out the righteousness of God. Perhaps this was the character of the penitent *lēstēs*. Should there be any truth in this view of his former condition,[14] it is certainly obscured by the name *thief*. He would more appropriately be called "the penitent *robber*."[15]

14. It certainly would help to explain his sudden conversion.
15. See my *Studies in the Gospels*, 4th ed., pp. 302ff.; Dean Stanley, *The Jewish Church*, 3:466.

45

plynō (4150) *niptō* (3538) *louō* (3068) — *Wash*

Unfortunately, only the English "to wash" is an adequate translation for the Greek words *plynō*, *niptō*, and *louō*, each of which the biblical writers used in distinct ways. Thus *plynein* always means "to wash inanimate things" (usually garments), as distinguished from living objects or persons.[1] But *plynein* is not only used for garments. In Luke 5:2 it refers to the washing or cleansing of nets.[2] When David exclaimed: "Wash [*plynon*] me thoroughly from my iniquity" (Ps. 51:2), this was not an exception to the rule. The mention of hyssop in verse 7 indicates that he had in mind the ceremonial purifications (i.e., by sprinkling) of the Levitical law, the purification of the garments of the unclean person,[3] though he may have foreseen a better sprinkling in the future.

Niptein and *louein* each refer to washing living persons. *Niptein*[4] and *nipsasthai* almost always refer to the washing of a part of the body;[5] and *louein* (whose meaning is closer to "to bathe" than to "to wash") and *lousthai* ("to

1. Cf. "clothing," Homer, *Iliad* 22.155; "outer garment," Plato, *Charmides* 161e; throughout the Septuagint; "robes," Rev. 7:14.

2. Cf. Polybius, 9.6, 3.

3. Lev. 14:9; Num. 19:6–7.

4. In Attic Greek, *niptein* replaced *nizein*.

5. This includes the hands (Mark 7:3; Exod. 30:19), the feet (John 13:5; Plutarch, *Theseus* 10), the face (Matt. 6:17), the eyes (John 9:7), and the back and shoulders (Homer, *Odyssey* 6.224).

plynō
niptō
louō

bathe *oneself*") always refer to the whole body, not just a part.[6] The restriction of *niptein* to persons, as opposed to things, is always observed in the New Testament, as it is elsewhere (with but few exceptions).[7] A single verse in the Septuagint (Lev. 15:11) uses all three of the words in their distinct meanings: "And whomever he who has the discharge touches, and has not rinsed [*neniptai*] his hands in water, he shall wash [*plynei*] his clothes and bathe [*lousetai*] his body in water."

In the Authorized Version, John 13:10 suffers the most by the translators' failure to distinguish between *niptein* (to wash a part of the body) and *louein* or *lousthai* (to wash the whole body): "*He that is washed* [*ho leloumenos*] needeth not save *to wash* [*nipsasthai*] his feet, but is clean every whit." The Latin Vulgate has the same defect: "He who has been washed [*lotus est*] needs only that he wash [*lavet*] his feet." De Wette tried to preserve the variation of words: "He who is bathed [*gebadet ist*] needs to wash [*waschen*] but his feet." The New King James Version is an improvement: "He who is bathed needs only to wash his feet, but is completely clean." Because Peter had not understood the symbolic nature of the foot washing, he exclaimed at first: "You shall never wash my feet!" But as soon as he comprehended the true meaning of Jesus' actions, he wanted to be completely washed: "Lord, not my feet only, but also my hands and my head!" Christ replied that this was not necessary because Peter had already received the washing of forgiveness that included the whole man. He was *leloumenos* (i.e., bathed all over his body), and this absolution not only did not need to be repeated but was incapable of repetition: "You are already clean because of the word which I have spoken to you" (John 15:3). Although Peter already possessed this all-inclusive forgiveness, he *did* need *to wash his feet*[8] to be clean. He needed to allow his Lord to cleanse him from the defilements that he (a justified and partially sanctified man) would acquire by living in a sinful world. Some have suggested that this was an allusion to the Levitical ordinance where Aaron and his successors in the priesthood were to be washed *once for all* from head to foot when they were officially consecrated (Exod. 27:4; 40:12). But afterwards, whenever they ministered before the Lord, they were to wash their hands and *their feet* in the brazen laver (Exod. 30:19, 21; 40:31). This view would have more to commend it if we did not find *hands and feet* in the same category there, whereas in John they are not merely separated but opposed to one another (John 13:9–10). The whole mystery of our justification (once for all, sufficient for every need, embracing our whole being) and sanctification (a daily process) is wrapped up in the antithesis between the two words. Augustine expressed this clearly:

> A person indeed is cleansed in holy baptism, not with the exception of his feet but totally; however when he lives afterward in human situations, he certainly abuses the ground. Accordingly human passions, without which there is no mortal life, are as feet when we are influenced by human situations. Therefore he daily washes our feet by interceding for us and daily we must wash our feet with the Lord's Prayer when we say, "Forgive us our debts."[9]

6. Thus "our bodies washed [*lelousmenoi*]," Heb. 10:22; cf. Exod. 29:4; Acts 16:33; 2 Pet. 2:22; Rev. 1:5; Plato, *Phaedo* 115a.

7. Thus, cups (Homer, *Iliad* 16.229), tables (*Odyssey* 1.112), and vessels (Lev. 15:12).

8. *Nipsasthai tous podas*.

9. *In Evangelium Johannis* 13.10.

46

phōs (5457) — Light
phengos (5338)
phōstēr (5458)
lychnos (3088) — Lamp
lampas (2985) — Torch

All of these words are translated by "light" in the Authorized Version, some occasionally and some always. Thus we have *phōs* in Matthew 4:16; Romans 13:12; and often; *phengos* only in Matthew 24:29; Mark 13:24; Luke 11:33; *phōstēr* only in Philippians 2:15 and Revelation 21:11; *lychnos* in Matthew 6:22; John 5:35; 2 Peter 1:19; and elsewhere—though this is often translated as "candle" (Matt. 5:15; Rev. 22:5); and *lampas* in Acts 20:8, though elsewhere it is translated as "lamp" (Matt. 25:1; Rev. 8:10) and as "torch" (John 18:3).

Previous grammarians distinguished *phōs* from *phengos* (different forms of the same word) by saying that *phōs* refers to sunlight or daylight and that *phengos* refers to moonlight. This distinction was only present in the Attic writers, and even they did not always observe it. Thus on three or four occasions Sophocles ascribed *phengos* to the sun,[1] though Plato used *phōs selēnēs* (4582, light of the moon).[2] The grammarians were correct to assert that

1. *Antigone* 800; *Ajax* 654, 840; *Trachiniae* 597.
2. *Republic* 7.516b; cf. Isa. 13:10; Ezek. 32:7.

phōs
phengos
phōstēr
lychnos
lampas

phengos usually refers to moonlight or to starlight and that *phōs* refers to sunlight or to daylight. Plato contrasted these two words as "light [*phōs*] of day" and "lights [*phengē*] of night."[3] As with other finer distinctions of the Greek language, this is observed in the New Testament. Wherever moonlight is meant, *phengos* is used;[4] *phōs* is used to refer to sunlight (Rev. 22:5). Thus *phōs*, not *phengos*, is the true antithesis of darkness (*skotos*, *4655*).[5] Generally *phōs* is the more absolute designation of light. Thus Habakkuk 3:4 states: "His [God's] brightness [*phengos*] will be like the light [*phōs*]."[6]

Phōstēr also is translated "light" in our English versions, as in Philippians 2:15: "Among whom you shine as *lights* in the world."[7] It would be difficult to improve on this translation, though it fails to reveal Paul's entire intention. The *phōstēres* in Philippians 2:15 are the heavenly bodies,[8] mainly the sun and moon, the "lights" or "great lights" to which Moses referred in Genesis 1:14, 16.[9] In Ecclesiasticus 43:7 the moon is referred to as *phōstēr*, and in Wisdom of Solomon 13:2 "the lights [*phōstēres*] of heaven" is exactly equivalent to "the lights [*phōstēres*] in the world."[10] It would be difficult to improve on our translation of Revelation 21:11: "*Her light* [*ho phōstēr autēs*] was like a stone most precious." In this passage our translators correctly reverted to Wycliffe's translation and replaced "her shining," which appeared in intermediate versions and which *must* have conveyed a wrong impression to the English reader, with "her light." But because of its ambiguity, even the present translation is not altogether satisfactory. Some readers may still understand "her light" as the light that the heavenly city will diffuse, when actually *phōstēr* refers to the light-giver. "Her *lumen* [source of light]" is the Vulgate's translation. In verse 23 we discover the source of this light: "The Lamb is its light."[11]

Our translators could have distinguished *lychnos* and *lampas* by translating *lampas* as "torch" (as they did only once—John 18:3), which would have left "lamp" (now wrongly appropriated by *lampas*) free. They could have translated *lychnos* as "lamp" wherever it occurs without using "candle" at all. But on the occasions where "candle" is inappropriate they reverted to "light," which almost completely obliterates the distinction between *phōs* and *lychnos* in our English versions.

3. *Republic* 6.508c.

4. Matt. 24:19; Mark 12:24; cf. Joel 2:10; 3:15.

5. Plato, *Republic* 7.518a; Matt. 6:23; 1 Pet. 2:9.

6. Cf. Euripides, *Helena* 530: "She says that she sees my spouse living as a brightness [*phengos*] in the light [*phaei* = *phōti*] of day." See Döderlein, *Lateinische Synonyme*, 2:69.

7. *Hos phōstēres en kosmō* (2889).

8. *Luminaria* in the Vulgate and *Himmelslichter* (heavenly lights) in German (De Wette).

9. Here *mĕ'ōrôt* (3974) is translated *phōstēres* in the Septuagint.

10. The "world" here is the *material* world, the *stereōma* (4733) or firmament, not the *ethical* world already referred to by "crooked and perverted nations."

11. *Ho lychnos autēs* is equivalent to *ho phōstēr autēs* in v. 11.

There would be many advantages to such a redistribution of terms, especially in accuracy of translation. *Lychnos* does not refer to a "candle"[12] but to an oil-fed hand-lamp. *Lampas* does not refer to a "lamp" but to a "torch," both in Attic and later Hellenistic Greek[13] and in the New Testament.[14] Our early translators used "brand" or "fire brand" (John 18:4) to translate *lampas*, which shows that they understood the force of the word. It may be argued that in the parable of the ten virgins the *lampades* are fed with oil and must necessarily be lamps, but this does not follow. In the East the torch, as well as the lamp, is fed in this manner: "The true Hindu way of lighting up is by torches held by men, who feed the flame with oil from a sort of bottle [the *angeion* (30) of Matt. 25:4], constructed for the purpose."[15]

Light

Lamp
Torch

Such an understanding would clarify several passages, especially where it is important to distinguish *phōs* and *lychnos*. In John 5:35 the Authorized Version (referring to John the Baptist) reads: "He was a burning and a shining *light*." In this passage the New King James Version follows the original[16] more closely and translates: "He was the burning and shining *lamp*."[17] This translation does not obliterate the antithesis between Christ, the *phōs alēthinon* (genuine light, John 1:8),[18] and the Baptist, a *lamp* kindled by the hands of another, whose brightness brings joy to men for a while but will one day be extinguished. The same contrast is intended here between *lychnos* and *phōs* as that found between *lychnos* and *phōsphoros* (5459) in 2 Peter 1:19, only here it is transferred to the highest sphere of the spiritual world. This was Shakespeare's thought when he wrote those glorious lines: "Night's *candles* are burnt out, and jocund *Day* / Stands tiptoe on the misty mountain-tops."

12. *Candela* in Latin from *candeo* (shine, glitter), the *white* wax light and then any kind of taper.

13. Polybius, 3.93.4; Herodian, 4.2; Plutarch, *Timoleon* 8; *Alexander* 38; Judg. 7:16; 15:4.

14. For proof that *lampas* in Rev. 8:10 should be translated "torch" (the German *Fackel*, De Wette), see Aristotle, *De mundo* 4.

15. Elphinstone, *History of India*, 1:333.

16. *Ekeinos ēn ho lychnos ho kaiomenos kai phainōn*.

17. The Vulgate correctly reads: "He was the burning and shining *lamp*" (*Ille erat* lucerna *ardens et lucens*).

18. *Phōs ek phōtos* (Light of light). He is the Eternal *Light* that has never been kindled and that cannot be quenched.

47

charis (5485) — Grace, Favor, (Free) Gift, Mercy

eleos (1656)

We have often noted how frequently Greek words are glorified and transformed when adopted for Christian use. These words seem to have waited for this adoption to reveal all the rich, deep meanings they contained or might be made to contain. *Charis* is such a word, and because it refers to the heart or essence of the Greek mind, it will be beneficial to sketch the history of its development. *Charis*[1] is first of all that property that produces joy in its hearers or beholders. As Plutarch correctly explained, "Nothing is so productive of joy as *charis*."[2] *Charis* also referred to the presence of grace or beauty, which were the most joy-inspiring of all qualities for the Greek.[3] *Charis* often is used this way in the Septuagint (Ps. 45:2; Prov. 10:32),[4] Apocrypha (Ecclus. 24:16; 40:22, "charm [*charis*] and beauty"), and New Testament (Luke 4:22; and perhaps Eph. 4:29).

1. Connected with *chairein* (5463).

2. *Maxime cum principibus philosopho esse disserendum* 3. Cf. Pott, *Etymologische Forschungen*, vol. 2, pt. 1, p. 217.

3. This is the same as the German *Anmuth* (charm); thus Homer, *Odyssey* 2.12; 6.237; Euripides, *Troiades* 1108, "beauty [*charites*] of maidens"; Lucian, *Zeuxis* 2, "Attic beauty [*charis*]."

4. *Charis* often translates the Hebrew *ḥēn* (2580), though *areskeia* (699; Prov. 31:30), *eleos* (Gen. 19:19), and *epicharis* (L-S 672, charming; Nah. 3:4) also are used.

charis

eleos

Over a period of time, *charis* ceased to refer to grace and beauty as qualities and came to refer to gracious or beautiful things, acts, thoughts, speech, or persons. It came to refer to grace that embodied and expressed itself in gracious actions toward objects, not to "favor" in the sense of beauty. Thus *charis* helps in tracing the history of Greek. In classical Greek and in the Septuagint (Esther 5:3), *charin* often was used to mean "to seek, receive, and give favor." *Charis* also is used in the New Testament to refer to a merely human grace and favor (thus Acts 2:47; 25:3; 2 Cor. 9:19). *Charis* also came to refer to the thankfulness that is a response to the favor, a usage found frequently in the New Testament (Luke 17:9; Rom. 6:17; 2 Cor. 8:16), though we will not discuss this nuance since we are only discussing *charis* as it relates to *eleos*.

Charis received its highest consecration in the New Testament, where its meaning was not changed but ennobled and glorified. *Charis* was lifted from referring to an earthly benefit to referring to a heavenly one, from signifying the favor, grace, and goodness of man to man, to signifying the favor, grace, and goodness of God to man. In New Testament usage *charis* denotes the grace of the worthy to the unworthy, of the holy to the sinful.[5] It had never had this meaning before, even in the Greek Old Testament, where the Hebrew word that approximates the meaning of *charis* in the New Testament is *ḥsd* (2617), which is not translated by *charis* (except in Esther 2:9) but usually by *eleos* (Gen. 24:12; Job 6:14; Dan. 1:9; and often).

An anticipation of *charis*'s glorification, however, can be seen in the ethical terminology of the Greeks. For the Greeks, *charis* implied a favor that was freely done without claim or expectation of return, a usage that predisposed *charis* to receiving its new religious emphasis and the dogmatic significance with which it refers to the absolute freeness of the lovingkindness of God to men. In his definition of *charis*, Aristotle stressed that it is conferred freely with no expectation of return; its only motive is the bounty and generosity of the giver. Aristotle said: "Let *charis* be that quality by which he who has it is said to render favor [*charin*] to one who is in need, not in return for anything, nor that anything be given to him who renders it, but that something be given to that one in need."[6] *Charis* is opposed to *misthos*.[7] In Romans 11:6 Paul placed *charis* and *erga* (*2041*) in direct antithesis, which shows that they are mutually exclusive. The essence of *charis* is that it is unearned and unmerited;[8] indeed, it is *demerited*, as the faithful man will freely acknowledge.

Although *charis* is related to *sins* and is the attribute of God that they evoke, God's *eleos*, the *free gift* for the forgiveness of sins, is related to the *misery* that sin brings. God's tender sense of our misery displays itself in his ef-

5. It did not correspond merely to the German *Gunst* (favor) or *Huld* (kindness) but to *Gnade* (grace) as well.

6. *Rhetorica* 2.7. Also see *charis kai dōrea* (*1431*), Polybius, 1.31.6 (cf. Rom. 3:24; *dōrean tē autou chariti*; 5:15, 17; 12:3, 6; 15:15; Eph. 2:8; 4:7); *charis* also is used with *eunoia* (*2133*; Plato, *Leges* 11.931a; Plutarch, *Quomodo adulator ab amico internoscatur* 34); *philia* (*5373*; *Lycurgus* 4); and *praotēs* (*4236*; *Adversus Colotem* 2).

7. *3408*; *Lycurgus* 15.

8. As Augustine frequently urged: "Grace, unless it is free, is not grace."

forts to lessen and entirely remove it—efforts that are hindered and defeated only by man's continued perverseness. As Bengel said: "Grace removes guilt, mercy removes misery."

It is worthwhile to consider how *charis* was used before it came to refer to God's mercy on all his works. Aristotle defined *eleos* this way: "Let mercy [*eleos*] be a certain grief for an apparently destructive and painful evil toward one who experienced what was undeserved in respect to what he himself or one of his family might expect to suffer."[9] Aristotle's definition shows how much *charis* had to be modified before it could be used to refer to the *eleos* of God. Grief cannot and does not touch God, in whose presence is fullness of joy. Nor does God demand *unworthy* suffering[10] to move him. Indeed, in a world of sinners there is no absolutely unworthy suffering. God transcends all chance and change and cannot be involved in the misery he beholds. It is not surprising that the Manichaeans and others who desired a God as unlike man as possible protested the attribution of *eleos* to him. They used this as a weapon in their warfare against the Old Testament, where God is not ashamed to proclaim himself a God of pity and compassion (Pss. 78:38; 86:15; and often). The Manichaeans were aided in this by the Latin word *misericordia* (tender-heartedness); they appealed to its etymology and demanded whether the *miserum cor* (miserable heart) could be found in God.[11] With respect to this "blemish of a petty mind," as he called it, Seneca observed: "Mercy is a neighbor of misery, for it possesses and draws something from it."[12] Augustine correctly answered that this and all other words used to express human affections required certain modifications to remove the infirmities of human passions before they could be ascribed to God. Such infirmities were accidental; the essentials remained unchanged. Thus Augustine stated: "Likewise concerning mercy, if you would remove the emotion of participating misery for the one you pity, *so that there remains a calm benevolence for healing and freeing from misery*, a certain recognition of divine mercy is acknowledged."[13] There is always an element of grief in man's pity; John of Damascus listed *eleos* as one of the four forms of *lypē* (*3077*).[14] This is not the case with God's pity. The *charis* of God, the gift of his free grace that is displayed in the forgiveness of sins, is extended to men as they are *guilty*, his *eleos* as they are *miserable*. The lower creation is the object of God's *eleos*, inasmuch as it has been affected by man's sin,[15] but his *charis* is extended to man alone as the only one who needs it or is capable of receiving it.

9. *Rhetorica* 2.8.

10. See the Stoic definition of *eleos* (Diogenes Laërtius, 7.1.63). Cicero said: "Mercy is grief from the pity for another who is *afflicted unjustly*. For no one is moved to pity by the punishment for the murder of parents or for a traitor" (*Tusculanae disputationes* 4.8.18).

11. Cf. Virgil, *Georgica* 2.498–99.

12. *De clementia* 2.6.

13. *De doctrina Christiana* 2.2. Cf. *De civitate Dei* 9.5; Anselm, *Proslogium* 8; and Suicer, *Thesaurus* under this word.

14. The other three are *achos* (L-S 297, pain), *achthos* (L-S 296, burden), and *phthonos* (5355; *De fide orthodoxa* 2.14).

15. Job 38:41; Ps. 147:9; Jon. 4:11; Rom. 8:20–23.

charis

eleos

In the divine mind, and in the order of our salvation as God conceives it, God's *eleos* precedes his *charis*. God so *loved* the world with a pitying love (*eleos*) that he *gave* his only begotten Son (*charis*) that the world through him might be saved (cf. Luke 1:78–79; Eph. 2:4). But in the order of the manifestation of that salvation, God's grace precedes his mercy, *charis* comes before *eleos*. The same people are the subjects of both, since they are both guilty and miserable, yet the righteousness of God[16] demands that the guilt should be absolved before the misery can be assuaged: only the forgiven may be blessed. God must pardon before he can heal; men must be justified before they can be sanctified. Just as the righteousness of God absolutely requires relating the two terms, so does man's moral constitution, which links misery with guilt and makes the first the inseparable companion of the second. As a result, in each of the apostolic salutations where these words occur, *charis* precedes *eleos*,[17] an order that could not have been reversed. In the more usual Pauline salutations, *charis* precedes *eirēnē* (*1515*; 1 Cor. 1:3; 2 Cor. 1:2; and often).[18]

16. It is as necessary to maintain as his love.

17. Zech. 12:10; 1 Tim. 1:2; 2 Tim. 1:2; Titus 1:4; 2 John 3; cf. Wisd. of Sol. 3:9.

18. On the distinction between the words of this section, see the excellent remarks in Delitzsch, *An die Ebräer*, p. 163.

48

theosebēs (2318) — *Worshiper of God*
eusebēs (2152) — *Pious*
eulabēs (2126) — *Devout*
thrēskos (2357) — *Religious*, *Godly*
deisidaimōn (1174) — *Superstitious*

Theosebēs is applied to Job three times (1:1, 8; 2:3) but occurs only once in the New Testament (John 9:31), as does *theosebia* (*2317*; 1 Tim. 2:10; Gen. 20:11; cf. Job 28:28). Though it is rare in the Septuagint (Isa. 24:16; 26:7; 32:8), *eusebēs* is common in the Apocrypha (Ecclus. 11:22; 12:2, 4) and is found more frequently in the New Testament with dependent words (1 Tim. 2:2; Acts 10:2; 2 Pet. 2:9; and often). Before considering the relation of *theosebēs* and *eusebēs* to the other words in this group, we should note a subordinate distinction between them. By virtue of its derivation, *theosebēs* implies piety *toward* God or *toward the gods*; *eusebēs* refers to piety in human relations (e.g., toward parents or others).[1] According to its etymology, *eusebēs* only implies "worship" (that is, "worthship") and reverence that is well and rightly directed. It has the same double meaning as the Latin *pietas* (piety and dutifulness), which is not just "uprightness toward the gods" or "the skill of

1. Euripides, *Electra* 253–54.

theosebēs
eusebēs
eulabēs
thrēskos

deisidaimōn (1174)

cultivating the gods."[2] This double meaning, though helpful, occasionally proves embarrassing. For accuracy and precision, Augustine defined *pietas* as what *eusebeia (2150) may* mean and what *theosebeia* alone *must* mean, piety *toward God*.[3] Plato defined *eusebia* as "uprightness concerning the gods,"[4] and the Stoics called it "knowledge of worshiping the gods,"[5] though not every reverencing of the gods was *eusebia*; only a correct reverencing of them *aright* (*eu*) was. *Eusebia* is the standing word used to refer to this piety, both in itself[6] and as the correct mean between *atheotēs*[7] and *deisidaimonia*[8] and between *asebeia* and *deisidaimonia*.[9] Josephus also contrasted *eusebia* with *eidōlolatreia* (*1495*). The *eusebēs* is the antithesis of the *anosios*;[10] he is *philotheos*[11] and "sensible concerning the gods."[12] Eusebius correctly described Christian *eusebeia* as "uprightness toward the one and only God as truly existing and confessed, and a resulting upright life."[13]

Although most of the information about *eulabēs* has been covered previously in section *10*, some additional material needs to be added. Earlier I observed that *eulabeia (2124)* changed from signifying caution and carefulness in human relationships to signifying caution and carefulness in our relationship with God.[14] The only places in the New Testament where *eulabēs* occurs are Luke 2:25; Acts 2:5; 8:2 (cf. Mic. 7:2). *Eulabēs* is usually translated "devout," a translation that cannot be improved.[15] On all of these occasions *eulabēs* refers to Jewish or Old Testament piety. In the first instance it is applied to Simeon, in the second to those Jews who came to Jerusalem from distant parts to keep the commanded feasts, and in the third instance to the *andres eulabeis* (devout men) who carried Stephen to his burial and who probably were not Christian brothers but devout Jews. By this courageous act they demonstrated their sorrow over the slaughtered saint and so separated themselves in spirit from the bloody deed and, if possible, from the judgments that would befall the city where the murder occurred. Whether they came to believe in the crucified Christ as witnessed to by Stephen we are not told, though we may well presume this to be the case.

2. Cicero, *De deorum natura* 1.41.

3. "Which the Greeks call either *eusebeian* or more distinctly and more fully *theosebeian*," *Epistulae* 167.3; *De trinitate* 14.1; *De civitate Dei* 10.1; *Enchiridion* 1.

4. Plato, *Definitions* 412c.

5. Diogenes Laërtius, 7.1.64, 119.

6. Xenophon, *Agesilaus* 3.5; 11.1.

7. L-S 31, godlessness.

8. *1175*, superstition; Plutarch, *De superstitione* 14.

9. Philo, *Quod deus sit immutabilis* 3, 4.

10. *462*; Xenophon, *Apologia Socratis* 19.

11. *5377*; Lucian, *Calumniae non temere credendum* 14.

12. Xenophon, *Memorabilia* 4.3, 2. For additional remarks about the Greek use of *eusebeia*, see Nägelsbach, *Nachhomerische Theologie*, p. 191.

13. *Praeparatio evangelica* 1, p. 3.

14. The German *Andacht* (devotion) had much the same history. See Grimm, *Wörterbuch* under this word.

15. It is the Latin *religiosus* (devout) but not our *religious*.

Worshiper of God
Pious
Devout
Religious
Godly
Superstitious

The piety of man toward God consists of fear and love. The Old Testament emphasized fear, the New Testament love.[16] *Eulabēs* is an excellent word for describing piety under the old covenant. According to Luke 1:6, Zacharias and Elizabeth "were both righteous before God, walking in all the commandments and ordinances of the Lord blameless" and performing all their prescribed duties. When used in their religious senses, *eulabēs* and *eulabeia* include the accurate and scrupulous performance of prescribed tasks where the danger of negligence in God's service and the need to preserve unaltered what God has commanded are recognized.[17]

On several occasions Plutarch exalted the *eulabeia* of the Romans in the handling of divine things and contrasted it with the comparative carelessness of the Greeks. Thus after giving other examples he said: "Of late times also they did renew and begin a sacrifice thirty times one after another, because they thought still there fell out one fault or other in the same; so holy and devout were they to the gods"[18] Elsewhere, Plutarch portrayed Aemilius Paulus[19] as someone who was famous for his *eulabeia*. The following is a portion of that lengthy passage:

> When he did anything belonging to his office of priesthood, he did it with great experience, judgment, and diligence; leaving all other thoughts, and without omitting any ancient ceremony, or adding to any new; contending oftentimes with his companions in things which seemed light and of small moment; declaring to them that though we do presume the gods are easy to be pacified, and that they readily pardon all faults and scrapes committed by negligence, yet if it were no more but the respect of the commonwealth's sake they should not slightly or carelessly dissemble or pass over faults committed in those matters.[20]

In one passage Euripides portrayed *eulabeia* as a divine person, "most beneficial of the gods."[21]

But if *eulabēs* refers to the anxious and scrupulous worshiper who never changes or omits anything because he is afraid of offending, *thrēskos* (James 1:26) refers to the Latin *religiosus* (devout) who zealously and diligently performs his outward service to God. Although the word does not occur anywhere else in Greek secular literature, its meaning may be determined by working back from *thrēskeia*,[22] which primarily refers to the ceremonial ser-

16. There was love in the fear of God's saints then, as there must be fear in their love now.

17. Cicero's well-known words in which he deduced *religio* (devotion to the gods) from *relegere* (to go through again) are appropriate here: "Those who diligently repeat all things which pertain to the worship of the gods, and as it were *go through them again* [*relegerent*], are called *devout* [*religiosi*]" (*De deorum natura* 2.28). Cf. Pott, *Etymologische Forschungen*, 5:369.

18. *Marcius Coriolanus* 25.

19. Ibid., chap. 3.

20. This is from St. Thomas North's somewhat loose, though reliable, translation (p. 206). Cf. Aulus Gellius (2.28): "The ancient Romans were *very pious* and *most cautious* in establishing religious rites and in giving attention to their immortal gods."

21. *Phoenissae* 794.

22. 2356. *Thrēskos* is a synonym for the Latin *cultus* (worship) or more exactly for the Latin *cultus exterior* (external worship).

theosebēs
eusebēs
eulabēs
thrēskos

deisidaimōn (*1174*)

vice of religion,[23] the external framework of which *eusebeia* is the animating soul. Plutarch's suggested derivation of *thrēskos* from Orpheus the *Thracian*,[24] who inaugurated the celebration of religious mysteries, is etymologically worthless. That etymology does, however, emphasize the celebration of divine functions as fundamental.

James' choice of *thrēskos* and *thrēskeia* (1:26, 27) is both delicate and precise. "If any man," he would say, "seems to himself to be *thrēskos*, a diligent observer of the functions of religion, if any man would render a pure and undefiled *thrēskeia* to God, let him understand that this does not consist in outward purifications or ceremonial observances; there is a better *thrēskeia* than thousands of rams and rivers of oil, namely, to do justly and to love mercy and to walk humbly with his God" (Mic. 6:7–8). Or, according to his own words, "to visit orphans and widows in their trouble, and to keep oneself unspotted from the world" (cf. Matt. 23:23). James was not affirming, as we sometimes hear, that these duties are the sum total or even the great essentials of true religion, but he declared them to be the body, the *thrēskeia* of which godliness or the love of God is the animating soul. His intention is somewhat obscured in English because our translations "religious" for *thrēskos* and "religion" for *thrēskeia* have lost their original meanings. James claimed that the new dispensation was superior to the old because the *thrēskeia* of the new consists in acts of mercy, love, and holiness. The new dispensation has *light for its garment*, its very *robe* is righteousness. In that way James explained the superiority of the new dispensation over the old, whose *thrēskeia* at best was merely ceremonial and formal, whatever inner truth it might embody. Coleridge made these same observations,[25] though he deemed our translations of *thrēskos* and *thrēskeia* erroneous. They are, however, not so much erroneous as obsolete—an explanation Coleridge suggested, though he was not aware of the meaning of "religion" in the time of the translators. Milton offered several more examples, characterizing some heathen idolatries as being "adorned with gay *religions* full of pomp and gold."[26] Our *Homilies* supply many more examples: "Images used for no *religion* or superstition rather, we mean of none worshipped, nor in danger to be worshipped or any, may be suffered."[27] An instructive passage on the merely *external* character of *thrēskeia*[28] occurs in Philo.[29] He rejected those who wanted to be counted among the *eusebeis* on the basis of various washings or costly offerings to the temple: "For he wanders from the path toward *piety* [*eusebeian*] when he deems *ceremony* [*thrēskeian*] a substitute for holiness." The tendency of *thrēskeia* to deteriorate into superstition and service of false gods[30] itself indicates that it was more

23. Lord Brooke grandly named her the "mother of form and fear."

24. *Alexander* 2.

25. *Aids to Reflection*, 1825, p. 15.

26. *Paradise Lost*, bk. 1.

27. In the homily *Against Peril of Idolatry*.

28. For the translators of the Authorized Version, this same external character was part of the meaning of "religion."

29. *Quod deterius potiori insidiari soleat* 7.

30. Wisd. of Sol. 14:18, 27; Col. 2:18.

closely related to the form than to the essence of piety. Thus Gregory Nazianzene remarked: "I understand *ceremony* [*thrēskeian*] and the reverence of demons, but *piety* [*eusebeia*] is the adoration of the Trinity."[31]

Worshiper of God
Pious
Devout
Religious
Godly
Superstitious

Deisidaimōn, the last word of this group, and *deisidaimonia* at first had honorable uses that were equivalent to *theosebēs*.[32] It is possible that the Latin *superstitio* (superstition) and *superstitiosus* (superstitious) initially had the same meaning. There seem to be traces of this use of *superstitiosus* in Plautus,[33] though since no one has yet solved the riddle of this word,[34] it is impossible to say whether this is correct. By Cicero's time *superstitiosus* had certainly left its better meaning behind.[35] Initially, the philosophers understood *deisidaimonia* unfavorably. Ast affirmed that it first occurred in an ill sense in Polybius,[36] but Jebb[37] quoted a passage from Aristotle[38] that showed that this meaning was not unknown to him. As soon as the philosophers began to see fear as a disturbing and not as a positive element in piety,[39] it was almost inevitable that they would adopt *deisidaimonia*,[40] whose etymology implies and involves fear. The philosophers then used *deisidaimonia* to denote what they condemned: the "empty fear of the gods,"[41] a phrase in which the emphasis should be on *fear*, not on *empty*. Augustine remarked: "*Varro* differentiates a pious person [*religiosum*] from a superstitious one [*superstitioso*] by this distinction, so that he says gods are feared by the superstitious; by the pious, however, they are *revered* as parents, not *feared* as enemies."[42] Although Baxter does not have an identical emphasis, his definition of superstition is also a good one: "A conceit that God is well pleased by overdoing in external things and observances and laws of men's own making."[43]

Even after *deisidaimonia*'s meaning changed to an ignoble one,[44] its higher meaning did not completely disappear. *Deisidaimonia* remained a "middle term" to the last; its sense, whether good or bad, depended on the user's intention. *Deisidaimōn*[45] and *deisidaimonia*[46] occur in a good sense, even in

31. *Carmina* 2.34.150, 151.

32. Xenophon, *Cyropaedia* 3.3.26.

33. *Curculio* 3.27; *Amphitruo* 1.1.169.

34. Pott (*Etymologische Forschungen*, 2:921) resumed the latest investigations on the derivation of *superstitio*. For the German *Aberglaube* (superstition) as a synonym for *Ueberglaube* (transcending belief), see Herzog, *Real-Encyclopädia* under this word.

35. *De deorum natura* 2.28; *Divinatio in caecilium* 2.72; cf. Seneca: "Piety cultivates the gods, superstition [*superstitio*] profanes them."

36. 6.56.7.

37. *Characters of Theophrastus*, p. 264.

38. *Politica* 5.11.

39. Therefore fear was something to be carefully eliminated from the true idea of piety. See Plutarch, *De recta ratione audiendi* 12; and Wyttenbach, *Animadversiones in Plutarchum*, 1:997.

40. From *deidō* (L-S 373, fear).

41. Cicero, *De deorum natura* 1.41.

42. *De civitate Dei* 6.9.

43. *Catholic Theology*, preface.

44. Theophrastus defined *deisidaimonia* as "timidity concerning demoniac power" and more vaguely by Plutarch as "a deep feeling which suspects the good to be evil" (*De superstitione* 6).

45. Xenophon, *Agesilaus* 11.8; *Cyropaedia* 3.3.58.

46. Polybius, 6.56.7; Josephus, *Antiquitates Judaicae* 10.3.2.

theosebēs
eusebēs
eulabēs
thrēskos

***deisidaimōn* (1174)**

Paul's memorable discourse on Mars' Hill. To the Athenians Paul said: "I perceive that in all things you are *hōs deisidaimonesterous*" (Acts 17:22). This does not mean "too superstitious," as it is translated in the Authorized Version, or *allzu abergläubisch* (too superstitious) as Luther translated it, but *religiosiores* (rather pious), as Beza translated it in Latin, or *sehr gottesfürchtig* (very religious), as De Wette translated it in German, or "very religious," as it is translated in the New King James Version. Paul's habit was not to affront and thereby alienate his hearers, especially at the beginning of a discourse intended to win them to the truth. Deeper reasons than prudence would have prevented him from such expressions: he was aware of the religious element in heathenism, however overlaid or obscured it was by falsehood and error. For these reasons, interpreters like Chrysostom made *deisidaimonesterous* equivalent to *eulabesterous* (rather reverent) and understood it as praise. But we must avoid this extreme. Paul tactfully and truthfully selected a word that almost imperceptibly slipped from praise to blame. In his comments on Acts 17:22, Bengel said: "*Deisidaimōn* in itself is a middle term and for that reason has a placid ambiguity very fitting for the beginning of the speech." Paul gave his Athenian hearers their due honor as zealous worshipers of the superior powers, so as far as their knowledge reached.[47] Paul did not squander words of highest praise on the Athenians but reserved these words for the true worshipers of the true God. This is the case in the one passage where *deisidamōn* occurs, as well as in the one passage where *deisidaimonia* occurs (Acts 25:19). In that passage Festus may have spoken with an implied slight of the *deisidaimonia* or overstrained way of worshiping God[48] that he believed was common to Paul and his Jewish accusers, but he would scarcely have referred to it as a "superstition" before Agrippa, who was himself an expert in the customs and questions of the Jews (Acts 26:3, 27). Festus certainly did not intend to insult Agrippa.

47. They were *theosebestatoi* (*2318*), according to Sophocles (*Oedipus Coloneus* 256), and *eusebestatoi pantōn tōn Hellēnōn* (the pious of all the Greeks), as Josephus called them. According to Aeschylus (*Eumenides* 867), their land was *theophilestatē* (*2321*). Cf. the beautiful chorus in *The Clouds* of Aristophanes (299–313).

48. De Wette translated *deisidaimonia* as *Gottesverehrung* (respect for God).

49

kenos (2756) *mataios* (3152) — Empty, Vain

Although *kenos* and *mataios* do not occur together in the New Testament, they are used together in the Septuagint (Job 20:18; Isa. 37:7; cf. 49:4; Hos. 12:1), in Clement of Rome,[1] and in classical Greek.[2] We will only investigate the ethical uses of *mataios* and *kenos*, since this is the only way that *mataios* is used in Scripture and since *kenos* must be compared to it in terms of similar usage.

Kenos means "empty" or "leer" in English,[3] and *mataios* means "vain."[4] *Kenos* implies hollowness, *mataios* aimlessness.[5] Thus *kenai elpides* (*1680*)[6] are empty hopes, hopes that are not built on a solid foundation. In the New Testament, *kenoi logoi*[7] are words that have no inner substance and kernel of truth, hollow sophistries and apologies for sin; *kopos* (2873) *kenos* is labor that yields no return (1 Cor. 15:58), as is *kenophōniai*.[8] Suidas said that *kenologia*[9]

1. *Epistula* 1.6.
2. Sophocles, *Electra* 324; Aristotle, *Ethica Nicomachea* 1.2; Plutarch, *Adversus Colotem* 17.
3. *Gehaltlose* in German and *inanis* in Latin.
4. *Eitel* (idle) or *erfolglose* (futile) in German and *vanus* in Latin.
5. Or if we may use the word, the "resultlessness," as it is connected with *matēn* (*3155*).
6. Aeschylus, *Persae* 804; cf. Job 7:6; Ecclus. 31:1, where they are joined with *pseudeis* (*5571*).
7. *3056*; Eph. 5:6; cf. Deut. 32:47; Exod. 5:9.
8. *2757*; 1 Tim. 6:20; 2 Tim. 2:16.
9. L-S 938, empty talk; Plutarch, *De communibus notitiis contra Stoicos* 22.

and *kenodoxia*[10] refer to "some empty opinion about oneself." Paul reminded the Thessalonians (1 Thess. 2:1) that his coming to them was not *kenē*, not without the demonstration of the Spirit and power. When used to refer to people instead of things, *kenos* implies not only an absence of good but the presence of evil, since man's moral nature permits no vacuum. *Kenos* is used this way in James 2:20, the only passage where it occurs in the New Testament. *Anthrōpos* (444) *kenos* refers to someone who does not possess any higher wisdom but who is puffed up with a vain conceit of his own spiritual insight.[11] Also note the "worthless [*kenoi*] men" of Judges 9:4. Plutarch stated: "We regard those who in their walk flatter themselves and carry their neck high as foolish and empty [*kenous*]."[12] Also of interest is the Greek proverb: "Empty persons [*kenoi*] think about empty things [*kena*]."[13]

But if *kenos* expresses the emptiness of anything that is not filled with God, then *mataios* refers to the aimlessness (lacking object and end) and vanity of everything that does not have God, who should be the only true and ultimate aim of any intelligent creature. When used to refer to natural things, *mataion*[14] means to build houses of sand on the seashore, to chase the wind, to shoot at the stars, to pursue one's own shadow. Pindar correctly described the *mataios* as one "hunting for vain things with idle hopes."[15] The toil that can result in nothing is *mataios*,[16] grief without a basis is *mataios*,[17] an "empty [*mataios*] prayer" is one that by the nature of things cannot be fulfilled,[18] and the prophecies of the false prophet that God will not fulfill are *manteiai mataiai*.[19] So in the New Testament *mataioi kai anōpheleis zētēseis* (Titus 3:9) are idle and unprofitable questions whose discussion cannot lead to any advancement in true godliness.[20] *Mataiologoi*[21] are vain talkers whose speech results only in poverty or worse (Isa. 32:6), and *mataioponia*[22] is labor that by its very nature is in vain.

Mataiotēs (3153) was not used in secular Greek, and had it been, it could never have imparted the depth of meaning it has in Scripture. The heathen world was too hopelessly debased in vanity to be aware of its own condition, to be capable of judging itself. One must at least be partially delivered from the *mataiotēs* to be able to recognize it for what it is. When the Preacher exclaimed "all is vanity" (Eccles. 1:2), it is clear that something in him was *not* vanity, or else he could never have arrived at this conclusion. Hugh of St.

10. 2754; Phil. 2:3.
11. *Aufgeblasen* (puffed up) as Luther has it.
12. *De recta ratione audiendi* 5.
13. Gaisford, *Paroemiae Graecae*, p. 146.
14. Gregory of Nyssa, *Homily on Ecclesiastes* 1.
15. *Pythia* 3.37.
16. Plato, *Leges* 735b.
17. *Axiochus* 369c.
18. Euripides, *Iphigenia Taurica* 633.
19. Ezek. 13:6, 7, 8; cf. Ecclus. 31:5.
20. Cf. *mataiologia* (3150; 1 Tim. 1:6; Plutarch, *De liberis educandis* 9).
21. 3151; Titus 1:10.
22. Clement of Rome, 9.

Victor said: "There was something in him which was not vanity and that was able to speak not aimlessly against vanity." However, some intimations of his cry are apparent in the moral waste of the old heathen world, perhaps most frequently and distinctly in Lucretius. The great pathetic passages in his poem may be summed up briefly in these words: "The human race strives for the empty and futile always, and squanders a lifetime on idle concerns." But if these confessions are comparatively rare elsewhere, they are frequent in Scripture. In fact *vanity* is the keyword in Ecclesiastes. In that book *mataiotēs*, or its Hebrew equivalent *hebel* (1892), occurs nearly forty times. Vanity is the sum the Preacher gave to the total good of man's life and labors apart from God. The false gods of heathendom are eminently *ta mataia*.[23] The *mataiousthai* (3154) is ascribed to the followers of idols,[24] because by following vain things they become *mataiophrones*[25] like the vain things they follow.[26] Their whole conversation is vain (1 Pet. 1:18) because the *mataiotēs* reaches to the very center of their moral being, the *nous* (3563) itself (Eph. 4:17). Nor is this all; this *mataiotēs* or *douleia tēs phthopas* (bondage of corruption)[27] extends to the entire creation that was made dependent on man. With a certain blind consciousness, this creation longs for a deliverance it is never able to grasp because its restitution can only follow man's. Olshausen clearly remarked:

> Every natural human being, every animal, every plant strives to get beyond itself, to realize an ideal, in the realization of which it has its *eleutheria* [*1657*], that is, a state of being consistent with its divine design. However its inherent transitoriness (Ps. 39:6; Eccles. 1:2, 14), that is, its deficient supply of life, the perishableness derived from it and destined to come to an end, namely in death, does not permit any created thing to attain its goal; each individual member of a species begins its life-cycle anew and strives unsuccessfully to overcome the impossibility of completing itself.[28]

23. Acts 14:15; cf. 2 Chron. 11:15; Jer. 10:15; Jon. 2:8.
24. 2 Kings 17:15; Jer. 2:5; 28:17–18; Rom. 1:21.
25. L-S 1084, weak-minded; 3 Macc. 6:11.
26. Wisd. of Sol. 13:1; 14:21–31.
27. Rom. 8:21. The phrases are interchangeable; the end of each is death.
28. On Rom. 8:21–22. There is an excellent article on this "vanity of the creature" in the *Zeitschrift für Lutherische Theologie*, 1872, pp. 50ff. and in another by Köster in the *Theologische Studien und Kritiken*, 1862, pp. 755ff.

50

himation (2440) — Cloak, Coat, Tunic, Garment, Robe

chitōn (5509)
himatismos (2441)
chlamys (5511)
stolē (4749)
podērēs (4158)

This section will not be a treatise on clothing, since Ferrarius, Braun, and others have written a great deal about this topic. Instead, I will briefly explain a few of the words most frequently used in the New Testament to refer to garments.

Himation[1] is most common word used to refer to garments in a general sense (Matt. 11:8; 26:65). When used more restrictively, *himation* refers to the large upper garment that a man could sometimes sleep in (Exod. 22:26), the cloak as distinguished from the *chitōn* or close-fitting inner vest.[2] *Endyein*

1. It is properly a diminutive of *hima*, which is equivalent to *heima* (L-S 487, garment), though like so many of our own words (*pocket* and *latchet*) it has quite lost the force of a diminutive.

2. Thus we have *periballein himation* (to throw about a cloak). The cloak is called *peribolaion* (4018) in Exod. 22:7 and *peribolē* (L-S 1369, garment) by Plutarch (*Conjugalia praecepta* 12).

himation

chitōn
himatismos
chlamys
stolē
podērēs

chitōna literally means "to go into a tunic."[3] *Himation* and *chitōn* often occur together to refer to the upper and the under garment.[4] In Matthew 5:40 Jesus instructed his disciples: "If anyone wants to sue you and take away your *tunic* [*chitōna*], let him have your *cloak* [*himation*] also." Here the despoiler begins with the less costly under garment, translated "tunic," and proceeds to the more costly outer garment. Since this process is a legal one, this is a natural sequence. But in Luke 6:29 the order is reversed: "And from him who takes away your *cloak* [*himation*], do not withhold your *tunic* [*chitōna*] either." In this context Jesus is clearly referring to an act of violence, and so the cloak or outer garment would be named first because it would be seized first. In the Aesopic fable[5] the violent wind makes the traveler wrap his *himation* around him more closely, but when the sun begins to shine, he first discards his *himation* and then his *chitōn*. A *gymnos* (*1131*) was one who had laid aside his *himation* and was clad only in his *chitōn*. This did not mean "naked," as it appears in many translations (John 21:7), suggesting indecency, but stripped for toil.[6] Joseph left his *himation* in the hands of his temptress (Gen. 39:12), but in Jude 23 *chitōn* is correct.

Himatismos appeared comparatively late and belonged to koine Greek. It usually referred to stately or costly garments—the "vesture" of kings.[7] It was used to refer to Solomon in all of his glory,[8] and it was associated with gold and silver as part of a precious spoil.[9] It is used with such terms as *endoxos*,[10] *poikilos*,[11] *diachrysos*,[12] and *polytelēs*.[13] It was also the name given to Jesus' *chitōn*,[14] which was one woven piece[15] and which was so desirable that even the rude Roman soldiers were unwilling to tear and destroy it.

The purple robe that the mockers in Pilate's judgment hall scornfully placed on Jesus is called a *chlamys* (Matt. 27:28–31), a very appropriate word for the context. *Chlamys* so obviously refers to a garment of dignity and office that *chlamyda peritithenia* (to put on a robe) was a proverbial phrase for assuming a magistracy.[16] This might be a *civil* magistracy, but *chlamys*[17] usually refers to the robe of military officers, captains, commanders, or *imperators*

3. Dio Chrysostom, *Oratio* 7.111.
4. Matt. 5:40; Luke 6:29; John 19:23; Acts 9:39.
5. Plutarch, *Conjugalia praecepta* 12.
6. Cf. Isa. 20:2; 57:7; Job 22:6; James 2:15. In Latin, *nudus ara* means "without the toga," "in one's tunic" (cf. Virgil, *Georgica* 1.299).
7. Cf. Gen. 41:42; Ps. 102:26; Rev. 19:13.
8. 1 Kings 10:5; cf. 22:30.
9. Exod. 3:22; 12:35; cf. Acts 20:33.
10. *1741*; Luke 7:25; cf. Isa. 3:18.
11. *4164*; Ezek. 16:18.
12. L-S 420, interwoven with gold; Ps. 44:10.
13. *4185*; 1 Tim. 2:9; cf. Plutarch, *Apophthegmata Laconica* 7.
14. Matt. 27:35; John 19:24.
15. *Arrhaphos* (*729*).
16. Plutarch, *An seni respublica gerenda sit* 26.
17. It was equivalent to the Latin *paludamentum* (military cloak), not *sagum* (coarse woolen blanket).

(emperors).[18] The use of *chlamys* in the passion narrative implies that Christ was arrayed in the cast-off cloak of some high Roman officer.[19] Matthew's use of *kokkinos* (*2847*) confirms this supposition (Matt. 27:28). The *chlamys* was "scarlet," the color worn by Roman officers of rank.[20] The other evangelists described it as "purple,"[21] but this does not affect our conclusion because the "purple" of antiquity was an indefinite color.[22]

Stolē[23] is any stately robe, especially a long sweeping garment that reaches to the feet or a garment that has a train that sweeps the ground. Most frequently a *stolē* was worn by women,[24] which explains the Latin use of *stola* (a long robe worn by women, a noble woman). Among the things that the emperor Marcus Antoninus learned from his tutor, the famous Stoic philosopher Rusticus, was not to stalk about the house in a *stolē*.[25] It was, on the contrary, the custom and pleasure of the scribes to "go around in long robes,"[26] to display themselves before men. *Stolē* is always used to refer to the holy garments of Aaron and his descendants[27] and to refer to any garment of special solemnity, richness, or beauty.[28]

Podērēs[29] designates "a long garment reaching to the ankle."[30] Thus we have *aspis* (*785*) *podērēs*,[31] *podēres endyma*,[32] and *podērēs pōgōn*,[33] which are respectively a shield, a garment, and a beard that reaches to the feet. *Podērēs* differs very little from *stolē*. Indeed the same Hebrew word that is translated *podērēs* in Ezekiel 9:2–3 is translated *stolē* in Ezekiel 10:2 and *stolē hagia* (*40*) in Ezekiel 10:6–7. At the same time, in the list of the high-priestly garments this *stolē* or *stolē hagia* signifies the whole array of the high priest, and the *podērēs* (*chitōn podērēs*)[34] is distinguished from it and refers to only one portion, namely the robe or *chetoneth*.[35]

18. 2 Macc. 12:35.

19. It would have been easy for the mockers to secure such a cloak within the praetorium.

20. In Latin it is *chlamys coccinea* (Lampridius, *Alexandri Severi vita* 40), and in Greek *chlamys periporphyros* (robe edged in purple; Plutarch, *Praecepta gerendae reipublicae* 20).

21. Mark 15:17; John 19:2.

22. Braun, *De vestitutu sacro Hebraeo*, 1:220; Gladstone, *Studies on Homer*, 3:457.

23. From *stellō* (*4724*), our English "stole."

24. The Trojan women are *helkesipeploi* (with dragging robes) in Homer.

25. *Mē en stolē kat' oikon peripatein* (*Meditations* 1.7).

26. Mark 12:38; cf. Luke 20:46.

27. Exod. 28:2; 29:21; "a robe [*stolē*] of honor" in Ecclus. 50:11.

28. "Garment [*stolē*] of ministry" (Exod. 31:10); cf. Esther 6:8, 11; Jon. 3:6; Mark 16:5; Luke 15:22; Rev. 6:11; 7:9.

29. It was naturalized in ecclesiastical Latin as *podēris* (of which the second syllable is short).

30. It is properly an adjective and is equivalent to the Latin *talaris* (belonging to the ankles).

31. Xenophon, 6.2, 10. It is equal to *thyreos* (*2375*; Eph. 6:16).

32. *1742*; Wisd. of Sol. 18:24.

33. L-S 1560, beard; Plutarch, *Quomodo adulator ab amico internoscatur* 7.

34. Plutarch called it this in his strangely inaccurate chapter about the Jewish festivals (*Septem sapientium convivium* 4.6.6).

35. Exod. 28:2, 4; Ecclus. 45:7–8.

himation

chitōn
himatismos
chlamys
stolē
podērēs

Other words that might be included in this group are *esthēs*,[36] *esthēsis*,[37] and *endyma*,[38] but it would be difficult to assign each of these a distinct meaning.

36. 2066; Luke 23:11.
37. 2067, Luke 24:4.
38. Matt. 22:12.

51

euchē (2171) — *Vow*
proseuchē (4335) — *Prayer*
deēsis (1162) — *Request*
enteuxis (1783) — *Intercession*
eucharistia (2169) — *Thanksgiving*
aitēma (155) — *Petition*
hiketēria (2428) — *Supplication*

Four of these words occur together in 1 Timothy 2:1, and as Flacius Illyricus justly observed: "Which group of words I far from doubt Paul brings together not by chance."[1] I propose to consider these words and the larger group to which they belong.

In the New Testament, *euchē* is used once to refer to a prayer (James 5:15) and twice to refer to vows (Acts 18:18; 21:23).[2] Origen[3] has a long discussion on the distinction between *euchē* and *proseuchē* and between *euchesthai* (2172) and *proseuchesthai* (4336), but he only notes the obvious: the concept of the vow or dedicated thing is more common in *euchē* and *euchesthai* than is the

1. *Clavis*, see under the word *oratio*.
2. Cf. Plato (*Leges* 801a): "Vows [*euchai*] are requests from the gods."
3. *De oratione* 2, 3, 4.

euchē
proseuchē
deēsis
enteuxis
eucharistia
aitēma
hiketēria

concept of prayer. A more interesting treatment of the words and the difference between them may be found in Gregory of Nyssa.[4]

Proseuchē and *deēsis* often occur together in the New Testament[5] and in the Septuagint,[6] and many attempts (mostly unsuccessful) have been made to distinguish them. For example, Grotius argued that they are respectively the Latin *precatio* and *deprecatio*; the first seeks to obtain good, the second to avert evil. Augustine[7] observed that this distinction between *precatio* and *deprecatio* had almost disappeared in his day. Theodoret anticipated Grotius and explained *proseuchē* as "requests for good things" and *deēsis* as "supplication brought for deliverance from some distressing things."[8] Gregory of Nazianzus said: "Think of supplication [*deēsin*] as the request for what is lacking." This arbitrary distinction, however, is not supported by the words or their usage. Calvin more correctly understood *proseuchē*[9] as "prayer in general" and *deēsis*[10] as "prayer for particular benefits": "*Proseuchē* is the entire genus of prayer, *deēsis* is when a specific thing is requested—as genus and species." Bengel's distinction amounts to nearly the same thing: "*Deēsis* (from *dei* [it is necessary]) is an imploring for a favor in a certain particular need; *proseuchē* (*oratio*) is through any presentation of wishes and desires before God."

Although Calvin and Bengel correctly noted one point of distinction between the words, they failed to observe that *proseuchē* is restricted to sacred uses. *Proseuchē* always refers to prayer *to God*; *deēsis* is not used with such a restriction. Fritzsche rightly argued:

> *Hē proseuchē* and *hē deēsis* differ as *precatio* [prayer] and *rogatio* [entreaty]. *Proseuchesthai* and *hē proseuchē* are sacred words, for we pray [*precamur*] to God; *deisthai* and *hē deēsis* at times are used for a sacred matter and at times for secular things, for we can ask both God and human beings.[11]

It is the same distinction that we find between the English *prayer*[12] and *petition*.[13]

Enteuxis is used in the New Testament only in 1 Timothy 2:1 and 4:5,[14] and once in the Apocrypha (2 Macc. 4:8). The Authorized Version's "intercession" is an unsatisfactory translation because of our current under-

4. *De oratione dominica orationes* 2, at the beginning.
5. Phil. 4:6; Eph. 6:18; 1 Tim. 2:1; 5:5.
6. Ps. 6:10; Dan. 9:21, 23; cf. 1 Macc. 7:37.
7. His treatment of the more important words of this group (*Epistulae* 149, parr. 12–16; cf. Bishop Taylor, *Preface to Apology for Set Forms of Liturgy*, par. 31) yielded interesting but few definite or valuable results.
8. This last definition is a reference to Aristotle (*Rhetorica* 2.7): "Supplications [*deēseis*] are the desires for those things in particular which are accompanied with grief if they do not materialize."
9. It is equivalent to *precatio*.
10. It is equivalent to *rogatio*.
11. On Rom. 10:1.
12. Though too often it is debased to mundane uses.
13. It is the same as the difference in German between *Gebet* (prayer) and *Bitte* (petition).
14. But *entynchanein* (1793) occurs four or five times.

standing of this word. *Enteuxis* does not necessarily refer to prayer in relation to others, as it now does, to a pleading that is either for them or against them (in 1 Tim. 4:5 this meaning is impossible).[15] It certainly cannot refer only to a pleading against our enemies, as Theodoret's words ("*enteuxis* is an accusation against those who do wrong"[16]) imply. Hesychius defined *enteuxis* as "a request for vindication in behalf of someone." But as its connection with *entynchanein*[17] implies, it refers to free, intimate prayer that boldly draws near to God.[18] When the Authorized Version was made, "intercession" did not have its current limited meaning of prayer *for others* (see Jer. 27:18; 36:25). The Vulgate uses *postulationes* (demands), but Augustine[19] preferred *interpellationes* (appeals) because it emphasized the *parrhēsia* (3954; the freedom and boldness of access) that constitutes the fundamental meaning of *enteuxis*.[20] Origen[21] also understood boldness of approach to God and asking him for some great thing (he cites Josh. 10:12) to be the fundamental concepts of *enteuxis*. *Enteuxis* might mean more than this, however, for Plato used it to refer to a possible encounter with pirates.[22]

In the Authorized Version, *eucharistia* is translated "thankfulness" (Acts 24:3), "giving of thanks" (1 Cor. 14:16), "thanks" (Rev. 4:9), and "thanksgiving" (Phil. 4:6). *Eucharistia* is rarely used outside the New Testament, except in sacred Greek. We will not discuss the special meaning the Greek *eucharistia* and the English *eucharist* have acquired from Holy Communion, the church's most important act of thanksgiving for all the benefits she has received from God. Regarded as one manner of prayer, *eucharistia* expresses what should always be present in our devotions: the grateful acknowledgment of past mercies as distinct from seeking future ones.[23] This aspect of prayer will exist in heaven (Rev. 4:9; 7:12), being larger, deeper, and fuller there, since only there will the redeemed know how much they owe to their Lord. In the very nature of things, all other forms of prayer will cease, because all other prayers will have come to fruition.

Aitēma occurs twice in the New Testament in the sense of "a petition of men *to God*," both times in the plural (Phil. 4:6; 1 John 5:15). It is not, however, restricted to this meaning (Luke 23:24; Esther 5:7; Dan. 6:7). In a *proseuchē* of any length there will probably be many *aitēmata*, because they make up the several requests of the *proseuchē*. For example, in the Lord's Prayer there are seven *aitēmata*, though some have regarded the first three as

15. It is incorrect to translate *di' enteuxeōs* in 2 Macc. 4:8 as "by intercession." This phrase probably refers to a confidential interview between Jason and Antiochus.

16. On Rom. 11:2. Theodoret failed to observe that "against" is part of the meaning of *kata*.

17. "To fall in with a person," or "to draw close to him so as to enter into familiar speech and communion with him" (Plutarch, *Conjugalia praecepta* 13).

18. Gen. 18:23; Wisd. of Sol. 8:21; cf. Philo, *Quod deterius potiori insidiari soleat* 25; "supplications and loud shouting" in Plutarch, *Phocion* 17.

19. *Epistulae* 149, parr. 12–16.

20. *Interpellare* (to interrupt another in speaking) always implied forwardness and freedom.

21. *De oratione* 14.

22. *Republic* 298d.

23. Phil. 4:6; Eph. 5:20; 1 Thess. 5:18; 1 Tim. 2:1.

euchē
proseuchē
deēsis
enteuxis
eucharistia
aitēma
hiketēria

euchai and only the last four as *aitēmata*. Witsius stated: "A petition is a part of a prayer, so that if you call the entire Lord's Prayer a prayer, indeed its individual parts or requests are petitions."[24]

Hiketēria, when used with *rhabdos* (4464) or *elaia* (1636),[25] was originally an adjective that gradually acquired substantival power and appeared alone. Plutarch explained *hiketēria* as "a branch from the sacred olive bound with white wool"[26]—the olive branch encased in white wool and held up by the suppliant as a token of his character.[27] A deprecatory letter that Antiochus Epiphanes is said to have written on his deathbed to the Jews is described as "having the position of a supplication [*hiketērias*]."[28] Agrippa designated his letter to Caligula as "a writing which I offer for a supplication [*hiketērias*]."[29] It is easy to trace the steps by which this symbol of supplication came to signify the supplication itself. Indeed, the only time *hiketēria* is used in the New Testament (Heb. 5:7), it is joined with *deēsis* and refers to the supplication itself.[30]

For the most part, however, these words do not refer to different kinds of prayer but to different aspects of prayer. Witsius stated:

> It seems to me that one and the same thing is designated by various names for the various aspects involved. Our prayers are called *deēseis* inasmuch as by them we make known our needs, for *deesthai* [*1163*] is "to stand in need"; they are *proseuchai* inasmuch as they contain our *solemn vows—aitēmata* in that they bring our *petitions* and desires—*enteuxeis* in that God allows us to approach him without fear and with self-confidence and on *friendly terms*, for *enteuxis* is a conference and gathering of *friends*—that *eucharistia* is an *act of thanks* for benefits already received is a fact too well-known to be reminded.[31]

24. *De Oratione Dominica*.

25. Or when used with other words such as *hilastērion* (*2435*), *thysiastērion* (*2379*), *dikastērion* (L-S 429, law court), and words of the same termination (see Lobeck, *Pathos sermonis Graeci*, p. 281).

26. *Theseus* 18. Cf. Wyttenbach, *Animadversiones in Plutarchum*, 13:89; and Wunder on Sophocles, *Oedipus tyrannus* 3.

27. Aeschylus, *Eumenides* 43, 44; cf. Virgil: "He extends with his hand a branch of peace-bearing olive. . . . He wished to extend branches adorned with a fillet" (*Aeneid* 8.116, 128; cf. 11.101).

28. 2 Macc. 9:18.

29. Philo, *Legatio ad Gaium* 36.

30. This is often true elsewhere (Job 41:3 [40:27 in LXX]; Polybius, 3.112.8).

31. *De Oratione Dominica* par. 4. On the Hebrew correlatives to the several words of this group see Vitringa, *De synagoga* 3.2.13.

52

asynthetos (802) *aspondos* (786)

Covenant Breaker Irreconcilable Implacable

Asynthetos occurs only once in the New Testament (Rom. 1:31) and several times in the Septuagint (Jer. 3:8–11). *Aspondos*, which is not used in the Septuagint, occurs only in 2 Timothy 3:3 in the New Testament. The best critical editions omit it from Romans 1:31, where it appears in some manuscripts.

The distinction between the scriptural uses of *asynthetos* and *aspondos* is not difficult to explain, but it is questionable whether *asynthetos* has exactly this meaning anywhere else. In its extrascriptural uses, *asynthetos* is frequently united with *haplous* (573) or with *akratos*,[1] and has the passive sense of "not put together" or "not made up of several parts."[2] Paul used *asynthetoi* in an active sense to refer to those who are in covenant and treaty with others but who refuse to abide by these covenants and treaties.[3]

1. *194*; Plutarch, *De communibus notitiis contra Stoicos* 48.

2. This is evidently its sense in the Vulgate, which translates it *incompositus* (not compounded). This explains the "dissolute" of the Rheims Version.

3. "Not abiding by the treaties" (Hesychius); "by no means holding fast to the agreements" (Erasmus); in German *bundbrüchig* (covenant breaking), not *unverträglich* (irreconcilable) as Tittmann maintains; "covenant breakers" in the Authorized Version. The word is associated with *astathmētos* (L-S 260, unstable) by Demosthenes, *De falsa legatione* 383.

asynthetos
aspondos

Worse than the *dysdialytoi*,[4] who are only "hard to be reconciled," the *aspondoi* are the absolutely irreconcilable[5]—those who will not be *atoned*, or set at one. They are at war and refuse to lay aside their enmity or to listen to terms of accommodation.[6] Plutarch opposed *dysdialytoi* and *eudiallaktos*.[7] The phrase *implacable* [*aspondoi*] *and unannounced war* is proverbial in Greek.[8] Thus "an unannounced war" does not refer to a war that is not duly announced by the authorities but to a war where the "the communications of war" (Virgil) are wholly suspended—no herald or flag of truce is allowed to pass between the parties, no terms of reconciliation are heard.[9] The word also appears in this sense in the phrases *implacable* [*aspondos*] *battle and irreconcilable strife*,[10] *unappeasable grudge*,[11] *implacable* [*aspondos*] *enmity*,[12] and *an implacable* [*aspondos*] *god*.[13]

Asynthetos presumes the existence of a state of peace that such people unrighteously interrupt, and *aspondos* presumes a state of war that the *aspondoi* refuse to bring to an equitable close. Calvin missed the force of each word and translated *aspondoi* as *foedifragi* (treaty breakers) and *asynthetoi* as *insociabiles* (incompatible). Theodoret made a similar mistake when he wrote: "*Asynthetoi* are those who welcome an unsociable and evil life; *aspondoi* are those who transgress fearlessly what has been agreed."[14] The proper equivalents may be found by reversing the meanings ascribed to these words by Calvin and Theodoret.

Additional agreement and confirmation of the meanings of these words may be found in the distinction that Ammonius drew between *synthēkē*[15] and *spondē*.[16] *Synthēkē* assumes peace because it is a further agreement, perhaps a treaty of alliance between those already on generally amicable terms. Thus there was a *synthēkē* between the several states that recognized the leadership of Sparta in the Peloponnesian War; at the end of the war, each state was to have the same territory with which it began the war.[17] But *spondē* (truce)—more often in the plural—refers to a war of which *spondē* is the cessation, though it may only be a temporary armistice.[18] It is true that a *synthēkē*

4. Aristotle, *Ethica Nicomachea* 4.5, 10.

5. "Implacable [*aspondoi*] and irreconcilable" in Philo, *Quis rerum divinarum heres sit* 50.

6. "Unappeasable, who once injured do not allow reconciliation" (Estius); *unversöhnlich* (irreconcilable) in German and "implacable" in the Authorized Version.

7. L-S 709, easy to reconcile; *De Alexandri magni fortuna aut virtute* 4.

8. Demosthenes, *De corona* 79; Philo, *De praemiis et poenis* 15; Lucian, *Revivescentes sive piscator* 36.

9. This type of war was waged by the Carthaginians with their rebellious mercenaries in the interval between the first and second Punic Wars.

10. Aristaenetus, 2, 14.

11. Nicander, *Theriaca* 367; quoted by Blomfield, *Agamemnon*, p. 285.

12. Plutarch, *Pericles* 30.

13. Euripides, *Alcestis* 431.

14. On Rom. 1:31.

15. L-S 1717, treaty.

16. L-S 1629, truce.

17. Thucydides, 5.31.

18. Homer, *Iliad* 2.341.

(treaty) may be attached to a *spondē* (truce) as terms of alliance consequent on terms of peace. In this sense *spondē* and *synthēkē* are used together in Thucydides (4.18), but they are different things. There *spondē* refers to a cessation of war, to a state of peace, to a truce; *synthēkē* adds to this the idea of a further agreement or alliance. *Eusynthetos*[19] could be the exact opposite of *asynthetos*, but it is not found with that meaning in our lexicons or in any Greek author. However, *eusynthesia*[20] is found in Greek literature, *asynthesia*[21] in the Septuagint (Jer. 3:7), and *athesia*[22] often in Polybius (2.32).

19. L-S 734, easy to deal with.
20. L-S 734, observance of treaties.
21. L-S 265, breach of covenant.
22. L-S 31, faithlessness, fickleness.

53

makrothymia (3115) — Long Suffering, Patience

hypomonē (5281) — Endurance

anochē (463) — Forbearance

Makrothymia and *hypomonē* are used together in Colossians 1:11.[1] Chrysostom distinguished them in the following way. *Makrothymei* (3114), he argued, refers to a man who has power to avenge himself but who refrains from doing so; *hypomenei* (5278) refers to a man who must endure, either patiently or impatiently, and who virtuously chooses the former. Chrysostom concluded by arguing that Christians usually would be called to exercise the former virtue among themselves (1 Cor. 6:7) and the latter in their dealings with those outside the church. He wrote:

> *Makrothymia* is toward one another and *hypomonē* is toward those outside, for a person *makrothymei* toward those against whom it is possible also to avenge himself, and *hypomenei* toward those against whom it is not possible to avenge himself.

In the light of Hebrews 12:2–3, however, this distinction cannot be maintained. In Hebrews 12:2–3, *hypomenē* is ascribed to Jesus, who willingly bore,

1. They also occur together in the same context in 2 Cor. 6:4, 6; 2 Tim. 3:10; James 5:10–11; cf. Clement of Rome, 58; Ignatius, *Epistulae* 3.

makrothymia

hypomonē
anochē

but not because he could not avoid bearing; in fact he could have summoned twelve legions of angels to his aid had he wanted to do so (Matt. 26:53). Perhaps, then, a closer examination will reveal a more satisfactory distinction between these words.

Makrothymia belongs to a later stage of Greek. Although it occurs in the Septuagint, it does not have the exact sense there (or elsewhere) that it does in the New Testament. Thus in Isaiah 57:15 *makrothymia* refers to a patient holding out under trial (more like *hypomonē*), not to long suffering under provocation.[2] Plutarch[3] also used *makrothymia* in a different sense from its New Testament usage. Plutarch used *anexikakia*[4] to refer to the long suffering *of men* and *megalopatheia*[5] to refer to the long suffering *of God*. In ecclesiastical Latin, *makrothymia* is translated by *longanimitas* (long suffering), which the Rheims Version tried to introduce into English in the form of "longanimity."[6] Instead we preferred "long suffering"—a long holding out of the mind before it gives way to action or passion (generally passion)—or the Pauline "bearing with one another in love" (Eph. 4:2). Anger is usually, but not universally, the passion that is repressed. The *makrothymos* (cf. *3115* and *3116*) is one who is "slow to anger," and the word is exchanged for "controlling anger" (Prov. 16:32) and is set over against "a wrathful man" (15:18). It is not necessarily anger that is repressed. When the historian of the Maccabees described how the Romans had won the world "by their policy and their *patience*" (1 Macc. 8:4), *makrothymia* refers to the Roman persistency that would never make peace under defeat. The true antithesis of that sense of *makrothymia* is *oxythymia*.[7]

But *hypomonē*[8] is usually known in heathen ethics as *karteria*[9] or as *karterēsis*.[10] Following some heathen moralists, Clement of Alexandria described *hypomonē* as "the knowledge of what things are to be borne and what are not."[11] *Hypomonē* is equivalent to the Latin *perseverantia* (perseverance) and *patientia* (patience)[12] taken together, or, more accurately, to *tolerantia*

2. Cf. Jer. 15:15; 1 Macc. 8:4, where its use is also unlike its New Testament use.

3. *Lucullus* 32.

4. Cf. 420; *De capienda ex inimicis utilitate* 9; cf. Epictetus, *Enchiridion* 10.

5. L-S 1087, patience; *De sera numinis vindicta* 5. In fact he may have coined this word.

6. This attempt failed, though there is no reason why "longanimity" should not have had the same success as "magnanimity." It was allowed and used by both Jeremy Taylor and Bishop Hall.

7. L-S 1235, quickness to anger. This word belonged to the best time of the language, and was employed by Euripides (*Andromacha* 729), as *oxythymos* was by Aristotle (*Rhetorica* 2.12; cf. *oxycholos* [L-S 1237, quick to anger] in Solon).

8. Chrysostom called it the "queen of virtues."

9. Cf. *2594*. If we accept the *Definitions* ascribed to Plato, then there is a slight distinction between these two words: "*Karteria* is the endurance of grief for the sake of the noble; *hypomonē* is the endurance of toils for the sake of the noble." The words are joined by Plutarch, *Apophthegmata Laconica* 2.

10. L-S 880, patient endurance.

11. *Stromata* 2.18; cf. Plutarch, *Placita philosophorum* 4.23.

12. According to Cicero: "*Patientia* is the voluntary and long endurance of arduous and difficult things for the sake of honor and service; *perseverantia* is the stable and constant persisting in

(endurance).

> In this noble word *hypomonē* there always appears (in the New Testament) a background of courage (cf. Plato, *Theaetetus* 177b, where "to endure courageously" is opposed to "to flee cowardly"); it does not mark merely the *endurance*, the *sustinentia* (Vulg.), or even the *patientia* (Clarom.), but the *perseverantia*, the *brave* patience with which the Christian contends against the various hindrances, persecutions, and temptations that befall him in his conflict with the inward and outward world.[13]

Although it comes from a more noble root, *hypomonē* is the "stout endurance" of Archilochus.[14] Cocceius described *hypomonē* in this way:

> *Hypomonē* is concerned with contempt for the goods of this world and in the brave acceptance of afflictions with the giving of thanks—especially with steadfast loyalty and esteem—so that in no way does it allow itself to be shaken or to be weakened or to be hindered from performing its own work and task.[15]

We may now distinguish *makrothymia* and *hypomonē* in a way that will be valid wherever they occur. *Makrothymia* refers to patience with respect to persons, *hypomonē* with respect to things. A man is *makrothymei* if he has to relate to injurious persons and does not allow himself to be provoked by them or to burst into anger (2 Tim. 4:2). A man is *hypomenei* if he is under a great siege of trials and he bears up and does not lose heart or courage.[16] Therefore we should speak of the *makrothymia* of David (2 Sam. 16:10–13) and the *hypomonē* of Job (James 5:11). Although both virtues are ascribed to the saints, only *makrothymia* is ascribed to God. There is a beautiful account of God's *makrothymia* in Wisdom of Solomon 12:20, though the word itself is not used. Men may tempt and provoke God, and he may and does display an infinite *makrothymia* with regard to them.[17] God allows men to resist him; he respects their wills, even when they are used to fight him. Things, however, cannot resist God or be a burden to him. Therefore *hypomonē* is not a characteristic of God nor is it ascribed to him.[18] When God is called "the God of patience" (*hypomonēs*, Rom. 15:5) this does not mean "God whose own attribute is *hypomonē*" but "God who gives *hypomonē* to his servants and saints."[19] In the same way "the God of grace" (1 Pet. 5:10) refers to God who is the Au-

---

a matter duly considered" (*De inventione rhetorica* 2.54). Cf. *Tusculanae disputationes* 4.24, where he deals with *fortitudo* (courage); and Augustine, *Quaestiones* 83, quaestio 31.

13. Ellicott on 1 Thess. 1:3.

14. *Fragmenta* 8.

15. On James 1:12. For some other definitions, see the article *Geduld* (endurance) in Herzog's *Real Encyclopädie*.

16. Rom. 5:3; 2 Cor. 1:6; cf. Clement of Rome, *Epistula* 1, par. 5.

17. Exod. 34:6; Rom. 2:4; 1 Pet. 2:20.

18. As Chrysostom correctly observed. Yet see Augustine, *De patientia*, par. 1.

19. Tittmann, p. 194: *Theos tēs hypomonēs* (God who bestows patience); cf. Ps. 70:5, LXX.

makrothymia

hypomonē
anochē

thor of grace, and "the God of peace" (Heb. 13:20) refers to God who is the Author of peace.[20]

Anochē is commonly used in the plural in classical Greek and usually refers to a truce or suspension of arms, the Latin *indutiae* (armistice). *Anochē* is translated "forbearance" in both of its New Testament occurrences (Rom. 2:4; 3:25). Origen distinguished *anochē* and *makrothymia* in this way:

> Forbearance [*anochē*] seems to differ from patience [*makrothymia*] in this respect, that those who transgress in weakness rather than intentionally are said to be *propped up* [*sustentari*], but those who with an evil mind rejoice as it were in their sins must be said to be *carried with patience* [*ferri patienter*].[21]

Origen failed to note that the distinction between *anochē* and *makrothymia* is not merely one of degree. The *anochē* is temporary and transient, like our "truce"; it has its own provisional character, and after a certain period of time, unless other conditions intervene, it will pass away. This may also be true of *makrothymia* in general and certainly it is true of the divine *makrothymia* (Luke 13:9). But this trait is not inherent in *makrothymia*. We can imagine a *makrothymia* that is unworthy of honor and that would *never* be exhausted, but *anochē* implies its own provisional character. Fritzsche distinguished *anochē* and *makrothymia* this way:

> *Hē anochē* denotes *indulgence*, when without pursuing your right continuously, you give time for reflecting to the one who has harmed you; *hē makrothymia* signifies *clemency*, when tempering your anger you do not immediately avenge the wrong, but you leave an opportunity for repenting to the one who has transgressed.[22]

Elsewhere Fritzche made an even finer distinction: "*Hē anochē* is that one closes the eyes to others' transgressions, not that one refrains from punishing another's transgression, which is *makrothymia*."[23] It is most appropriately employed in Romans 3:26 in relation to the *paresis* (3929) *hamartiōn*[24] that occurred before the atoning death of Christ, as contrasted with the *aphesis* (859) *hamartiōn* (forgiveness of sins) that resulted from his death.[25] This forbearance or suspension of God's wrath, this truce with the sinner does not imply that God's wrath will not finally be executed. God's wrath will certainly be exercised unless the sinner meets the new conditions of repentance and obedience (Luke 13:9; Rom. 2:3–6).[26]

20. Cf. *Theos tēs elpidos* (the God of hope; Rom. 15:13).
21. *Commentary on the Romans* 2.4. The Greek original is lost.
22. On Rom. 2:4.
23. On Rom. 3:26.
24. 266; the passing over of sins in Rom. 3:25.
25. See section 33.
26. At the beginning of his first sermon *On the Mercy of the Divine Judgments*, Jeremy Taylor distinguished the two words, though not very sharply.

54

strēniaō (4763) *tryphaō* (5171) *spatalaō* (4684)

Live in Luxury and Pleasure

Although *strēniaō*, *tryphaō*, and *spatalaō* each refer to excess, wanton, dissolute, self-indulgent, prodigal living, they have different shades of meaning.

Strēniaō occurs only twice in the New Testament (Rev. 18:7, 9); *strēnos* (4764) occurs once (Rev. 18:3; cf. 2 Kings 19:28), as does the compound *katastrēniaō* (2691; 1 Tim. 5:11). *Strēniaō* originated in the New or Middle Comedy and was used by Lycophron,[1] Sophilus,[2] and Antiphanes,[3] but was rejected by the Greek purists. Phrynichus claimed that only a madman would use it if he could use *tryphan* instead.[4] Although *tryphan* was preferred in Greek usage, it appears only once in the New Testament (James 5:5), as does *entryphan*.[5] *Tryphan* and *tryphē*[6] belong to the best age and to the most classical writers in the language. Closer examination will show that the words have different meanings and that frequently one could not be used in place of the

1. As quoted in Athenaeus, 10.420b.
2. Ibid. 3.100a.
3. Ibid. 3.127d.
4. Lobeck, *Phrynichus*, p. 381.
5. *1792*; 2 Pet. 2:13.
6. *5172*; Luke 7:25; 2 Pet. 2:13.

other. *Strēnian*[7] correctly refers to the insolence of wealth, to the wantonness and petulance that result from being full from eating.[8] It does not designate luxurious effeminacy, and in fact Pape relates *strēnos* to the Latin *strenuus* (vigorous).[9] *Strēnos* always implies strength or vigor,[10] such as that displayed by the inhabitants of Sodom (Gen. 19:4–9).

Tryphē and *tryphan*,[11] however, do refer to effeminacy or brokenness of spirit through self-indulgence. Thus *tryphē* is related to *chlidē*,[12] *polyteleia*,[13] *malakia*,[14] and *rhathymia*.[15] According to Clement of Alexandria: "For what else is *hē tryphē* than pleasurable gluttony and superfluous excess for the enjoyment of relaxation?"[16] When *tryphē* is used with *hybris*,[17] and when *tryphan* is used with *hybrizein*,[18] they mean "insolence." As Menander said: "They were arrogant where excessive *tryphē* occurred." Occasionally *tryphē* has a good sense and is used to refer to the triumph and exultation of the saints of God.[19] In Genesis 2:15 the garden of Eden is referred to as "a paradise of *tēs tryphēs*."

Spatalan[20] is more closely related to *tryphan*[21] than to *strēnian*, though it inherently refers to wastefulness.[22] Thus Hottinger said: "*Tryphan* concerns delights and exquisite pleasure; *spatalan* concerns extravagance and prodigality." Tittmann wrote: "*Tryphan* is rather the softness of a luxurious life; *spatalan* denotes more wantonness and prodigality." Theile took them in reverse order: "They are compared as preceding and subsequent: to live with excess and then to squander or to live luxuriously and then to live wantonly."

If we have accurately understood the differences between these words, then *spatalan* would correctly be applied to the prodigal son, who wasted his substance in riotous living (Luke 15:13), *tryphan* to the rich man who fared sumptuously every day (Luke 16:19), and *strēnian* to Jeshurun, who grew fat and kicked (Deut. 32:15).

7. It is equivalent to *ataktein* (*812*) in Suidas and to "being haughty because of wealth" in Hesychius.

8. This is similar to the Latin *lascivire* (to be wanton).

9. See too Pott, *Etymologische Forschungen* 2.2.357.

10. German *Uebermuth* (arrogance).

11. This word is related to *thryptein* (L-S 807, to enfeeble) and to *thrypsis* (L-S 808, weakness).

12. L-S 1994, effeminacy; Philo.

13. Cf. *4185*; Plutarch, *Marcellus* 3.

14. *3119*; *Quomodo adolescens poetas audire debeat* 4.

15. L-S 1564, sluggishness; *Marcellus* 21. Cf. Suicer, *Thesaurus* under this word and note the other words to which it is related elsewhere (Plato, 1 *Alcibiades* 122b).

16. *Stromata* 2.20.

17. *5196*; Aristophanes, *Ranae* 21; Strabo, 6.1.

18. *5195*; Plutarch, *Praecepta gerendae reipublicae* 3.

19. Chrysostom, *In Matthaeum* 67, 668; Ps. 35:9; Isa. 66:11; Ezek. 34:13. This is also true of *entryphan* (Isa. 55:2).

20. It occurs only in 1 Tim. 5:6; James 5:5; cf. Ecclus. 21:17; Ezek. 16:49; Amos 6:4 [the last two are instructive passages].

21. The two are associated in James 5:5.

22. It is equivalent to *analiskein* (*355*) in Hesychius, and this is consistent with its derivation from *spaō* (4685) and from *spathaō* (L-S 1623, to squander).

55

thlipsis (2347) *stenochōria* (4730)

Tribulation Affliction Anguish Distress Burden

Thlipsis and *stenochōria* are often used together. In three of the four passages where *stenochōria* occurs in the New Testament, it is associated with *thlipsis*.[1] The verbs *thlibein* (2346) and *stenochōrein*[2] also are used together. Because *stenochōria* always occurs last whenever it is used with *thlipsis*, and because of the antithesis between these words in 2 Corinthians 4:8,[3] *stenochōria* appears to be the stronger of the two words, whatever their difference in meaning.

Thlipsis and *stenochōria* refer to the same thing under different images. *Thlipsis*[4] properly means "pressure."[5] I could have said *angor* (anguish), since

1. Rom. 2:9; 8:35; 2 Cor. 6:4; cf. Deut. 28:55; Isa. 8:22; 30:6.

2. 4729; 2 Cor. 4:8; cf. Lucian, *Nigrinus* 13; Artemidorus, 1.79; 2.37.

3. *Thlibomenoi, all' ou stenochōroumenoi* (hard pressed . . . yet not crushed).

4. It is used with *basanos* (931) in Ezek. 12:18; its synonym *thlimmos* occurs in Exod. 3:9; Deut. 26:7.

5. The Latin is *pressura* (pressure) and *tribulatio* (tribulation). *Tribulatio* is only found in ecclesiastical Latin where it has a metaphorical sense—that which presses upon or burdens the spirit.

Cicero referred to this as "*pressing* grief,"[6] except that the connection of *angor* with the German *Angst* (anguish) and *enge* (narrow or confined)[7] makes it more appropriate to reserve this word for *stenochōria*.

The proper meaning of *stenochōria* is "narrowness of room," "confined space,"[8] and the painfulness that is the result. "Narrow straits" (*aporia stenē*) and *stenochōria* appear together in Isaiah 8:22. Thucydides used *stenochōria* literally (7.70). Sometimes *stenochōria* is used in place of *dyschōria*.[9] Plutarch[10] contrasted *stenochōria* with *anesis* (425). In the Septuagint *stenochōria* refers to the straitness of a siege (Deut. 28:53, 57). It appears in a secondary and metaphorical sense once in the Old Testament—"anguish [*stenochōria*] of spirit" (Wisd. of Sol. 5:3)—which is its only sense in the New Testament. The appropriateness of this image is attested by the frequency with which a state of joy is referred to in the psalms (and elsewhere) as a bringing into a large room.[11] Whether Aquinas intended to provide an etymology (he probably did), he certainly uttered a truth when he said: "Joyfulness is like width."

The literal meaning of *thlipsis* is illustrated by the penalty prescribed by ancient English law for those who refused to plead: they were pressed and crushed to death by heavy weights that were placed on their chests. It was *stenochōria* when Tamerlane, who had vanquished Bajazet, carried him about in an iron cage.[12] Since we do not know if Bajazet suffered because of his narrow confines, perhaps it would be better to refer to the *oubliettes*, in which Louis XI shut up his victims, or to the "little-ease"[13] that was used to torture the Roman Catholics in Queen Elizabeth's reign: "It was of so small dimensions and so constructed that the prisoners could neither stand, walk, sit, nor lie in it at full length."[14] In Romans 2:9 Paul said that both *thlipsis* and *stenochōria* would be the portion of the lost.[15]

6. *Tusculanae disputationes* 4.8.

7. See Grimm, *Wörterbuch*, under the word *Angst*; and Max Müller, *On the Science of Language*, 1861, 1:366.

8. The Latin *angustiae*.

9. L-S 462, lack of room.

10. *Septem sapientium convivium* 5.6.

11. *Platysmos* (cf. *4116*), Ps. 118:5; 2 Sam. 22:20; Ecclus. 47:12; Clement of Rome, *Epistulae* 1, par. 3; Origen, *De oratione* 30; *eurychōria*, Marcus Antoninus, 9.32.

12. If the story is true.

13. *Little-ease* is not in our dictionaries, but it was an early English expression for any place or condition of extreme discomfort.

14. Lingard.

15. On these considerations, see Gerhard, *Loci theologici* 31.6.52.

56

haplous (573)
akeraios (185)

akakos (172)

adolos (97)

Single
Sincere
Harmless
Simple
Good
Pure

Haplous, *akeraios*, *akakos*, and *adolos* refer to the rarest and best Christian virtues, perhaps to the same virtue seen in terms of different images. The meanings of these terms are only slightly different.

Haplous occurs only twice in the New Testament (Matt. 6:22; Luke 11:34), but *haplotēs* (572) occurs seven or eight times, always in Paul's epistles. *Haplōs* (574) occurs only once (James 1:5). It would be impossible to improve on "single,"[1] the translation of the Authorized Version, since it comes from *haploō*[2]—that which is *spread out*, without folds or wrinkles. *Haplous* means exactly the opposite of *polyplokos*[3] in Job 5:13. *Haplous* is

1. See a good note in Fritzsche, *Commentary on the Romans*, 3:64, denying that *haplotēs* ever means "liberality," which often appears in our translation.

2. L-S 191, spread out. It is similar to the Latin *expando* (spread out) and *explico* (unfold).

3. L-S 1441, complex, cunning.

haplous
akeraios
akakos
adolos

equivalent to the Latin *simplex*,[4] which also had an honorable use. This singleness, simplicity, or absence of folds is part of the etymology of *haplous* and is predominant in its meaning "a mind alien to cunning, fraud, pretense, deceit, evil, and the desire to harm others."[5]

This understanding of *haplous* is confirmed by the words with which it is associated: *alēthēs*,[6] *aponēros*,[7] *gennaios*,[8] *akratos*,[9] *monoeidēs*,[10] *asynthetos*,[11] *monotropos*,[12] *saphēs*,[13] *akakos*,[14] and *hygiēs*.[15] And it is even more apparent from the words with which *haplous* is contrasted: *poikilos*,[16] *polyeidēs*,[17] *polytropos*,[18] *peplegmenos*,[19] *diplous*,[20] *epiboulos*,[21] and *pantodapos*.[22] *Haplotēs*[23] is also associated with *eilikrineia*[24] and *akakia*,[25] and in the Septuagint these latter two words are used indiscriminately to translate the Hebrew word that we translate as "integrity" (Ps. 7:8; Prov. 19:1) or "simplicity" (2 Sam. 15:11). *Haplotēs* is associated with *megalopsychia*[26] and with *agathotēs*.[27] It is contrasted with *poikilia*,[28] *polytropia*,[29] *kakourgia*,[30] *kakoētheia*,[31] and *dolos*.[32] Aquila translated the Hebrew *tām*[33] as *haplous*. As with at least one other word of this group (and many others that express the same virtue), *haplous* is often used to refer to a foolish simplicity that is unworthy of the Christian. For in addition

4. This does not mean "without folds" but "one-folded," since *semel* (once) and not *sine* (without) is its first syllable. Cf. the German *einfaltig* (simple); see Donaldson, *Varronianus*, p. 390.

5. Suicer; cf. Herzog, *Real Encyclopädia*, under the article *Einfalt*, 3:723.

6. *227*; Xenophon, *Anabasis* 2.6.22; Plato, *Leges* 5.738e; and often.

7. L-S 210, harmless; Theophrastus.

8. L-S 344, noble; Plato, *Republic* 361b.

9. *194*; Plutarch, *De communibus notitiis contra Stoicos* 48.

10. L-S 1144, one in kind; *De animae procreatione in Timaeo* 21.

11. 802, similar to the Latin *incompositus* (not put together); ibid.; Basil, *Adversus Eunomium* 1.23.

12. L-S 1445, one of a kind; *Homilia in principium proverbiorum* 7.

13. L-S 1586, clear, plain; Alexis, in Meineke's *Fragmenta Comoeda Graeca*, p. 750.

14. Diodorus Siculus, 13.76.

15. *5199*; Demosthenes, *Orationes* 37.969.

16. *4164*; Plato, *Theaetetus* 146d.

17. L-S 1438, of diverse kinds; *Phaedrus* 270d.

18. Cf. *4187*; *Hippias Minor* 364e.

19. *4120*; Aristotle, *Poetica* 13.

20. *1362*; ibid.

21. Cf. *1917*; Xenophon, *Memorabilia* 3.1.6.

22. L-S 1300, of every kind; Plutarch, *Quomodo adulator ab amico internoscatur* 7.

23. See 1 Macc. 1:37.

24. *1505*; 2 Cor. 1:12.

25. Philo, *De opificio mundi* 41.

26. L-S 1088, greatness of soul; Josephus, *Antiquitates Judaicae* 7.13.4.

27. Cf. *18*; Wisd. of Sol. 1:1.

28. Plato, *Republic* 404e.

29. Cf. *4187*.

30. Cf. *2557*; Theophylact.

31. *2550*; Theodoret.

32. *1388*; Aristophanes, *Plutus* 1158.

33. 8535; Gen. 25:27. The Septuagint translates this by *aplastos* (L-S 190, unaffected, natural).

to simplicity, the Christian should be *phronimos* (*5429*) as well (Matt. 10:16; Rom. 16:19). Although Basil the Great[34] used *haplous* in this way, it does not appear in this sense anywhere else in biblical Greek.

Akeraios[35] occurs only three times in the New Testament (Matt. 10:16; Rom. 16:19; Phil. 2:15). A mistaken etymology equated it with *akeratos*[36] and derived it from *a* (*1*) and *keras*,[37] which means "without horn to push or hurt."[38] Thus several times in the Authorized Version *akeraios* is translated "harmless." In each case, however, the translators placed more correct translations in the margin, for example, "simple" (Matt. 10:16) and "sincere" (Phil. 2:15). In Romans 16:19, however, just the opposite is true: "simple" stands in the text with "harmless" in the margin. The fundamental notion of *akeraios*,[39] is the absence of any foreign substance or influence: "The one undefiled by evil, but single and simple."[40] When Philo spoke of the harshly conditioned favor that Caligula granted the Jews, he called it a "favor not unmixed," obviously referring to its etymology. Philo said: "Likewise however, even giving the favor, he did not give it unmixed [*akeraion*], but mingled with it a more painful fear."[41] Wine that is not mixed with water is called *akeraios*,[42] as is unalloyed metal. Plato used *akeraios* with *ablabēs*[43] and with *orthos*.[44] Plutarch associated it with *hygiēs*[45] and contrasted it with *taraktikos*.[46] Clement of Rome[47] compared it with *eilikrinēs* (*1506*). *Akeraios* refers to something in its true and natural condition[48] and in this regard is similar to *holoklēros* (*3648*). The predominant idea of *holoklēros*, however, is completeness; *akeraios* primarily refers to freedom from disturbing elements.

Akakos is used only twice in the New Testament (Rom. 16:18; Heb. 7:26). There are three stages of development in this word's history, two of which are apparent from its New Testament usage; the third is found elsewhere. In Hebrews 7:26 *akakos* is applied to Christ the Lord, so that the absence of all evil implies the presence of all good, and in that passage *akakos* is associated with other noble terms. The Septuagint uses *akakos* in all of its various senses, sometimes employing it in the highest sense to which we just referred. Thus

34. *Epistulae* 58.

35. It does not occur in the Septuagint.

36. L-S 49, without horns.

37. *2768*; cf. *keraizein* (L-S 940, ravage, slaughter) and similar to the Latin *laedere* (to wound) and from *keratizein* (L-S 941, to butt with horns) in the Septuagint.

38. Even Bengel fell into this notion: "*Akeraioi*: without horn, hoof, tooth, sting" (on Matt. 10:16).

39. As of *akēratos*, which has the same derivation from *a* and *kerannymi* (*2767*).

40. *Etymologica magna*.

41. *Legatio ad Gaium* 42.

42. Athenaeus, 2.45.

43. L-S 2, harmless; *Republic* 1.342b.

44. *3717*; *Politicus* 268b.

45. *5199*; *De communibus notitiis contra Stoicos* 31.

46. Cf. *5015, 5016, 5017*; *De defectu oraculorum* 51.

47. *Epistula* 1, par. 2.

48. Polybius, 2.100.4; Josephus, *Antiquitates Judaicae* 1.2.2. This is similar to the Latin *integer* (whole).

haplous
akeraios

akakos

adolos

Job is described as "a person free of evil [*akakos*], genuine, blameless, God-fearing, shunning evil" (Job 2:3). In Job 8:20 the *akakos* is opposed to the *asebēs* (765). In Psalm 25:21 *akakos* is used with *euthēs*,[49] and Plutarch[50] used *akakos* with *sōphrōn* (4998). In the second stage of its development, *akakos* refers to the same absence of harm, but from a negative, not a positive, viewpoint: "a docile [*akakon*] lamb,"[51] "a gentle [*akakos*] and young girl,"[52] and "gentle [*akakos*] and unmeddling."[53] This use of *akakos* does not occur in the New Testament. It is easy to trace the progression of *akakos* to its third stage of development, where it came to mean "easily deceived," then "*too* easily deceived,' and finally *akakia* comes to refer to excessive simplicity.[54] Someone who means no evil to others often fears no evil from others; having truth in his own heart, he believes truth exists in everyone's heart. This noble quality in our world can be pushed too far—where with regard to malice we are to be "babes, but in understanding be mature" (1 Cor. 14:20) and "simple concerning evil" yet "wise in what is good" (Rom. 16:19).[55] The use of *akakos* in Romans 16:18 refers to a confidence that is degenerating into a readiness to be deceived and to be led away from the truth.[56] For a somewhat contemptuous use of *akakos*, see Plato[57] and Plutarch: "The wise do not praise the simplicity [*akakian*] which is embellished by inexperience with evil, but regard it as silliness and ignorance of what it is especially fitting to know."[58] Especially noteworthy are the words that the author of *Second Alcibiades* puts into the mouth of Socrates:

> Those who have a large portion of folly we term crazed, and those with a slightly smaller portion silly and stupid; but of the people who wish to use euphemistic names some call them high-minded, others refer to them as good-hearted, and still others speak of them as simple [*akakous*] and inexperienced and senseless.[59]

Shakespeare had the rogue Autolycus say: "What a fool Honesty is, and Trust, his sworn brother, a very simple gentleman."[60]

The second and third stages of *akakos* are separated by so fine a line (and often run into one another), that it is not surprising that some see only two

49. L-S 715, righteous.
50. *Quomodo quis suos in virtute sentiat profectus* 7.
51. Jer. 11:19.
52. Plutarch, *Mulierum virtutes* 23.
53. Demosthenes, *Orationes* 47.1164.
54. Aristotle, *Rhetorica* 2.12.
55. Cf. Jeremy Taylor's Sermon *On Christian Simplicity, Works*, Eden's edition, 4:609.
56. "Astonished and simple [*akakoi*]," Plutarch, *De recta ratione audiendi* 7; cf. Wisd. of Sol. 4:12; Prov. 1:4, where Solomon declares the purpose of his proverbs: "to give prudence to the simple [*akakois*]"; 8:5; and in 14:15 Solomon wrote: "The simple [*akakos*] believes every word."
57. *Timaeus* 91d, with Stallbaum's note.
58. *Demosthenes* 1.
59. 140c.
60. *Winter's Tale*, act iv, sc. 3.

stages, rather than three, in the development of this word. Basil the Great, for example, wrote:

Single
Sincere
Harmless
Simple
Good
Pure

> We think of *akakian* in two ways: either as the estrangement from sin, kept straight by reason through long attention to and practice of good endeavors, as cutting away any root of evil and maintaining its complete absence—such an appellation we accept for one who is *akakos*; or *akakia* is the thus far inexperience with evil, because of a young age frequently or because of the pursuance of certain types of life, some of which are not affected by exposure to certain evils—like some of those who dwell in the countryside, not acquainted with the vices of commerce nor with duplicity in the courtroom. Such people we call *akakous*—not as being separated from evil by choice, but as not yet having been exposed to evil habits.[61]

It is apparent that *akakos* has run the same course and has the same moral history as *chrēstos* (5543), *haplous*, *euēthēs*,[62] and as the French *bon* (good)[63] and *bonhomie*,[64] and as the English "silly," "simple," "daft," and as the German *einfaltig* (silly, foolish) and *gütig* (good-natured).

Adolos, the last word of this beautiful group, occurs only once in the New Testament (1 Pet. 2:2) and is translated "sincere" in the Authorized Version—"the *sincere* milk of the word."[65] The New King James Version translates it "pure." *Adolos* is not used in the Septuagint or in the Apocrypha, but *adolōs*[66] appears once in the latter (Wisd. of Sol. 7:13). Plato used *adolos* with *hygiēs*[67] and Philemon with *gnēsios*.[68] It is difficult, if not impossible, to ascribe an ethical province to *adolos* that is not already occupied by other words in this group. *Adolos* designates the same excellent virtue under another image: if the *akakos* has nothing of the serpent's *tooth*, the *adolos* has nothing of the serpent's *guile*; if *akakos* means "unwillingness to hurt and lack of malice," then *adolos* means "the absence of fraud and deceit." It is like Nathaniel "in whom is no guile" (John 1:47). We conclude that just as the *akakos*[69] contains no harmfulness, so the *adolos*[70] has no guile, the *akeraios*[71] contains no foreign mixture, and the *haplous*[72] has no folds.

61. *Homilia in principium proverbiorum* 11.
62. L-S 713, good-hearted. It is often used with this word, as by Diodorus Siculus, 5.66.
63. Thus Jean le Bon becomes "John the heedless."
64. Good-nature, simplicity, credulity.
65. The early English use of "sincere" meant unmixed, unadulterated, and for that "milk of the word" which would *not* be "sincere," cf. 2 Cor. 4:2.
66. L-S 24, without fraud.
67. *Epistulae* 8.355e.
68. *1103*; Meineke, *Fragmenta comicorum Graecorum*, p. 843.
69. As the Latin *innocens* (harmless).
70. As the Latin *sincerus* (sincere).
71. As the Latin *integer* (whole).
72. As the Latin *simplex* (single).

57

chronos (5550) *kairos* (2540)

Time Season Opportunity

Chronoi and *kairoi* occur together several times in the New Testament, always in the plural (Acts 1:7; 1 Thess. 5:1), as well as in the Septuagint and in the Apocrypha.[1] Grotius thought that the difference between *chronos* and *kairos* was that the *chronoi* were longer than the *kairoi*. According to him: "*Chronoi* are larger divisions of time as years, *kairoi* are smaller divisions as months and days."[2] This distinction, if not inaccurate, is certainly insufficient and fails to touch the heart of the matter.

Chronos is simply time as such or the succession of moments.[3] Plato called it a "moving representation of eternity,"[4] and Philo called it a "dimension of the movement of the heavens."[5] According to Severianus: "*Chronos* is length, *kairos* is favorable opportunity."[6] *Kairos*[7] is time as it brings forth its

1. Wisd. of Sol. 7:18; 8:8 (both instructive passages); Dan 2:12, and in the singular in Eccles. 3:1; Dan 7:12 (but in this last passage the reading is doubtful).

2. On Acts 1:7. Cf. Bengel: "*Kairoi* are parts of *chronoi*."

3. Matt. 25:19; Heb. 4:7; Rev. 10:6.

4. *Timaeus* 37d; cf. Hooker, *Ecclesia politica* 5.69.

5. *De opificio mundi* 7. It is the German *Zeitraum* (time-period) as distinguished from *Zeitpunkt* (point in time); cf. Demosthenes (1357), where both words occur.

6. Suicer, *Thesaurus* under this word.

7. It is derived from *keirō* (2751), as the Latin *tempus* (time) comes from *temno* (to cut).

several births: "the time [*kairos*] of harvest" (Matt. 13:30), "the season [*kairos*] of figs" (Mark 11:13); Christ died "in due time (*kata kairon*, Rom. 5:6). Ecclesiastes 3:1–8 is actually a miniature essay on the word.[8] *Chronos* embraces all possible *kairoi*, and since it is the more inclusive term, it is frequently used where *kairos* would have been equally suitable, though the reverse is not true. In *chronos tou tekein* (the time of bringing forth, Luke 1:57) and *plērōma* (*4138*) *tou chronou* (Gal. 4:4), which refers to the fullness or to the ripeness of time for the manifestation of the Son of God, we would have expected *tou kairou* or *tōn kairōn* instead.[9] The "times [*chronoi*] of restoration" (Acts 3:21) are identical with the "times [*kairoi*] of refreshing," which are mentioned in verse 19. Thus it is possible to speak of the *kairos chronou*, as Sophocles did: "May reason preclude from you the opportune moment [*kairon*] of time [*chronou*],"[10] but not of the *chronos kairou*. Olympiodorus remarked: "*Chronos* is the interval at which something is done; *kairos* is the time [*kronos*] suitable for the action. Thus *chronos* can be *kairos*, but *kairos* is not *chronos*; it is the appropriateness [*eukairia*] of what is done occurring in time [*chronō*]."[11] According to Ammonius: "*Kairos* indicates quality of time [*chronou*]; *chronos* indicates quantity." *Eukairos chronos* (a fitting time) occurs in a fragment of Sosipatros.[12]

Consequently, when the apostles asked, "Lord, will you at this time restore the kingdom to Israel?" he answered: "It is not for you to know times or seasons" (Acts 1:6–7). "The times" (*chronoi*) are (in Augustine's words) "the very divisions of time," that is, the duration of the church's history; but "the seasons" (*kairoi*) are the joints or articulations in these times, the critical epoch-making periods foreordained by God[13] or the "preappointed times" in Acts 17:26.[14] *Kairoi* refers to the gradual and perhaps unobserved ripening and maturing process that results in grand decisive events that close one period of history as they inaugurate another. Examples of such decisive events in history include the noisy end of the old Jewish dispensation, the recognition of Christianity as the religion of the Roman Empire, the conversion of the Germanic tribes settled within the limits of the empire and the conversion of those outside of it, the great revival that occurred with the first institution of the Mendicant orders, and more importantly the Reformation. The most decisive event of all will be the second coming of the Lord in glory (Dan. 7:22).

There is not an adequate Latin word for *kairoi*. According to Augustine, who complained of this deficiency:

8. See Keil on this passage.
9. This last phrase actually occurs in Eph. 1:10.
10. *Electra* 1292.
11. Suicer, *Thesaurus* under this word.
12. Quoted by Athenaeus, 9.22.
13. *Kairoi protetagmenoi*.
14. Cf. Augustine, *De doctrina Christiana* 11.13, who calls God "the controller of time."

Greek speaks of *chronos* or *kairos*. Our people call either word "time," whether *chronos* or *kairos*, although these two possess a differentiation which must not be neglected. The Greeks indeed use *kairos* as a particular time—not however as one which passes in an alteration of divisions, but as one which is perceived on occasions fitting and suitable in some respect, as time for harvesting, gathering of grapes, warmth, cold, peace, war, and anything similar. They speak of *chronoi* as the very divisions of time.[15]

Augustine did not recognize *tempestivitas* (timeliness), which is used by Cicero. This complaint is confirmed by the Vulgate, where various words are used to translate *kairoi* whenever it occurs with *chronoi*. In those cases, *kairoi* cannot be translated by *tempora* (times) because *chronoi* is. Thus it is translated in various ways such as "times and moments" (Acts 1:7; 1 Thess. 5:1), "times and ages" (Dan. 2:21), and "times and generations" (Wisd. of Sol. 8:8). A modern Latin commentator on the New Testament has "times and divisions" and Bengel has "intervals and times." It might be argued that *tempora et opportunitates* (times and opportune times) would fulfill all the necessary conditions. Augustine anticipated this suggestion and demonstrated its insufficiency by arguing that *opportunitas* (opportune time) refers to a *convenient*, favorable season,[16] but *kairos* may refer to a most inconvenient and unfavorable time that is nevertheless essentially the critical nick of time. *Kairos* itself does not determine whether this critical time is positive or negative—helpful or harmful. "Whether the time is convenient or inconvenient, it is called *kairos*." It is usually, however, the former: "*Kairos* is for men like a very great chief over every work."[17]

15. *Epistulae* 197.2.

16. *Eukairia* (2120).

17. Sophocles, *Electra* 75, 76. On the distinction between *chronos kairos* and *aiōn*, see Schmidt, *Synonymik*, 2:54ff.

58

pherō (5342) — Bring

phoreō (5409) — Bear, Wear

Lobeck distinguishes *pherō* and *phoreō* in this way:

> Between *pherō* and *phoreō* it is agreed that there is this difference, that the former indicates a simple and transitory act, while the latter signifies a continuation of the same act; for example, to bear [*pherein*] a message is to bring news of something (Herodotus 3.53 and 122; 5.14), while to repeatedly bear [*phoreein*] a message is to perform a duty for someone (Herodotus 3.34). Hence we also are said to wear [*phorein*] those things which we carry around, with which we are clothed and have put on, so that we wear [*phorein*] a cloak, garment, ring, and whatever pertains to the attire of the body.[1]

Lobeck acknowledged that this distinction is not consistently observed, even by the best Greek authors. The New Testament authors, however, always followed this rule—another example of their accuracy that so often takes us by surprise.

Phorein occurs six times in the New Testament[2] and invariably expresses not an accidental and temporary bearing but a habitual and continuous one. "For thus *phorein* differs from *pherein* so that the latter is 'to bear' and the for-

1. *Phrynichus*, p. 585.
2. Matt. 11:8; John 19:5; Rom. 13:4; 1 Cor. 15:49, twice; James 2:3.

pherō

phoreō

mer is 'to be accustomed to bear.' "[3] A sentence in Plutarch where both *pherō* and *phoreō* occur provides an excellent illustration of their differences. Plutarch described Xerxes as "angered at the Babylonian defectors, he overpowered them and commanded them not to bear [*pherein*] arms, but to play string instruments and flutes, to keep brothels and engage in trade, and to wear [*phorein*] elaborate garments."[4] Arms are only borne occasionally, therefore *pherein*; but since garments are habitually worn, *phorein* replaces *pherein* in the second clause.

3. Fritzsche, on Matt. 11:8.
4. *Regum et imperatorum apophthegmata*.

59

kosmos (2889) *aiōn* (165) — World, Age

The Authorized Version translates *kosmos* as "world" everywhere except in 1 Peter 3:3. And this is also the Authorized Version's usual translation of *aiōn*.[1] The Authorized Version translates *kosmos* as "age" only in Ephesians 2:7 and in Colossians 1:26. Although "age" may sound inadequate now, had it been used more frequently, it might have expanded gradually so that it adapted itself to the larger meaning of *kosmos*. It is unfortunate that the translators of the Authorized Version did not devise some means to distinguish between *kosmos*[2] and *aiōn*.[3] Indeed the Latin, no less than the Greek, has two words where we have used only one. This deficiency is evident in all of those passages[4] that refer to the end or consummation of the *aiōn*,[5] as well as in those that speak of "the wisdom *of this world*" (1 Cor. 2:6), "the god *of this world*" (2 Cor. 4:4), and "the children *of this world*" (Luke 16:8). The New King James Version improved many of these passages by translating *aiōn* as "age."

1. See Eph. 2:2, 7; Col. 1:26. This does not include *eis aiōna*.
2. It is equivalent to the Latin *mundus* (world), the spatial world.
3. It is equivalent to the Latin *saeculum* (age), the temporal world.
4. Such as Matt. 13:39; 1 Cor. 10:11.
5. There are none that refer to the end of the *kosmos*.

kosmos
aiōn

Kosmos[6] has an interesting history for several reasons. Suidas traced its development through four successive meanings: "*Ho kosmos* signifies in Scripture four things: goodly appearance, the whole, orderliness, magnitude." Originally *kosmos* meant "ornament," which is its primary meaning in the Old Testament[7] and a meaning it has once in the New Testament (1 Pet. 3:3).[8] Next *kosmos* came to mean "order" or "arrangement" and then "beauty"—as springing out of these—"goodly appearance," and "orderliness" (according to Suidas) or (according to Hesychius) *kallōpismos*,[9] *kataskeuē*,[10] *taxis* (5010), *katastasis*,[11] and *kallos*.[12] Pythagoras was the first to use *kosmos* to refer to the sum total of the material universe,[13] and according to Plutarch,[14] he did this to express his sense of the universe's beauty and order. According to others, Pythagoras only used *kosmos* to refer to heaven because of its well-ordered arrangement, not to the whole material universe.[15] This is often the way *kosmos* is used in Xenophon,[16] Isocrates,[17] Plato,[18] and Aristotle.[19] Augustine described the Latin *mundus* (world) as "the arrangement and regulation of each single thing formed and distinguished," which is nearly the same as the Greek *kosmos*. This similarity gave rise to Augustine's profound play on words: "O *munde immunde*" (O filthy clean). Thus Pliny stated: "What the Greeks with a name of embellishment have called *kosmon*, we have termed *mundum* from its perfect and absolute *elegance*."[20] And Cicero said: "The Greeks well name it *kosmon* as noted for its variety, we refer to it as a *shining mundum*."[21]

From its use as referring to the material universe,[22] *kosmos* came to refer to the external framework of things where man lives and moves and is himself

6. It is used with *komein* (L-S 975, to take care of) and is similar to the Latin *comere* (to care for) and *comptus* (adorned).

7. Thus the stars are "the adornment [*kosmos*] of the sky," Deut. 17:3; Isa. 24:21; cf. 41:18; Jer. 4:30; Ezek. 7:20; Ecclus. 43:9.

8. Although some translate it as "adorning."

9. L-S 869, adorning.

10. L-S 911, artistic construction.

11. L-S 913, settled system.

12. L-S 869, beauty.

13. For a history of this new use, see a note in Humboldt's *Cosmos*, 1846, English edition, p. 371.

14. *Placita philosophorum* 1.5.

15. Diogenes Laertius, 8.48.

16. *Memorabilia* 1.1.11.

17. 1.179.

18. *Timaeus* 28b. Plato also used it in the larger and more ideal sense as including heaven and earth and gods and men (*Gorgias* 508a).

19. *De mundo* 2. Cf. Bentley, *Works*, 1:391; 2:117.

20. *Historia naturalis* 2.3.

21. *De universo* 10. Cf. *De deorum natura* 2.22. But on the inferiority of *mundus* to *kosmos* as a philosophical expression, see Sayce, *Principles of Comparative Philology*, p. 98.

22. This is frequently found in Scripture (Matt. 13:35; John 17:5; 21:25; Acts 17:4; Rom. 1:20).

the moral center.[23] In that sense, *kosmos* is nearly equivalent to *oikoumenē*,[24] and then to the people themselves, to the sum total of persons living in the world.[25] From that meaning an ethical use of *kosmos* developed that referred to all who were not of the *ekklēsia* (1577)[26] and who therefore were alienated from the life of God and were his enemies because of their wicked deeds.[27] It is hardly necessary to remind the reader of the immense role that this sense of *kosmos* plays in John's theology, both in his record of Jesus' sayings and in his own writings.[28] This last sense of *kosmos* was utterly unknown to the entire heathen world, which had no sense of the opposition between God and man, the holy and unholy, though this sense was latent but not distinct in the Old Testament.[29]

Aristotle's etymology of *aiōn*—"receiving its name from *aei einai* [always being]"[30]—must be rejected as incorrect. It is more likely that *aiōn* derives from *aō* and *aēmi* (to breathe). Like *kosmos*, *aiōn* has a primary and physical meaning and an additional secondary and ethical meaning. *Aiōn*'s primary meaning refers to time—short or long—in its unbroken duration. In classical Greek, *aiōn* often refers to the duration of a human life.[31] But the essential meaning of *aiōn* is time as the condition for all created things and as the measure of their existence. Thus Theodoret wrote:

> *Ho aiōn* is not any substance, but it is an irresistible thing, accompanying those who have a mortal nature; for the interval from the constituting of the world [*kosmou*] to its consummation is called *aiōn—aiōn* then is the interval yoked to created nature.

Aiōn came to mean all that exists in the world under conditions of time: "The totality of what is discernible in the passage of time, the world inasmuch as it is active in time."[32] Ethically speaking, *aiōn* refers to the course and current of this world's affairs. But since the world's course of affairs is sinful, it is not surprising that "this age"—as contrasted with "that age" (Luke 20:35) and "the coming age" (Mark 10:30) and "the age about to come" (Matt. 12:32)—like *kosmos* soon acquired an unfavorable meaning. The "kingdoms of the world [*kosmou*]" in Matthew 4:8 are the "kingdoms of this age [*aiōnos*]" in

23. John 16:21; 1 Cor. 14:10; 1 John 3:17.

24. Matt. 24:14; Acts 19:27.

25. John 1:29; 4:42; 2 Cor. 5:19.

26. Origen indeed (*Commentarii in evangelium Joannis* 38) mentioned someone in his day who interpreted *kosmos* as the church because it is the *ornament* of the *world* (*kosmos ousa tou kosmou*).

27. 1 Cor. 1:20, 21; 2 Cor. 7:10; James 4:4.

28. John 1:10; 7:7; 12:31; 1 John 2:16; 5:4. It occurs in his Gospel and epistles more than a hundred times and most often in this sense.

29. Zezschwitz, *Profangräcität und Biblischer Sprachgeist*, pp. 21–24. For these various meanings of *kosmos* and the confusion that may result, see Augustine, *Contra Pelagium* 6.3, 4.

30. *De caelo* 1.9.

31. It is equivalent to *bios* (979) and was used in place of that word by Xenophon, *Cyropaedia* 3.3.24; cf. Plato, *Leges* 3.701c; Sophocles, *Trachiniae* 2; *Electra* 1085: "You have chosen a most lamentable life [*aiōna*]"; Pindar, *Olympia* 2.120: "They live a tearless life [*aiōna*]."

32. C.L.W. Grimm; thus see Wisd. of Sol. 13:8; 14:6; 18:4; Eccles. 3:11.

Ignatius.[33] God delivered us by his Son "from the present evil age [*aiōnos*]" (Gal. 1:4); Satan is "god of this age [*aiōnos*]" (2 Cor. 4:4);[34] and sinners walk *kata ton aiōna tou kosmou toutou* (Eph. 2:2). This last phrase is translated too weakly in our Authorized Version[35] as "*according to the course* of this world." Ephesians 2:2 is particularly instructive since *kosmos* and *aiōn* are both used. Bengel's excellent remarks are worth noting:

> *Aiōn* and *kosmos* are different. The former controls and as it were shapes the later; *kosmos* is more outward and *aiōn* is more subtle. *Aiōn* is a term used not only physically, but also morally, denoting a quality of people living in it; and thus *aiōn* refers to a long succession of times when an evil age succeeds an evil age.

Compare Windischmann's remarks:

> *Aiōn* dare never be taken to denote only time, but rather as embracing everything caught up in time, the world and its glory, people and their natural unredeemed doings and strivings, in contrast to yonder eternal kingdom of the Messiah, which only begins in the here and now and yearns to be perfected.[36]

We attach an ethical meaning to "the times," as well as to "the age," "the spirit or genius of the age," and *der Zeitgeist* (the spirit of the time). *Aiōn* includes all the thoughts, opinions, maxims, speculations, impulses, and aspirations present in the world at any given time, which may be impossible to accurately define but which still constitute a real and effective power—the moral or immoral atmosphere we breathe. Bengel called it the subtle shaping spirit of the *kosmos*, or world of people, who are living alienated and apart from God. *Saeculum* (age/spirit of the age) in Latin acquired the same sense, as in the familiar epigram of Tacitus: "*Saeculum* [age] is said to corrupt and to be corrupted."[37]

The use of *aiōnes* in Hebrews 1:2 and 11:3, however, does not follow the preceding distinction between *aiōn* and *kosmos*. In both of these passages *aiōnes* refers to the worlds as seen in other than temporal terms. Some expositors—especially modern Socinian ones[38]—have attempted to explain *aiōnes* in Hebrews 1:2 as the successive dispensations, the *chronoi kai kairoi* of the divine management. However plausible this explanation might be if we take the verse in isolation, the use of *aiōnes* in Hebrews 11:3 is decisive. In both passages *aiōnes* can only mean "the world," not "the ages." I have called the Hebrews passages the only exceptions, for I do not believe that 1 Timothy 1:17 is a third. In that passage *aiōnes* does not refer to "the worlds" in the usual concrete meaning of the term but to the "the ages," the temporal peri-

33. *Epistula ad Romanos* 6.
34. Cf. Ignatius: "the ruler of this age [*aiōnos*]" (*Epistulae* 1).
35. As in earlier versions.
36. On Gal. 1:4.
37. *Germania* 19.
38. Although they are not without forerunners who did not have their motivation.

ods whose sum and aggregate foreshadow the conception of eternity. This usage agrees with the more common *temporal* meaning of *aiōn* in the New Testament. The "King of *tōn aiōnōn*"[39] thus refers to the sovereign dispenser and disposer of the ages, where the mystery of God's purpose with man unfolds.[40] Etymologically our English *world* more nearly represents *aiōn* than does the Greek *kosmos*. The old *Weralt* (in modern German *Welt*) is composed of two words, *Wer* (man) and *Alt* (age or generation). Thus the basic meaning of *Weralt* is "generation of men."[41] The notion of space unfolds from this expression of time, as *aiōn* passed into the meaning of *kosmos*.[42] In the earliest German records, however, *Weralt* is used first as an expression of time and only derivatively as one of space.[43] Grimm, however, thought that *world* is equivalent to *whirled*.[44] For the Hebrew equivalents of the words for time and eternity, see Conrad von Orelli.[45] For their Greek and Latin equivalents—such as there are—see Pott.[46]

39. Cf. Clement of Rome, *Epistula* 1, par. 13: "The Creator and Father of *tōn aiōnōn*."

40. See Ellicott, *in loco*.

41. Pott, *Etymologische Forschungen*, vol. 2, pt. 1, p. 125.

42. Grimm, *Deutsche Mythologie*, p. 752.

43. Rudolf von Raumer, *Die Einwirkung des Christenthums auf die Alt-hochdeutsche Sprache*, 1845, p. 375.

44. *Kleine Schriften*, 1:305.

45. *Die Hebräischen Synonyma der Zeit und Ewigkeit*, Leipzig, 1871.

46. *Etymologische Forschungen* 2.2.444.

60

neos (3501) *kainos* (2537)

New Young

Some scholars have denied that there is any difference between *neos* and *kainos* in the New Testament. Such scholars gain plausible support for their position from the fact that both of these words are translated by "new" in the Authorized Version and often are used interchangeably.[1] Although they contend that *neos* and *kainos* have the same force and significance, this does not follow and in fact is not the case. The same man or the same wine may be *neos* or *kainos* or both, according to one's perspective.

Neos refers to something new in *time*, to something that recently has come into existence.[2] Thus the young are *hoi neoi* or *hoi neōteroi*, the generation that has lately come into being. *Neoi theoi* (*2316*) refers to the young race of gods—Jupiter, Apollo, and the other Olympians[3]—as contrasted with Saturn, Ops, and the dynasty of elder deities whom they dethroned. *Kainos* refers to something new in *quality* and is contrasted with that which has seen service—the outworn, the exhausted, or that which is marred through age. Thus "a piece of unshrunk cloth" (Matt. 9:16) may be contrasted with "a piece

1. *Neos anthrōpos* (*444*; Col. 3:10) and *kainos anthrōpos* (Eph. 2:15) are translated by "the new man." *Nea diathēkē* (*1242*; Heb. 12:24) and *kainē diathēkē* (Heb. 9:15) are translated by "a new covenant." *Neos oinos* (*3631*; Matt. 9:17) and *kainos oinos* (Matt. 26:29) are translated by "new wine."

2. See Pott, *Etymologische Forschungen*, 1:290–92.

3. Aeschylus, *Prometheus vinctus* 991, 996.

from a new [*kainou*] garment" (Luke 5:36); the latter is "a new garment," the former a threadbare and outworn one. *Kainoi askoi* (*779*) are "new wine-skins" (Matt. 9:17; Luke 5:38) that have not lost their strength and elasticity through age and use. This also is the sense of *kainos ouranos* (*3772*; 2 Pet. 3:13), "a new heaven," as compared with one that has grown old and shows signs of decay and dissolution (Heb. 1:11–12). Similarly, the phrase *kainai glōssai* (*1100*; Mark 16:17) does not refer to the recent commencement of the miraculous speaking with tongues but to the dissimilarity of these tongues to any that had occurred before. Therefore these tongues were called *heterai* (*2087*) *glōssai* (Acts 2:4), unusual tongues that were different from any previously known. This sense of the unusual in *kainos* comes out very clearly in a passage from Xenophon: "Either a new [*kainēs*] rule beginning or the *customary* one remaining."[4] The *kainon mnēmeion* (*3419*) in which Joseph of Arimathea laid the body of Jesus (Matt. 27:60; John 19:41) was not a tomb that recently had been hewn from rock but one that never had been used at all, one where no dead person had lain to make the place ceremonially unclean (Matt. 23:27; Num. 11:16; Ezek. 39:12, 16). This tomb might have been created a hundred years before and therefore not be *neon*, but if it had never been used before, it would still be *kainon*. Even in the midst of the humiliations of his earthly life, a divine decorum attended Christ (cf. Luke 19:30; 1 Sam. 6:7; 2 Kings 2:20).

Kainos often implies the secondary notion of praise, for frequently the new is better than the old. Thus in the kingdom of glory, everything will be new: "the new Jerusalem" (Rev. 3:12; 21:2), the "new name" (2:17; 3:12), "a new song" (5:9; 14:3), "a new heaven and new earth" (21:1; cf. 2 Pet. 3:13), "all things new" (Rev. 21:5). *Kainos* does not necessarily imply superiority. Sometimes the old is better than the new, as is the old friend (Ecclus. 9:10) and the old wine (Luke 5:39). Frequently *kainos* may refer only to the novel and strange as contrasted (even unfavorably) with the known and familiar. *Neoi theoi* was a title given to the younger generation of gods. The charge against Socrates, however, was that he had introduced *kainous theous* or *kaina daimonia* (*1140*) into Athens,[5] phrases that imply a novel pantheon of gods that Athens had not previously worshiped. Plato said: "These are new [*kaina*] and strange names of diseases."[6] Similarly, those who exclaimed "What new [*kainē*] doctrine is this?" when they heard Christ's teaching, intended anything but praise (Mark 1:27). The *kainon* is the *heteron*, the qualitatively other; the *neon* is the *allo* (*243*), the numerically distinct.

We will now apply this distinction to the interpretation of Acts 17:21. Luke described the Athenians as spending their leisure[7] in the marketplace. We might have expected to find *ti neōteron* here, especially since previously Demosthenes had portrayed the same Athenians as haunting the marketplace with this same aim: "Inquiring at the marketplace whether anything new

4. *Cyropaedia* 3.1.10.

5. Plato, *Apologia Socratis* 26b; *Euthyphro* 3b; cf. *xena* (*3581*) *daimonia*, Acts 17:18.

6. *Republic* 3.405d.

7. All their life was leisure; or, to adopt Fuller's pun, "vacation being their whole vocation."

[*neōteron*] is said." Elsewhere, however, Demosthenes described the Athenians as Luke did: "Is anything new [*kainon*] said?"[8] But the meaning of the two passages is not exactly identical. The *neōteron* of the first implies that it is always the *latest* news the Athenians sought: "They at once were despising the new and were seeking the newer."[9] The *kainon* of the second passage refers to something not only new but sufficiently diverse from what had gone before to stimulate a jaded curiosity.

This distinction becomes even more apparent if we pursue these words into their derivatives and compounds. Thus *neotēs*[10] is youth; *kainotēs*[11] is newness or novelty; *neoeidēs* refers to youthful appearance; and *kainoeidēs* implies novel or unusual appearance. *Neologia* (had such a word existed) would have referred to a new development of words as distinguished from the older language, or as we would say, to "neologies." *Kainologia*, which exists in later Greek, refers to a novel, abnormal invention of words that are constructed on different laws from those previously recognized. A *philoneos* is a lover of youth;[12] a *philokainos* is a lover of novelty.[13]

There is a passage in Polybius[14] where *neos* and *kainos* occur in close proximity but are not employed rhetorically, each having its own significance. In describing a stratagem whereby the town of Selge was almost surprised and taken, Polybius remarked that though many cities had been lost through a similar device, we are still *new and young* in regard to such deceits[15] and capable of being deceived again. In that passage, *kainoi* is applied to men on the basis of their inexperience, and *neoi* is applied to them on the basis of their youth. Although inexperience and youth often go together—Plutarch joined *neos* and *apeiros* (*552*)[16]—this is not necessarily the case. An old man may be raw and unpracticed in the affairs of the world and so *kainos*; and there have been many young men, *neoi* in age, who were well skilled in worldly affairs.

If we apply this distinction to the New Testament, it becomes apparent that the same man, wine, and covenant each may be described as *neos* and as *kainos* in ways that convey different meanings.[17] When a man is transformed by becoming obedient to the truth, in relation to time we subsequently call him *neos anthrōpos*. The old man in him[18] has died and a new man has been born. Now let us view the same mighty transformation in relation to quality and condition. When a man who through long contact with the world and

8. *Philippica* 1.43.

9. As Bengel on Acts 17:21 has it.

10. *3503*; 1 Tim. 4:12; cf. Ps. 103:5: "So that your youth [*neotēs*] is renewed like the eagle's."

11. *2538*; Rom. 6:4.

12. Lucian, *Amores* 24.

13. Plutarch, *De musica* 12.

14. 5.75, 4. Other such passages include Aeschylus, *Persae* 665; Euripides, *Medea* 75, 78; and Clement of Alexandria, *Paedagogus* 1.5.

15. *Kainoi tines aiei kai neoi pros tas toiautas apatas pephykamen.*

16. *De recta ratione audiendi* 17.

17. For example, the "new [*neos*] man" of Col. 3:10 and the "new [*kainos*] man" of Eph. 2:15.

18. This is an appropriate name, since it dates back to Adam.

sinful habits throws off his old life like a snake casts off its shriveled skin, he emerges as "a new [*kainē*] creature" from his heavenly Maker's hands and has a "new [*kainon*] spirit" (Ezek. 11:19). This is the *kainos anthrōpos*, one who is prepared to walk "in newness of life"[19] through the renewal (*anakainōsis*) of the Spirit (Titus 3:5). "We have become new [*kainoi*], being created again from the beginning."[20]

Sometimes, though not always, *neos* and *kainos* may be used interchangeably. For example, Clement of Alexandria[21] said of those who are Christ's, "they must be new [*kainous*], having partaken of a new [*kainon*] Word [Christ]." It would be impossible to substitute *neous* or *neou* in that passage. Consider the verbs *ananeoun*[22] and *anakainoun*.[23] Everyone needs both *ananeousthai* and *anakainousthai*. It is the same marvelous and mysterious process, brought about by the same almighty agent, but seen from different perspectives. *Ananeousthai* is to be made *young* again, and *anakainousthai*[24] is to be made *new* again. Chrysostom realized this distinction and based a separate exhortation on each word, as the following passages show. The first passage reads: "Be renewed [*ananeousthe*], Paul says, in the spirit of your mind. . . . to be renewed [*ananeousthai*] is when that which has grown old is made young again [*ananeōtai*] and becomes changed. . . . The young [*neos*] is strong, does not have a wrinkle, and is not carried about."[25] The second passage reads: "What we do in the case of houses, always restoring them when they become dilapidated, do also in the case of yourself. Have you sinned today? Have you worn out your life? Do not despair nor lose heart, but renew [*anakainison*] it by repentance."[26]

Depending on the point of view, new wine may be characterized as *neos* or as *kainos*. As *neos*, it is tacitly set over against the vintage of past years; as *kainos*, we may assume it to be austere and strong, in contrast with *chrēstos* (5543), sweet and mellow through age (Luke 5:39). The covenant of which Christ is the mediator is a *diathēkē nea*, as compared with the Mosaic covenant, confirmed nearly two thousand years before (Heb. 12:24). The covenant that Christ established is a *diathēkē kainē*, when compared with the Mosaic covenant, because the Mosaic covenant is exhausted with age and has lost its vigor, energy, and quickening power.[27]

A Latin grammarian distinguished *recens* and *novus* in the following way: "*Recens* refers to *time*, *novum* refers to a condition."[28] By substituting *neos* for

19. *En kainotēti zōēs* (2222), Rom. 6:4.
20. *Epistle of Barnabas*, 16.
21. *Paedagogus* 1.6.
22. 365; Eph. 4:23.
23. 341; Col. 3:10.
24. Or *anakainizesthai* (340).
25. *In epistulam ad Ephesios*, 13.
26. *In epistulam ad Romanos*, 20.
27. Heb. 8:13; cf. Marriott's *Eirēnika*, pt. 2, pp. 110, 170.
28. Cf. Döderlein, *Lateinische Synonyme*, 4:64.

recens and *kainos* for *novum*, we may summarize the central distinction between *neos* and *kainos*: "*Neos* refers to *time*, *kainos* refers to a condition."[29]

29. Lafaye (*Dictionnaire des Synonymes*, p. 798) distinguished *nouveau* (equivalent to *neos*) and *neuf* (equivalent to *kainos*) in the same way: "That which is *nouveau* puts in its appearance for the first time; that which is *neuf* comes to be a fact without as yet serving any purpose. An invention is *nouvelle*, an expression is *neuve*."

61

methē (3178) *Drunkenness*
potos (4224) *Drinking Party*
oinophlygia (3632) *Excess of Wine*
kraipalē (2897)
kōmos (2970) *Revelry*

Methē, *potos*, *oinophlygia*, *kōmos*, and *kraipalē* refer from different perspectives to riotousness and excessive drinking of wine .

Methē (Luke 21:34; Rom. 13:13; Gal. 5:21) and *potos* (only in 1 Pet. 4:3) may be distinguished as an abstract and a concrete. *Methē*[1] means "drunkenness" (Joel 1:5; Ezek. 39:19); *potos*[2] refers to a drinking bout, a banquet, or a symposium. *Potos* does not necessarily imply excessiveness,[3] though it does provide an opportunity for excess.[4]

Oinophlygia, which is translated as "excess of wine" in the Authorized Version, occurs in the New Testament only in 1 Peter 4:3 and never in the Sep-

1. *Methē* is stronger and expresses a worse excess than *oinōsis* (L-S 1208, drunkenness), from which it is distinguished by Plutarch, *De garrulitate* 4; *Septem sapientium convivium* 3.1; cf. Philo, *De plantatione* 38. *Methē* was defined by Clement of Alexandria as "a rather excessive use of unmixed wine."

2. Hesychius used *potos* as a synonym for *euōchia* (L-S 740, feasting); cf. Polybius, 2.4.6.

3. Gen. 19:3; 2 Sam. 3:20; Esther 6:14.

4. 1 Sam. 25:36; Xenophon, *Anabasis* 7.3, 13: "When the drinking bout [*potos*] was advancing."

methē
potos
oinophlygia
kraipalē
kōmos

tuagint, though *oinophlygein*[5] is used in Deuteronomy 21:20 and Isaiah 56:22. Because *oinophlygia* refers to something worse than *methē*, Philo[6] listed it among the "extreme lusts."[7] Strictly speaking, *oinophlygia* means "insatiate desire for wine"[8] or "insatiate desire."[9] Commonly, however, *oinophlygia* is used to refer to a debauch, to an extravagant indulgence in alcoholic beverages[10] that may permanently damage the body.[11] According to Arrian,[12] this type of fatal orgy was responsible for the death of Alexander the Great.

Kōmos is found only in the plural in the New Testament, where it is translated in the Authorized Version once as "rioting" (Rom. 13:13) and twice as "revelings" (Gal. 5:21; 1 Pet. 4:3). *Kōmos* unites the concepts of rioting and revelry.[13] At the same time, *kōmos* often refers to the company of revelers themselves—to a festive company that is not necessarily riotous and drunken.[14] Generally, however, *kōmos* refers to excess and is applied in a special sense to troops of drunken revelers[15] who at the end of their revels, with garlands on their heads, with torches in their hands, and with shouting and singing[16] pass to the harlots' houses or wander through the streets insulting everyone they meet.[17] In the indignant words of Milton: "When night darkens the streets, then wander forth the sons of Belial, *flown with insolence and wine*." Plutarch characterized the mad drunken march of Alexander and his army through Carmania on their return from their Indian expedition as a *kōmos*.[18]

Kraipalē[19] is another word whose derivation remains obscure. In the New Testament it occurs only in Luke 21:34, where it is translated as "surfeiting," "carousing," or "dissipation." It does not occur in the Septuagint, though the

5. L-S 1207, to be drunk.

6. *De ebrietate* 8.

7. Cf. Xenophon (*Oeconomicus* 1.22): "Slaves of gluttony, sexual intercourse, drunkenness [*oinophlygia*]."

8. Andronicus of Rhodes.

9. Philo, *De vita Mosis* 3.22; it is the German *Trinksucht* (drinking mania).

10. See Basil, *In ebriosos* 7.

11. Aristotle, *Ethica Nicomachea* 3.5.15.

12. 7.24, 25, adopting one of the reports current in antiquity.

13. *Kōmos* is similar to the Latin *comissatio* (reveling), which is connected with *kōmazein* (L-S 1017, to make merry), and not with the Latin *comedo* (to eat together, consume). For example, *kōmos kai asōtia* (*810*; 2 Macc. 6:4), "frantic *kōmoi*" (Wisd. of Sol. 14:23), and "drinking bouts and revelings [*kōmoi*] and ill-timed festivities" (Plutarch, *Pyrrhus* 16; cf. Philo, *De cherubim* 27, who has a striking description of the other vices most closely associated with *methē* and *kōmoi*).

14. Thus see Euripides, *Alcestis* 816, 959.

15. In *Agamemnon* 1160, the troop of Furies who have this name are *drunk* with blood.

16. Plutarch, *Alexander* 38.

17. Theophylact called the songs themselves the *kōmoi*, defining the word thus: "the songs with drunkenness and lewdness." Cf. Meineke, *Fragmenta Comoeda Graeca*, p. 617, and the graphic description in Juvenal's third Satire, 278–301.

18. *Alexander* 37. On possible, or rather on impossible, etymologies of *kōmos*, see Pott, *Etymologische Forschungen* 2.2.551.

19. The Latin *crapula* (inebriation), is more limited; cf. "the drunkenness [*methē*] of yesterday" (Ammonius) and "the distress and unpleasantness from drunkenness [*epi tē methē*]" (Clement of Alexandria, *Paedagogus* 2.2).

verb *kraipalaō*[20] is used three times (Ps. 78:65; Isa. 24:20; 29:9). The early sense of the English word *fulsomeness*[21] would express *kraipalē* very well, though *fulsomeness* refers to the disgust and loathing that arise from eating too much meat and drinking too much wine, while *kraipalē* refers only to the latter.

Drunkenness
Drinking Party
Excess of Wine

Revelry

20. L-S 989, to have a sick headache after a debauch.
21. See my *Select Glossary of English Words*, under the word *fulsome*.

62

kapēleuō (2585) — Corrupt

doloō (1389) — Handle Deceitfully, Peddle

In 2 Corinthians 2:17, Paul claimed that he was not "as many, *which corrupt* [*kapēleuontes*] the Word of God." Shortly thereafter, in 2 Corinthians 4:2, Paul disclaimed "*handling deceitfully* [*dolountes*] the Word of God." Neither *kapēleuō* nor *doloō* appear elsewhere in the New Testament. Their contexts and characters make it evident that these words must have similar meanings. Although translators frequently have assumed that *kapēleuō* and *doloō* are absolutely identical and have translated them by one word,[1] this is incorrect. When examined more closely, it becomes apparent that *kapēleuein*, whether used literally or figuratively,[2] refers to all that *doloun* does plus something more. Whether or not the Authorized translators understood this distinction, they did not obliterate it.

The history of *kapēleuein* is not difficult to follow. The *kapēlos* is properly the huckster or petty retail trader, as contrasted with the *emporos* (*1713*) or merchant who sells in large quantities.[3] Although it may refer to *any* such peddler, the *kapēlos* is predominantly the retail vendor *of wine*.[4] The wine

1. The Vulgate uses *adulterantes* (falsifying, counterfeiting) in both places. According to Chrysostom, *kapēleuein* is equivalent to *notheuein* (L-S 1178, to consider spurious).

2. Paul used the word figuratively.

3. *Kapēleuein* and *kapēlos* are used together in Ecclus. 26:29.

4. Lucian, *Hermotius* 58.

kapēleuō

doloō

trade exposed its vendors to numerous temptations (Ecclus. 25:29): to mix their wine with water (Isa. 1:22) or otherwise to tamper with it or to sell it in short measure. Because they generally yielded to these temptations, *kapēlos* and *kapēleuein*[5] became terms of contempt. *Kapēleuein* refers to any shameful traffic and gain done by the *kapēlos*.[6] *Doloun*, however, is only one aspect of *kapēleuein*—namely, the tampering with or adulterating the wine by adding a foreign substance to it. *Doloun* does not suggest that this was done for the purpose of making a disgraceful profit and may refer only to the tampering itself, as the following phrase from Lucian indicates: "The philosophers sell their learning just as the hucksters [*kapēloi*]—indeed in many cases after adulterating it and tampering [*dolōsantes*] with it and using false measures."[7] Here *doloun* refers only to one aspect of the deceitful handling by the *kapēlos*.

Doloun certainly implies no more than simply falsifying, but *kapēleuein* includes the intention of making an unworthy profit. Surely here is a *moment* in the sin of the false teachers that Paul, in disclaiming the *kapēleuein*, intended to disclaim for himself. And Paul did this quite emphatically in as many words in 2 Corinthians (12:14; cf. Acts 20:33), because according to Scripture, the idea of making an unworthy profit is a hallmark of false prophets and false apostles,[8] who through covetousness make merchandise of souls.[9] This distinction must be maintained. The false teachers in Galatia might undoubtedly have been charged as *dolountes ton logon* (3056)—mingling vain human traditions with the pure word of the gospel, building in hay, straw, and stubble with its silver, gold, and precious stones—but there is nothing that would lead us to charge them as *kapēleuontes ton logon tou Theou* (2316)—working this mischief for filthy lucre's sake.[10]

Bentley[11] strongly maintained this distinction:

> Our English Translators have not been very happy in their version of this passage [2 Cor. 2:17]. We are not, says the Apostle, *kapēleuontes ton logon tou theou*, which our Translators have rendered, "we do not corrupt," or (as in the margin) "deal deceitfully with," "the word of God." They were led to this by the parallel place, ch. 4 of this Epistle, v. 2, "not walking in craftiness," *mēde dolountes ton logon tou theou*, "nor handling the word of God deceitfully"; they took *kapēleuontes* and *dolountes* in the same adequate notion, as the vulgar Latin had done before them, which expresses both by the same word, *adulterantes verbum Dei*; and so, likewise, Hesychius makes them synonyms, *ekkapēleuein*,

5. Like the Latin *caupo* (huckster) and *cauponari* (to trade).

6. Plato, *Republic* 7.525d; *Protagoras* 313d; Becker, *Charikles*, 1840, p. 256.

7. *Hermotius* 59.

8. For the meanest clings to the highest, and untruthfulness in highest things is exposed to lowest temptations.

9. Paul noted this in Titus 1:11; Phil. 3:19; cf. 2 Pet. 2:3, 14, 15; Jude 11, 16; Ezek. 13:19. See Ignatius (the longer recension) where, no doubt with a reference to this passage and showing how the writer understood it, the false teachers are denounced as "hurricanes for wealth" and as "merchandisers of Christ, trafficking in Jesus and deceitfully making gain [*kapēleuontes*] from the message of the gospel."

10. See Deyling, *Obsessiones sacrae*, 4:636.

11. "Sermon on Popery," *Works*, 3:242.

doloun. Doloun, indeed, is fitly rendered "adulterare"; so *doloun ton chryson, ton oinon*, to adulterate gold or wine, by mixing worse ingredients with the metal or liquor. And our Translators had done well if they had rendered the latter passage, not adulterating, not sophisticating the word. But *kapēleuontes* in our text has a complex idea and a wider signification; *kapēleuein* always comprehends *douloun*; but *douloun* never extends to *kapēleuin*, which, besides the sense of adulterating, has an additional notion of unjust lucre, gain, profit, advantage. This is plain from the word *kapēlos*, a calling always infamous for avarice and knavery: *perfidus hic caupo* [this treacherous huckster] says the poet, as a general character. Thence *kapēlein*, by an easy and natural metaphor, was diverted to other expressions where cheating and lucre were signified: *kapēleuein ton logon*, says the apostle here, and the ancient Greeks, *kapēleuein tas dikas, tēn eirēnēn, tēn sophian, ta mathēmata*, to corrupt and sell justice, to barter a negotiation of peace, to prostitute learning and philosophy for gain. Cheating, we see, and adulterating is part of the notion of *kapēleuein*, but the essential of it is sordid lucre. So *cauponari* in the well-known passage of Ennius, where Pyrrhus refuses to treat for the ransom for his captives, and restores them gratis: 'I do not demand gold, nor shall you give me a price, war is not for one trading, but for one waging battle.' And so the Fathers expound this place. . . . So that, in short, what Paul says, *kapēleuontes ton logon*, might be expressed in one classic word—*logemporoi* [merchants of the word], or *logopratai* [sellers of the word][12] where the idea of gain and profit is the chief part of the signification. Wherefore, to do justice to our text, we must not stop lamely with our Translators, "corrupters of the word of God"; but add to it as its plenary notion, "corrupters of the word of God *for filthy lucre*."

Corrupt
Handle Deceitfully
Peddle

If Bentley was correct, it follows that "deceitfully handling" would be a more accurate (though not a perfectly adequate) translation of *kapēleuontes* and "who corrupt" of *dolountes*, than the reverse, which our Authorized Version actually offers.

12. So *logopōloi* (sellers of the word) in Philo, *De congressu eruditionis gratia* 10.

63

agathōsynē (19) *chrēstotēs* (5544) — Goodness Kindness

Agathōsynē is one of many words where revealed religion has enriched the later language of Greece. *Agathōsynē* occurs only in the Greek translations of the Old Testament (2 Chron. 24:16; Neh. 9:25; Eccles. 9:18), in the New Testament, and in writings directly dependent on these. The grammarians never acknowledged or gave it[1] their stamp of approval and insisted that *chrēstotēs*[2] should always be used in its place.[3] In the New Testament, *agathōsynē* occurs four times, always in the writings of Paul,[4] where it is consistently translated "goodness" in the Authorized Version. Sometimes the lack of a more special and definite word is felt, as in Galatians 5:22, where *agathōsynē* is one of a long list of Christian virtues or "fruits of the Spirit." Although in that passage it must refer to a single, separate virtue, the translation "goodness" seems to embrace them all. Favorinus explained *agathōsynē* as "the completed virtue," but this is less than satisfactory,[5] though it is difficult to suggest any other translation and even more difficult to determine the central force of *agathōsynē* than of *chrēstotēs*. The difficulty in precisely defining

1. Or *agathotēs* (L-S 4, goodness).
2. As we shall see, this word is not absolutely identical with *agathōsynē*.
3. Lobeck, *Pathos sermonis Graeci*, p. 237.
4. Rom. 15:14; Gal. 5:22; Eph. 5:9; 2 Thess. 1:11.
5. Sometimes *agathōsynē* is contrasted with *kakia* (2549), as in Ps. 53:3–4, and obtains this larger meaning.

agathōsynē occurs primarily because there are no helpful passages in classical Greek literature where the word is used. Although classical usage can never be the absolute standard by which we define the meaning of words in Scripture, we feel a loss when there are no classical instances to use for comparison.

It is prudent first to consider *chrēstotēs*. After determining its range of meaning, it will be easier to ascertain what *agathōsynē* means.

Like *agathōsynē*, *chrēstotēs*[6] occurs in the New Testament only in Paul's writings, where it is used with *philanthrōpia*,[7] *makrothymia* (*3115*), and *anochē*[8] and contrasted with *apotomia*.[9] The Authorized Version translates it by "good" (Rom. 3:12), "kindness" (2 Cor. 6:6; Eph. 2:7; Col. 3:12; Titus 3:4), and "gentleness" (Gal. 5:22). The Rheims Version translates it by "benignity" (a great improvement over "gentleness" in Gal. 5:22) and "sweetness" (2 Cor. 6:6), which better captures the central meaning of this word. Plato defined *chrēstotēs* as "sincerity of character with prudence,"[10] and Favorinus explained it as "good-heartedness, being sympathetic toward a neighbor and regarding his possessions as one's own." Clement of Rome used *chrēstotēs* with *eleos*,[11] Plutarch used it with *eumeneia*[12] and with *haplotēs* (*572*) and *megalophrosynē*.[13] Lucian used it with *oiktos*,[14] and Plutarch used *chrēstos* (*5543*) with *philanthrōpos*.[15] When speaking of the *chrēstotēs* of Isaac,[16] Josephus displayed insight into the ethical character of the patriarch.[17]

Calvin had too superficial a view of *chrēstotēs* when he wrote:

> Kindness—for so it has been agreed to translate *chrēstotēta*—is what we render to loved ones. Meekness [*prautēs*, *4240*], which follows, extends wider than *chrēstotēs*, for meekness exists especially in facial expression and speech, while *chrēstotēs* is also an inward feeling.[18]

Rather than being a virtue that refers only to a person's words and countenance, *chrēstotēs* refers to a virtue that pervades and penetrates the whole nature, that mellows anything harsh and austere. Thus wine that has been mellowed with age (Luke 5:39) is *chrēstos*, and Christ's yoke is *chrēstos*, because it has nothing harsh or galling about it (Matt. 11:30). Cocceius distinguished *chrēstos* and *agathōsynē* this way:

6. *Chrēstotēs* is a beautiful word that expresses a beautiful virtue. Cf. *chrēstoētheia* (L-S 2007, goodness of heart) in Ecclus. 37:13.

7. *5363*; Titus 3:4; cf. Lucian, *Timon* 8; Plutarch, *Demetrius* 50.

8. *463*; Rom. 2:4.

9. *663*; Rom. 9:22.

10. *Definitions* 412e.

11. *1656*; *Epistula 1 ad Corinthios* 9.

12. L-S 721, goodwill; *De capienda ex inimicis utilitate* 9.

13. L-S 1087, generosity; *Galba* 22.

14. Cf. *3627*; *Timon* 8.

15. *Septem sapientium convivium* 1.1.4.

16. *Antiquitates Judaicae* 1.18.3.

17. See Gen. 26:20–22.

18. On Col. 3:12.

> From this example it is clear that this word [*chrēstotēs*] indicates a certain generosity and eagerness to do good. The other word [*agathōsynē*] implies kindness, agreeableness of manners, eloquence, earnestness of character, and every amiability joined with propriety and dignity.[19]

Even that statement, however, is not exactly correct. If the words are contrasted, kindness belongs more to the *chrēstotēs* than to the *agathōsynē*. Jerome's excellent statement is more germain to the matter:

> *Benignitas* [friendliness] or *suavitas* [kindness]—since among the Greeks *chrēstotēs* signifies each—is a gentle, charming, and calm virtue, suited to the company of all good people, attracting their friendship, delightful in encouragement and moderate in manners. Also the Stoics define it thus: *chrēstotēs* is a virtue willingly ready to do good. *Agathōsynē* is not much different, for it also seems ready to do good. But it differs in that it can be more harsh and with a countenance wrinkled by strict standards for one to do well and to excel in what is demanded, without being pleasant to associates and attracting crowds by its sweetness. Also the followers of Zeno define it as follows: *agathōsynē* is a virtue which is beneficial, or a virtue which promotes usefulness, or a virtue for its own sake, or a disposition which is the source of all benefits.[20]

Jerome's statement essentially agrees with the distinction drawn by Basil: "I think *chrēstotēs* is more extensive in doing good to those who in any way at any time have need of it; *agathōsynē* is more narrow and uses words of justice in its well-doing."[21] Lightfoot found more activity in the *agathōsynē* than in the *chrēstotēs*: "They are distinguished from one another as character from activity; *chrēstotēs* is potential *agathōsynē*, while *agathōsynē* is energizing *chrēstotēs*."[22]

A man may display his *agathōsynē*, his zeal for goodness and truth, in rebuking, correcting, and chastising. Although Christ was still in the spirit of this virtue when he drove the buyers and sellers out of the temple (Matt. 21:13) and when he uttered all those terrible words against the scribes and the Pharisees (Matt. 23), we could not say that his *chrēstotēs* was shown in these acts of righteous indignation. Rather, his *chrēstotēs* was displayed in his reception of the penitent woman (Luke 7:37–50; cf. Ps. 25:6–7) and in all his other gracious dealings with the children of men. Thus we might speak[23] of the *chrēstotēs tēs agathōsynēs* of God, but scarcely of the converse. This *chrēstotēs* was so predominantly a part of the character of Christ's ministry that it is not surprising to learn from Tertullian[24] how "Christus" became "Chrestus" and "Christiani" became "Chrestiani" on the lips of the hea-

19. On Gal. 5:22, quoting Titus 3:4, where *chrēstotēs* occurs.
20. *Epistula ad Galatios* 5.22.
21. *Prologus 3: prooemium in regulas brevius tractatus* 214.
22. On Gal. 5:22.
23. The *Apostolic Constitutions* (2.22) do speak in this way.
24. *Apologeticum* 3.

then, though with an undertone of contempt.[25] The world expresses contempt for goodness that seems to have only the harmlessness of the dove and not the wisdom of the serpent. Such a contempt would be justified for a goodness that has no edge, no sharpness, no righteous indignation against sin or willingness to punish it. Sometimes *chrēstotēs* degenerated into this and ended up being not goodness at all, as evidenced in this striking fragment of Menander: "What now by some is called kindness [*chrēstotēs*] has set loose entire lives to vice, for no one is punished for his wrongs."[26]

25. The *chrēstos*, as we learn from Aristotle, was called "foolish" by those who take everything in a negative sense (*Rhetorica* 1.9.3; cf. Eusebius, *Praeparatio evangelica* 5.5.5).

26. Meineke, *Fragmenta Comoeda Graeca*, p. 982.

64

diktyon (1350) *amphiblēstron* (293) *sagēnē* (4522) — Net

Although *diktyon*, *amphiblēstron*, and *sagēnē* are usually translated by "net," it is possible to distinguish these words more accurately.

Diktyon[1] is the more general term for nets, including the hunting net, the net used to catch birds (Prov. 1:17), and the fishing net. In the New Testament *diktyon* has only the latter meaning (Matt. 4:20; John 21:6). Often in the Septuagint *diktyon* is used in the figurative sense in which Paul used *pagis*,[2] with which it is associated (Job 18:8; Prov. 29:5).

Amphiblēstron and *sagēnē* are types of fishing nets. These two words are used together in Habakkuk 1:15 and in Plutarch,[3] who joined *gripos*[4] with *sagēnē* and *hypochē*[5] with *amphiblēstron*. The *amphiblēstron*[6] is a casting net.[7] When skillfully cast from the shore or over the shoulder from a boat, this net

1. *Diktyon* is equivalent to the Latin *rete* (net) and is derived from *dikein* (to cast), which appears again in *diskos* (a quoit).

2. *3803*; Rom. 2:9; 1 Tim. 3:7.

3. *De sollertia animalium* 26.

4. L-S 360, haul of fish.

5. L-S 1902, a round fishing net.

6. It only occurs twice in the New Testament (Matt. 4:18; Mark 1:16; cf. Eccles. 9:12; Ps. 14:10. *Amphibolē* (L-S 90, fishing net) occurs in Oppian (*Halientica* 4.149).

7. In Latin it is either *jaculum* or *rete jaculum* (Ovid, *Ars amatoria* 1.763) or *funda* (Virgil, *Georgica* 1.141).

spreads out into a circle[8] as it falls on the water, where it sinks swiftly because of its lead weights and encloses whatever is below it. Its circular, bell-like shape made it suitable for use as a mosquito net.[9] An *amphiblēstron* is the garment in whose deadly folds Clytemnestra entangled Agamemnon;[10] it was the fetter used to fasten Prometheus to his rock;[11] and it was the envenomed garment that Deianira gave to Hercules.[12]

Sagēnē, which occurs only once in the New Testament (Matt. 13:47; cf. Isa. 19:8; Ezek. 26:8)[13] is the long-drawn net or sweep-net.[14] Its ends are taken by boats to the open sea where they are drawn together, thus capturing all that the net encircles. The Vulgate translates *sagēnē* by *sagena* (fishing net).[15] In classical Latin, a *sagēnē* is referred to as an *everriculum* (drag-net),[16] because it *sweeps* the bottom of the sea. Since it was a *panagron*,[17] or take-all,[18] the Greeks gave the name of *sagēneuein*[19] to a device reportedly used by the Persians to clear a conquered island of its inhabitants.[20] Virgil described fishing first by using *amphiblēstron* and then by using *sagēnē*: "One, seeking its depth, beats the wide steam with a net, another draws the wet nets from the sea."[21]

Thus Jesus' use of *sagēnē* in a parable to describe the wide and all-embracing character of his future kingdom is very appropriate (Matt. 13:47). Neither *amphiblēstron* nor *diktyon* (which *might* have meant no more than *amphiblēstron*) would have been as suitable.

8. *Amphiballetai* (is thrown around).

9. According to Herodotus (2.95), the Egyptian fishermen used it for this purpose, but see Blakesley, *Herodotus* (2.95).

10. Aeschylus, *Agamemnon* 1353; *Choephoroe* 490; cf. Euripides, *Helena* 1088.

11. Aeschylus, *Prometheus vinctus* 81.

12. Sophocles, *Trachiniae* 1052.

13. It comes from *sattō*, *sesaga* (L-S 1585, pack, stuff); cf. the Latin *onero* (to load, to burden).

14. *Vasta sagena* (huge fishing net), as Manilius called it.

15. It is called "seine" or "sean" in Cornwall, where it is frequently used.

16. Cicero, playing upon Verres's name, called him *everriculum in provincia* (the drag-net in the province).

17. L-S 1295, catching all.

18. Homer, *Iliad* 5.487.

19. L-S 1580, to sweep away an entire population.

20. Herodotus, 3.149; 6.31; Plato, *Leges* 3.698d. Curiously enough, the same device was actually tried, though with little success, in Tasmania not many years ago (see Bonwick's *Last of the Tasmanians*).

21. *Georgica* 1.141.

65

lypeō (3076) — *Grieve*

pentheō (3996) — *Be Sorrowful*, *Lament*

thrēneō (2354) — *Mourn*

koptō (2875) — *Wail*

Lypeō, *pentheō*, *thrēneō*, and *koptō* refer to the *sense* of grief or to its *utterance*. In sensing grief, there are degrees of intensity; grief is verbally manifested in different forms.

Lypein[1] is a general term that is used to express various forms of grief. *Lypein* is contrasted with *chairein*,[2] just as *lypē* (3077) is contrasted with *chara*[3] or with *ēdonē*.[4] Unlike the grief expressed by *pentheō*, *thrēneō*, and *koptō*, *lypē* refers to an inward grief that does not necessarily manifest itself outwardly, unless the grieving person chooses to reveal it (Rom. 9:2).

Penthein is a stronger term than *lypein*. *Penthein* is not merely *dolere* (to be in pain) or *angi* (to suffer pain) but *lugere* (to mourn, to bewail). Like *lypein*,

1. Matt. 14:9; Eph. 4:30; 1 Pet. 1:6.
2. *5463*; Aristotle, *Rhetorica* 1.2; Sophocles, *Ajax* 555.
3. *5479*; John 16:20; Xenophon, *Hellenica* 7.1.22.
4. *2237*; Plato, *Leges* 733.

lypeō

pentheō

thrēneō
kopto

penthein primarily means to lament for the dead[5] but also includes any other passionate lamenting,[6] since *penthos* is a form of *pathos*,[7] a grief so all-encompassing that it cannot be hidden. As Spanheim noted:

> For *penthein* among the Greeks corresponds to the words *bkh* [1058], *klaiein* [2799], *thrēnein* and *hylōyl* [1984], *ololyzein* [3649] and thus denotes not only grief felt inwardly but also expressed outwardly.[8]

According to Chrysostom, the *penthountes* of Matthew 5:4 are "those who grieve [*lypoumenoi*] with intensity," those whose grief is so great that it manifests itself externally. Thus *penthein* is often joined with *klaiein*,[9] and we have the phrase *penthōn kai skythrōpazōn* (cf. 4659) in Psalm 35:14. Gregory of Nyssa defined *penthos* more generally: "*Penthos* is the mournful disposition of the soul brought about by the loss of anyone of those who are close to the heart."[10] Since Gregory was not distinguishing synonyms, however, he was not careful to make fine distinctions.

Thrēnein[11] means "to bewail," "to make a *thrēnos*."[12] *Thrēnein* may refer to mere wailing or lamentation,[13] to breaking out in unstudied words (like an Irish wake), or it may take the more elaborate form of a poem. The beautiful lamentation that David composed over Saul and Jonathan is introduced in the Septuagint with *ethrēnēse Dabid ton thrēnon touton* (2 Sam 1:17). The sublime dirge over Tyre is also called a *thrēnos*.[14]

Koptein (Matt. 24:30; Luke 23:27; Rev. 1:7) means "to strike" and was an act that commonly accompanied a *thrēnein*. More specifically, *koptein* means "to strike the breast as an outward sign of grief" (Nah. 2:7; Luke 18:13). So *kopetos*[15] is *thrēnos* "with the sound of hands,"[16] and, as with *penthein*, is often a token of grief for the dead.[17] Plutarch[18] joined *olophyrseis*[19] and *kopetoi*[20] as two of the more violent manifestations of grief and condemned both for their excesses.

5. Cicero, *Tusculanae disputationes* 1.13; 4.8: "Lamentation [*luctus*], grief from the bitter death of one who had been dear"; "to lament [*penthein*] a corpse" (Homer, *Iliad* 19.225); "to lament [*penthein*] those who have perished" (Xenophon, *Hellenica* 2.2, 3).

6. Sophocles, *Oedipus tyrannus* 1296; Gen. 37:34.

7. 3806; see Plutarch, *Consolatio ad Apollonium* 22.

8. *Dubia evangelica* 81.

9. 2 Sam. 19:1; Mark 16:10; James 4:9; Rev. 18:15.

10. Suicer, *Thesaurus* under *penthos* (3997).

11. It is joined with *odyresthai* (cf. 3602; Plutarch, *Quomodo quis suos in virtute sentiat profectus* 5) and with *katoikteirein* (cf. 3627; Plutarch, *Consolatio ad Apollonium* 11).

12. 2355. It is equivalent to the Latin *nenia* (dirge over the dead).

13. *Thrēnos kai klauthmos* (2805; Matt. 2:18).

14. Ezek. 26:17; cf. 2 Chron. 35:25; Amos 8:10; Rev. 18:11.

15. 2870; Acts 8:2.

16. Hesychius.

17. Gen. 23:2; 2 Kings 3:31. It is the Latin *plangere* (to strike, to beat); "striking lacerated breasts" in Ovid, *Metamorphoses* 6.248; cf. Sophocles, *Ajax* 615–17. It is connected with the Latin *plaga* (a blow) and *plēssō* (4141).

18. *Consolatio ad uxorem* 4.

19. L-S 1219, lamentation.

20. Cf. *Fabius Maximus* 17: "female lamentations."

66

hamartia (266)	*Sin*
hamartēma (265)	
parakoē (3876)	*Disobedience*
anomia (458)	*Unrighteousness*
	Lawlessness
paranomia (3892)	*Breaking the Law*
parabasis (3847)	*Transgression*
paraptōma (3900)	*Trespass*
	Fault
agnoēma (51)	*Error*
hēttēma (2275)	*Failure*

This group contains numerous words—*hamartia, hamartēma, parakoē, anomia, paranomia, parabasis, paraptōma, agnoēma, hēttēma*—and more can easily be added. It is not difficult to see why: sin[1] may be viewed from an infinite number of aspects in all languages. The diagnosis of sin primarily belongs to

1. Augustine defined sin as "any deed or word or desire against eternal law" (*Contra Faustum* 22.27; cf. the Stoic definition of *hamartēma* as "a prohibition of the law"; Plutarch, *De Stoicorum repugnantiis* 11). Sin is "the willingness to allow or retain what righteousness forbids and from what a free person abstains" (*Contra Julium Pelagium* 1.47).

hamartia
hamartēma
parakoē
anomia

paranomia
parabasis
paraptōma

agnoēma
hēttēma

Scripture, where it is viewed from the greatest number of perspectives and described with many various images. When sin is viewed as the missing of a mark or aim, it is referred to as *hamartia* or as *hamartēma*. When seen as the transgressing of a line, sin is termed *parabasis*. When understood as disobeying a voice, sin is called *parakoē*. When perceived as falling where one should have stood upright, sin is labelled *paraptōma*. When portrayed as the ignorance of what one should have known, sin is termed *agnoēma*. When depicted as the diminishing of what should have been given in full measure, sin is called *hēttēma*. When viewed as the nonobservance of a law, sin is termed *anomia* or *paranomia*. When seen as a discord in the harmonies of God's universe, sin is referred to as *plēmmeleia*.[2] Sin may be described in ways almost beyond number.

We will begin our study of this word group with *hamartia*, the word most frequently used to describe sin. *Hamartia*'s etymology is uncertain and so cannot help us accurately define the word or distinguish it from the other words in this group. Suidas derived *hamartia* from *marptō*,[3] as though *hamartia* came from *hamarptia* (a failing to grasp). Buttmann's conjecture[4] that *hamartia* belongs to the root *meros* (*3313*), *meiromai*, on which a negative intransitive verb (to be without one's share of, to miss) was formed,[5] has found more favor.[6] Only this, however, is obvious: when sin is contemplated as *hamartia*, it is regarded as a failing (or missing) of the true end and scope of our lives, namely God.[7]

A slighter understanding of sin and its evil goes hand in hand with a slighter ethical significance in the words used to express it. Nowhere in classical Greek do *hamartia* and *hamartanein* (*264*) have the depth of meaning they have acquired in revealed religion. They run the same course there that all ethical terms seem to have run. Employed first about natural things, *hamartia* and *hamartanein* were then applied to the moral or spiritual realm.[8] Initially *hamartanein* meant to miss a mark and was the exact opposite of *tychein* (*5177*). Thus over and over in Homer we read of the warrior *hamartei*, who hurls his spear but who fails to strike his foe.[9] *Tōn hodōn hamartanein*[10] is to miss one's way. Next, *hamartia* was applied to the intellectual realm. Thus we read of the poet *hamartanei*, who selects a subject that is impossible to treat

2. L-S 1418, fault, error; lit. a false note.

3. L-S 1081, take hold of.

4. *Lexilogus*, p. 85, English ed.

5. See Xenophon, *Cyropaedia* 1.6.13.

6. See a long note by Fritzsche on Rom. 5:12, with excellent philology and abominable theology.

7. It is "the vanishing of the good" according to Oecumenius, or "the failure to obtain the good" and "to miss the mark or to shoot at aimless things," according to Suidas, or "the turning aside from what is noble—whether by nature or by law," according to another authority. We may compare it to the German *fehlen* (to miss, to make a mistake).

8. The human mind delights to trace the analogy between the former and the latter.

9. *Iliad* 4.491. This occurs approximately a hundred times in this work.

10. Thucydides, 3.98.2.

poetically or who seeks results that lie beyond the limits of his art.[11] *Hamartia* constantly is contrasted with *orthotēs*.[12] *Hamartia* is so far removed from any necessary ethical significance that Aristotle sometimes (if not always) withdrew it from the realm of right and wrong.[13] The *hamartia* is a mistake (perhaps a fearful one), like that of Oedipus, but nothing more.[14] Elsewhere, however, *hamartia* can be as close in meaning to our use of *sin* as any word used in heathen ethics.[15]

Hamartia refers to sin in the abstract as well as to sin in the concrete—to the act of sinning and to the actual sin.[16] *Hamartēma*,[17] however, never refers to sin as sinfulness or to the act of sinning. Instead, *hamartēma* refers to sin in terms of its separate consequences and acts of disobedience to a divine law.[18] There is the same difference between *anomia* and *anomēma*,[19] between *asebeia* and *asebēma*,[20] and between *adikia* and *adikēma*.[21] This is brought out in Aristotle's[22] contrast of *adikon*[23] and *adikēma*: "*To adikēma* and *to adikon* are different. *Adikon* is by nature or by order; but whenever this very thing is committed, it is an *adikēma*."[24] Clement of Alexandria[25] has a long but not very profitable discussion on the distinction between *hamartia* and *hamartēma*, between *adikia* and *adikēma*, and between other words in this group.

Asebeia is used with *adikia*,[26] just as *asebēs* (765) is used with *adikos*, *anosios*,[27] and *hamartōlos*.[28] *Asebeia* is positive and active irreligion—a deliberate withholding from God of his dues of prayer and service, as if one were in battle array against him. The Authorized Version always translates *asebeia* as "ungodliness," and the Rheims Version always translates *asebeia* as "impiety"

11. Aristotle, *Poetica* 8 and 25. Thus we have "an error [*hamartia*] of opinion" (Thucydides, 1.32) and "fault [*hamartēma*] of judgment" (2.65).

12. L-S 1249f., correctness; Plato, *Leges* 1.627d; 2.668c; Aristotle, *Poetica* 25.

13. *Ethica Nicomachea* 5.8.7.

14. *Poetica* 13; cf. Euripides, *Hippolytus* 1426.

15. Plato, *Phaedrus* 113e; *Republic* 2.366a; Xenophon, *Cyropaedia* 5.4.19.

16. The Latin *peccatio* (sin; A. Gellius, 13.20, 17) no less than *peccatum* (the sin).

17. It only occurs in Mark 3:28; 4:12; Rom. 3:25; 1 Cor. 6:18.

18. In the Greek schools it is opposed to *katorthōma* (2735). In their controversy with the Roman Catholic Church, the Pelagians claimed that Chrysostom sided with them on the subject of the moral condition of infants. Augustine (*Contra Julium Pelagium* 6.2) replied by quoting the exact words of Chrysostom, showing that he had pronounced infants to be free not of *hamartia*, or sin, but of *hamartēmata*, the several acts and results of sin. Only in this sense were they partakers of the *anamartēsia* (sinlessness) of Christ.

19. This word is not in the New Testament but is found in 1 Sam. 25:28; Ezek. 16:49.

20. It is not found in the New Testament but occurs in Lev. 18:17.

21. 92; Acts 18:14.

22. *Ethica Nicomachea* 5.7.

23. 94. It is equivalent to *adikia*.

24. Cf. an instructive passage in Xenophon (*Memorabilia* 2.2, 3): "Cities have pronounced death as the punishment for the great wicked actions [*adikēmasi*], as though people cease from sin [*adikian*] through fear of greater evil."

25. *Stromata* 2.15.

26. Xenophon, *Apologia Socratis* 24; Rom. 1:8.

27. 462; Xenophon, *Cyropaedia* 8.8.27.

28. 268; 1 Tim. 1:9; 1 Pet. 4:18.

hamartia
hamartēma
parakoē
anomia

paranomia
parabasis
paraptōma

agnoēma
hēttēma

and *asebēs* as "impious," though neither of these words occur in our English Bible. The *asebēs* and the *dikaios* are always opposed to one another (cf. Gen. 18:23) as the two who wage on earth the great warfare between light and darkness and between right and wrong.

Parakoē occurs only once in the New Testament (Rom. 5:19)[29] and never in the Septuagint, though *parakouein*[30] is used several times in the Septuagint in the sense of "to disobey."[31] In its strictest sense, *parakoē* is a failing to hear or an incorrect hearing. The sense of active disobedience that results from this inattentive or careless hearing is superinduced on the word, or perhaps the sin is already committed in failing to listen when God is speaking. Bengel has a good note:

> *Para* [*3844*] in *parakoē* expresses as suitably as possible the reason for the origin of Adam's fall. Does one inquire how the mind and will of any upright person was able to suffer defeat or to receive injury? Answer—the mind and will wavered at the same time through carelessness; nothing can be assumed prior to carelessness, just as the relaxing of the guards is the beginning of the capturing of a city. *Parakoē*, disobedience, indicates such carelessness.[32]

Frequently in the Old Testament, disobedience is described as a refusing to hear (Jer. 11:10; 35:17) and it appears literally as such in Acts 7:57. In Hebrews 2:2, where *parakoē* is joined with and follows *parabasis*, the writer is implying that every actual transgression embodied in an outward act of disobedience was punished as was every refusal to hear, though such refusals might not have resulted in outwardly disobedient acts.

Generally we have translated *anomia* as "iniquity" (Matt. 7:23; Rom. 6:19; Heb. 10:17), once as "unrighteousness" (2 Cor. 6:14), and once as "transgression of the law" (1 John 3:4). *Anomia* is contrasted with *dikaiosynē*[33] and used with *anarchia*[34] and *antilogia*.[35] *Anomos* is used negatively at least once in the New Testament to refer to a person without law or to whom a law had not been given.[36] Elsewhere *anomia* is used of the greatest enemy of all law, the man of sin, the lawless one (2 Thess. 2:8). In 2 Thessalonians 2:8 *anomia* does not refer to one living without law but to one who acts contrary to law, as also is the case with *paranomia*, which occurs only in 2 Peter 2:16 (cf. Prov. 10:29), and with *paranomein* (*3891*) in Acts 23:3. It follows that where there is no law (Rom. 5:13), there may be *hamartia* or *adikia* but not *anomia*, which Oecumenius defined as "the error against the adopted law" or as Fritzsche stated, "the contempt for the law or the permissiveness of morals by which the law is violated." Thus the Gentiles who do not have a law (Rom. 2:14)

29. Here it is opposed to *hypakoē* (*5218*); 2 Cor. 10:6; Heb. 2:2.
30. *3878*; in the New Testament it occurs only in Matt. 18:17.
31. Esther 3:3, 8; Isa. 65:12.
32. On Rom. 5:19.
33. *1343*; 2 Cor. 6:14; cf. Xenophon, *Memorabilia* 1.2.24.
34. L-S 120, lawlessness; Plato, *Republic* 9.575a.
35. *485*; Ps. 55:10.
36. 1 Cor. 9:21; cf. Plato, *Republic* 302e, "a lawless monarchy."

might be charged with sin; but since they were sinning without law,[37] they could not be charged with *anomia*. Behind the law of Moses that the Gentiles never had is another law, the original law and revelation of the righteousness of God that is written on the hearts of all (Rom. 2:14–15). Since this law is never completely obliterated in the human heart, all sin, even that of the darkest and most ignorant savage, must still in a secondary sense remain as *anomia*, a violation of this older, though partially obscured, law. Thus Origin stated:

> Guilt indeed has this differentiation from sin, in that guilt refers to those things which are done against law; hence also the Greek language calls it lawlessness [*anomian*]. But that can also be called a sin which is committed against what nature teaches and conscience censures.[38]

It is the same with *parabasis*. There must be something to transgress before there can be a transgression. Sin occurred between the time of Adam and Moses, a fact attested to by death. Those people who lived between the law that was given in paradise (Gen. 2:16–17) and the law that was given from Sinai sinned, though not "according to the likeness of the transgression of Adam" (*parabaseōs*, Rom. 5:14). With the coming of the law at Sinai, for the first time there was the possibility of transgressing that law (Rom. 4:15). *Parabasis*[39]—some act that is excessive or enormous—is the term especially used to refer to such transgressions or trespasses. Cicero wrote: "To sin is as if to leap across lines."[40] According to Paul, a *parabasis*, seen as the transgression of a given commandment, is more serious than *hamartia*.[41] From this viewpoint, and with reference to this very word, Augustine often drew a distinction between the *peccator* (sinner) and the *praevaricator* (transgressor), and between the *peccatum* (sin, *hamartia*) and the *praevaricatio* (transgression, *parabasis*). Thus Augustine stated:

> Every transgressor indeed is a sinner because he sins with the law, but not every sinner is a transgressor because some sin without a law. For where there is no law, there is neither a transgressor.[42]

The Latin word *praevaricator* (one who does not walk straight) introduces a new image, not that of overstepping a line but that of halting on unequal feet, though this imagery had faded from the word by the time Augustine used it. Augustine's motive in using *praevaricator*, or collusive prosecutor, was that this word dealt unjustly *with a law*. In Augustine's language, one who is under

37. *Anomos* is equivalent to *chōris* (5565) *nomou* (3551), Rom. 2:12; 3:21.

38. *Commentarii in Romanos* 4.5. Cf. Xenophon, *Memorabilia* 4.4.18, 19.

39. It is derived from *parabainein* (3845) and is similar to the Latin *transilire lineam* (to leap across the line) and to the French *forfait* (a grave transgression).

40. *Paradoxa Stoicorum* 3. Cf. the Homeric *hyperbasiē* (L-S 1860, transgression); *Iliad* 3.107 and often.

41. Rom. 2:23; 1 Tim. 2:14; cf. Heb. 2:2; 9:15.

42. *Narratio in Psalma* 118; *Sermones* 25.

hamartia
hamartēma
parakoē
anomia

paranomia
parabasis
paraptōma

agnoēma
hēttēma

no express law and sins is a *peccator* (sinner), but the one who has such a law and sins is a *praevaricator* (transgressor).[43] Before the law came men might be the former, but after the law they could only be the latter. In the first there is *implicit* disobedience, in the second *explicit* disobedience.

Paraptōma occurs only in later Greek and then rarely.[44] Cocceius wrote: "If we look at the origin of the word, it signifies those actions for which someone falls and lies prostrate, so that he cannot rise and stand before God." In Ephesians 2:1, where *paraptōmata* and *hamartia* occur together, Jerome distinguished them (apparently in agreement with others) in this way: the former are sins suggested to the mind and partially entertained and welcomed there; the latter are embodied in actual deeds:

> They say that *paraptōmata* are, as it were, the beginnings of sins, when a silent thought has crept in while we are drowsy but does not drive us to ruin. Sin, however, exists when something actually is done and reaches its conclusion.

This distinction is unwarranted, except insofar as sins of thought partake more of the nature of infirmity and have less aggravation than the same sins consummated and embodied in actions. Thus *paraptōma* sometimes is used to designate sins that are not the gravest or the worst, as is clearly the case in Galatians 6:1, where the Authorized Version translated it as "fault," and not obscurely, as it seems to be in Romans 5:15, 17–18. Polybius used *paraptōma* to refer to an error, to a mistake in judgment, to a blunder.[45] In another inadequate distinction, Augustine[46] described *paraptōma* as the negative omission of good, as contrasted with *hamartia*, the positive doing of evil.

Paraptōma has not always been understood so mildly[47] and certainly is not used that way in Ephesians 2:1, "dead in *trespasses* [*paraptōmasi*] and sins." In Ezekiel 18:26 *paraptōma* refers to mortal sin. In Hebrews 6:6 *parapesein* (3895) is equivalent to the "sinning [*hamartanein*] willingly" of Hebrews 10:26 and to the "departing from the living God" of Hebrews 3:12. A passage in Philo[48] that closely resembles the two in the Epistle to the Hebrews expressly precludes a weaker understanding of *paraptōma*. In this passage Philo used *paraptōma* to describe a man who had reached an acknowledged pitch of godliness and virtue but who had fallen from that state: "He was lifted up to the height of heaven and is fallen down to the depth of hell."

Agnoēma occurs in the New Testament only in Hebrews 9:7,[49] though *agnoia* (52) is used in the same sense of sin in Psalm 25:7 (and often), and

43. This is equivalent to *parabatēs* (Rom. 2:25; James 2:9), a name the church fathers always gave to Julian the Apostate.

44. Longinus used it to refer to literary faults (*De sublimitate* 36).

45. 9.10.6; cf. Ps. 19:12–13, where it is contrasted with the *hamartia megalē* (3173). For other examples, see Cremer, *Biblisch-Theologische Wörterbuch*, p. 501.

46. *Quaestiones ad Leviticum* 20.

47. See Jeremy Taylor, *Doctrine and Practice of Repentance*, 3.3.21.

48. 2.648.

49. See Theoluck, *On the Hebrews*, *Appendix*, p. 92. It also occurs in Jth. 5:20; 1 Macc. 13:39; Tob. 3:3.

agnoein (50, to sin) occurs in Hosea 4:15; Ecclesiasticus 5:15; and Hebrews 5:2. Sin is referred to as an *agnoēma* when one tries to make excuses for it (as far as this is possible), to regard it in the mildest possible light.[50] Although there is always an element of ignorance in every human transgression (making it human and not devilish), this mitigates but does not eliminate the sin; it makes forgiveness possible but not necessary. As Jesus said, "Father, forgive them, for they do not know what they do" (Luke 23:34). And Paul said, "I obtained mercy because I did it ignorantly in unbelief" (1 Tim. 1:13).[51] No human sin, except perhaps the sin against the Holy Spirit,[52] is committed with a complete recognition of the true nature of the evil that is chosen and of the good that is forsaken. Many passages in Plato identify vice with ignorance and even claim that no man is voluntarily evil.[53] Whatever exaggerations Plato's statements may contain, sin is always to a greater or lesser degree an *agnoēma*. The more the *agnoein* (as opposed to the "sinning willingly" of Heb. 10:26) predominates, the greater the extenuation of the sinfulness. Therefore the one New Testament use of *agnoēma* (Heb. 9:7) is very appropriate. In Hebrews 9:7, the *agnoēmata* (errors) of the people for which the high priest offered sacrifice on the great Day of Atonement were not willful transgressions; they were not "presumptuous sins" (Ps. 19:13) that willingly were committed against the conscience and with a high hand against God. Those who committed such sins were cut off from the congregation; there was no provision in the levitical constitution for the forgiveness of such sin (Num. 15:30–31). Rather, these were sins that resulted from the weakness of the flesh, from an imperfect insight into God's law, and from a lack of due circumspection[54] that afterwards were viewed with shame and regret. The same distinction exists between *agnoia* and *agnoēma* as the one between *hamartia* and *hamartēma* and between *adikia* and *adikēma*: the former is often more abstract, and the latter is always more concrete.

Hēttēma is not used in classical Greek, though *hētta*, a briefer form of the word, is contrasted with *nikē* (3529), as defeat is opposed to victory.[55] *Hēttēma* is used once in the Septuagint (Isa. 31:8) and twice in the New Testament (Rom. 11:12; 1 Cor. 6:7), but only in 1 Corinthians 6:7, where it refers to a coming short of duty, to a fault, does it have an ethical sense.[56] According to Gerhard: "*Hēttēma* is a decrease, a lack, from *hēttasthai*, to be defeated, since sinners succumb to the temptations of the flesh and of Satan."[57]

50. See Acts 3:17.

51. Here, as someone has noted correctly, "the expression combines guilt and excuse."

52. This may be the reason why it is unforgivable (Matt. 12:32).

53. Also see what is said qualifying or guarding this statement in Archer Butler, *Lectures on Ancient Philosophy*, 2:285.

54. "Willingly," Lev. 4:13; cf. 5:15–19; Num. 15:22–29.

55. It has gone through much the same stages as the Latin *clades* (loss, defeat).

56. It is equivalent to the German *Fehler* (a mistake) and the Latin *delictum* (a wrong).

57. *Loci theologica* 11.

hamartia
hamartēma
parakoē
anomia

paranomia
parabasis
paraptōma

agnoēma
hēttēma

Plēmmeleia[58] occurs frequently in the Old Testament (Lev. 5:15; Num. 18:9; and often), as well as in later ecclesiastical Greek,[59] but not in the New Testament. Properly speaking, *plēmmeleia*[60] is a discord or disharmony.[61] Augustine's Greek was faulty when he related *plēmmeleia* and *melei* (3199), "it is a concern,"[62] and made *plēmmeleia* equivalent to *ameleia* (carelessness). Instead, *plēmmeleia* refers to sin that is regarded as a discord or disharmony in the great symphonies of the universe: "Disproportioned sin jarred against nature's chime, and with harsh din broke the fair music that all creatures made to their great Lord."

Delitzsch made the following observation on the more important Hebrew terms that more or less correspond with the ones we have just studied:

> Sin is called *pōša'* [6586] as being a tearing away from God, a breach of fidelity, a falling from the state of grace, in Greek *asebeia*; *ḥaṭā'āh* [2401] is a missing the mark set by God, a deviation from what pleases God, achieving what is contrary to God, in Greek *hamartia*; *'āôn* [5771] is a perverting what is right, a misdeed, an incurring of guilt, in Greek *anomia* or *adikia*.[63]

58. L-S 1418, fault, error; lit. a false note.

59. Thus see Clement of Rome, *Epistula 1 ad Corinthios* 41.

60. It is derived from *plēmmelēs* (one who sings out of tune; *plēn* [4133] and *melos* [L-S 1099, song, tune]), as *emmelēs* is "one who is in tune," and *emmeleia* is "the right modulation of the voice to the music."

61. "Disharmony [*plēmmeleia*] and without metre" (Plutarch, *Septem sapientium convivium* 9.14.7).

62. *Quaestiones ad Leviticum* 3.20.

63. On Ps. 32:1. Cf. Hupfeld on the same passage.

67

archaios (744) *palaios* (3820) — Old

It would be a mistake to attempt to distinguish *archaios* and *palaios* on the basis of which term expresses the greatest antiquity, since sometimes this is expressed by one word and then the other. *Archaios* refers to that which was *from the beginning*.[1] If we accept this as the *first* beginning of all, it must be older than a person or a thing that is merely *palaios*—having existed a long time ago.[2] But since there may be later beginnings, it is quite possible to view the *palaios* as older than the *archaios*. Donaldson wrote:

> As the word *archaeology* is already appropriated to the discussion of those subjects of which the antiquity is only comparative, it would be consistent with the usual distinction between *archaios* and *palaios* to give the name of *palaeology* to those sciences which aim at reproducing an absolutely primeval state or condition.[3]

I fail to trace such a strong or constant sense of a more primeval state or condition in the uses of *palaios* as Donaldson's statement implies. Thus compare Thucydides, 2.15: "This has happened from the very ancient [*archaiou*] of time," from the prehistoric time of Cecrops, with 1.18: "Sparta was well gov-

1. *Archēn* (746), *ap' archēs*.
2. *Palai*, 3819.
3. *New Cratylus*, p. 19.

erned from very ancient [*palaitatou*] time," from very early times but still within the historic period. Here the words are used in exactly the opposite sense.

It is not always possible to determine the difference between *archaios* and *palaios*. Often these words are used together as merely cumulative synonyms or with no greater antiquity predicated by one than by the other.[4] Etymologically the words are often used indifferently—that which was from the beginning is generally from a long time ago, and that which was from a long time ago often will be from the beginning. Thus the *archaia phōnē* (5456) of one passage in Plato[5] is exactly equivalent to the *palaia phōnē* of another.[6] The *archaioi theoi* (*2316*) of one passage in the *Euthyphro* are the *palaia daimonia* (*1140*) of another. *Hoi palaioi* and *hoi archaioi* both refer to the ancients.[7] There cannot be much difference between *palaioi chronoi*[8] and *archaiai hēmerai*.[9]

But whenever the emphasis is on going back to a beginning (whatever that beginning may be), *archaios* is the preferred term. Thus *archaia* and *prōta* (*4413*) are used together in Isaiah 33:18. Satan is the "serpent of old" (Rev. 12:9; 20:2), since his malignant work against God reaches back to the earliest epoch in human history. The world before the flood (which was from the first) is *ho archaios kosmos*.[10] Mnason was *archaios mathētēs* (*3101*; Acts 21:16), "an old disciple," not in the sense that English readers almost inevitably take the words—"an *aged* disciple"—but one who had been a disciple from the commencement of the faith, from the day of Pentecost or before it. Although he probably was advanced in years, this is not the emphasis here. The original founders of the Jewish commonwealth, who gave the law with authority, are *hoi archaioi*.[11] *Pistis* (*4102*) *archaia*[12] is the faith that was from the beginning, "once delivered to the saints." In a passage where both words occur, Plato[13] traced the language's finer distinctions in a way that determined the respective uses of these words. In a passage in Sophocles, Deianira speaks of the poisoned shirt, her gift from Nessus, in this way: "I had a gift, given long ago [*palaion*] by a monster of olden time [*archaiou*] hidden in an urn of bronze."[14]

Archaios[15] often designates something that is both ancient and venerable, something that is honorable because of its antiquity,[16] just as its opposite *mod-*

4. Plato, *Leges* 865d; Demosthenes, 22.597; Plutarch, *Consolatio ad Apollonium* 27; Justin Martyr, *Cohortatio ad Graecos* 5.

5. *Cratylus* 418c.

6. Ibid. 398d.

7. Plutarch, *Consolatio ad Apollonium* 14 and 33.

8. *5550*; 2 Macc. 6:21.

9. *2250*; Ps. 44:1.

10. *2889*; 2 Pet. 2:5.

11. Matt. 5:21, 27, 33; cf. 1 Sam. 24:14; Isa. 25:1.

12. Eusebius, *Historica ecclesiastica* 5.28, 9.

13. *Timaeus* 22b.

14. *Trachiniae* 546. Aeschylus (*Eumenides* 727–28) furnishes a third passage.

15. Like the Latin *priscus* (old).

16. Thus "the ancient [*archaios*] Lord" (Xenophon, *Anabasis* 1.9.1; cf. Aristophanes, *Nubes* 961).

ern is always used disparagingly by Shakespeare. This is the point where the meaning of *archaios* and *palaios* diverge. These words do not share secondary meanings; each has its own proper domain. I noted that the honor of antiquity is sometimes expressed by *archaios*, though *palaios* also may have this meaning. But that which is ancient also is old-fashioned, ill-adapted to the present, part of a world that has passed away.[17] *Archaios* often has this additional sense of old-world fashion and refers to something that not only is antique but that also is antiquated and out-of-date.[18] This can be seen even more strongly in *archaiotēs*,[19] which only has this meaning.[20]

Although the meaning of *archaios* moves in that direction,[21] the meaning of *palaios* diverges in another.[22] What has existed for a long time has been exposed to, and perhaps suffered from, the wrongs and injuries of time. Only *palaios* means old in the sense of more or less worn out.[23] Thus we have "an old [*palaion*] garment" (Matt. 9:16), "old [*palaioi*] wineskins" (Matt. 9:17), "old [*palaioi*] wineskins torn and mended" (Josh. 9:4), and "old [*palaia*] rags (Jer. 38:11). Although *hoi archaioi* could never be used to refer to the old men of a living generation as compared with that generation's young men, this is always the meaning of *hoi palaioi*. Thus we read of "young and old [*palaios*]"[24] and of "aged and old [*palaioi*]."[25] This is also true of words formed on *palaios*, as in Hebrews 8:13: "Now what is becoming obsolete [*palaioumenon*] and growing old is ready to vanish away."[26] Plato used *palaiotēs* (*3821*) and *saprotēs* (cf. *4550*) together.[27] Whenever *palaios* means that which is worn out or wearing out by age, it requires *kainos* (*2537*) as its opposite.[28] When it does not denote something that is worn out, there is nothing to prevent *neos* (*3501*) from being used as its opposite.[29] *Kainos* also may be contrasted with *archaios*.[30]

17. We find an example of this in that "antique" and "antic" are only different spellings of the same word.

18. It is not merely *alterthümlich* (ancient) but *altfränkisch* (antiquated); Aeschylus, *Prometheus vinctus* 325; Aristophanes, *Plutus* 323; *Nubes* 915; *Pax* 554, "to rejoice is now antiquated [*archaion*] and stale."

19. L-S 251, old-fashionedness.

20. Plato, *Leges* 2.657b.

21. There is no example of this meaning in the New Testament.

22. There are many New Testament examples of *palaios*.

23. This is also the case for *vetus* (old); cf. Tertullian's pregnant antithesis (*Adversus Marcum* 1.8): "If God is aged [*vetus*], He will not be; if He is new [*novus*], He was not."

24. Homer, *Iliad* 14.108; and often.

25. Philo, *De vita contemplativa* 8; cf. Job 15:10.

26. Cf. Ecclus. 14:17; Luke 12:33; Heb. 1:11.

27. *Republic* 10.609e; cf. Aristophanes, *Plutus* 1086; "aged [*palaia*] and rotten [*sapra*] dregs."

28. Josh. 9:13; Mark 2:21; Heb. 8:13. Sometimes this will be true on other occasions (Herodotus, 9.26, twice).

29. Lev. 26:10; Homer, *Odyssey* 2.293; Plato, *Cratylus* 418b; Aeschylus, *Eumenides* 778, 808.

30. 2 Cor. 5:17; Aristophanes, *Ranae* 720; Isocrates, 15.82; Plato, *Euthyphro* 3b; Philo, *De vita contemplativa* 10.

68

aphthartos (862) — Incorruptible, Immortal

amarantos (263), *amarantinos* (262) — Unfading

The reign of sin and its results—imperfection, decay, and death—throughout this fallen world are so pervasive that in describing the glory, purity, and perfection of the higher world that is our goal, we are almost inevitably compelled to use negatives. We contrast the leading features and characteristics of this world with those of the higher order. This is especially the case in 1 Peter 1:4, where two of the three synonyms used in the New Testament to describe the higher order occur. Peter magnified the inheritance reserved in heaven for the faithful by using three negatives.[1] This inheritance is *aphthartos* (without our corruption), *amiantos* (283) (without our defilement), and *amarantos* (without our withering and fading away). Peter depicted what the heavenly inheritance is by describing what it is not. We will not distinguish *amiantos* from *aphthartos* and *amarantos*, since the distinction is too apparent for useful synonymous discrimination.

Aphthartos, which is used in later Greek, is not found in the Septuagint and occurs only twice in the Apocrypha (Wisd. of Sol. 12:1; 18:4). Properly speaking, only God is *aphthartos*, a fact that heathen theology recognized just as clearly as biblical theology. Thus Plutarch quoted the grand saying of the

1. He hardly had any choice in the matter.

aphthartos

amarantos

amarantinos

Stoic philosopher Antipater of Tarsus: "We regard God as a blessed and incorruptible [*aphtharton*] creature."[2] Plutarch also associated *aphthartos* with *isotheos*,[3] *aidios*,[4] *anekleiptos*,[5] *agennētos*,[6] *agenētos*,[7] and *apathēs*.[8] Philo related *aphthartos* to *olympios*[9] and to other corresponding words. On one occasion in the New Testament (1 Tim. 1:17), *aphthartos* is translated as "immortal," though there is a clear distinction between it and *athanatos* (cf. *110*) or "he who has *athanasian*" (1 Tim. 6:16). In other places in the New Testament (1 Cor. 9:25; 15:52; 1 Pet. 1:23), *aphthartos* is translated as "incorruptible," a translation that is to be preferred in 1 Timothy 1:17 as well. In this verse *aphthartos* means that God is exempt from wear and final perishing—that *phthora* (*5356*) that time and sin bring to everything except God, to those whom God has not given his *aphtharsia*.[10]

Amarantos occurs once in the New Testament (1 Pet. 1:4) and once in the Apocrypha, where it is joined with *lampros*.[11] *Amarantinos* also occurs only once in the New Testament (1 Pet. 5:4), and perhaps since it is a name given to a crown, it should be translated "of amaranths." Our version, however, has not distinguished *amarantos* and *amarantinos* but has translated both by the phrase *that does not fade away*.[12] Even the Rheims translators, who had the Vulgate's *immarcescibilis* before them, did not use it. *Amarantos* affirms that the heavenly inheritance is exempt from the swift withering that befalls all earthly loveliness. The most exquisite beauty of the natural world, the flower, is also the shortest-lived,[13] the quickest to fade and die.[14] Such fading and dying, however, is not part of the inheritance of unfading loveliness that is reserved in heaven for the faithful.

What does *amarantos* predicate of the heavenly inheritance that is not already indicated by *aphthartos*? Essentially, nothing. *Amarantos* does, however, imply a pledge that the delicate grace, beauty, and bloom of the heavenly inheritance will not wither and wane any more than its solid and substantial worth will depart. Not only can decay and corruption not touch it, but it will wear its freshness, brightness, and beauty forever. Estius stated: "It is unfading [*immarcescibilis*] in that it retains its vigor and grace like the amaranth flower, so that at no time does loathing or weariness creep upon its possessor."

2. *De Stoicorum repugnantiis* 38; cf. Diogenes Laërtius, 10.1.31.139.
3. L-S 837, godlike; *Non posse suaviter vivi secundum Epicurum* 7.
4. *126*; *Adversus Colotem* 13.
5. *413*; *De defectu oraculorum* 51.
6. L-S 8, unbegotten; *De Stoicorum repugnantiis* 38.
7. L-S 8, uncreated; *De E apud Delphos* 19.
8. L-S 174, not suffering; *De defectu oraculorum* 20.
9. L-S 1219, Olympian.
10. *861*; 1 Cor. 15:42; cf. Isa. 51:6; Heb. 1:10–12.
11. *2986*; Wisd. of Sol. 6:12.
12. No doubt our modern English translators considered "immarcescible" too pedantic. This word was used by Bishops Hall and Taylor and other scholarly writers of the seventeenth century.
13. *Breve lilium* (the brief lily).
14. Job 14:2; Pss. 37:2; 103:15; Isa. 40:6–7; Matt. 6:30; James 1:9; 1 Pet. 1:24.

69

metanoeō (3340) *metamelomai* (3338) — *Repent*

Reformation theologians frequently argued that *metanoia* (*3341*) and *metameleia*[1] and their verbs *metanoein* and *metamelesthai* are quite distinct. On the one hand, *metameliea* and its verb express a desire that an action might be undone, express regrets or even remorse, but do not imply an effective change of heart. On the other hand, *metanoia* and its verb refer to a true change of heart toward God.[2] According to Chillingworth:

> To this purpose it is worth the observing, that when the Scripture speaks of that kind of repentance, which is only sorrow for something done, and wishing it undone, it constantly useth the word *metameleia*, to which forgiveness of sins is nowhere promised. So it is written of Judas the son of perdition (Matt. 27:3), *metamelētheis apetrepse*, he repented and went and hanged himself, and so constantly in other places. But that repentance to which remission of sins and salvation is promised, is perpetually expressed by the word *metanoia*, which signifieth a thorough change of the heart and soul, of the life and actions.[3]

Before proceeding further, let me correct a slight inaccuracy in Chillingworth's statement. *Metameleia* does not occur in the New Testament and is

1. L-S 1114, regret, repentance.

2. Beza was the first to make this distinction, and he was followed by many others; cf. Spanheim, *Dubia evangelica*, 3:9.

3. *Sermons before Charles I*, p. 11.

found only once in the Septuagint (Hos. 11:8). Since this is a work on New Testament synonyms, the comparison and distinction can be made only between the verbs, though what is true of them also will be true of their nouns. But still another qualification needs to be made. Jeremy Taylor remarked:

> The Greeks use two words to express this duty, *metameleia* and *metanoia*. *Metameleia* is from *metameleisthai, post factum angi et cruciari*, "to be afflicted in mind," "to be troubled for our former folly"; it is *dysarestēsis epi pepragmenois*, saith Favorinus, "a being displeased for what we have done," and it is generally used for all sorts of repentance; but more properly to signify either the beginning of a good, or the whole state of an ineffective, repentance. In the first sense we find it in Matthew, *hymeis de idontes ou metamelēthēte hysteron tou pisteusai autō*, "and ye, seeing, did not repent that ye might believe Him." Of the second sense we have an example in Judas, *metamelētheis apestrepse*, he "repented" too, but the end of it was he died with anguish and despair. . . . There is in this repentance a sorrow for what is done, a disliking of the thing with its consequences and effect, and so far also it is a change of mind. But it goes no further than so far to change the mind that it brings trouble and sorrow, and such things as are the natural events of it. . . . When there was a difference made, *metanoia* was the better word, which does not properly signify the sorrow for having done amiss, but something that is nobler than it, but brought in at the gate of sorrow. For *hē kata Theon lypē*, "a godly sorrow," that is *metameleia*, or the first beginning of repentance, *metanoian katergazetai*, "worketh this better repentance," *metanoian ametamelēton* [278] and *eis sōtērian* [4991].[4]

Later Taylor admitted that "however the grammarians may distinguish them, yet the words are used promiscuously" and that it is not possible to distinguish them in a rigid fashion. Although this is partially true, it is possible to show that each word has a predominant use. There was a well-known conflict between the early Reformers and the Roman Catholic theologians over whether *paenitentia* (repentance), as the Catholics held, or *resipiscentia* (reformation), as Beza and others affirmed, was the better Latin translation of *metanoia*. There was much to be said on both sides. Had *metameleia* and not *metanoia* been the disputed word, the Catholics would have had a more favorable position. Augustine stated: "*Paenitentia* is a certain defense of one grieving, always punishing himself for having committed what pained him."[5]

Properly speaking, *metanoein* is "to know *after*" as *pronoein* (4306) is "to know *before*"; *metanoia* is "*after*knowledge," as *pronoia* (4307) is "*fore*knowledge." As Clement of Alexandria said:

> If he perceived afterwards [*metenoēsen*] what he had done wrong, if he has understood where he had made a mistake and has had a change of heart, that very thing is—after he has realized these things—*metanoia* or late knowledge.[6]

4. *On the Doctrine and Practice of Repentance*, ch. 2, 1, 2.
5. *De veris et falsis poenis*, chap. 8.
6. *Stromata* 2.6.

And Stobaeus stated: "The wise man must not know after [*metanoein*] but know before [*pronoein*]."[7] The next step that *metanoia* signifies is the change of mind that results from this afterknowledge. Thus Tertullian wrote: "In the Greek language the word for repentance is not derived from the admission of a fault but from a change of mind."[8] The third stage of *metanoia* results from this change of mind and consists of regret for the course of action that was pursued and of *dysapestēsis* (displeasure) with oneself. Tertullian defined it as "a certain suffering of the mind which comes from a displeasure about a previous opinion,"[9] for this was all that the heathen understood by it. At this stage of its meaning, *metanoia* was associated with *dēgmos*,[10] *aischynē*,[11] and *pothos*.[12] Last of all *metanoia* signifies a resulting change of conduct. This change of mind and consequent change of action, however, may be a change for the worse or a change for the better. The change signified by *metanoia* does not necessarily imply a *resipiscentia* (reformation) as well. That idea is a Christian addition to *metanoia*. Thus A. Gellius stated:

> We are accustomed then to say we regret [*paenitere*] when the deeds which we ourselves have done, or have been done through our will and plan, begin to displease us and we change our opinion about them.[13]

Similarly, Plutarch[14] told of two murderers who spared a child but who afterwards "repented" (*metenoēsan*) and sought to slay it. Plutarch used *metameleia* in the sense of repenting of something that is good,[15] thus validating Tertullian's complaint:

> What the pagans irrationally might include under the act of regret will be sufficiently clear from that fact alone that they apply it also to their good deeds: one regrets loyalty, love, sincerity, patience, mercy when any of these has fallen on the thankless.[16]

The regret that is part of the meaning of *metanoia* may be (and often is) quite unconnected with any sense of wrongdoing, with any sense of violating a moral law. This type of regret may simply be what our fathers used to call "hadiwist."[17] Sometimes, though rarely, *metanoia* has an ethical meaning, as

7. *Florilegium* 1.14.
8. *Adversus Marcionem* 2.24.
9. *De paenitentia* 1.
10. L-S 384, suffering; Plutarch, *Quomodo adulator ab amico internoscatur* 12.
11. *152*; Plutarch, *De virtute morali* 12.
12. L-S 1427, regret; Plutarch, *Pericles* 10; cf. Lucian, *De saltatione* 84.
13. 17.1.6.
14. *Septem sapientium convivium* 21.
15. *De sera numinis vindicta* 11.
16. *De paenitentia* 1.
17. *Had-I-wist*, "I should have acted otherwise," is better; thus see Plutarch, *De liberis educandis* 14; *Septem sapientium convivium* 12; *De sollertia animalium* 3: "grief through pain, which we call repentance [*metanoian*]"; "displeasure with oneself, proceeding from pain, which we call repentance" (Holland).

is the case in two other passages in Plutarch.[18] In the former passage, Plutarch's use of *metanoia* is in harmony with its use in Romans 2:4; in the latter passage, Plutarch used *metameleia* and *metanoia* interchangeably.

Only in Scripture and in the works of those who were dependent on Scripture does *metanoia* predominantly refer to a change of mind, to taking a *wiser* view of the past, to "the soul's perception of the wicked things it has done" (Favorinus), to a regret for the ill done in the past that results in a change of life for the better, to "a turning about of one's life."[19] Or as Plato had already described it, *metanoia* refers to "a turning from shadows to light"[20] and to "a turning about, a turning around of the soul."[21] This meaning was neither an etymological component of the word nor its primary meaning but was imported into it. This usage did not occur frequently in the Septuagint or in the Apocrypha[22] but is common in Philo, who related *metanoia* and *beltiōsis*[23] and who explained *metanoia* as a "change to the better."[24] In the New Testament,[25] *metanoein* and *metanoia* are always used in an ethical sense to refer to "a radical transformation in the lifestyle of people, accompanied by painful remorse" (Delitzsch).

The meanings of *metanoein* and *metanoia* gradually expanded until they came to express the mighty, Spirit-wrought change in mind, heart, and life known as repentance.[26] A similar honor was partially bestowed on *metameleia* and *metamelesthai*. Plutarch called the first word "a saving demon," explained it as "the shame from pleasures which are contrary to law and uncontrollable,"[27] and associated it with *barythymia*, heaviness of heart.[28] *Metamelesthai* is used five times in the New Testament, *metameleia* not at all. In one case, *metamelesthai* is used to refer to Judas Iscariot's sorrow (Matt. 27:3), which resulted in his death. On another occasion (Heb. 7:21), *metamelesthai* does not refer to man's repentance but to God's change of mind.

Metanoia occurs twenty-five times in the New Testament and *metanoein* thirty-five times. Those who deny any discernible difference between these words (either in profane or in sacred Greek) point to passages in secular Greek where *metameleia* is used in all the senses claimed for *metanoia* and to other passages where the two are used interchangeably to refer to remorse.[29] In sacred Greek they point to passages in the New Testament where

18. *De sera numinis vindicta* 6; *De tranquillitate animi* 19.

19. Clement of Alexandria, *Stromata* 2.245a.

20. *Republic* 7.532b.

21. Ibid. 7.521c.

22. Yet see Ecclus. 44:15; Wisd. of Sol. 11:24; 12:10, 19; and for the verb, Jer. 8:6.

23. L-S 313, improvement; *De Abrahamo* 3.

24. Ibid.; cf. *De praemiis et poenis* 2.

25. It should be noted how rarely Paul used these words: *metanoein* only once (2 Cor. 12:21) and *metanoia* only four times (Rom. 2:4; 2 Cor. 7:9–10; 2 Tim. 2:25).

26. "Such a virtuous alteration of the mind and purpose as begets a like virtuous change in the life and practice" (Kettlewell).

27. *De genio Socratis* 22.

28. L-S 307, heaviness of heart; *An vitiositas ad infelicitatem sufficiat* 2. Plato joined it with *tarachē* (L-S 1758, disturbance; *Republic* 9.577e; cf. Plutarch, *De cohibenda ira* 16).

29. Plutarch, *De tranquillitate animi* 19.

metamelesthai implies all that *metanoein* would (Matt. 21:29, 32). Although all of that is true, there is a distinct preference in sacred and profane Greek to use *metanoia* as the word that best expresses the nobler form of repentance. This is in keeping with what we would have expected from the relative etymological force of the words. The one who has *changed his mind* about the past is on the road to changing everything, but the one who has an *after care* may have little more than a selfish dread of the consequences of his actions.[30]

We may sum up the long dispute on the relation of these words by quoting from Bengel, who distinguishes them but who does not push the distinction too far.

> From its origin *metanoia* is properly of the mind and *metameleia* is of the will, since the former would indicate a change of opinion and the latter a change in anxiety or in eagerness. . . . Either term therefore is used for a person who repents of an act or a plan—whether the repentance is good or bad, whether for a good thing or a bad thing, whether it occurs with a change of deeds in the future or without it. However if you consider the use, *metameleia* generally is a middle term and refers usually to individual actions, while *metanoia* especially in the New Testament is used in a good sense, which denotes the reformation of the whole life and of ourselves in a measure—or it is the entire happy reminiscence after error and sins, with our beloved ones joining in, which produces worthy fruits. Hence it happens that *metanoein* often occurs in the imperative mood, *metameleisthai* never—but in other places where *metanoia* is read one may substitute *metameleia*, but not the reverse.[31]

30. Aristotle, *Ethica Nicomachea* 9.4.10: "The common people are full of regret [*metameleias*]."

31. *Gnomon Novi Testamenti*; *2 Cor. 7:10*. Cf. Witsius, *De Oeconomico Foedere Dei* 3.12.130–36; Girdlestone, *Old Testament Synonyms*, pp. 153ff.

70

morphē (3444) *schēma* (4976) *idea* (2397)

Form *Fashion* *Appearance* *Countenance*

Morphē, *schēma*, and *idea* are not used frequently in the New Testament. *Morphē* occurs only twice (Mark 16:12; Phil. 2:6),[1] as does *schēma* (1 Cor. 7:31; Phil. 2:8), and *idea* appears only once (Matt. 28:3). *Morphē* means "form,"[2] *schēma* means "fashion,"[3] and *idea* means "appearance."[4] The first two words frequently are used together[5] and are objective. The "form" and the "fashion" of something would exist even if it were alone in the universe, whether anyone were there to behold it or not. *Idea*[6] is subjective, in that the "appearance" of a thing implies someone to whom this appearance is made; there must be a "seer" before there can be a "seen."

The best way to study the distinction between *morphē* and *schēma* and to estimate its importance is to study the use of these words in Philippians 2:6–8. In this great doctrinal passage Paul says that the eternal Word

1. But cf. *morphōsis* (3446; Rom. 2:20; 2 Tim. 3:5).
2. It is equivalent to the Latin *forma* and to the German *Gestalt*.
3. *Habitus* in Latin and *Figur* in German.
4. The Latin *species* and the German *Erscheinung*.
5. Plutarch, *Septem sapientium convivium* 8.2.3.
6. It is equivalent to *eidos* (1491; John 5:37).

sisted "in the *form* of God" before his incarnation,[7] assumed "the *form* of a servant" at his incarnation,[8] and was "found in *appearance* as a man" after his incarnation and during his walk on earth.[9] The fathers were inclined to use the first phrase (*en morphē theou hyparchōn*) against the Arians,[10] as did the Lutherans against the Socinians. The fathers understood this phrase as a statement that proved the absolute divinity of the Son of God, because they understood *morphē* as equivalent to *ousia* (*3776*) or to *physis* (*5449*). But it is now generally acknowledged that this cannot be maintained. Doubtless Paul's words in Philippians 2:6–8 contain a proof of the divinity of Christ, though this is present implicitly, not explicitly. Although *morphē* is not equivalent to *ousia*, no one who is not God could be *en morphē theou*. Thus Bengel correctly noted: "The form of God is not his divine nature, although he who exists in the form of God is God." This is true because *morphē*[11] signifies the form as it expresses the inner life—not "being" but "mode of being," or better "mode of existence," and only God could have the mode of existence of God. But Jesus, who had thus been from eternity *en morphē theou* (John 17:5), took at his incarnation *morphēn doulou*. The veracity of his incarnation is implied here; there was nothing docetic or fantastic about it. His manner of existence was now that of a *doulos*, that is, of a *doulos tou theo*, for in the midst of all our Lord's humiliations he was never a *doulos anthrōpōn*. From time to time he was man's *diakonos*;[12] this was part of his *tapeinōsis* (*5014*), which is mentioned in the next verse. But he was never man's *doulos*. On the contrary, they were his. With respect to God, he emptied himself of his glory, so that from that manner of existence in which he thought it not robbery to be equal with God, he became God's servant.

The next clause, "and being found in appearance (*schēmati*) as a man," helps us distinguish *schēma* and *morphē*. The truth of the Son's incarnation was expressed by *morphēn doulou labōn*. The words that follow declare the outward facts that were known by his fellow men, with an emphasis on *heuretheis*. By men, Christ was *found* in fashion as a man—the *schēma* signifying his whole outward presentation. Bengel correctly stated: "*schēma* is his character, manner of life, dress, food, posture, speech, and actions." In these there was no difference between Jesus and other men. The *superficial* character of *schēma* appears in its association with words such as *chrōma*[13] and *hypographē*.[14] Plutarch defined *schēma* this way: "It is an appearance and outline and boundary of a body."[15]

7. *En morphē theou* (*2316*) *hyparchōn* (*5225*).

8. *Morphēn doulou* (*1401*) *labōn* (*2983*).

9. *Schēmati heuretheis* (*2147*) *hōs anthrōpos* (*444*).

10. Cf. Hilary, *De trinitate* 8.45; Ambrose, *Epistula* 46; Gregory of Nyssa, *Contra Eunomium* 4.

11. Like the Latin *forma* and the German *Gestalt*.

12. *1249*; Matt. 20:28; John 13:4–5.

13. L-S 2012, color; Plato, *Gorgias* 20; *Theaetetus* 163b.

14. L-S 1877, outline; *Leges* 5.737d.

15. *Placita philosophorum* 14. *Schēma* and *morphē* are used in an instructive antithesis by Justin Martyr (1 *Apologia* 9).

The distinction between *schēma* and *morphē* is clearly expressed in the compound verbs *metaschēmatizein* (3345) and *metamorphoun* (3339). If a Dutch garden were changed into an Italian one, this would be *metaschēmatismos*; but if I were to transform a garden into something wholly different, such as a city, this would be *metamorphōsis*. It is possible for Satan *metaschēmatizein* himself into an angel of light (2 Cor. 11:14); he can assume this outer appearance. But it would be impossible to apply the *metamorphousthai* to any of his changes, for this would imply not an external but an internal change—a change of essence that is quite beyond his power. The variation of words in Romans 12:2 is fine and subtle, though "con*formed*" and "trans*formed*" inadequately represent it. "Do not fall in," says the apostle, "with the fleeting fashions of this world, nor be yourselves fashioned to them (*mē syschēmatizesthe* [4964]), but undergo a deep abiding change (*alla metamorphousthe*) by the renewing of your mind, such as the Spirit of God alone can work in you" (cf. 2 Cor. 3:18). In commenting on this verse, Theodoret called particular attention to this variation of the word—a variation that would take the highest skill of the English scholar to reproduce in his own language. "He was teaching how much present circumstances differ from virtue, for the former he was calling *schēma* but virtue he terms *morphē*; *morphē* is indicative of genuinely important values, while *schēma* is a thing easy to undo." Meyer perversely rejected this and noted: "Both words are contrasted only by the prepositions without any difference in the root words."[16] One can understand a commentator overlooking but not denying the significance of this change of roots.[17]

Form
Fashion
Appearance
Countenance

At the resurrection of the dead, Christ will transfigure (*metaschēmatisei*) the bodies of his saints (Phil. 3:21; cf. 1 Cor. 15:53). On this Calov remarked:

> That transformation [*metaschēmatismos*] brings about not a change of *substance* but a change of *accidence*, not in regard to the *essence* of our body but in respect to its *qualities*, with its essence being preserved.

The changes of heathen deities into wholly different shapes were *metamorphōseis*. *Metaschēmatismos* refers to a transition but not to an absolute disruption of continuity. The butterfly, a prophetic type of man's resurrection, is immeasurably more beautiful than the grub from which it unfolds. But when Proteus successively transformed himself first into a flame, then into a wild beast, and finally into a running stream,[18] this was not merely a change of *schēma* but of *morphē*.[19] When Mark recorded that after his resurrection Christ appeared to the disciples *en hetera* (2087) *morphē* (Mark 16:12), the words indicate the vast mysterious change that his body had undergone.[20]

16. Fritzsche is in agreement (Rom. 12:2).
17. For the very different uses of each word, see Plutarch, *Quomodo adulator ab amico internoscatur* 7, where both occur.
18. Virgil, *Georgica* 4.442.
19. Cf. Euripides, *Hecuba* 1266.
20. This is in keeping with the *metemorphōthē* of Matt. 17:2 and Mark 9:2.

morphē
schēma
idea

The transformation on the mount was a prophetic anticipation of this change.[21]

Morphē refers to something's essence.[22] An object cannot be conceived of apart from its "formality," using this word in its old logical sense. *Schēma* refers to something's accidental properties—not to its essence but to its qualities and whatever changes it may undergo. *Schēma* leaves the essence untouched and the thing itself essentially or "formally" the same as it was before. Thus we may speak of "an essence [*morphē*] of nature" and of "a quality [*schēma*] of habit." Thus the *schēma basilikon*[23] is the whole outward adornment of a monarch—diadem, tiara, scepter, and robe[24]—all of which he might lay aside and still remain king. It does not belong to the man as a part of himself. Thus Menander wrote: "An evil man assuming a meek posture [*schēma*] lies as a concealed trap for his neighbors."[25] The *schēma tou kosmou* (2889) passes away (1 Cor. 7:31); here the image is probably drawn from the shifting scenes of a theater. The *kosmos* itself abides; there is no *telos* (5056) *tou kosmou* but only *tou aiōnos* (165) or *tōn aiōnōn*.[26]

The use of *forma* and *figura* in Latin corresponds respectively with *morphē* and *schēma*. Although *figura formae* occurs frequently,[27] *forma figurae* never occurs.[28] The contrast in English between "de*formed*" and "dis*figured*" functions in a similar manner. A hunchback is "deformed," but a man that has been beaten on the face may be "disfigured"; the deformity is bound up in the very existence of the one; the disfigurement of the other may disappear in a few days. "Transformed" and "transfigured" display the same distinction.

The only New Testament use of *idea* (Matt. 28:3) is poorly translated as "countenance."[29] "Appearance" would be better. *Idea* refers to "a sight occurring to the eyes"—not to the thing itself but to the thing as it is seen. Plato wrote: *platte idean thēriou poikilou* (fashion to thyself the image of a manifold beast);[30] *idea tou prosōpou* (the look of the countenance);[31] *idea kalos* (fair to look on);[32] *chionos idea* (the appearance of snow).[33] In the last clause of his definition, Plutarch said: "*Idea* is a property without a body—not that it

21. Cf. Dan. 4:33 (LXX), where Nebuchadnezzar described himself: "My form [*morphē*] has returned to me" (cf. 4:34 in other versions).

22. "Form [*morphē*] refers necessarily to substance or essence. Figure [*schēma*], on the contrary, is more independent of objects; it expresses something partially" (Lafaye, *Synonyme Français*, p. 617).

23. 937; Lucian, *Revivescentes sive piscator* 35; cf. Sophocles, *Antigone* 1148.

24. Cf. Lucian, *Hermotimus* 86.

25. Meineke, *Fragmenta comicorum Graecorum*, p. 985.

26. For some valuable remarks on the distinction between *morphē* and *schēma*, see the *Journal of Classical and Sacred Philology*, no. 7, pp. 113, 116, 121. An even more complete account is found in Bishop Lightfoot, *Commentary on the Philippians*, pp. 125–31.

27. "To preserve the old *figuram formae*"; cf. Cicero, *De deorum natura* 1.32.

28. See Döderlein, *Lateinische Synonyme*, 3:87.

29. In 2 Macc. 3:16 it is translated "face."

30. *Republic* 9.588c.

31. Plutarch, *Pyrrhus* 3; and often.

32. Pindar, *Olympia* 11.122.

33. Philo, *Quod deterius potiori insidiari soleat* 48.

subsists by itself, but it molds shapeless matter into a form and is the cause of its display."[34] This is consistently the meaning of *idea*.[35] The following quotation from Philo concerning his doctrine of the Logos (which was fundamentally different from John's and which actually was a denial of the most important element of John's doctrine) shows that this clearly is the case: "The divine Logos above the cherubims has not come into visible appearance [*idean*]."[36]

34. *Placita philosophorum* 1.9.

35. And of the *idein* (aorist of *3708*) lying at its own base.

36. *De cherubim* 19. On the distinction between *eidos* and *idea* in Platonic philosophy, see Stallbaum's note on Plato's *Republic* 10.596b; Donaldson's *Cratylus*, 3d ed., p. 105; and Thompson's note on Archer Butler's *Lectures*, 2:127.

71

psychikos (5591)

sarkikos (4559)

Natural
Sensual
"Soulish"
Fleshly
Carnal

Psychikos occurs six times in the New Testament. On three occasions, where it refers to the lowliness of the Christian's present *sōma* (4983) *psychikon* as contrasted with the glory of his future *sōma pneumatikon* (*4152*; 1 Cor. 15:44 [twice], 46), it does not have a distinctly ethical sense. In the other three cases, however, *psychikos* is used with a negative moral emphasis. Paul declared that the *psychikos* cannot and does not receive[1] the things of the Spirit of God (1 Cor. 2:14). James (3:15) characterized the wisdom that is *psychikē* as *epigeios* (*1919*, earthly) and as *daimoniōdēs* (*1141*, devilish). Jude described the *psychikoi* as "not having the Spirit" (v. 19). *Psychikos* does not appear in the Septuagint, but *psychikōs* is used twice in the Apocrypha (2 Macc. 4:37; 14:24) in the sense of "heartily."[2]

At first this use of *psychikos* (and the words with which it is associated) comes as something of a surprise, since in current parlance the soul is referred to as a person's highest part. We might expect to find *psychikos* closely related

1. Since it does not have an organ for their reception.
2. *Psychikōs* is equivalent to *ek psychēs* (5590); Col. 3:23.

psychikos

sarkikos

to *pneumatikos*, separated only by a slight shade of meaning. But this is not the case. The way *psychikos* is used in the New Testament should not surprise us, since it is characteristic of the inner differences between a Christian and a secular viewpoint. The meaning of *psychikos* is indicative of those better gifts and graces brought into the world by the gift of the Spirit. *Psychikos* is always used as the highest term in later classical Greek literature[3] and is opposed to *sarkikos*,[4] or, where there is no *ethical* antithesis, to *sōmatikos*.[5] In *Christian* terminology, then, *psychikos* must be replaced by an even loftier term. Secular Greek philosophy knew of nothing higher than the soul of man, but God's revelation reveals that the Spirit of God makes his habitation with people and calls out an answering spirit in them. There was some intimation of this higher level in the distinction Lucretius and others made between the *anima* (soul) and the *animus* (mind), which is a more noble term. According to Scripture, the *psychē*, no less than the *sarx* (4561), belongs to the lower region of man's being.[6] Since *psychikos* often is applied to man's lower level, it is no more honorable a word than *sarkikos*.[7] According to Scripture, the *psychikos* is one for whom the *psychē* is the highest motivation of life and action. On the one hand, such a person suppresses the *pneuma* (4151), the organ of the divine *pneuma*. On the other hand, the *pneuma* of the *psychikos* is as good as extinct, because the divine Spirit has never lifted such a person to the spiritual realm (Rom. 7:14; 8:1; Jude 19).[8]

According to Scripture, both the *sarkikos* and the *psychikos* are opposed to the *pneumatikos*. *Sarkikos* and *psychikos* refer to different ruling principles, each of which is antagonistic to the *pneuma*. When Paul reminded the Ephesians of how they once behaved, "fulfilling the desires *of the flesh* and *of the mind*" (Eph. 2:3), he described them first as *sarkikoi* and then as *psychikoi*. In unregenerate people, who live their lives apart from God, there are two forms of life. Although every unregenerate person partakes of both forms, either

3. It first appears in Aristotle.

4. Plutarch, *Non posse suaviter vivi secundum Epicurum* 14.

5. 4984; Aristotle, *Ethica Nicomachea* 3.10.2; Plutarch, *Placita philosophorum* 1.9; Polybius, 6.5.7.

6. The double use of *psychē* in Matt. 16:26 and Mark 8:35 may require a certain caution in this statement.

7. Hilary has not *quite* extricated himself from this idea. In the following passage he certainly ascribed more to the *psychikos* than the Scriptures do, though he clearly contrasted this person with the *pneumatikos*: "The apostle regards people as *sarkikos*, *psychikos*, and *pneumatikos*. The *sarkikos* neglects divine and human aspects as do animals; his life is a servant to the body, busily concerned with food, sleep, and passion. The *psychikos* judges what is decent and honorable with a criterion of human feelings, abstaining from all vices on the basis of his human intellect and determining what is advantageous and honorable by his own feeling—he spurns money, is frugal with food, is free of ambition, and resists passions. The *pneumatikos*, whose higher interests are directed to the Lord, regulates his actions by the knowledge of God, understanding and realizing what is his will and knowing the reason for his incarnation, his triumphant crucifixion, and his power over death as exemplified through his resurrection" (*Tractatus in Psalma* 14.3; cf. Irenaeus, 5.6).

8. For a good collection of passages from the Greek fathers on this use of *psychikos*, see Suicer, *Thesaurus*, under this word.

form may predominate. In the *sarkikoi*, the *sarx* predominates; in the *psychikoi*, the *psychē* rules. *Sarx* often is used in the New Testament to refer to the entire domain of our fallen nature, to the source of sin (Rom. 7:18; 8:5). Thus the *erga (2041) tēs sarkos* (Gal. 5:19–21) not only are sinful works done in and through the body but also include sinful acts of the mind. More than half of the sins listed in Galatians 5:19–21 belong to the latter class. Although *sarx* can include everything in man that is alienated from God and from his life, it is limited when contrasted with *psychē*.

Natural Sensual "Soulish" Fleshly Carnal

Bishop Reynolds' Latin sermon on 1 Corinthians 2:14 includes a helpful discussion on the difference between *sarkikos* and *psychikos*. The following is the most important paragraph:

> It is true that—since people consist of flesh [*sarx*] and soul, although the soul is the more significant part of a person—our apostle very frequently terms the unregenerate *sarkikoi* because their desire is prone to vices and their impulses incline to concupiscence. He names people of this type from their most significant part, demonstrating that he understands them not to be those who are slaves of passion and who bury their natural talent through crass concupiscence (for these the apostle calls 'brute beasts' [*aloga zōa*, 2 Pet. 2:12]), but persons eager for wisdom, who are accustomed to respect only those things which are foolish and absurd. Thus *psychikoi* are those who "do not have the Spirit" (Jude 19), however much they shine with the most exquisite natural gifts, cultivate the mind, the most excellent part, with all types of education, and direct their life very strictly according to the dictates of reason. Finally he calls *psychikoi* those to whom he previously had appealed as the wise, the scribes, the scholars, and the leaders of that age that they suppress any natural or acquired rank, in order that human reason may be able to increase with its natural strength—"*psychikos* is one who yields in everything to the reasonings of the soul [*psychē*], not thinking there is need for help from above," as Chrysostom has rightly stated—he is one who has nothing extraordinary in himself except a rational soul, the light and guidance of which alone he follows.[9]

Grotius made similar observations:

> A *psychikos* person is not the same as a *sarkikos* individual. *Psychikos* is one who is led only by the light of human reason; *sarkikos* is one who is controlled by bodily desires. But usually *psychikoi* are in some way *sarkikoi* as the Greek philosophers, fornicators, corrupters of boys, snatchers of fame, slanderous, envious. Nothing else is denoted here (1 Cor. 2:14) but a person who thrives on human reason alone such as most of the Jews and the Greek philosophers.[10]

The question of how to translate *psychikos* is not easy to answer. "Soulish," which some have proposed, has the advantage of having the same relation to "soul" that *psychikos* does to *psychē*,[11] but the word would certainly convey no meaning at all to ordinary English readers. Wycliffe translated *psychikos* as

9. *Animalis Homo, Works*, London, 1826, 4:349.
10. *Annotationes in Novum Testamentum*, 1 Cor. 2:14.
11. And the Latin *animalis* (animate or living) does to *anima* (soul).

psychikos

sarkikos

"beastly,"[12] which is equivalent to "animal" (*animalis* occurs in the Vulgate). The Rhemish Version has "sensual," and this was adopted by the Authorized Version in James 3:15 and Jude 19, instead of "fleshly," which appears in Cranmer's Version and in the Geneva Version. The other three times *psychikos* is used in the New Testament, it is translated as "natural." "Sensual" and "natural" are both unsatisfactory translations, but "sensual" is even more so now than at the time when our Authorized Version was made. The meanings of *sensual* and of *sensuality* have been modified considerably and now imply a deeper degradation than they formally did.[13]

12. This did not have our meaning of "bestial." See my *Select Glossary*, under this word.

13. On the relations of the *psychē* to the *sarx* and to the *pneuma*, there is an interesting, though difficult, passage in Delitzsch's *Psychology*, Eng. Ver., pp. 109–28.

72

sarkikos (4559) — Carnal, Fleshly

sarkinos (4560) — Of Flesh

Our discussion of the relation between *psychikos* (5591) and *sarkikos* naturally leads us to examine the relation between *sarkikos* and another form of the word, *sarkinos*. *Sarkinos* occurs three or four times in the New Testament. It appears only once in the Textus Receptus (2 Cor. 3:3). The evidence overwhelmingly favors accepting it in Romans 7:14 and in Hebrews 7:16, and the evidence strongly favors accepting it in 1 Corinthians 3:1.

Words ending in *-inos*[1] are common in the New Testament. Thus we have *thyinos*,[2] *hyalinos*,[3] *hyakinthinos*,[4] *dermatinos*,[5] and *akanthinos*.[6] *Sarkinos*, the only form of this word recognized in classical Greek, is another example.[7] In 2 Corinthians 3:3, *sarkikos* is correctly translated "of flesh"—being composed of the substance of flesh. I am unable to confirm that the word *fleshen* ever ex-

1. They are called *metousiastika* (L-S 1121, denoting participation) and frequently designate the substance of which things are made. See Donaldson, *Cratylus*, 3d ed., p. 458; Winer, *Grammatik*, par. 16.3; Fritzsche, *Epistula ad Romanos*, 2:46.

2. *2367*, "of thyine wood" (Rev. 18:12).

3. *5193*, "of glass," "glassen" (Rev. 4:6).

4. *5191*; Rev. 9:17.

5. *1193*; Matt. 3:4.

6. *174*; Mark 15:17.

7. *Sarkikos*, like the Latin *carnalis* (fleshly, carnal), was a result of the ethical necessities of the church.

sarkikos

sarkinos

isted in English, but had it existed and survived, it would be an even better translation, since *of flesh* or *fleshy* may mean *carnosus* (fleshy, abounding in flesh), which is also the case with *sarkinos*.[8] *Fleshen*, however, *must* mean what *sarkinos* means here, namely *carneus* or "having flesh for its material." The former existence of a word like *fleshen* is not improbable, since many such forms once were used that now have passed away.[9] The demise of such words is unfortunate, since they added to the language. German uses both *steinig* (full of stones) and *steinern* (consisting of stones), and Latin has *lapidosus* (full of stones) and *lapideus* (consisting of stones), and *saxosus* (full of rocks) and *saxeus* (consisting of rocks). We might have used *stony* and *stonen*—a "stony" place is one where there are many stones; a "stonen" vessel would be a vessel made of stone.[10] A "glassy" sea is a sea resembling glass; a "glassen" sea is a sea made of glass. *Fleshly*, *fleshy*, and *fleshen* would have been useful, just as *earthly*, *earthy*, and *earthen* each have a proper use.

"Fleshly"[11] lusts are lusts existing in the ethical domain of the flesh, lusts that have their source in that rebellious region of man's corrupt and fallen nature. This is the case with the "fleshly [*sarkikai*] lusts" in 1 Peter 2:11. The man who allows the *sarx* (4561) a position that does not belong to it is *sarkikos*. *Sarx*'s proper place is under the dominion of the *pneuma* (4151), where it receives a law. *Sarx* becomes the source of all sin and opposition to God when this position is reversed and *sarx* becomes the ruler rather than the ruled. When Paul said that the Corinthians were *sarkinoi* (1 Cor. 3:1), this was a serious charge, though not as grave as if he had written *sarkikoi*. In 1 Corinthians 3:1, Paul was not charging the Corinthians with positive active opposition to the Spirit of God[12] but only with intellectually and spiritually pausing at the threshold of the faith (cf. Heb. 5:11–12). Although they might have been carried great distances by the mighty transforming powers of the Spirit freely given to them by God, they were making no progress and were content to remain where they were. Paul did not charge the Corinthians with being *anti*spiritual but *un*spiritual—being flesh and little else, when they might have made spiritual progress. In verses 3 and 4, where Paul leveled the more serious accusation that the Corinthians were allowing the *sarx* to work actively as a ruling principle, he used a different word. Not only were the Corinthians *sarkinoi*,[13] but they also were *sarkikoi*—full of "envy, strife, and divisions."

On the one hand, it is not easy to suggest a way that our Authorized translators could have distinguished between *sarkinos* and *sarkikos* in 1 Corinthians 3. In all likelihood, however, this was not a difficulty for them, since they ac-

8. Plato, *Leges* 10.906c; Aristotle, *Ethica Nicomachea* 3.9.3.

9. For example, *stonen, hornen, hairen, clayen* (all in Wycliffe's Bible), *threaden* (Shakespeare), *tinnen* (Sylvester), *milken, breaden, reeden*, and many more (see my *English Past and Present*, 10th ed., p. 256).

10. See John 2:6; Rev. 9:20 in Wycliffe's version, where the word is found.

11. "Carnal" is the more frequent translation in English, but in fixing the relations between *sarkikos* and *sarkinos*, it will be more convenient to employ "fleshly" and "fleshy."

12. This is evident from the "as to babes in Christ," which he used to explain it.

13. No person or church can remain for long at this point.

cepted the Textus Receptus, which does not use two different words. On the other hand, in 2 Corinthians 3:3 the translators' task was plain, and they correctly translated *sarkinai plakes* (4109) as "*fleshy* tables." Erasmus observed that *sarkinos*, not *sarkikos*, is used in this passage "in order that you may understand material and not quality." Paul was drawing a contrast between the tables of stone, where the law of Moses was written, and the tables of flesh, where Christ's law is written, and he was exalting the latter over the former. "Fleshy" is not a dishonorable term in this passage but indicates the superiority of the new law over the old. The latter is graven on dead tables of stone, the former on the hearts of living men (cf. Jer. 31:33; Ezek. 11:19; 36:26; Heb. 8:10; 10:16).

73

pnoē (4157)
pneuma (4151)
anemos (417)
lailaps (2978)
thyella (2366)

Wind

Storm
Tempest

We will discuss *pneuma* in its natural, earthly sense, not in its supernatural, heavenly meaning.[1] *Pnoē*, *pneuma*, and *anemos* designate earthly things and differ from one another exactly as do the Latin *aër* (air), *spiritus* (breeze), and *ventus* (wind). Seneca noted: "Motion separates breeze [*spiritus*] from wind [*ventus*], for a more violent breeze [*spiritus*] is wind [*ventus*]; a lightly flowing breeze [*spiritus*] in turn is air [*aër*]."[2]

Pnoē and *pneuma* frequently occur together, as in Isaiah 42:5 and 57:16. *Pnoē* refers to a lighter, gentler motion of the air than *pneuma*, just as *aura* (gentle breeze) refers to a lighter motion than *ventus* (wind). Aristotle remarked: "The breezes [*pneumata*] blowing in the atmosphere we call winds [*anemous*], but those accompanied by dampness we term vapors [*ekpnoai*]."[3] Pliny recognized a similar distinction: "Air [*aër*] is moved by some breeze [*spiritu*]; more often however it causes gentle breezes [*auras*] than winds

1. Augustine discussed the relations between *pnoē* and *pneuma* in its higher sense in *De civitate Dei* 13.22; cf. *De anima et huius origine* 1.14, 19.

2. *Quaestiones naturales* 5.13.

3. *De mundo* 4.10.

pnoē
pneuma
anemos
lailaps
thyella

[*ventos*]."[4] Philo stated: "He spoke of *pnoē* but not *pneuma* as there is a difference; for *pneuma* is thought of according to its strength and vigor and force, while *pnoē* is a gentle breeze and a quiet and calm exhalation."[5] In one of its two New Testament occurrences (Acts 2:2), however, *pnoē* is used with *biaia* (972) and clearly refers to a strong and vehement wind (cf. Job 37:9). As De Wette observed, this may be accounted for by the fact that on this occasion it was necessary to reserve *pneuma* for the higher spiritual gift of which *pnoē* was the sign and symbol. To have used *pneuma* would have introduced a perplexing repetition.

Pneuma is seldom used in the New Testament (John 3:8; Heb. 1:7)[6] to mean "wind," though often it is used in that sense in the Septuagint (Gen. 8:1; Eccles. 11:5; Ezek. 37:9). *Rûaḥ* (7307) in Ecclesiastes 11:5 is translated by "spirit," not "wind" (Job 1:19; Ps. 148:8), in our Authorized Version, which is unfortunate because it obscures the remarkable connection between the Preacher's saying and Jesus' words to Nicodemus (John 3:8). Jesus loved to use the Old Testament. His words "the wind blows where it wishes" echo the words of Ecclesiastes "and you do not know what is the way *of the wind*." The Preacher had already indicated that the winds are symbols for mysteries that are higher than man can trace. *Pneuma* often appears in the Septuagint in connection with *pnoē* but generally is used in a figurative sense (2 Sam. 22:16; Job 33:4; Isa. 42:5; 57:16).

Aristotle gave this account of *anemos*: "Wind [*anemos*] is nothing but a large amount of air flowing together, which is also called *pneuma* [breeze]."[7] Hippocrates said: "Wind [*anemos*] is a current and stream of air."[8] Like *ventus* and *wind*, *anemos* is usually the strong, often tempestuous, wind.[9] It is interesting to observe that in the inspired account of Jesus' conversation with Nicodemus (which probably took place in Aramaic), the writer did not use *anemos* but *pneuma* to draw an analogy between the natural world and the mysterious movements[10] of the Holy Spirit. Undoubtedly the writer chose *pneuma* because there is nothing fierce or violent in the measured operation of the Spirit. When Paul wanted to describe men violently blown about on a sea of error, however, he described them as "tossed to and fro and carried about with every wind [*anemō*] of doctrine" (Eph. 4:14; cf. Jude 12 with 2 Pet. 2:17).

The derivation of *lailaps* is uncertain. This word is probably formed by reduplication and is meant to imitate in sound what it represents. It occurs three times in the New Testament (Mark 4:37; Luke 8:23; 2 Pet. 2:17) and slightly more often in the Septuagint. It refers to a formidable kind of squall.

4. *Epistulae* 5.6.

5. *Legum allegoriarum libri* 1.14.

6. Its occurrence in Heb. 1:7 is not certain.

7. *De mundo* 4.

8. *De flatebus* 3.

9. 1 Kings 19:11; Job 1:19; Matt. 7:25; John 6:18; Acts 27:14; James 3:4; Plutarch, *Conjugalia praecepta* 12.

10. They were not to be traced by human eye.

J.H.H. Schmidt has a careful and full discussion on the whole group of words used for wind and weather and associated phenomena.[11] Concerning *lailaps* he wrote: "The ancients quite generally understood it to denote a storm raging back and forth unstably, breaking forth from dark clouds and accompanied by torrential rains." The examples he gave support this statement. As Hesychius explained, it is "a whirling of wind [*anemou*] with rain." Suidas added the further notion of darkness.[12] Homer always associated *kelainē*[13] and *eremnē*[14] with *lailaps*, implying that the darkness that accompanies the latter should not be ignored.[15]

Wind

Storm
Tempest

Whenever it occurs in the Septuagint (Deut. 4:11; 5:22; Exod. 10:22), *thyella* is used with *gnophos* (*1105*). In the New Testament, *thyella* is used only in Hebrews 12:18, where it sounds more like its Septuagintal usage than other words the writer might have employed. Schmidt distinguished *thyella* from the Homeric *aella*,[16] but we will not discuss these differences. *Thyella* often refers to a wilder and fiercer natural phenomenon than *lailaps* and frequently refers to the conflicted mingling of many opposing winds,[17] as in a turbulent cyclone.

11. *Synonymik*, 2:218ff. As one might expect, the Greek language is singularly rich in these words.

12. "Rain and darkness accompanied by winds [*anemōn*]."

13. L-S 936, black, dark.

14. L-S 685, murky, dark.

15. *Iliad* 11.747; 16.384; 20.51.

16. L-S 27, stormy wind, whirlwind.

17. Homer, *Odyssey* 5.319; 12.290.

74

dokimazō (1381)

peirazō (3985)

Prove
Test
Try
Examine
Tempt

Dokimazō and *peirazō* often are used together, as in 2 Corinthians 13:5 and Psalm 94:10.[1] Although our Authorized Version translates both words by "prove" (Luke 14:19; John 6:6), "try" (1 Cor. 3:13; Rev. 2:2), and "examine" (1 Cor. 11:28; 2 Cor. 13:5), they are not perfectly synonymous. *Dokimazein* is translated by four other words in the Authorized Version: "discern" (Luke 12:56), "like" (Rom. 2:18), "approve" (Rom. 2:18), and "allow" (Rom. 14:22). *Dokimazein* always includes the idea of proving whether a thing is worthy *to be received* and is closely related to *dechesthai* (*1209*). In classical Greek *dokimazein* is the technical word used for putting money to the *dokimē* (*1382*, proof) by use of the *dokimion* (*1383*, test).[2] Whatever passes this test is *dokimos* (*1384*), and whatever fails is *adokimos* (96). These words are not, at least immediately, connected with *dokimazein* but with *dechesthai*. Because this proving is through fire (1 Cor. 3:13), *dokimazein* and *pyroun* (4448) often are used together (Ps. 95:9; Jer. 9:7). In the New Testament *dokimazein* al-

1. In Heb. 3:9 the better reading is *en dokimasia* (L-S 442, testing).
2. Plato, *Timaeus* 65c; Plutarch, *De defectu oraculorum* 21.

dokimazō

peirazō

most always implies that the test is victoriously surmounted and the *proved* is also *approved* (2 Cor. 8:8; 1 Thess. 2:4; 1 Tim. 3:10). Similarly, in English we speak of *tried* men,[3] meaning not only those who have been tested but those who have stood the test.[4] Sometimes *dokimazein* implies the further step of choosing the approved, not just approving the proved.[5]

Not only does the *dokimasia* usually result in victory, but it implies that the trial itself was made in the expectation of such an outcome, or at least without a contrary anticipation. The ore is thrown into the refining pot[6] in the expectation that though it may be mingled with dross, it is not *all* dross, and some good, purified metal will emerge from the fiery trial (Heb. 12:5–11; 2 Macc. 6:12–16). In the tests that God brings as the refiner of his church, his intention is not to find his saints pure gold[7] but to make them pure by purging out their dross.[8] He is the "God who tests [*tō dokimazontai*] our hearts" (1 Thess. 2:4; cf. Ps. 17:3; Jer. 11:20). Job used an equivalent word: "When he has tested [*diekrine*] me, I shall come forth as gold" (Job 23:10). God's people pray to him in words like Abelard's (who expounded the sixth petition of the Lord's Prayer): "Grant that through trial we be approved, not disapproved." This is the point of divergence between *dokimazein* and *peirazein*, as we shall now see.

Testing *may* have a different intention and outcome, especially in the case of the false-hearted and those who only seem to belong to God. Testing will cause its recipients to *appear* as what they always have *been*. This is predominantly, though not exclusively, the sense of *peirazein*. Nothing in the word requires it to refer to a trial given with the intention of entangling the person in sin. *Peirazein*[9] properly means "to make an experience of,"[10] "to pierce or search into,"[11] or "to attempt" (Acts 16:7; 24:6). Later *peirazein* signified testing whose intention was to discover whether a person or thing was good or evil, or strong or weak (Matt. 16:1; 19:3; 22:18; 1 Kings 10:1); or, if the outcome already was known to the tester, to reveal the same to the one being tested, as when Paul commanded the Corinthians, *heautous peirazete*, "try" or "examine yourselves" (2 Cor. 13:5). In this way sinners are said to tempt God,[12] to put him to the test by refusing to believe his word until he manifests his power. We must stop at this stage of the word's history when we say that

3. They are equivalent to the *dedokimasmenoi*.

4. Then it is nearly equivalent to *axioun* (*515*; 1 Thess. 2:4; cf. Plutarch, *Theseus* 12).

5. Xenophon, *Anabasis* 3.3.12; cf. Rom. 1:28.

6. This image always underlies the Old Testament use of the word (Ps. 66:10; Prov. 8:10; 17:3; 27:21; Jer. 9:7; Zech. 13:9; Ecclus. 2:5; Wisd. of Sol. 3:6; cf. 1 Pet. 1:7).

7. For God knows they are not.

8. He never intends to show that they are all dross.

9. It is connected with the Latin *perior* (to experience) and *experior* (to try) and *peiraō* (*3987*).

10. *Peiran lambanein*, Heb. 11:29, 36.

11. Thus the wicked are said to be those that "search into [*peirazousi*] death" (Wisd. of Sol. 2:24; cf. 12:26; Ecclus. 39:4).

12. Matt. 4:7 (*ekpeirazein*, *1598*); Acts 5:9; 1 Cor. 10:9; Wisd. of Sol. 1:2.

God "tempts" people.[13] God tempts people only in the sense we have just discussed—for the purpose of self-knowledge—and so that they may (and often do) emerge from testing holier, humbler, and stronger than they were before.[14] As Augustine wrote:

> In the statement "God tempts no one" [James 1:13] God must be understood not as tempting in every manner but in a certain manner of temptation, in order that the statement in Deuteronomy 13:3 may not be false, "Your God is tempting you," and that we may not deny that Christ is God or say that the evangelist is untruthful when we read in John 6:6 that Jesus questioned his disciple testing him. There is a testing which leads to sin, in which respect God tempts no one; there is also a testing which proves faithfulness, in which respect God deigns to test.[15]

Thus James was able to say, "Count it all joy when you fall into various *trials* [*peirasmois*]" (1:2; cf. v. 12) and to affirm that God tempts no man (1:13).

But *peirazein* developed another meaning. The sad fact is that people often do break down under temptation, and this gave *peirazein* the predominant sense of putting to the test with the intention and the desire that the "proved" may not turn out "approved" but "reprobate" and break down under the test. Consequently, *peirazein* is applied to the solicitations and suggestions of Satan (Matt. 4:1; 1 Cor. 7:5; Rev. 2:10) that always are made with a malicious hope. Satan is called the *tempter* (Matt. 4:3; 1 Thess. 3:5), and he reveals himself as such (Gen. 3:1, 4–5; 1 Chron. 21:1).

In conclusion we may say that though *peirazein* may rarely be used of God, *dokimazein* could not be used of Satan, since he never proves in order to approve, nor tests that he may accept.

13. Heb. 11:17; cf. Gen. 22:1; Exod. 15:25; Deut. 13:3.

14. As Oecumenius said: "For the sake of training and public proclamation."

15. *Sermones* 71, chap. 10. Cf. *Sermones* 57, chap. 9; *Ennarationes in Psalma* 55.1; *Sermones* 2, chap. 3: "God tempts in order that he may teach; the devil tempts in order that he may deceive."

75

sophia (4678) *phronēsis* (5428) *gnōsis* (1108) *epignōsis* (1922)

Wisdom Prudence Knowledge

Sophia, *phronēsis*, and *gnōsis* are used together in the Septuagint in Daniel 1:4, 17, where they all are ascribed to God. *Phronēsis* is not used in the New Testament in this sense.[1] *Sophia* and *gnōsis* are used in Romans 9:33, and *phronēsis* and *sophia* are used in the Septuagint in Proverbs 3:19 and in Jeremiah 10:12. There have been various attempts to assign each of these words its own meaning, and though these attempts differ from one another, they commonly recognize *sophia* as the highest and most noble of these terms. Clement of Alexandria referred to it as "knowledge of divine and human matters"[2] and elsewhere added (as did the Stoics before him) "also of their causes."[3] Augustine made this distinction between *sophia* and *gnōsis*: "These are usually distinguished so that wisdom [*sophia*] pertains to the understand-

1. Eph. 1:8 is not a case in point.

2. *Paedagogus* 2.2.

3. *Stromata* 1.5. Plato called *philosophia* (5385) "a longing after knowledge of what always exists" (*Definitiones* 414) and "a longing after divine wisdom" (as quoted by Diogenes Laërtius, 3.63). Philo described it as "a devotion to wisdom" (*De congressu eruditionis gratia* 14), and Seneca called it "an eagerness for virtue through virtue itself" (*Epistulae* 89.7). On the relation of *philosophia* to *sophia*, see Clement of Alexandria, *Stromata* 1.5. The word first appears in Herodotus, 1.50. For a sketch of its history, see Ueberweg, p. 1.

ing of eternal matters, but knowledge [*gnōsis*] to those things which we experience through the senses of the body."[4]

Philo made a similar distinction between *sophia* and *phronēsis*. He defined *phronēsis* as the "mean between craftiness and folly."[5] According to Philo, "wisdom [*sophia*] pertains to the service toward God, knowledge [*phronēsis*] to the management of human life."[6] The following statement from Cicero confirms this as a standard distinction:

> The chief of all virtues is that wisdom which the Greeks call *sophian*; for we understand knowledge, which the Greeks term *phronēsin*, as something else, as the science of what is to be sought and what is to be shunned; that wisdom which I call "the chief" is the science of divine and human causes.[7]

In making this distinction, Cicero followed Aristotle, who was careful to emphasize the *practical* character of *phronēsis* and who contrasted it sharply with *synesis* (4907), the critical faculty. One acts, the other judges. Aristotle described *phronēsis* in this way: "It is the true character functioning through reason concerning what is good and evil for man."[8] Elsewhere Aristotle said: "It is the virtue of thought by which people are able to deliberate concerning the good and the evil related to happiness."[9] Aristo the Peripatetic wrote: "The virtue which contemplates what should and should not be done is called *phronēsis*."[10] It is plain from these references and quotations that the church fathers based their distinctions between these words on the works of heathen philosophers, widening and deepening the meaning of the words, as inevitably is the case when the ethical and philosophical terms of a lower viewpoint are assumed into the service of a higher one.[11]

In Scripture *sophia* is ascribed only to God or to good men, though it is used in an ironic sense by adding "of this world" (1 Cor. 1:20), "of this age" (1 Cor. 2:6), or similar words (2 Cor. 1:12). None of the children of this world are called *sophoi* without this tacit or expressed irony (Luke 10:21). They are never more than those "professing to be wise" (Rom. 1:22). If *sophia* includes striving after the best ends as well as using the best means—mental excellence in its highest and fullest sense[12]—then wisdom cannot be separated from goodness. Long ago Plato noted: "All knowledge [*epistēmē*] separated from justice and the rest of virtue appears to be knavery and not wisdom

4. *De divinis quaestionibus* 2, quaestio 2. For a much fuller discussion to the same effect, see *De trinitate* 12.22–24; 14.3.

5. *Mesē panourgias kai mōrias phronēsis* (*Quod deus sit immutabilis* 35).

6. *De praemiis et poenis* 14.

7. *De officiis* 2.43. Cf. *Tusculanae disputationes* 4.26; Seneca, *Epistulae* 85.

8. *Ethica Nicomachea* 6.5.4.

9. *Rhetorica* 1.9.

10. See Plutarch, *De virtute morali* 2; cf. chap. 5, where he has an excellent discussion that discriminates between these two terms.

11. Cf. Zeller, *Philosophie der Griechen* 3.1.222.

12. Cf. Aristotle, *Ethica Nicomachea* 6.7.3.

[*sophia*]."[13] Socrates of Xenophon[14] refused to separate or even to distinguish by definition *sophia* from *sōphrosynē* (4997), *diakaiosynē* (1343), or any other virtue. The true antithesis to *sophos* (4680) is *anoētos*,[15] not *asynetos* (801). Although the *asynetos* may only be intellectually deficient, the *anoētos* always has a moral fault beneath the intellectual. The *nous* (3563), the highest knowing power in man and the faculty that apprehends divine things, is the ultimate seat of the error.[16] *Anoia*[17] always refers to foolishness that is related to and that derives from wickedness. *Sophia* refers to the wisdom that is related to goodness, or to goodness itself as seen from one viewpoint, as the wisdom only the good can possess. Ammon, a modern German rationalist, helpfully defines the *sophos* or *sapiens* (wise) as one who is "trained in the knowledge of the best and of the proper means for attaining it."

Phronēsis is a middle term between *sophia* and *gnōsis*, since it refers to the right use and application of the *phrēn* (5424). *Phronēsis* may be related to *sophia* (Prov. 10:23),[18] though it also may be related to *panourgia*.[19] *Phronēsis* involves the skillful adaptation of means to achieve desired ends, though it does not indicate whether the ends themselves are good.[20] *Phronēsis* always is used in the New Testament to refer to a praiseworthy prudence.[21] *Phronēsis* does not refer to wisdom itself, nor does *phronimos* (5429) refer to the wise. Augustine correctly objected to the use of *sapientissimus* (very wise) in his Latin Version for *phronimōtatos* in Genesis 3:1: "Through the misuse of a term wisdom [*sapientia*] refers to something evil."[22] Frequently the same objection has been raised against the Authorized Version's translations "*wise* [*phronimoi*] as serpents" (Matt. 10:16) and "*wiser* [*phronimōteroi*] than the children of light" (Luke 16:8).[23]

Bengel made the following distinction between *sophia* and *gnōsis*:

> It is certain that when these terms are ascribed to God, they differ only in their objects; cf. Romans 11:33. When they are attributed to the faithful, *sophia* extends further in length, width, depth, and height than *gnōsis*. *Gnōsis* is like a vision, while *sophia* is like a vision with refinement. *Gnōsis* concerns things to be

13. *Menexenus* 19. Ecclus. 19:20, 22 offers a fine parallel to this.

14. *Memorabilia* 3.9.

15. 453; Rom. 1:14.

16. Luke 24:25, "O foolish ones, and slow of heart"; cf. Gal. 3:1, 3; 1 Tim. 6:9; Titus 3:3.

17. 454; Luke 6:11; 2 Tim. 3:9.

18. They are used interchangeably by Plato (*Symposium* 202a).

19. 3834; Job. 5:13; Wisd. of Sol. 17:7.

20. On the different kinds of *phronēsis* and the very different senses in which it is employed, see Basil the Great, *Homilia in principium proverbiorum*, par. 6.

21. "The wisdom [*phronēsei*] of the just," Luke 1:17; and "in all wisdom [*sophia*] and prudence [*phronēsei*]," Eph. 1:8.

22. *De genesi ad litteras* 11.2; cf. *Contra gaudium* 1.5.

23. The Old Italic perhaps goes to the opposite extreme by translating *phronimoi* as *astuti* (cunning), though Augustine assured us (*Epistulae* 167.6) that this word did not have in later Latin as evil a connotation as it did in classical Latin.

done, and *sophia* concerns eternal matters; therefore it is not stated that *sophia* must vanish (1 Cor. 13:8).[24]

In comparing *epignōsis* with *gnōsis*, the *epi* (*1909*) must be regarded as an intensive use of a preposition that gives the compound word a greater strength than the simple word alone possesses, as is true of the words *epipotheō*[25] and *epimeleomai* (*1959*). Correspondingly, if *gnōsis* is the Latin *cognitio* (knowledge) and the German *Kenntniss* (knowledge), then *epignōsis* is a "greater and more accurate knowledge" (Grotius) and *Erkenntniss* is a "deeper and more intimate knowledge and acquaintance." *Epignōsis* is not "*re*cognition" in the Platonic sense of reminiscence as distinguished from cognition, as Jerome (on Eph. 4:13) and some moderns have argued. Paul exchanged *ginōskō* (*1097*), which expresses present and fragmentary knowledge, for *epignōsomai* (*1921*), when he wished to refer to future knowledge that is intuitive and perfect (1 Cor. 13:12). It is difficult to see how this distinction, which the Authorized translators made no attempt to maintain, could have been preserved in an English translation. Bengel, however, preserved the distinction by using *nosco* (know) and *pernoscam* (know thoroughly). According to Culverwell,

> *Epignōsis* and *gnōsis* differ. *Epignōsis* is the complete comprehension after the first knowledge [*gnōsin*] of a matter. It is bringing me better acquainted with a thing I knew before; a more exact viewing of an object that I saw before afar off. That little portion of knowledge which we had here shall be much improved, our eye shall be raised to see the same things more strongly and clearly.[26]

All Paul's uses of *epignōsis* justify and bear out this distinction.[27] This same intensive use of *epignōsis* is confirmed by similar passages in the New Testament[28] and in the Septuagint.[29] It also was recognized by the Greek fathers. Thus Chrysostom stated: "You knew [*egnōte*], but it is necessary to know thoroughly [*epignōnai*]."[30]

24. *Gnomon, in 1 Corinthios* 12.8.
25. *1971*; 2 Cor. 5:2.
26. *Spiritual Optics*, p. 180.
27. Rom. 1:28; 3:20; 10:2; Eph. 4:13; Phil. 1:9; 1 Tim. 2:4; 2 Tim. 2:25; cf. Heb. 10:26.
28. 2 Pet. 1:2, 8; 2:20.
29. Prov. 2:5; Hos. 4:1; 6:6.
30. On Col. 1:9. On the whole subject of this section, see Lightfoot on Col. 1:9.

76

laleō (2980) | *Say*
legō (3004) | *Speak* | *Tell* | *Talk*
(*lalia* [2981] | (*Speech* | *Talk*
logos [3056]) | *Word*)

In dealing with synonyms of the New Testament, we do not need to examine earlier or even contemporary uses of words that lie completely outside of its sphere, as long as these uses do not illustrate and have not affected their scriptural use. As a result, all of the contemptuous uses of *lalein* (to talk at random, one who is *athyrostomos*[1]) and of *lalia* (chatter, an illogical mixture of words[2]) may be dismissed and set aside. The antithesis in Eupolis, "very good at chattering [*lalein*] but unable to speak [*legein*]," sheds little, if any, light on the meaning of *laleō* and *legō*.

The distinction between *laleō* and *legō* may be clarified by examining the two leading aspects in terms of which we may understand speech. Speech may

1. L-S 34, ever-babbling; lit. with no door to his lips.

2. Plato, *Definitiones* 416. I cannot believe that this is the correct translation of the word in John 4:42.

be understood as the articulate utterance of human language as contrasted with its absence. This absence may be due to choice, as is the case with those who hold their peace when they might speak; or it may be due to an undeveloped condition of the organs and faculties of speech, as is the case with infants (*nēpioi, 3516*); or it may be due to natural defects, as is the case with those born without hearing; or it may be due to an inherent inability to speak, as is the case with animals. Speech also may be understood as the orderly linking and knitting together in connected discourse of the inward thoughts and feelings of the mind: "To speak and to join together aptly chosen and selected words."[3] The first is *lalein*, which is equivalent to the Hebrew *dibbēr* (1699), to the German *lallen* (to mumble) and *sprecken* (to speak), and to the Latin *loqui*. The second is *legein*, which is equivalent to the Hebrew *'āmar* (559), to the Latin *dicere*, and to the German *reden* (to talk, to discourse). Ammonius wrote: "*Lalein* and *legein* differ; *legein* is the orderly presenting of discourse, while *lalein* is the disorderly uttering of chance phrases."

The dumb man (*alalos, 216*; Mark 7:37) whose speech was restored is called *elalēse* (Matt. 9:33; Luke 11:14) by the Gospel writers, who were not concerned to report what the man said but only that the previously mute man now was able to speak. Thus it is always *lalein* "in tongues" (Mark 16:17; Acts 2:4; 1 Cor. 12:30), since the sacred narrators emphasize the ecstatic utterance per se, not its content. *Lalein* may be ascribed to God himself, as in Hebrews 1:1–2, where the emphasis is on God speaking to men rather than on what God spoke.

If *lalein*[4] primarily refers to the articulated utterance of human language, then *legein*[5] primarily refers to the words that are uttered, to the verbally expressed thoughts of the speaker. Although *lalein* may be applied to a parrot or talking automaton (Rev. 13:15), since both produce sounds that imitate human speech, and though in poetry *lalein* may be ascribed to grasshoppers,[6] pipes, and flutes,[7] nothing lies behind these sounds, which therefore may not be referred to by *legein*. *Legein* always refers to the *ennoia* (*1771*) or thought of the mind (Heb. 4:12) as that which is correlative to spoken words and as their necessary condition. *Legein* means "to bring together words in a sentence," just as Aristotle defined *logos* as "a compound intelligible sound."[8] Similarly, Plutarch argued that *phrazein*[9] could not be predicated of monkeys and dogs—"for they utter sounds [*lalousi*] but do not explain [*phrazousi*]"[10]—but that *lalein* could.

Often when *lalein* and *legein* occur together in phrases like *elalēse legōn* (Mark 6:50; Luke 24:6), *lalētheis logos* (Heb. 2:2), and the like, each word re-

3. Valcknaer; cf. Donaldson, *Cratylus*, p. 453. Cf. the Latin *oratio* (discourse).
4. It is equivalent to the Latin *loqui*.
5. It is equivalent to the Latin *dicere*.
6. Theocritus, *Idyllia* 5.34.
7. Ibid. 20.28–29.
8. *Poetica* 20.11. See Malan, *Notes on the Gospel of St. John*, p. 3.
9. *5419*. It only occurs twice in the New Testament (Matt. 13:36; 15:15).
10. *Placita philosophorum* 5.20.

tains its own meaning. Thus in the first phrase, *elalēse* refers to opening the mouth to speak, as opposed to remaining silent (Acts 18:9), and *legōn* refers to what the speaker actually said. I do not believe there is any passage in the New Testament where the distinction between these words has not been observed. Thus in Romans 15:18; 2 Corinthians 11:17; and 1 Thessalonians 1:8, there is no difficulty in giving *lalein* its proper meaning—indeed all these passages gain rather than lose when this is done. In Romans 3:19 there is an instructive interchange of the words.

In the New Testament, *lalia* and *logos* follow the distinction described above. The one occasion when Jesus claimed *lalia* as well as *logos* for himself—"Why do you not understand my speech [*lalian*]? Because you are not able to listen to my word [*logon*]" (John 8:43)—shows that *lalia* and *lalein* do not mean anything disrespectful. To understand John 8:43 we must understand the contrast between *lalia* and *logos*, something that commentators have interpreted in different ways. Some, like Augustine, have failed to notice the difference between the two words. Others, like Olshausen, have noticed the difference but have denied that it has any significance. Others have admitted that there is a significant difference between the words but have failed to explain the difference correctly. The inability to understand Jesus' "speech" (*lalia*) is a consequence of refusing to hear his "word" (*logos*). This refusal is a deeper problem and the root of the trouble. To hear Jesus' "word" can mean nothing less than to open one's heart to the truth that Jesus speaks. Those who will not do this necessarily fail to understand Jesus' "speech," the outward form that his uttered "word" assumes. Those who belong to God hear God's words—his *rhēmata* (4487) as they are called in other passages (John 3:34; 8:47)—or his *lalia* as they are referred to here,[11] which those who do not belong to God do not and cannot hear. According to Melanchthon: "Those who are God's true sons and family cannot be unacquainted with the language of the paternal household."

11. Philo distinguishes the *logos* and the *rhēma* in terms of the whole and its parts (*Legum allegoriarum libri* 3.61): "*To rhēma* is a portion of *logos*." On the distinction between *rhēma tou theou* and *logos tou theou*, see the important remarks of Archdeacon Lee, *On Inspiration*, pp. 135, 539.

77

apolytrōsis (629) — *Redemption, Deliverance*

katallagē (2643) — *Reconciliation*

hilasmos (2434) — *Atonement, Propitiation*

The New Testament uses three major sets of images to explain the inestimable benefits of Christ's death and passion. Although these benefits transcend human thought and therefore cannot be expressed perfectly in language, they must nevertheless be described in words and in terms of human relationships. As in similar cases, Scripture approaches this central truth from many complimentary perspectives that compensate for one another's weaknesses and that serve to express the multifaceted nature of this truth. The three words used to represent these sets of images are *apolytrōsis* (redemption), *katallagē* (reconciliation), and *hilasmos* (propitiation). Almost every word and phrase that directly bears on this aspect of our salvation through Christ is related to one of these three words.

Apolytrōsis is the word that Paul preferred.[1] In drawing attention to this, Chrysostom correctly observed that Paul's use of *apo* (575) expresses the completeness of our redemption in Christ, a redemption not followed by any bondage: "He did not speak simply of a *lytrōsis* but of an *apolytrōsis* as we no

1. *Lytrōsis* (3085) occurs in the New Testament only in Luke 1:68; 2:38; Heb. 9:12.

longer return again to the same bondage."[2] *Apo* has the same force in *apokatallassein*,[3] which means "to reconcile absolutely,"[4] *apokaradokia* (603), and *apekdechesthai* (553; Rom. 8:19). Both *apolytrōsis*[5] and *lytrōsis* appear late in the Greek language;[6] *lytrōtēs* (3086) seems to be unique to the Greek Scriptures (Lev. 25:31; Ps. 19:14; Acts 7:35).

When Theophylact defined *apolytrōsis* as "the recall from captivity," he overlooked its most important aspect. *Apolytrōsis* is not just "recall from captivity" but "the rescue of captives from captivity through the payment of a ransom."[7] The idea of deliverance through a *lytron* (3083) or *antallagma*[8] (a price paid) is central to these words (Isa. 52:3; 1 Pet. 1:18–19), though in actual use it often is absent in words from this family (cf. Isa. 35:9). Thus *apolytrōsis* is related to an entire group of significant words, not only to *lytron*,[9] *antilytron*,[10] *lytroun*,[11] and *lytrōsis*,[12] but also to *agorazein*[13] and *exagorazein*.[14] Here is a point of contact with *hilasmos*, for the *lytron* paid in this *apolytrōsis* is identical with the *prosphora* (4376) or *thysia* (2378) that results in the *hilasmos*. *Apolytrōsis* also is related to all of the statements in Scripture that speak of sin as slavery, of sinners as slaves (John 8:34; Rom. 6:17, 20; 2 Pet. 2:19), and of deliverance from sin as freedom from or as cessation of bondage (John 8:33, 36; Rom. 8:21; Gal. 5:1).

Katallagē occurs four times in the New Testament but only once in the Septuagint and once in the Apocrypha. On one of these occasions (Isa. 9:5), *katallagē* simply means "exchange"; on the other (2 Macc. 5:20) it is used in the New Testament sense of being opposed to the wrath of God and refers to God's reconciliation and favor toward his people. It is clear that *synallagē*,[15] *synallassein*,[16] *diallagē*,[17] and *diallassein*[18] are more usual in earlier and in classical Greek.[19] Nevertheless, the grammarians were wrong who denounced *katallagē* and *katalassein* (2644) as words that were avoided by writers who

2. On Rom. 3:24.

3. 604; Eph. 2:16; Col. 1:20, 22.

4. See Fritzsche on Rom. 5:10.

5. It is not found in the Septuagint, but *apolytroō* occurs twice (Exod. 21:8; Zeph. 3:1).

6. Rost and Palm (*Lexicon*) give no earlier authority for them than Plutarch (*Aratus* 11; *Pompeius* 24).

7. Cf. Origen on Rom. 3:24.

8. 465; Matt. 16:26; cf. Ecclus. 6:15; 26:14.

9. Matt. 20:28; Mark 10:45.

10. 487; 1 Tim. 2:6.

11. 3084; Titus 2:14; 1 Pet. 1:18.

12. Heb. 9:12.

13. 59; 1 Cor. 6:20.

14. *1805*; Gal. 3:13; 4:5.

15. Ezek. 16:8, Aquila.

16. Acts 7:26.

17. Ecclus. 22:23; 27:21; cf. Aristophanes, *Acharnenses* 988.

18. *1259*; in the New Testament only in Matt. 5:24; cf. Judg. 19:3; 1 Esd. 4:31; Euripides, *Helena* 1235.

19. According to Clement of Alexandria (*Cohortatio ad gentes* 10), Christ is "our Reconciler [*dialaktēs*] and Savior."

strove for purity. No one should be ashamed of words that were used by Aeschylus,[20] Xenophon,[21] and Plato.[22]

There are two aspects to the Christian use of *katallagē*. First, *katallagē* refers to the reconciliation "by which God has reconciled himself to us." God laid aside his holy anger against our sins and received us into his favor by means of the reconciliation that was accomplished once for all by Christ on the cross. *Katallagē* is used this way in 2 Corinthians 5:18–19 and Romans 5:10, where *katallassesthai* is a pure passive: "We are received into grace by him with whom we had been in wrath." Second and subordinately, *katallagē* refers to the reconciliation "by which we are reconciled to God," the daily deposition of the enmity of the old man toward God under the operation of the Holy Spirit. This passive sense of *katallassesthai* appears in 2 Corinthians 5:20 (cf. 1 Cor. 7:11). All attempts to substitute the secondary for the primary meaning of *katallagē* are based on a foregone determination to deny the reality of God's anger against the sinner, not on unprejudiced exegesis. *Katallagē* is related to all the language of Scripture that describes sin as a state of enmity (*echthra, 2189*) with God (Rom. 8:7; Eph. 2:15; James 4:4) and sinners as God's enemies who are alienated from him (Rom. 5:10; Col. 1:21), that depicts Christ on the cross as the peace and as the maker of peace between God and man (Eph. 2:14; Col. 1:20), and with all invitations such as: "be reconciled to God" (2 Cor. 5:20).

The exact relationship between *katallagē* and *hilasmos* is somewhat confused for the English reader, because the word *atonement*, which the Authorized translators used once to translate *katallagē* (Rom. 5:11), has slowly changed in meaning. If a new translation were to be made, "atonement" would plainly be a better translation of *hilasmos*, which refers to propitiation. The central aspect of *hilasmos* is found in *atonement*, as we currently use this word, though this was not always the case. When our Authorized Version was made, atonement referred to reconciliation or the making up of a previous enmity. All of its uses in our early literature justify the etymology (which now is sometimes called into question) that "atonement" is "at-one-meet" and therefore equivalent to "reconciliation." Consequently "atonement" was then (though not now) the correct translation of *katallagē*.[23]

Hilasmos is used twice in the First Epistle of John (2:2; 4:10) but nowhere else in the New Testament.[24] I am inclined to think that the excellent word *propitiation*, which was used by our Authorized translators, did not exist in the English language when the earlier Reformed versions were made. The versions of Tyndale, Geneva, and Cranmer have "to make *agreement*" instead of

20. *Septem contra Thebas* 767.

21. *Anabasis* 1.6.2.

22. *Phaedo* 69a. Fritzsche (on Rom. 5:10) effectively disposed of Tittmann's fanciful distinction between *katallassein* and *diallassein*.

23. See my *Select Glossary* under the words *atone, atonement*. For a complete treatment of these words, see Skeat, *Etymological Dictionary of the English Language*, under "atonement," an article that leaves no doubt about their history.

24. For other examples of its use, see Plutarch, *Solon* 12; *Fabius Maximus* 18; *Camillus* 7: *theōn mēnis hilasmou kai charistēriōn deomenē*.

apolytrōsis

katallagē
hilasmos

"to be the *propitiation*" in 1 John 2:2 and "he that obtaineth grace" in 2 John 4:10. *Hilastērion* (2435) is also translated by "propitiation" (Rom. 3:25), though I think that is incorrect.[25] Other erroneous translations translate *hilastērion* as "the obtainer of mercy" (Cranmer) and "a pacification" (Geneva). The Rheims Version was the first to use "propitiation"; the Latin tendencies of this translation caused it to transfer this word from the Vulgate. *Hilasmos* is not used frequently in the Septuagint, though in some passages (Num. 5:8; Ezek. 44:27; cf. 2 Macc. 3:33) it was being prepared for its more solemn use in the New Testament. *Hilasmos* is related to the Greek *hileōs*[26] and *hilaskesthai*[27] and to the Latin *iram avertere* (to avert anger) and *ex irato mitem reddere* (to render mild from angered). Hesychius correctly, though inadequately, equated *hilasmos* (cf. Ps. 130:7; Dan. 9:9) with the following synonyms: *eumeneia*,[28] *synchōrēsis*,[29] *diallagē*, *katallagē*, and *praotēs* (4236). I say "inadequately" because none of the words that Hesychius offered as equivalents contain the essential notion of *hilasmos* and *hilaskesthai*: the *eumeneia* (goodwill) has been gained by means of some offering or other means of appeasing.[30] *Hilasmos* is more comprehensive than *hilastēs*,[31] the word Grotius proposed as its equivalent. Not only does Christ propitiate, as *hilastēs* (propitiator) would indicate, but he both propitiates and is himself the propitiation. In the language of the Epistle to the Hebrews, in offering himself he is both *archiereus* (749) and *thysia* or *prosphora*.[32] The two functions of priest and sacrifice (which were of necessity divided in the typical sacrifices of the law) met and were united in him, who was the sin-offering by and through whom the just anger of God against our sins was appeased. Without compromising his righteousness, God was enabled to show himself propitious to us once more. When used of Christ, *hilasmos* declares all of this. According to Cocceius: "*Hilasmos* is the death, accomplished for sanctification before God, of the bondsman who is willing to present an offering for sins and thus to remove condemnation."

Hilasmos is related to a larger group of words and images than either of the preceding terms. This group includes the words that set forth the benefits of Christ's death as a propitiation of God, as well as those that speak of him as a sacrifice or an offering (1 Cor. 5:7; Eph. 5:2; Heb. 10:14), as the Lamb of God (John 1:29, 36; 1 Pet. 1:19), and as the Lamb who was slain (Rev. 5:6, 8). A little more remote but still related are all of those words that describe Christ as washing us in his blood (Rev. 1:5). In comparison with *katallagē*,[33] *hilasmos*[34] is the deeper word and closer to the heart of the matter. If we had

25. See *Theologische Studien und Kritiken*, 1842, p. 314.

26. 2436, the Latin *propitius*.

27. 2433, the Latin *placare* (to appease).

28. L-S 721, favor, goodwill.

29. L-S 1669, agreement, forgiveness.

30. Cf. Herodotus, 6.105; 8.112; Xenophon, *Cyropaedia* 7.2.19; and Nägelsbach, *Nachhomerische Theologie*, 1:37.

31. L-S 828, propitiator.

32. For the difference between *thysia* and *prosphora*, see Mede, *Works*, 1672, p. 360.

33. It is equivalent to the German *Versöhnung* (reconciliation).

34. It is equivalent to the German *Versühnung* (propitiation).

only *katallagē* and the group of words and images that cluster around it to explain the benefits of Christ's death, they would show that we *were* enemies and by that death were made friends. But *katallagē* does not explain *how* we were made friends. It does not necessarily imply satisfaction, propitiation, the Mediator, the High Priest—all of which are found in *hilasmos*.[35] I conclude this discussion with Bengel's excellent note on Romans 3:24:

> *Hilasmos* (expiation or propitiation) and *apolytrōsis* (redemption) have fundamentally a single benefit—namely, the restitution of a lost sinner. It is *apolytrōsis* in reference to an enemy, and *katallagē* in respect to God. And here these terms, *hilasmos* and *katallagē*, again differ. *Hilasmos* (propitiation) removes an offense against God; *katallagē* (reconciliation) has two fronts and removes (a) God's displeasure toward us (2 Cor. 5:19) and (b) our alienation from God (2 Cor. 5:20).

35. See two admirable articles, *Erlösung* (redemption) and *Versöhnung* (reconciliation) by Schoeberlein in Herzog's *Real-Encyclopädie*.

78

psalmos (5568) *Psalm*
hymnos (5215) *Hymn*
ōdē (5603) *(Spiritual) Song*

Psalmos, *hymnos*, and *ōdē* are all used together in the same order in Ephesians 5:19 and Colossians 3:16, passages that are nearly identical (cf. Ps. 66: title).[1] Some expositors refuse to attempt to distinguish these words, arguing that Paul did not intend to classify different forms of Christian poetry. Although this statement is true, Paul would not have used three words if one would have served his purpose equally well.[2] Although it is reasonable to question whether "psalms," "hymns," and "spiritual songs" can be differentiated and whether Paul did so, it is nevertheless true that each word must have its own distinctive meaning. Even though we may discern these meanings, we may not be able to classify the Christian poetry of the apostolic age under these three heads.

Remarkably, the psalms of the Old Testament have no single, well recognized, and universally accepted name by which they are designated in the Hebrew Scriptures.[3] They were first called *Psalmos*[4] in the Septuagint, a title that properly means "touching," then "touching of the harp or other stringed

1. *Asma* (L-S 258, song, lyric ode) occurs frequently in the Septuagint but does not occur in the New Testament.

2. There is evidently no temptation to rhetorical amplification here.

3. Delitzsch, *Kommentar über den Psalter*, 2:371; Herzog, *Real-Encyclopädie*, 12:269.

4. From *psaō* (cf. 5567).

instruments with the finger or with the plectrum,"[5] then "the instrument itself," and finally "the song sung with this musical accompaniment." The last meaning is the one used in the Septuagint and by the church. In the *Lexicon* ascribed to Cyril of Alexandria, *psalmos* is defined as "a musical composition, when an instrument is struck rhythmically in harmonious modes."[6] Basil the Great emphasized the differences between the "psalm" and the "ode" or "spiritual song." According to Basil, "it is a song [*ōdē*] and not a psalm [*psalmos*] because by voice alone, without any instrument accompanying it, it has been transmitted with melodious utterance."[7] In all probability the *psalmoi* of Ephesians 5:19 and Colossians 3:16 are the inspired psalms of the Hebrew canon. This is certainly true on all other occasions when *psalmos* occurs in the New Testament, with the possible exception of 1 Corinthians 14:26, though this passage also probably refers to the Old Testament psalms. The "psalms" the apostle wanted the faithful to sing to one another are the psalms of David, Asaph, or some of the other sweet singers of Israel. Because of the nearly synonymous words that are used with it, *psalmos* seems to have this narrow meaning.

Although by right of primogeniture "psalms" is the oldest form and occupies the foremost place in the church, the church is not restricted to singing only "psalms" but is free to bring new things as well as old out of her treasure house. Thus, in addition to inheriting the psalms bequeathed to her by the Jews, the church will produce "hymns and spiritual songs" of her own. A new salvation demands a new song (Rev. 5:9), as Augustine often delighted to remind us.

The essential idea of a Greek *hymnos* was that it addressed or praised a god or a hero (a deified man). Callisthenes reminded Alexander that by claiming hymns or allowing them to be addressed to him, he was implicitly accepting not human but divine honors.[8] The gradual breakdown of the distinction between the human and the divine that marked the fallen days of Greece and Rome—a time when men usurped divine honors—resulted in *hymnos* increasingly being applied to men, though not without remonstrance.[9] When *hymnos* was adopted by the church, this essential distinction still belonged to it. A "psalm" might be a *De profundis* ("Out of the Depths"), the story of man's deliverance, or a commemoration of mercies he had received. The same sort of thing could be said of the "spiritual song," but a "hymn" (more or less) must always be a *Magnificat* (cf. Luke 1:46–55), a direct address of praise and glory to God. Thus Jerome wrote: "In brief, one must sing hymns, which proclaim the power and majesty of God and always marvel at his bene-

5. *Psalmoi toxōn*, Euripides, *Ion* 174; cf. *Bacchae* 740, the twangings of the bow strings.

6. Cf. Clement of Alexandria, *Paedagogus* 2.4.

7. *Homilia in Psalma* 44. Cf. *In Psalma* 29:1, to which Gregory of Nyssa (*In Psalma* 100:3) agreed.

8. "Hymns are composed for gods, praises for human beings" (Arrian, 4.11).

9. Athenaeus, 6.62; 15.21–22.

fits and deeds."[10] Gregory of Nyssa wrote: "A hymn [*hymnos*] is a praise dedicated to God for the benefits we have."[11] In several places Augustine gave what he considered to be the three essentials of a hymn: it must be sung; it must be praise; it must be to God. Thus Augustine wrote:

> Hymns are praises to God with singing; hymns are songs containing praises to God. If there is praise but not to God, it is not a hymn; if there is praise and it is to God but is not sung, it is not a hymn. It is necessary, therefore, to be a hymn that it have three things: praise, and to God, and singing.[12]

Again Augustine noted:

> Do you know what a hymn is? It is a song with praise to God. If you praise God but do not sing, you do not call it a hymn; if you sing but do not praise God, you do not call it a hymn; if you praise something which does not pertain to God's praise, even if it is in song, you do not call it a hymn. A hymn, therefore, has these three elements: a song, praise, to God.[13]

According to Gregory Nazianzene: "Laudation [*epainos*] is to speak well of anything I possess; praise [*ainos*] is an august laudation [*epainos*] to God; the hymn [*hymnos*] is praise [*ainos*] with melody, as I believe."

Although the church had freely adopted the term *hymnos* by the fourth century,[14] it is not clear that it had done so earlier. The authority of Paul's usage notwithstanding, *hymnos* does not appear in the writings of the apostolic fathers, Justin Martyr, or in the *Apostolic Constitutions*. Tertullian used it only once.[15] This may be due to *hymnos*'s association with heathenism and profane usages that desecrated the term. There were so many hymns to Zeus, Hermes, Aphrodite, and other heathen deities that the early Christians instinctively shrunk from using the term.

What was the character of the "hymns" that Paul desired the faithful to sing among themselves? We may assume that these hymns followed the rules and directly addressed praise to God. Inspired specimens of *hymnoi* are found in Luke 1:46–55, 68–79; and Acts 4:24. Paul and Silas probably sung *hymnoi* from the depths of the Philippian dungeon.[16] The *Te Deum*, the *Veni Creator Spiritus*, and many other examples show how noble and magnificent unin-

10. *In Ephesios* 5:19. Cf. Origen, *Contra Celsum* 8.67, and a precious fragment, probably from the Presbyter Caius, preserved by Eusebius (*Historia ecclesiastica* 5.28): "Great psalms [*psalmoi*] and songs [*ōdai*], composed originally by faithful brethren, sing of the Word of God, Christ, commemorating his Deity."

11. *In Psalma* 100:3; the whole chapter is interesting.

12. *Ennarationes in Psalma* 82:1.

13. *Ennarationes in Psalma* 148:14. It is not very easy to follow Augustine in his distinction between a "psalm" and a "canticle." He acknowledged his own lack of clarity; thus see *Ennarationes in Psalma* 67:1: "In a psalm there is fullness of sound, in a canticle joy"; cf. *In Psalma* 4:1; and Hilary, *Prologus in Librum Psalmorum*, paragraphs 19–21.

14. This is apparent from the previous quotations.

15. *Ad uxores* 2.8.

16. "They were singing hymns [*hymnoun*] to God," Acts 16:25.

spired hymns can be. Even if we lacked supporting evidence, we could be certain that the church used hymns to praise God for the new, marvelous, heavenly world into which she had been brought. There is, however, abundant evidence to this effect. More than one fragment of a very early hymn is probably embedded in Paul's own epistles.[17] It seems quite impossible that the Christian church, as it moved away from the Jewish synagogue, would fall into the mistake later made by some Reformed churches of using only "psalms" in the liturgy. The early church used "hymns" and sang them to Christ as to God,[18] though this practice occurred more frequently in Gentile, than in Jewish, churches.[19]

Ōdē[20] is the only word of this group used in Revelation (5:9; 14:3; 15:3). Paul used it twice and added *pneumatikē* (*4152*) to it, probably because *ōdē* by itself might refer to any kind of song—battle, harvest, festal, or hymeneal.[21] When *pneumatikē* was applied to "songs," it did not imply that they were divinely inspired any more than the *anēr* (*435*) *pneumatikos* is an inspired man (1 Cor. 3:1; Gal. 6:1). These songs were composed by spiritual men about spiritual topics. How are we to distinguish these "spiritual songs" from the "psalms" and "hymns" that Paul grouped with them? If the "psalms" represent the heritage of sacred song that the Christian church derived from the Jewish Scriptures, then the "hymns" and "spiritual songs" are what the church itself produced, with the following qualification. Hymns were a direct address to God, but Christian thought and feeling soon expanded to a wider range of poetic utterances. In Herbert's *Temple*, Vaughan's *Silex Scintillans*, and Keble's *Christian Year*, there are many poems that are certainly not "psalms," nor do they possess the characteristics of "hymns." These "spiritual songs" are found in almost all of our collections of so-called "hymns," though it would be more correct to call them "spiritual songs." Calvin would only agree in part with the distinctions we have made:

> Under these three terms Paul has included every type of songs, which usually are distinguished as follows—a psalm is one in which some musical instrument besides the voice accompanies the singing; a hymn strictly speaking is a song of praise, either with mere voice or otherwise sung; an ode contains not only praises but exhortations and other admonitions.[22]

17. Eph. 5:14; 1 Tim. 3:16; 2 Tim. 2:11–14; cf. Rambach, *Anthologie*, 1:33; and Neale, *Essays on Liturgiology*, pp. 413, 424.

18. Pliny, *Epistulae* 10.96.

19. For an etymological perspective on *hymnos*, see Pott, *Etymologische Forschungen*, vol. 2, pt. 2, p. 612.

20. It is equivalent to *aoidē* (L-S 172, song).

21. Because of their backgrounds, *psalmos* and *hymnos* did not require qualifying adjectives.

22. Cf. Vollbeding's *Thesaurus*, 2:27ff.; a treatise by J. Z. Hillger, *De psalmorum, hymnorum, et odarum discrimine*; Palmer in Herzog's *Real-Encyclopädie*, 5:100ff.; Deyling, *Obsessiones sacrae*, 3:430; Lightfoot, *On Colossians* 3:16; and the article *Hymns* in Dr. Smith's *Dictionary of Christian Antiquities*.

79

agrammatos (62)

idiōtēs (2399)

Unlearned
Uneducated
Uninformed
Ignorant
Untrained

Agrammatos and *idiōtēs* are used together in Acts 4:13. *Agrammatos* is not used elsewhere in the New Testament; *idiōtēs* is used four other times (1 Cor. 14:16, 23, 24; 2 Cor. 11:6). When they are used together, it seems that *idiōtēs* is stronger than *agrammatos* and adds something to it. Apparently this is the way the Authorized translators understood these words, for they translated *agrammatos* as "unlearned," and *idiōtēs* as "ignorant." Bengel said: "*Agrammatos* is 'uninformed,' *idiōtēs* is 'more uninformed.' "

It is not difficult to define *agrammatos*, which corresponds exactly to our *illiterate*.[1] Plato used *agrammatos* with *oreios*[2] and with *amousos*,[3] and Plutarch contrasted it with *memousōmenos*.[4]

Idiōtēs has a wider range of meaning and is a far more complex and subtle term. Initially, *idiōtēs* referred to a private person who was occupied with his

1. *Grammata mē memathēkōs* (not having learned letters), John 7:15; Acts 26:24; 2 Tim. 3:15.

2. Cf. *3714*, rugged as the mountaineer; *Crito* 109d.

3. L-S 85, rude; *Timaeus* 23b.

4. L-S 1149, being educated and accomplished; *Adversus Colotem* 26.

agrammatos

idiōtēs

own concerns,[5] as contrasted with the political person (a man without public office as opposed to one who holds an office). Because one of the strongest convictions in the Greek mind was that a person's true education consisted in public life, *idiōtēs* became tinged with contempt and scorn. The *idiōtēs* stayed at home while others worked.[6] Our ancestors demeaningly referred to such a person as a "house-dove'—unexercised in business, unaccustomed to deal with other people, impractical. Plato joined *idiōtēs* with *apragmōn*.[7] Plutarch used it with *apraktos*[8] and contrasted it with the *politikos*[9] *kai praktikos*.[10] More than this, however, the *idiōtēs* often is boorish, an association that resulted in *idiōtēs* being used with *agroikos*,[11] *apaideutos*,[12] and with other similar words.[13]

The history of *idiōtēs* does not stop here, though we have traced it as far as is necessary to explain its association in Acts 4:13 with *agrammatos* and to contrast the two terms. To explain why Paul used *idiōtēs* in 1 Corinthians 14:16, 23–24 and in what sense requires pursuing its etymology further. There is a unique feature to *idiōtēs* that is best communicated by citing a few examples. *Idiōtēs* always refers to the negation of some particular skill, knowledge, profession, or standing with which it is contrasted. For example, if the *idiōtēs* is contrasted with the *dēmiourgos*,[14] the *idiōtēs* is the unskilled man who is contrasted with the skilled artificer. The *idiōtēs* may possess any other dexterity but that of the *dēmiourgos*. If the *idiōtēs* is contrasted with the *iatros* (*2395*), the *idiōtēs* is one who is ignorant of the physician's art.[15] If the *idiōtēs* is contrasted with the *sophistēs*,[16] the *idiōtēs* is unacquainted with the sophist's dialectical skill.[17] If the *idiōtēs* is contrasted with the *philologos*,[18] the *idiōtēs* has no interest in those earnest studies. When contrasted with poets, prose writers are *idiōtai*. When compared with the *athlētai*,[19] those unpracticed in gymnastic exercises are *idiōtai*. When contrasted with their prince,[20] the

5. *Ta idia* (*2398*).

6. Plutarch called the *idiōtēs* an *oikouros* (*3626*); *Maxime cum principibus philosopho esse disserendum*.

7. L-S 229, free from business; *Republic* 10.620c; cf. Plutarch, *De virtute et vitio* 4.

8. L-S 229, inactive, idle; *Maxime cum principibus philosopho esse disserendum* 1.

9. L-S 1435, relating to citizens.

10. L-S 1458, active, practical.

11. L-S 15, rustic, boorish, rude; Chrysostom, *In epistulam 1 ad Corinthios* 3.

12. *521*; Plutarch, *Comparatio Aristidis et Catonis* 1.

13. There is an excellent discussion on the successive meanings of *idiōtēs* in Bishop Horsley's *Tracts in Controversy with Dr. Priestly, Appendix, Disquisition Second*, pp. 475–85. Our English "idiot" also has an instructive history. This quotation from Jeremy Taylor (*Dissuasive from Popery*, pt. 2, bk. 1, par. 1) will show how it was used two hundred years ago: "S. Austin affirmed that the plain places of Scripture are sufficient to all laics, and all *idiots* or private persons." See my *Select Glossary* under this word for other examples of this same use.

14. *1217*; Plato, *Theages* 124c.

15. Plato, *Republic* 3.389b; Philo, *De confusione linguarum* 7.

16. L-S 1622, sophist.

17. Xenophon, *De venatione* 13; cf. *Hiero* 1.2; Lucian, *Revivescentes sive piscator* 34; Plutarch, *Septem sapientium convivium* 4.2.3.

18. *5378*; Sextus Empiricus, *Adversus mathematicos et grammaticos*, par. 235.

19. L-S 32, athletes; Xenophon, *Hiero* 4.6; Philo, *De septem orbis spectaculis* 6.

20. *De Abrahamo* 33.

underlings in the harvest field are *idiōtai kai hypēretai* (5257), as distinguished from the *hēgemones*.[21] The weak are *idiōtai* (*aporoi*[22] and *adoxoi*[23] are qualitative adjectives) as contrasted with the strong.[24] Finally, all of those in the congregation of Israel are *idiōtai* as contrasted with the priests.[25] Based on these examples, we must conclude that the *idiōtai* in 1 Corinthians 14:16, 23–24 are plain believers who have no special spiritual gifts, as distinguished from those who possess such gifts, that is, the lay members of the church as contrasted with those who minister the word and sacraments, for it is always the word with which *idiōtēs* is combined and contrasted that determines its meaning.

Unlearned Uneducated Uninformed Ignorant Untrained

When the Pharisees recognize Peter and John as men *agrammatoi kai idiōtai*, the first word expresses their lack of book learning,[26] their lack of acquaintance with teaching such as that Paul had received at Gamaliel's feet. The second word emphasizes the apostles' lack of the sort of education that is gained by mingling with people who have important affairs to transact and by transacting such affairs. Apart from the higher training of the heart and intellect that is obtained by direct communion with God and his truth, books and public life (literature and politics) are the world's two most effective instruments of mental and moral training. The second is immeasurably more effective than the first. One is *agrammatos* who has not shared in the first; one is *idiōtēs* who has had no part in the second.

21. Philo, *De somniis* 2.4.
22. L-S 215, helpless.
23. L-S 24, obscure.
24. Philo, *De creationis principibus* 5; cf. Plutarch, *Regum et imperatorum apophthegmata* 1.
25. Philo, *De vita Mosis* 3.29.
26. The Pharisees confined this to the Old Testament (the *hiera grammata* or "sacred writings") and to the glosses of their own doctors on these.

dokeō (1380) *phainomai (5316)*

Seem Be Considered Appear

The translators of the Authorized Version did not always observe the distinction between *dokein*[1] and *phainesthai*.[2] *Dokein* refers to a person's subjective mental estimate or opinion about something. A person's *doxa (1391)* may be right[3] or wrong, since it always involves the possibility of error.[4] *Phainesthai*, however, refers to how a thing shows and presents itself phenomenally and does not imply the presence of an observer; it suggests an opposition to the *nooumenon* (apprehending), not to the *on* (being). Thus when Plato said of certain heroes in the Trojan war that "they appeared [*ephanēsan*] ready for war,"[5] he did not mean that they *seemed* good for the war and really were not but that they *showed* themselves to be good (the tacit assumption is that they really were). So when Xenophon wrote "there appeared [*ephaineto*] footprints of horses,"[6] he implied that horses actually had left their footprints on the

1. It is equivalent to the Latin *videri* (to seem).
2. It is equivalent to the Latin *apparere* (to appear).
3. Acts 15:28; 1 Cor. 4:9; 7:40; cf. Plato, *Timaeus* 51d; *doxa alēthēs* (true opinion).
4. 2 Macc. 9:10; Matt. 6:7; Mark 6:49; John 16:2; Acts 27:13; cf. Plato, *Republic* 423a; *Gorgias* 458a, *doxa pseudēs* (false opinion); Xenophon, *Cyropaedia* 1.6.22; *Memorabilia* 1.7.4, *ischyron, mē onta, dokein* (to have a false reputation for strength).
5. *Republic* 408a.
6. *Anabasis* 1.6.1.

dokeō

phainomai

ground. Had Xenophon used *dokein*, he would have implied that Cyrus and his company took for horses' tracks what may or may not have been horses' tracks.[7] Zeune wrote: "To seem [*dokein*] is discerned in an opinion, which can be false and groundless; but to appear [*phainesthai*] usually is in reality outside the mind, inasmuch as no judgment is involved."[8]

Even in passages where *dokein* and *einai* (*1511*) may be used interchangeably, *dokein* does not lose the meaning that Zeune gave it. *Dokein* always includes a predominant reference to public opinion and estimate, rather than to actual being. The former, however, may be the faithful reflection of the latter (Prov. 27:14). There is no irony or depreciation in Paul's use of *hoi dokountes* in Galatians 2:2 and of *hoi dokountes einai ti* in verse 6.[9] Clearly Paul intended no slight by his words, since he used them to characterize the chief of his fellow apostles. Instead, Paul's words refer to the apostles' reputation in the church, not to their own intrinsic worth, though their reputation may have been the true measure of their worth.[10] When Christ referred to "those who are considered [*hoi dokountes*] rulers over the Gentiles" (Mark 10:42), he did not cast doubt on the reality of their rule (cf. Matt. 20:25), though these words may contain a slight hint of the contrast between the worldly appearance of greatness and its heavenly realities.[11]

On the one hand, our mental conceptions may or may not correspond to something in the world. On the other hand, appearance may or may not have an underlying reality. *Phainesthai* is often synonymous with *einai* and *ginesthai*.[12] Plato contrasted the *phainomena* with "the things which truly exist,"[13] as the reflections of things seen in a mirror, as appearances that have no substance, such as the display of goodness made by the hypocrite (Matt. 23:28). In the latter case, however, we should not assume that the meaning of *phainesthai* shades into that of *dokein* or that the distinction between the two words breaks down. The distinction still stands: one word refers to something objective, the other to something subjective. Thus the contrast in Matthew 23:27–28 is not between what *other men took* the Pharisees to be and what they really were but between what *they showed themselves* to be to other men ("you also outwardly appear [*phainesthe*] righteous to men") and what they really were.

Dokein always signifies a subjective estimate of a thing, not the objective appearance and qualities it actually possesses. Consequently, the Authorized translation of James 1:26 is not perfectly satisfactory: "If any man among you *seem to be religious* [*dokei thrēskos einai*], and bridleth not his tongue, but

7. Cf. *Memorabilia* 3.10.2.

8. Thus *dokei phainesthai* (it seems to appear); Plato, *Phaedrus* 269d; *Leges* 12.960d.

9. Exactly the same phrases occur in Plato (*Euthydemus* 303d), where they are joined with *semnoi* (*4586*).

10. It is equivalent to *episēmoi* (*1978*; Rom. 16:7). Cf. Euripides (*Troiades* 608), where *ta dokounta* is contrasted with "that which in no way exists" (*Hecuba* 295). In Porphyry (*De abstinentia* 2.40) *hoi dokountes* is contrasted with "the masses."

11. Cf. Josephus, *Antiquitates Judaicae* 19.6.3; Winer, *Grammatik*, par. 67.4.

12. *1096*; Matt. 2:7; 13:26.

13. *Republic* 596e.

deceiveth his own heart, this man's religion is vain." As it now reads, this verse must have perplexed many. How can a man "seem to be religious," that is, present himself to others as such, when his religious pretensions are belied and refuted by the license of an unbridled tongue? But the verse becomes clear when the words are correctly translated (as in the New King James Version): "If anyone among you *thinks he is* religious[14] and does not bridle his tongue." Here *dokei* expresses a person's own mental estimate of his spiritual condition, an estimate that the following words declare to be altogether erroneous. Compare Hebrews 4:1, where for *dokē* the Vulgate correctly has *existimetur* (is thought). If the Vulgate's translation of *dokein* here is correct and our Authorized translation is wrong, elsewhere the Vulgate's translation of *phainesthai* is wrong, and the Authorized Version is correct. In Matthew 6:18 ("that thou appear not unto men to fast") the Vulgate has *ne videaris* (that you not seem), though in verse 16 it correctly has *ut appareant* (that they not appear). The disciples in this verse (v. 18) are not warned against the hypocrisy of wishing to be perceived as having fasted when they had not, as *ne videaris* might imply, but against the ostentation of wishing *to be known* to fast when they did, which plainly is the meaning of the original *hopōs mē phanēs*.

Seem
Be Considered
Appear

The force of *phainesthai* displayed in Matthew 6:18 was overlooked in the Authorized Version's translation of Philippians 2:15, not by confusing *phainesthai* with *dokein* but by confusing *phainesthai* with *phainein*. The Authorized Version translates *en hois phainesthe hōs phōstēres en kosmō* (Phil. 2:15) as "among whom *ye shine* as lights in the world." Instead of using "ye shine," the Authorized Version should have used "ye are seen" or "ye appear." To justify "ye shine," which is common to all the versions of the English Hexapla, Paul should have written *phainete*,[15] not *phainesthe*. It is noteworthy that though the Vulgate has *lucetis* (you shine), sharing and anticipating our error, an earlier Latin Version did not. This is evident from the form of the verse quoted by Augustine: "In which you *appear* as lights in the sky."[16]

14. Cf. Gal. 6:3, where *dokei* is correctly so translated, as it is in the Vulgate: *se putat religiosum esse* (thinks himself to be religious).

15. Cf. John 1:5; 2 Pet. 1:19; Rev. 1:16.

16. *Ennarationes in Psalma* 147:4.

81

zōon (2226)

thērion (2342)

Animal
Living Creature
Beast

In numerous passages, *zōon* and *thērion* may be used interchangeably,[1] though this does not prove that there is no distinction between them. In a few other passages, one word is appropriate and the other is not, or one word is more suitable than the other. These passages reveal the difference between *zōon* and *thērion*.

Zōon and *thērion* are not coordinate terms. *Thērion* is completely subordinate to *zōon*. As the lesser term, *thērion* is "included in" *zōon*, the greater term. All creatures that live on earth, including man himself,[2] are *zōa*.[3] According to the *Definitions* of Plato, God himself is "an immortal creature [*zōon*]," the only one to whom life by absolute right belongs.[4] *Zōon* is not used in the New Testament to designate man,[5] still less to designate God. God is not merely living but absolute life, the one fountain of life, "self-existent" (*autozōon*), and the "source of life" (*pēgē zōēs*). Therefore *zōē* (*2222*), the better and more reverent term, is used to describe God (John 1:4; 1 John 1:2). In

1. Plutarch, *De capienda ex inimicis utilitate* 2.

2. "A rational and social creature [*zōon*]," as Plutarch (*De amore prolis* 3) grandly described him.

3. Aristotle, *Historia animalium* 1.5.1.

4. "We say that God is a most noble eternal creature [*zōon*]," Aristotle (*Metaphysica* 12.7).

5. But see Plato, *Politicus* 271e; Xenophon, *Cyropaedia* 1.1.3; Wisd. of Sol. 19:20.

zōon its ordinary use, *zōon* is synonymous with the English *animal* and often[6] is used with *alogon* (249) or similar terms (2 Pet. 2:12; Jude 10).

thērion *Thērion* seems to be a diminutive of *thēr*.[7] Like *chrysion* (5553), *biblion* (975), *phortion* (5413), *angeion* (30), and many other words,[8] *thērion* has left behind whatever diminutive force it once may have possessed. *Thērion* already had lost this force by the time the *Odyssey* was composed, as the phrase *mega* (3173) *thērion* (large beast) attests.[9] *Thērion* does not exclusively refer to mischievous and ravening beasts (cf. Exod. 19:13; Heb. 12:20), though such animals are generally intended (Mark 1:13; Acts 28:4–5). *Thēria* in Acts 11:6 is distinguished from "four-footed animals." Schmidt correctly noted: "In *thērion* there is a very strong connotation of ferocity and cruelty." Although there are numerous passages in the Septuagint where beasts of sacrifice are mentioned, they are never called *thēria*. Evidently, *thērion* primarily has a brutal or bestial connotation that does not draw attention to the similarity between man and inferior animals that makes the latter an appropriate representative and substitute that may be offered for the former. This also explains the frequent application of *thērion* and *thēriōdēs*[10] to fierce and brutal men.[11]

All of this makes us regret[12] that the Authorized Version uses "beast" to translate *thērion* and *zōon* in the Book of Revelation, thereby obliterating the distinction between them. *Thērion* and *zōon* both play important roles in the Book of Revelation, and both belong to its higher symbolism. They are used in spheres as far removed as heaven is from hell. The *zōa* (living creatures) that stand before the throne, who contain the fullness of creaturely life as it gives praise and glory to God,[13] constitute a part of the heavenly symbolism. The *thēria* are the first and second beasts that rise up—one from the bottomless pit (Rev. 11:7) and the other from the sea (13:1). One makes war upon the two witnesses, and the other opens his mouth in blasphemies. Together they form part of the hellish symbolism. To confuse these distinct symbols under the common designation *beast* would be an oversight, even if that name were suitable for both. It is a more serious error when the word used brings out, as *thērion* does, the predominance of the lower animal life and the translation of that word is then applied to the glorious creatures in the very court of heaven. This error is common to most English translations. It is surprising that the Rheims Version did not escape this, since the Vulgate translates *zōa* by *animalia* (animals)[14] and *thērion* only by *bestia* (beast). If *zōa* always were translated "living creatures," it would unmistakably relate these symbols to Ezekiel 1:5, 13–14 (and often), where the Authorized Version translates *ḥayāh* (2416) as "living creature" and the Septuagint uses *zōon*.

6. Plutarch, *De garrulitate* 22; Heb. 13:11.

7. L-S 799, beast of prey. In its Aeolic form, *phēr* reappears as the Latin *fera* (wild animal), in its more usual shape in the German *Thier* (animal), and in the English *deer*.

8. See Fischer, *Prologus de Vitali Lexe N.T.*, p. 256.

9. 10.181; cf. Xenophon, *Cyropaedia* 1.4.11.

10. L-S 800, savage. This is the same as the Latin *bestia* (beast) and *bellua* (brute).

11. Titus 1:12; 1 Cor. 15:32; Josephus, *Antiquitates Judaicae* 17.5.5; Arrian, *In Epictetum* 2.9.

12. Broughton expressed this regret almost as soon as our Authorized Version was published.

13. Rev. 4:6–9; 5:6; 6:1; and often.

14. *Animantia* (living creatures) would have been even better.

82

hyper (5228) / *anti* (473)

For (the Sake of) / *In Behalf of* / *Instead of*

Many New Testament passages use *hyper* in phrases like "in behalf of [*hyper*] all," "in behalf of us," and "in behalf of the sheep."[1] To preserve the emphasis in these passages on the all-important truth of the vicarious nature of Christ's sacrifice, some scholars argue that *hyper* should be seen as the equivalent of *anti*. Because *anti* is the preposition first of equivalence[2] and then of exchange,[3] they conclude that *hyper* must have the same force in all of these passages. If this is correct, then each of these passages would become a *dictum probans* (demonstrating statement) for the vital truth that Christ suffered not merely *on our behalf* and *for our good* but also *in our stead*, that he bore the penalty of our sins that otherwise we would have had to bear. Although this has been denied, *hyper* sometimes has this meaning. Thus Plato wrote: "I will answer *in your stead*" (*egō* [*1473*] *hyper sou apokrinoumai* [*611*]).[4]

1. Luke 22:19–20; John 10:15; Rom. 5:8; Gal. 3:13; 1 Tim. 2:6; Titus 2:14; Heb. 2:9; 1 Pet. 2:21; 3:18; 4:1.

2. Homer, *Iliad* 9.116–17.

3. Matt. 5:38; 1 Cor. 11:15; Heb. 12:2, 16.

4. *Gorgias* 515c. Cf. Xenophon, *Anabasis* 7.4.9: *Ethelois an hyper toutou apothanein* (Wouldst thou die instead of this lad?), as the context and the words "if he should strike him instead of [*anti*] that one" make abundantly clear. Cf. Thucydides, 1.141; Euripides, *Alcestis* 712; Polybius, 3.67.7; Philem. 13; and perhaps 1 Cor. 15:29.

hyper

anti

In most passages, however, *hyper* means no more than "on behalf of" or "for the good of."[5] If Scripture only stated that Christ died "in behalf of [*hyper*] us" and that he tasted death "in behalf of [*hyper*] everyone," we would have no undeniable New Testament proof that his death was vicarious—that he died in our stead and bore our sins and their penalty on the cross—though we might find evidence for that elsewhere (e.g., Isa. 53:4–6). Only by beginning with the New Testament's teaching that Christ died "instead of [*anti*] many" (Matt. 20:28), that he gave himself as an *antilytron* (487, ransom; 1 Tim. 2:6), and by using this as an interpretive starting point can we claim that those verses which teach that Christ died *for us* also teach that he died *in our stead.* The preposition *hyper* is used in these passages with both of these meanings. It expresses the fact that Christ died *for our sakes*[6] and *in our stead. Anti* expresses only the latter.

Tischendorf[7] has some excellent remarks on this matter, though we have partially anticipated them.

> There were those who tried to show only from the nature and use of the preposition *hyper* that Paul taught the vicarious satisfaction of Christ. Others in turn have denied that the preposition *hyper* has been used correctly by the authors of the New Testament for *anti* in an attempt to prove the contrary. Error has been committed by each group. The preposition alone supports equally each part of the opinions—I say "equally each." For there are at hand, contrary to the opinion of very many, passages taken from many writers of the ancient Greeks which clearly show that the preposition *hyper* signifies "in the place of" and "in the stead of" someone; and no one can doubt that Paul himself applied this preposition with the same meaning, also in passages which do not pertain to our topic (cf. Philem. 13; 1 Cor. 15:29; 2 Cor. 5:20). If, however, it is asked why the apostle employed chiefly this preposition of uncertain and fluctuating meaning in a subject so important, the preposition itself is more fitting than others to describe Christ's death for us. Indeed no one denies that in this word lies the chief point, that Christ died for the benefit of human beings—and he did it in such a way that he died in the place of human beings. For the joint meaning of both beneficial and vicarious the apostle admirably employed the preposition *hyper*. Thus Winer contends most correctly, as is his custom, that we are not allowed in important passages which describe the death of Christ to assume that the preposition *hyper* simply equals *anti*. It is clearly the *pro* [for] of Latin and the *für* [for] of German. As often as Paul teaches that Christ died for us he did not wish the concept of benefit to be disassociated from the very concept of vicarious, and in my judgment by that expression he did not wish the one ever to be excluded from the other.

5. Matt. 5:44; John 13:37; 1 Tim. 2:1; and continually.

6. Here it touches more nearly on the meaning of *peri* (*4012*), Matt. 26:28; Mark 14:24; 1 Pet. 3:18. *Dia* (*1223*) occurs once in this connection (1 Cor. 8:11).

7. *Doctrina Pauli de vi mortis Christi satisfactoria.*

83

phoneus (5406) *anthrōpoktonos* (443) *sikarios* (4607) — Murderer

Phoneus, *anthrōpoktonos*, and *sikarios* are all translated "murderer" in the Authorized Version. Although this is a proper translation of *phoneus* (Matt. 22:7; 1 Pet. 4:15; Rev. 21:8), it is too general for *anthrōpoktonos* and *sikarios* and ignores characteristic meanings of these words.

Anthrōpoktonos, which corresponds exactly to the English *manslayer* and *homicide*, is found in the New Testament only in the writings of John (8:44; 1 John 3:15, twice).[1] *Anthrōpoktonos* is particularly appropriate on Christ's lips in John 8:33; no other word would have been as suitable. John 8:33 alludes to Satan's great and only too successful assault on the natural and spiritual life of all mankind. By planting sin (and its result, death) in the authors of the human race, Satan infected all of Adam and Eve's descendants. Satan was truly *ho anthrōpoktonos*, for he would gladly have slain not just one particular person but the entire race.

Sikarios occurs only once in the New Testament, on the lips of a Roman officer (Acts 21:38). It is one of many Latin loan words that the Romans introduced into their eastern provinces. Unlike the West, the East refused Latinization and retained its own language. The *sicarius* derived his name from the *sica*, a short sword, poniard, or stiletto that he wore and was prompt

1. *Anthrōpoktonos* also is found in Euripides (*Iphigenia Taurica* 390).

phoneus
anthrōpoktonos
sikarios

to use; he was a hired mercenary or swordsman. In the long agony of the Republic, the Antonies and Clodiuses kept troops of *sicari* in their pay, often using them as bodyguards to inspire fear and, if necessary, to remove obnoxious persons. The Latin *sicarius* found its way into Palestine and the Greek spoken there. Josephus[2] gave full details about the *sicari*. They were the "assassins"[3] who arose in the latter days of the Jewish commonwealth, when all societal ties were fast dissolving. They were an ominous token of Rome's approaching doom. Concealing their short swords under their garments and mingling with the multitude at the great feasts, the *sicari* would stab their enemies and then join the bystanders in exclamations of horror, thus effectively averting suspicion from themselves.

Phoneus may refer to any murderer. *Phoneus* is the genus of which *sikarios* is a species. The *sikarios* is an assassin who uses a particular weapon and follows his trade of blood in a special manner. *Anthrōpoktonos* refers to a murderer *of men*, a homicide. *Phoneus* may be used more vaguely. A wicked man might be characterized as *phoneus tēs eusebeias* (*2150*, a destroyer of piety), even though he does not directly attack men's lives. A traitor or tyrant might be characterized as *phoneus tēs patridos* (a destroyer of the fatherland).[4]

2. In two instructive passages, *De bello Judaico* 2.13.3; *Antiquitates Judaicae* 20.8.6.
3. I believe this to be the best translation of Acts 21:38.
4. Plutarch, *Praecepta gerendae reipublicae* 19; such uses of the word are not infrequent.

84

kakos (2556) *ponēros (4190)* *phaulos (5337)* — Wicked Evil Bad

Because that which is morally evil may be seen from several viewpoints, various terms, such as *kakos*, *ponēros*, and *phaulos*, are used to express different aspects of this concept.

Kakos and *ponēros* are used in Revelation 16:2 and *kakia* (2549) and *ponēria* (4189) in 1 Corinthians 5:8. The *dialogismoi* (1261) *kakoi* of Mark 7:21 are referred to as *dialogismoi ponēroi* in the parallel passage in Matthew (15:19). The distinction between *kakos* and *ponēros* is best understood by studying *ponēros*. *Kakos* is constantly used in antithesis to *agathos*[1] and less frequently as the antithesis of *kalos*.[2] *Kakos* describes something that lacks the qualities and conditions that would make it worthy of its name.[3] *Kakos* was first used in a physical sense. Thus the *kaka heimata*[4] are "mean or tattered garments"; *kakos iatros*[5] is a "physician lacking the skill which physicians should possess"; and *kakos kritēs*[6] is an "unskillful judge." *Kakos* is used in Scripture without ethi-

1. *18*; Deut. 30:14; Ps. 33:14; Rom. 12:21; 2 Cor. 5:10; cf. Plato, *Republic* 10.608e.
2. *2570*; Gen. 24:50; 44:4; Heb. 5:14; Plutarch, *Regum et imperatorum apophthegmata* 20.
3. Cremer: "Thus *kakos* characterizes what is not as it should or could be according to prescriptions determined by its nature and its concept."
4. Homer, *Odysscy* 11.190.
5. *2395*; Aeschylus, *Prometheus vinctus* 5.473.
6. *2923*; Plutarch, *Apophthegmata Romana* 4.

cal connotations[7] and sometimes with one. The *kakos doulos*[8] is a "servant lacking that fidelity and diligence which are properly due from servants."[9]

As Ammonius called him, the *ponēros* is *ho drastikos kakou* (the active worker out of evil).[10] Beza made this distinction: "*Ponēros* signifies something more than *kakos* and beyond question it refers to a person who has been trained in every crime and completely prepared for inflicting injury to anyone."[11] According to its derivation, the *ponēros* is "one who furnishes trouble to others."[12] *Ponēria* is the *cupiditas nocendi* (desire of harming). Jeremy Taylor defined *ponēros* as an "aptness to do shrewd turns, to delight in mischief and tragedies; a loving to trouble our neighbor and to do him ill offices; crossness, perverseness, and peevishness of action in our intercourse."[13] The positive activity of evil is emphasized more by *ponēros* than by *kakos*. Thus *ponēros* constantly is contrasted with *chrēstos* (*5543*), the good contemplated as the useful.[14] If *kakos* is the French *mauvais* (bad) or *méchant* (wicked), then *ponēros* is the French *nuisible* (injurious), the Latin *noxious* (hurtful), and the English *noisome* in the older sense of this word. The *kakos* may be content to perish in his own corruption, but the *ponēros* is not content unless he is corrupting others and drawing them into his own destruction. "For they do not sleep unless they have done evil; and their sleep is taken away unless they make someone fall" (Prov. 4:16).[15] Thus *opson ponēron*[16] is an "unwholesome dish"; *asmata ponēra*[17] are "wicked songs" that by their wantonness corrupt the minds of the young; *gynē* (*1135*) *ponēra*[18] is a "wicked wife"; *ophthalmos* (*3788*) *ponēros* (Mark 7:22) is a "mischief-working eye." Satan is emphatically *ho ponēros* as the first author of all the mischief in the world.[19] "Ravening beasts" are always *thēria* (*2432*) *ponēra* in the Septuagint.[20] *Kaka thēria* (evil beasts) occurs once in the New Testament (Titus 1:12), but the meaning is not precisely the same, as the context sufficiently shows. Euripides testifies that the Greeks thought there was a more inborn and radical evil in the man who is *ponēros* than in the man who is *kakos*: "The evil person [*ponēros*] is in no way differ-

7. Prov. 20:17; Luke 16:25; Acts 28:5; Rev. 16:2.

8. *1401*; Matt. 24:48.

9. Cf. Prov. 12:12; Jer. 7:24; 1 Cor. 15:33; Phil. 3:2; Col. 3:5.

10. *Ponēros* is equivalent to the German *Bösewicht* (scoundrel).

11. *Annotationes in Mathaeum* 5.37.

12. J.H.H. Schmidt did not think that this was the relation between *ponos* (*4192*) and *ponēros*. Instead he claimed that this illustrated the aristocratic tendencies of the language. The feature of their poorer neighbors' life-style that must strike the leisured few the most is that the poorer neighbors are always at work. They are *ponēroi* or laborious, for their *ponoi* never cease. It is not long before a word constantly applied to the poor develops an unfavorable connotation. This is true with numerous words, such as our own "churl" or "villain." It is suggested that the poor also are the bad, moving the word into a lower sphere in agreement with this thought.

13. *Doctrine and Practice of Repentance* 4.1.

14. Isocrates, *Ad Demonicum* 1.6d; 8.184a; Xenophon, *Memorabilia* 2.6.20; Jer. 24:2–3. It is also associated with *achrēstos* (*890*; Demosthenes, *In Cononem* 1271).

15. Cf. the French *dépraver les femmes* (to corrupt ladies).

16. Plutarch, *Septem sapientium convivium* 2.

17. Plutarch, *Quomodo adolescens poetas audire debeat* 4.

18. Plutarch, *De virtute et vitio* 2.

19. Matt. 6:13; Eph. 6:16; cf. Luke 7:21; Acts 19:12.

20. Gen. 37:33; Isa. 35:9; cf. Josephus, *Antiquitates Judaicae* 7.5.5.

ent from the bad [*kakos*]."[21] In the context, Euripides meant that a man with an evil nature (*ponēros*) will *always* show himself so in his actions (*kakos*).

In most languages there are words like *phaulos* that portray the good-for-nothing aspect of evil, that show it as something that cannot produce any true gain. Thus we have the Latin *nequam* (worthless)[22] and *nequitia* (worthlessness),[23] the French *vaurien* (good-for-nothing), the English *naughty* and *naughtiness*, and the German *taugenichts* (good-for-nothing), *schlecht* (bad), and *schlechtigkeit* (badness, baseness).[24]

The central notion of *phaulos* is worthlessness.[25] *Phaulos* successively has the following meanings—light, unstable, blown about by every wind,[26] small, slight,[27] mediocre, of no account, worthless, and bad. *Phaulos* predominantly meant "bad" in the sense of worthless. Thus *phaulē aulētris*[28] is a bad flute-player, and *phaulos zōgraphos*[29] is a bad painter.

Phaulos and *spoudaios* (*4705*) are antithetical terms.[30] The Stoics divided all people into two classes, the *spoudaioi* and the *phauloi*.[31] *Phaulos* is contrasted with *chrēstos*,[32] *kalos*,[33] *epieikēs*,[34] and *asteios*.[35] *Phaulos* commonly is used with *achrēstos*,[36] *eutelēs*,[37] *mochthēros*,[38] *asthenēs*,[39] *atopos*,[40] *elaphros*,[41] *blaberos*,[42] *koinos*,[43] *akratēs*,[44] *anoētos*,[45] *akairos*,[46] *agennēs*,[47] and *agoraios*.[48] In the New Testament, *phaulos* reached the last stage of its meaning. "Those

21. *Hecuba* 596.
22. It is strictly opposed to *frugi* (useful).
23. See Ramsay on the *Mostellaria* of Plautus, p. 229.
24. Graff (*Alt-hochdeutsche Sprachschatz*, p. 138) similarly ascribed an original sense of weak, small, worth nothing to *bose* (*böse*) or "wicked." *Tugend* (virtue), however is equivalent to *taugend* (serving the purpose) and refers to virtue that is seen as usefulness.
25. Some have very questionably identified it with the German *faul* (worthless) and the English "foul."
26. See Donaldson, *Cratylus*, par. 152; "a synonym interchangeable with lightness," according to Matthäi.
27. *Schlecht* (bad) and *schlicht* (simple) in German are only different spellings of the same word.
28. *834*; Plato, *Symposium* 215c.
29. Plutarch, *Quomodo adulator ab amico internoscatur* 6.
30. Plato, *Leges* 6.757a; 7.814e.
31. The Stoics did not recognize a middle ethical position.
32. Plutarch, *Quomodo adolescens poetas audire debeat* 4.
33. Plutarch, *Quomodo adulator ab amico internoscatur* 9.
34. *1933*; Aristotle, *Ethica Nicomachea* 3.5.3.
35. *791*; Plutarch, *De Stoicorum repugnantiis* 12.
36. Plato, *Lysias* 204b.
37. L-S 734, cheap; *Leges* 7.806a.
38. L-S 1149, wretched; *Gorgias* 486b.
39. *772*; Euripides, *Medea* 803.
40. *824*; Plutarch, *Quomodo adolescens poetas audire debeat* 12; *Conjugalia praecepta* 48.
41. *1645*; Plutarch, *Quomodo adulator ab amico internoscatur* 32.
42. *983*; Plutarch, *Quomodo adolescens poetas audire debeat* 14.
43. *2839*; Plutarch, *De tuenda sanitate praecepta* 14.
44. *193*; *Gryllus* 8.
45. *453*; Plutarch, *De communibus notiis contra Stoicos* 11.
46. Cf. *171*; Plutarch, *Conjugalia praecepta* 14.
47. L-S 8, low-born, sordid; Plutarch, *Quomodo adulator ab amico internoscatur* 2.
48. *60*; Chariton.

who have done evil [*phaula*]" are directly contrasted with "those who have done good [*agathas*]." The former are condemned to "the resurrection of condemnation."[49] The same antithesis of *phaulos* and *agathos* occurs elsewhere.[50]

49. John 5:29; cf. 3:20; Titus 2:8; James 3:16; Aristotle, *Ethica Nicomachea* 2.6.18; Philo, *De Abrahamo* 3.

50. Phalaris, *Epistulae* 144; Plutarch, *Placita philosophorum* 1.8. For a good note on the word, see Schoeman, *Agis et Cleomenes*, p. 71.

85

eilikrinēs (1506)

katharos (2513)

Sincere
Pure
Clean
Clear

The difference between *eilikrinēs* and *katharos* is difficult to express, even though one may instinctively feel it. *Eilikrinēs* and *katharos* often are used together,[1] and words associated with one also are associated with the other.

Eilikrinēs occurs only twice in the New Testament (Phil. 1:10; 2 Pet. 3:1) and once in the Apocrypha (Wisd. of Sol. 7:25). *Eilikrineia* (1505) appears in the New Testament three times (1 Cor. 5:8; 2 Cor. 1:12; 2:17). The etymology of *eilikrinēs*, like that of its best English translation ("sincere"), is doubtful, and this uncertainty results in some unclarity about its breathing. Some scholars, such as Stallbaum,[2] relate *eilikrinēs* with *eilein* (1507), which refers to something that is cleansed by frequent rolling and shaking in a sieve. According to Lösner's more familiar and more beautiful, though somewhat speculative, etymology, *eilikrinēs* "is spoken of those subjects whose purity is compared to the splendor of the sun." One who is selected in the sun's warmth [*tē heilē*] is held up to the sunlight and proved and approved. Insofar as the uses

1. Plato, *Philebus* 52d; Eusebius, *Praeparatio evangelica* 15.15.4.
2. Plato, *Phaedo* 66a, note.

eilikrinēs

katharos

of *eilikrinēs* support either etymology, they strongly support the former.[3] *Eilikrinēs* does not refer so much to the clear and the transparent as to the purged, the winnowed, and the unmingled.[4] *Eilikrinēs* consistently is used with *amigēs*,[5] *amiktos*,[6] *apathēs*,[7] *akratos*,[8] *akraiphnēs*,[9] and *akeraios*.[10] In a similar vein, the *Etymologia magna* states: "*Eilikrinēs* signifies what is pure and unmingled with anything else."[11] Various passages might be cited where the notion of clearness and transparency predominates. In Philo,[12] "pure [*eilikrines*] fire" is contrasted with the "oven filled with smoke," but these instances are far fewer and may well be secondary and superinduced.

The ethical use of *eilikrinēs* and *eilikrineia* was distinctly felt for the first time in the New Testament. In classical Greek, there are only approximations of this use. Aristotle spoke of some who "not having tasted of sincere [*eilikrinous*] and noble pleasure, flee to bodily ones."[13] Theophylact correctly defined *eilikrineia* as "purity and guilelessness of thought without having anything shady or false." Basil the Great wrote: "I deem *eilikrines* to be undefiled and completed clear of any opposite quality."[14] This is the central meaning of *eilikrinēs* in the New Testament. The Corinthians were to purge the old leaven to keep the feast with the unleavened bread *of sincerity* (*eilikrineias*) and truth (1 Cor. 5:8). Paul rejoiced that he had conducted himself in the world in the simplicity and *sincerity* that come from God (*en eilikrineia theou*), not with fleshly wisdom (2 Cor. 1:12). Paul declared that he was not one of those who tamper with and adulterate (*kapēleuontes*, *2585*) the Word of God but that in Christ he spoke with *sincerity* (*ex eilikrineias*, 2 Cor. 2:17).

In its earliest use, *katharos*[15] meant "clean" in a physical or nonethical sense, as opposed to *rhyparos* (4508).[16] Thus *katharon sōma*[17] is the body that is not smeared with paint or ointment. *Katharos* often is used in this sense in the New Testament (Matt. 27:59; Heb. 10:22; Rev. 15:6). *Katharos* has another physical sense; it may be applied to that which is clear and transparent. Thus

3. There is an instinctive and traditional feeling that may lead to the correct use of a word long after the secret of its derivation has been completely lost.

4. Cf. Plato, *Axiochus* 370.

5. L-S 83, unmixed; Plato, *Menexenus* 245d; Plutarch, *Quaestiones Romanae* 26.

6. L-S 83, unmingled; Plutarch, *De defectu oraculorum* 34; cf. *De Iside et Osiride* 61.

7. L-S 174, without feeling; Plutarch, *Quomodo adulator ab amico internoscatur* 33.

8. *194*; Plutarch, *De animae procreatione in Timaeo* 27.

9. L-S 54, unmixed; Philo, *De opificio mundi* 2.

10. *185*; Clement of Rome, *Epistulae 1* 2. Cf. Xenophon, *Cyropaedia* 8.5.14; Philo, *De opificio mundi* 8; Plutarch, *Adversus Colotem* 5; *De facie in orbe lunae* 16: "It suffers the mixed, for it discards the pure [*to eilikrines*]."

11. Cf. an interesting discussion in Plutarch, *De E apud Delphos* 20.

12. *Quis rerum divinarum heres sit* 61.

13. *Ethica Nicomachea* 10.6.

14. *In regulas brevius tractatas*.

15. It is related to the Latin *castus* (pure) and the German *heiter* (clear).

16. This is the only meaning of *katharos* in Homer (*Odyssey* 6.61; 17.48).

17. 4983; Xenophon, *Oeconomicus* 10.7.

we have *katharos* and *diaugēs*.[18] Pindar,[19] Plato,[20] and the tragic poets, however, already used *katharos* in an ethical sense. And this ethical use of *katharos* is not uncommon in the Septuagint, where the word often designates "cleanness of heart" (Job 8:6; 33:9; Ps. 24:4), though more often in the Septuagint *katharos* merely refers to an external or ceremonial cleanness (Gen. 9:21; Lev. 14:7). *Katharos* frequently has the same domain of meaning as *eilikrinēs*. *Katharos* also is used with *alēthinos*,[21] *amigēs*,[22] *akratos*,[23] *achrantos*,[24] and *akēratos*.[25] *Katharos sitos* (*4621*) is wheat with the chaff winnowed away,[26] and *katharos stratos* (*4756*) is an army that is rid of the sick and ineffective.[27] In Xenophon, *katharos* refers to an army made up of the best materials, one that has not been lowered by the addition of mercenaries or cowards; it refers to the flower of the army with all of the "useless men" set aside.[28] Primarily, however, *katharos* refers to the pure as seen from the perspective of that which is clean and free from soil or stain. Thus we have "pure [*kathara*] and undefiled [*amiantos*] religion" (James 1:27), "free [*katharos*] from murder," and "free [*katharos*] from injustice."[29] *Katharon* and *koinon* (*2839*) are consistently set in antithesis to one another; *katharon* is used synonymously with *akatharton*.[30]

Sincere
Pure
Clean
Clear

We may conclude that the Christian virtue of *eilikrinēs* will exclude all double-mindedness, the divided heart (James 1:8; 4:8), the eye that is not single (Matt. 6:22), and all hypocrisies (1 Pet. 2:1). When the Christian is "pure [*katharos*] in heart," this excludes the *miasmata*,[31] the *molysmos*,[32] and the *rhyparia*[33] of sin. *Eilikrinēs* refers to the Christian's freedom from falsehoods. *Katharos* refers to the Christian's freedom from the defilements of the flesh and the world. If both of these words refer to the Christian's freedom from foreign mixture, this is truer of *eilikrinēs* (probably because of its etymology) than of *katharos*.

18. L-S 417, translucent; Plutarch, *De genio Socratis* 22.
19. *Pythia* 5.2, "pure [*kathara*] virtue."
20. *Republic* 6.496d, "clear [*katharos*] of injustice and unholy deeds."
21. *228*; Job 8:6.
22. Philo, *De opificio mundi* 8.
23. Xenophon, *Cyropaedia* 8.7.20; Plutarch, *Aemilius Paullus* 34.
24. L-S 297, undefiled; Plutarch, *De Iside et Osiride* 79.
25. L-S 49, undefiled; Plato, *Cratylus* 396b.
26. Xenophon, *Oeconomicus* 18.8.9.
27. Herodotus, 1.211; cf. 4.135.
28. Appian, 8.117.
29. Plato, *Republic* 6.496d; Acts 18:6.
30. *169*; Rom. 14:14, 20; Heb. 9:13.
31. *3393*; 2 Pet. 2:20; cf. Titus 1:15.
32. *3436*; 2 Cor. 7:1.
33. *4507*; James 1:21; 1 Pet. 3:21; Rev. 22:11.

86

polemos (4171)

machē (3163)

War
Fight
Battle
Strife

Polemos and *machē* often are used together,[1] as are *polemein* (4170) and *machesthai* (3164). The difference between *polemos* and *machē* is the same as that between the English words *war* and *battle*: *ho polemos Peloponnēsiakos* is "the Peloponnesian War"; *hē en Marathōni machē* is "the battle of Marathon." In dissuading the Athenians from yielding to the demands of the Spartans, Pericles[2] admitted that with their allies, the Spartans were a match for all the other Greeks together in a single battle. But Pericles denied that the Spartans and their allies would retain the same superiority in a war against those who had made different preparations:

> For in one battle [*machē*] the Peloponnesians and their allies were able to withstand all the Greeks, but they were unable to wage a war [*polemein*] against a similar hostile preparation.[3]

1. Homer, *Iliad* 1.177; 5.891; Plato, *Timaeus* 19e; Job 38:23; James 4:1.

2. He dealt with the words in this antithesis—*polemos* embraces the whole course of hostilities and *machē* the actual shock in arms of hostile armies.

3. Thucydides, 1.141. Cf. Tacitus, *Germania* 30: "You may see others go to battle, but the Chatti to war."

polemos

machē

Although *polemos* and *polemein* remain true to their primary meanings and do not acquire secondary ones, this is not the case with *machē* and *machesthai*. *Machē* and *machesthai* often designate contentions that fall far short of armed conflict. There are *machai* of every kind: *erōtikai* (of love),[4] *nomikai*,[5] *logomachiai*,[6] and *skiamachiai* (shadow-boxing).[7] Eustathius expressed these differences well:

> The terms wars [*polemoi*] and battles [*machai*] either refer to the same action in a parallel way, or there is a difference in the terms—if, for example, one is disputing with words, as *logomachia* [a battle about words] indicates. The poet himself later speaks of battling [*machessamenō*] over words (1.304). At all events, *machē* is a clash between men; *polemos* involves pitched battles and opportune times for fighting.[8]

Tittmann stated:

> They agree in that they denote an encounter, a strife, a fight; but *polemos* and *polemein* properly refer to a fight that takes place with the hands, while *machē* and *machesthai* refer to any strife—also of minds even if it does not result in beatings and killings. In the former the fight is thought of; in the latter it is sufficient to think of a strife which usually is not followed by a fight.[9]

Plato distinguished *stasis*[10] (insurrection or sedition) from *polemos*. According to Plato, the former refers to civil strife, the latter to foreign strife. "For in the case of enmity at home it is called *stasis*, but in a case involving foreigners it is called *polemos*."[11]

4. Xenophon, *Hiero* 1.35.
5. 3544, at law; Titus 3:9; cf. 2 Tim 2:23.
6. 3055, about words; 1 Tim. 6:4.
7. Cf. Prov. 26:20–21; John 6:52; 2 Tim. 2:24.
8. On Homer, *Iliad* 1.177.
9. *De Synonymis in Novo Testamento*, p. 66.
10. 4714; Mark 15:7; Luke 23:19; Acts 24:5; cf. Sophocles, *Oedipus Coloneus* 1228.
11. *Republic* 5.470b.

87

pathos (3806)
epithymia (1939)

hormē (3730)
orexis (3715)

Passion
Lust
Desire
Concupiscence
Impulse
Desire

Pathos is used three times in the New Testament, once in coordination with *epithymia*[1] and once in subordination to it.[2] In Romans 1:26, the *pathē atimias* (819, vile passions) are lusts that dishonor those who indulge in them. *Pathos* belongs to the terminology of the Greek schools. Thus Cicero wrote: "What the Greeks call *pathē* we prefer to term *passions* more than *maladies*."[3] After Cicero adopted Zeno's definition of *pathos* as "an emotion of the mind, turned from correct reason contrary to nature," he called it "a disturbed impulse of the mind."[4] According to Diogenes Laërtius, Zeno said: "*Pathos* itself is the irrational movement of the soul contrary to nature or an excessive im-

1. Col. 3:5; see Gal. 5:24, where *pathēmata* and *epithymiai* are used together.
2. *Pathos epithymias* (passion of lust), 1 Thess. 4:5.
3. *Tusculanae disputationes* 4.5. On this preference, see 3.10.
4. *De officiis* 2.5.

pathos
epithymia

pulse [*hormē*]."[5] Clement of Alexandria had this definition in mind when he distinguished *hormē* from *pathos*:

hormē
orexis

> *Hormē* is a thrust of the intellect toward something or from something; *pathos* is an excessive impulse [*hormē*] which goes beyond the limits of reason, or an impulse [*hormē*] carried beyond bounds and unpersuaded by reason.[6]

In the New Testament, *pathos* does not have as broad a sense as it did in the Greek schools. In the Greek schools, *pathos*'s meaning was so much broader than *epithymia*'s that the latter was only regarded as one of the several *pathē* of our nature and was used with *orgē* (3709), *phobos* (5401), and the rest.[7] In Scripture, however, *epithymia* is the more inclusive term and refers to the whole world of active lusts and desires—to all that the *sarx* (4561) as the seat of desire and the natural appetites impels. *Pathos* is the *morosa delectatio* (capricious delight). It is not so much a disease of the soul in its more active operations as the diseased condition from which these operations arise. Bengel correctly called *pathos* the *morbus libidinis* (the disease of passion), rather than the *libido* (lustfulness, as distinguished from lust).[8] According to Theophylact, "*pathos* is the frenzy of the body, like a fever or a wound or some disease." Godet wrote: "The term *pathē* (passions) has something more ignoble than the word *epithymiai* (lusts) in verse 24, for it includes a concept more marked by rebuke and shameful bondage."[9]

Aristotle defined *epithymia* as "a longing [*orexis*] for pleasure,"[10] and the Stoics explained it as "an irrational longing [*orexis*]." Cicero called it "an immoderate desire for the greatest good without being tempered by reason."[11] The Authorized Version usually translates *epithymia* as "lust" (Mark 4:19; and often), though sometimes as "concupiscence" (Rom. 7:8; Col. 3:5) or "desire" (Luke 22:15; Phil. 1:23). Occasionally, *epithymia* has a good sense in the New Testament,[12] though usually it means "depraved concupiscence," not merely "concupiscence." According to Origen,[13] this was its only sense in the Greek schools.[14] Thus we have *epithymia kakē* (2556), "evil desires" (Col. 3:5); *epithymiai sarkikai* (4559), "fleshly lusts" (1 Pet. 2:11); *neōterikai* (3512), "youthful lusts" (2 Tim. 2:22); *anoētoi* (453) *kai blaberai* (983), "foolish and harmful lusts" (1 Tim. 6:9); *kosmikai* (2886), "worldly lusts" (Titus 2:12); *phthoras* (5356), "corruption . . . through lust" (2 Pet. 1:4); *miasmou* (3394), "in the lust of uncleanness" (2 Pet. 2:10); *anthrōpōn* (444), "the lusts of men" (1 Pet. 4:2); *tou sōmatos* (4983), "the lusts of the body" (Rom. 6:12); *tou*

5. 7.1.63.
6. *Stromata* 2.13. See Zeller, *Philosophie der Griechen*, 3.1.208.
7. Aristotle, *Ethica Nicomachea* 2.4; Diogenes Laërtius, 7.1.67.
8. It is equivalent to the German *Leidenschaft*.
9. On Rom. 1:26.
10. *Rhetorica* 1.10.
11. *Tusculanae disputationes* 3.11.
12. Luke 22:15; Phil. 1:23; 1 Thess. 2:17; cf. Ps. 102:5; Prov. 10:24.
13. *Commentarii in evangelium Joannis*, vol. 10.
14. But see Aristotle, *Rhetorica* 1.11.

diabolou (*1228*), "the desires of the devil" (John 8:44); *tēs apatēs* (*539*), "the deceitful lusts" (Eph. 4:22); *tēs sarkos* (*4561*), "the lust of the flesh" (1 John 2:16); and *tōn ophthalmōn* (*3788*), "the lust of the eyes" (1 John 2:16). *Epithymia* also is used without a qualifying term.[15] Vitringa's definition of *epithymia* is correct: "That corrupt disposition of the will which leads to striving after what is acquired illegally or which strives in an irregular manner after what it acquires illegally."[16] This evil sense of *epithymia* also appears in other definitions, such as that of Clement of Alexandria: "An irrational pretext and longing [*orexis*] for what is gratifying."[17] Clement also noted: "Those who are skillful at these matters distinguish between *orexin* and *epithymias*; the latter they assign to areas of pleasure and wantonness as not directed by reason, and the former as an emotion guided by reason in areas which by nature are necessary."[18] Primarily, Clement pointed to Aristotle as one who is skillful.[19] Formerly, the English word *lust*, whose history is similar to that of *epithymia*, was harmless enough.[20] We have already traced the relation of *epithymia* to *pathos*.

Hormē occurs twice in the New Testament (Acts 14:5; James 3:4), and *orexis* occurs once (Rom. 1:27). Elsewhere, these words often are found together, as in Plutarch[21] and Eusebius.[22] On one occasion, Cicero translated *hormē* as *appetitio* (desire)[23] and as *appetitus animi* (desire of the *soul*) on another.[24] The Stoics said: "*Hē hormē* is a person's reason compelling him to act"[25] and further explained it as an "impulse of the mind" or "impulse of the soul toward something."[26] *Hormē* is *orexis* if it is *toward* a thing and *ekklisis*[27] if it is *from* a thing. When the Authorized translators translated *hormē* as "assault" (Acts 14:5), they ascribed more to it than it implies. Certainly there was no actual "assault" on the house where Paul and Barnabas stayed, for in this case it would have been unnecessary for Luke to tell us that they "became aware" (v. 6) of it. Rather there was only a purpose and intention of assault.[28] In James 3:4, the *hormē* of the pilot is not the "assault of the arms" but the "eager attempt of the will."[29]

15. Rom. 7:7; 1 Pet. 4:3; Jude 16; cf. Gen. 44:6; Ps. 106:14.
16. In the dissertation *De concupiscentia vitiosa et damnabili* (*Obsessiones sacrae*, pp. 598ff.).
17. *Stromata* 2.20.
18. Ibid. 4.18.
19. Thus see *Rhetorica* 1.10.
20. Thus see Deut. 7:7 in Coverdale's Version and my *Select Glossary* under this word.
21. *De amore prolis* 1; *De recta ratione audiendi* 18 (see Wyttenbach's note here).
22. *Praeparatio evangelica* 14.765d.
23. *De officiis* 2.5.
24. *De finibus* 5.7.
25. Plutarch, *De Stoicorum repugnantiis* 11.
26. See Zeller, *Philosophie der Griechen* 3.1.206.
27. L-S 509, turning away, avoidance.
28. In German a *Trieb* (impulse) or *Drang* (impetus), as Meyer gave it.
29. Cf. *hormē*, Sophocles, *Philoctetes* 237; Plutarch, *De recta ratione audiendi* 1; Prov. 3:25, and the many passages where *hormē* is joined with *proairesis* (L-S 1466, purpose, plan; Josephus, *Antiquitates Judaicae* 19.6.3).

pathos
epithymia

hormē
orexis

Although *hormē* frequently refers to a *hostile* motion toward an object for the purpose of propelling and repelling it further from itself,[30] *orexis*[31] always refers to reaching toward an object for the purpose of drawing the object to itself and making it its own. *Orexis* is commonly used to refer to the appetite for food,[32] as is the Latin *orexis* (appetite), which was used during Latin's "silver age."[33] In the Platonic *Definitions* (414b), philosophy is described as a "desire for the knowledge of the eternal entities." The context of the one passage in the New Testament where *orexis* occurs (Rom. 1:27) reveals Paul's view of the nature of the vile pleasures that the heathens reach out for and seek.[34]

30. As, for example, the *hormē* of the spear or the assaulting army.
31. From *oregesthai* (3713).
32. Plutarch, *De fraterno amore* 2; *Septem sapientium convivium* 6.2.1.
33. Juvenal, *Satura* 6.427; 11.127.
34. Cf. Plutarch, *Platonicae quaestiones* 21.

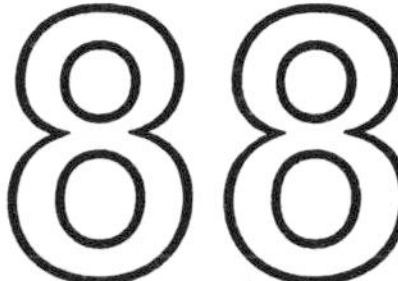

hieros (2413) hosios (3741) hagios (40) hagnos (53)

Sacred Holy Pure Chaste

Hieros[1] never implies moral excellence in the New Testament and seldom does elsewhere. *Hieros* is used twice in the New Testament (1 Cor. 9:13; 2 Tim. 3:15), once in the Septuagint (Josh. 6:8: "holy trumpets"), and four times in the Apocrypha (all in 2 Macc.). In each case *hieros* does not refer to persons, who alone are moral agents, but to things. Only rarely is *hieros* elsewhere applied to people. Thus in Aristophanes[2] *hieros anthrōpos* (444, sacred person) is a man initiated into the mysteries. Pindar[3] called kings *hieroi* because their dignity comes from the gods. According to Plutarch, the Indian gymnosophists were "sacred [*hieroi*] and independent men"[4] and "persons sacred [*hieroi*] and of divine power."[5] *Hieros*[6] is very close to the Latin *sacer*[7] and to our *sacred*. Because it refers to that which may not be violated, *hieros*

1. *Hieros* probably is the same word as the German *hehr* (sublime). See Curtius, *Grundzüge*, 5:369.
2. *Ranae* 652.
3. *Pythia* 5.97.
4. *De Alexandri magni fortuna aut virtute* 1.10.
5. *De genio Socratis* 20. Cf. *De defectu oraculorum* 2.
6. "Dedicated to God," according to Suidas.
7. "Whatever is devoted to the gods is called *sacrum*."

constantly is used with *abebēlos*,[8] *abatos*,[9] and *asylos*.[10] The inviolable character of *hieros* springs from its relations, near or remote, to God; *theios* (*2304*) and *hieros* often are used together.[11] At the same time, this relation is viewed merely as an external one. Thus Pillon wrote: "*Hagios* expresses the idea of native and inward or moral holiness, while *hieros*, as the Latin *sacer*, expresses only the idea of outward holiness or of an inviolability consecrated by law or custom."[12] Tittman stated: "In the word *hieros* strictly speaking nothing else is thought of except that some person or thing is sacred to God, without consideration of natural disposition or character—particularly what is devoted to sanctuaries." Thus the priest (*hiereus*, *2409*) is a *sacred* person in that he serves at God's altar. This does not in the least imply that he is a *holy* person as well. He may be a Hophni, a Caiaphas, or an Alexander Borgia.[13] The true antithesis to *hieros* is *bebēlos*[14] and, though not as perfectly, *miaros*.[15]

For analytical reasons, *hosios* is more often grouped with *dikaios* (*1342*) than with the words with which we will associate it below. *Hosios* and *dikaios* occur together in Plato,[16] Josephus,[17] and the New Testament (Titus 1:8), as do their derivatives *hosiōs* (*3743*) and *dikaiōs* (*1346*; 1 Thess. 2:10) and *hosiotēs* (*3742*) and *dikaiosynē*.[18] Many have argued that *hosios* describes a person who carefully performs his duties toward God and *dikaios* a person who carefully performs his duties toward people. In classical Greek there are many passages where such a distinction is explicit or implicit. According to Plato, for example, "doing proper things toward human beings would be doing *dikaia*, and toward the gods would be *hosia*."[19] Marcus Antoninus described Socrates as "*dikaios* in matters concerning humans, *hosios* in matters concerning the gods."[20] But there is nothing that warrants transferring this distinction to the New Testament or that restricts using *dikaios* to refer to a person who accurately fulfills the precepts of the second table of the law[21] or of using *hosios* to refer

8. L-S 2, inviolable; Plutarch, *Quaestiones Romanae* 27.

9. L-S 2, not to be trodden.

10. L-S 264, inviolate; Plutarch, *De genio Socratis* 24.

11. Plato, *Timaeus* 45a.

12. *Synonyme Grecs*. However, see Sophocles (*Oedipus Coloneus* 287), which appears as an exception to the absolute universality of this rule.

13. Grinfield, *Scholia in Novum Testamentum*, p. 397.

14. 952; Plutarch, *Quaestiones Romanae* 27.

15. L-S 1132, defiled, polluted; 2 Macc. 5:19.

16. *Theaetetus* 176b; *Republic* 10.615b; *Leges* 2.663b.

17. *Antiquitates Judaicae* 8.9.1.

18. *1343*; Plato, *Protagoras* 329c; Luke 1:75; Eph. 4:24; Wisd. of Sol. 9:3; Clement of Rome, *Epistulae 1 ad Corinthios* 48.

19. *Gorgias* 507b. This is not altogether true in the *Euthyphro*, where Plato regarded *to dikaion* or *dikaiosynē* as the sum total of all virtue, of which *hosiotēs* (piety) is only a part. In this dialogue (throughout a discussion on the *hosion*), Plato made Euthyphro say (12e): "This [i.e., *to hosion*] seems to me, O Socrates, to be the part of justice [*dikaiou*], religious and holy, which concerns service to the gods; that which concerns people is the remaining portion of justice [*dikaiou*]." Socrates admitted and allowed this; indeed Socrates himself forced Euthyphro to say it.

20. 7.66; cf. Plutarch, *Demetrius* 24; Charito, 1.10.4; and a large collection of passages in Rost and Palm's *Lexicon* under this word.

21. Thus see Luke 1:6; Rom. 1:17; 1 John 2:1.

to one who fulfills the demands of the first table of the law.[22] And, indeed, we would not expect to find such a distinction in the Bible, since Scripture views righteousness as a unit that grows from a single root, as obedience to a single law. There is no room for such an antithesis in Scripture. The one who loves his brother and fulfills his duties toward him loves him in God and for God. The second great commandment is not coordinated with the first (i.e., the "greatest") but subordinated to it and included in it (Mark 12:30–31).

If the Greek *hieros* is equivalent to the Latin *sacer* (sacred), then *hosios* is equivalent to *sanctus* (holy)[23]—"what is supported by ancient and prior holiness"[24]—and is the opposite of *pollutus* (polluted). Some ancient grammarians derived *hosios* from *hazesthai*,[25] the Homeric synonym for *sebesthai* (*4576*). Although this is the correct meaning of *hosios*, it is the wrong etymology. *Hosios*'s derivation remains doubtful.[26] In classical Greek *hosios* is used far more frequently to refer to things than to persons. When used with *boulē* (*1012*) or *dikē* (*1349*), *hosia* refers to the everlasting ordinances that no law or custom has constituted. Such ordinances are prior to all law and custom; they rest on the divine constitution of the moral universe and on man's relation to it—on the eternal law. In the noble words of Chrysippus, this eternal law is "king of all divine and human affairs."[27] Thus Homer wrote: "It is not divine law [*hosiē*] to plot evil against one another."[28] The *hosios*[29] is one who reverences these everlasting ordinances and admits his obligation to them. *Hosios* is used with *eusebēs*,[30] *euorkos*,[31] and *theios*.[32] More than once *hosios* is contrasted with *epiorkos*.[33] Things that violate the everlasting ordinances are *anosia* (*462*). For example, a Greek regarded the Egyptian custom of marriage between a brother and sister—even more the Persian custom of marriage between a mother and son—as *incestum* (incestuous). Plato described those customs that human laws necessarily refer to as abominable as "in no way holy."[34] This would also be true of the omission of burial rites by those from whom they were due, when it was possible to pay them—for example, if Antigone had obeyed Creon's edict and allowed her brother to remain unburied.[35] The nature and obligations of the *hosion* have never been more nobly declared than in the words the poet put in her mouth: "Nor did I believe that your decrees have so much force, so that a mortal man is able to prevail against the unwrit-

22. Thus see Acts 2:27; Heb. 7:26.
23. *Hosios* is equivalent to *sancitus*.
24. Popma; cf. Augustine, *De fide et symbolis* 19.
25. L-S 29, stand in awe of.
26. See Pott, *Etymologische Forschungen*, 1:126.
27. Cf. Euripides, *Hecuba* 799–801.
28. *Odyssey* 16.423.
29. *Hosios* is equivalent to the German *fromm* (pious).
30. *2152*; 2 Macc. 12:45.
31. L-S 725, keeping one's oath; Plato, *Republic* 263d.
32. Plutarch, *De defectu oraculorum* 40.
33. *1965*; Xenophon.
34. *Leges* 8.858b.
35. Sophocles, *Antigone* 74.

ten and firm divine laws [*nomima*] of the gods."[36] Because *hosion* is prior to and superior to all human laws, there is the same antithesis between *hosia* and *nomima* (cf. *3545*) as there is between the Latin *fas* (divine law) and *jus* (civil law).

In biblical Greek, *hosios*'s meaning was intensified, though its use remains faithful to its classical heritage. The Septuagint draws a striking distinction between *hosios* and *hagios*. Although *hosios* is used thirty times to translate *ḥāsîd*,[37] and *hagios* is used nearly a hundred times to translate *qādôš*,[38] *hosios* is never used for the latter or *hagios* for the former. I believe the same rule holds true universally for their cognates. Even more remarkable is the fact that of the other Greek words that are rarely used to translate *hosios* and *hagios*, none that is used for one is ever used for the other. Thus *katharos* (*2513*), which is used to translate the second of these Hebrew words (Num. 5:17), is never used to translate the first; and *eleēmōn*,[39] *polyeleos*,[40] and *eulabēs*[41] are used for the former but never for the latter.

Hagios[42] and *hagnos* often have been understood as different forms of the same word. They do share the common root *hag*, which reappears as *sac* in the Latin *sacer* (sacred), *sancio* (consecrate), and in many other Latin words. It is only natural that *hagios* and *hagnos* should have much in common, though they have different, clearly distinguishable spheres of meaning. Although *hagios* only occurs rarely in Attic Greek, Porson was incorrect to say[43] that it is *never* used by the tragic poets.[44] The basic idea of *hagios* is separation and consecration and devotion to the service of a deity. Thus *hieron mala hagion* is "a very holy temple."[45] The idea that such consecration may be *anathēma* (*334*) or *anathema* (*331*) is always present in *hagios*.[46] A closely related idea is that what is set apart from the world and consecrated to God should separate itself from the world's defilements and share in God's purity. In this way *hagios* quickly acquires a moral significance. The children of Israel must be "a consecrated [*hagion*] people," not merely in the sense of being God's inheritance, "a special people," but by separating themselves from the abominations of the heathen nations around them (Lev. 19:2; 11:44). Because he is absolutely separate from evil, and because he repels every possibility of sin or defilement

36. 453–55. Cf. an instructive passage in Thucydides, 2.52, where *hiera* and *hosia* occur together. Plato (*Leges* 9.878b) also used them together.

37. 2623; Deut. 33:8; 2 Sam. 22:26; Ps. 3:4.

38. 6918; Exod. 19:6; Num. 6:5; Ps. 16:3.

39. *1655*; Jer. 3:12.

40. L-S 1438, very merciful; Exod. 34:6.

41. *2126*; Mic. 7:2.

42. It is equivalent to *qādôš*. On the etymology of this word, see the article in Herzog's *Real-Encyclopädie* under *Heiligkeit Gottes*.

43. On Euripides, *Medea* 750; cf. Pott, *Etymologische Forschungen*, 3:577.

44. See Aeschylus, *Supplices* 851.

45. Xenophon, *Hellenica* 3.2.14.

46. As it is in the Latin *sacer* (sacred); see the previous discussion of *anathēma* and *anathema*. *Hagios* also is related to *hagēs*, *hagos* (L-S 9 and 14, pure, holy), which now is recognized not as another form of *hagos* (L-S 14, sacrifice) or as only the Ionic form of the same word but as fundamentally distinct. Cf. Curtius, *Grundzüge*, pp. 155ff.

and wars against these in every one of his creatures,[47] God has the highest right to the title of *hagios*.[48]

It is somewhat different with *hagnos*. *Hagneia*[49] is vaguely and superficially explained as "caution against sins toward the gods, normal service to a god's honor."[50] Clement of Alexandria described it as "abstinence from sins" or "to have holy thoughts."[51] Suidas more accurately defined it as "extreme prudence,"[52] and Favorinus called it "freedom from every physical and spiritual defilement." *Hagnos*[53] refers to that which is "pure." Sometimes this purity is only external or ceremonial, as in this line of Euripides: "I am pure [*hagnos*] in hands but not in thoughts."[54] In the Septuagint, *hagnos*'s highest meaning refers to ceremonial purification;[55] and in four of its seven uses in the New Testament, this also is true.[56] *Hagnos*, however, frequently refers to that which is pure in the highest sense. Frequently it is applied to heathen gods and goddesses: Ceres, Proserpine, Jupiter,[57] the Muses,[58] the Sea-nymphs,[59] and above all to Artemis, the virgin goddess in Homer. And in Scripture, *hagnos* is applied to God himself (1 John 3:3). Compared to the Septuagint's use of *hagios* (Ps. 12:6; Prov. 20:9), this nobler use of *hagnos* in the Septuagint is extremely rare. Because impurities like the fleshly ones that defile both the body and the spirit (1 Cor. 6:18–19) are the most serious type, *hagnos* predominantly is used to express freedom from these.[60] Sometimes in an even more restricted sense, *hagnos* expresses not only chastity but virginity, as in the oath taken by the priestesses of Bacchus: "I am clean and pure [*hagnē*] of intercourse with a man."[61] *Hagneia* sometimes has a similar limitation.[62]

47. When Quenstedt defined the holiness of God as "the highest holiness, free from every blemish," his statement is true as far as it goes, but it is not exhaustive. One side of this holiness—namely its intolerance of unholiness and active war against it—is not brought out.

48. Lev. 10:3; 1 Sam. 2:2; Rev. 3:7; 4:8.

49. 47; 1 Tim. 4:12; 5:2.

50. In the so-called *Definitions* of Plato (414a).

51. *Stromata* 5.1. In the vestibule of the temple of Aesculapius at Epidaurus the following lines, which rank among the noblest utterances of the ancient world, were inscribed (they are quoted by Theophrastus in a surviving fragment of his work, *De pietate*): "One must be pure [*hagnon*] as one enters a fragrant temple; purity [*hagneiē*] is to think of holy things [*hosia*]."

52. *Hagneia* is used with *sōphrosynē* (4997) twice in the apostolic fathers: Clement of Rome, *Epistula 1 ad Corinthios* 21; Ignatius, *Epistula ad Ephesios* 20.

53. Clement of Rome used *hagnos* with *amiantos* (*283*) (*Epistula 1 ad Corinthios* 29).

54. *Orestes* 1604; cf. *Hippolytus* 316–17. *Hagnizein* (48) is equivalent to the Latin *expiare* (to purify) in Sophocles, *Ajax* 640.

55. Josh. 3:5; 2 Chron. 24:5; cf. 2 Macc. 1:33.

56. John 11:55; Acts 21:24, 26; 24:18. This is also true of *hagnismos* (49), Acts 21:26.

57. Sophocles, *Philoctetes* 1273.

58. Aristophanes, *Ranae* 875; Pindar, *Olympia* 7.60; and Dissen's note.

59. Euripides, *Iphigenia Aulidensis* 982.

60. Plutarch, *Conjugalia praecepta* 44; *Quaestiones Romanae* 20; Titus 2:5; cf. Herzog, *Real-Encyclopädia*, see under *Keuschheit*.

61. Demosthenes, *In Neaeram* 1371. Cf. "untouched and pure [*hagnos*] of marriage" in Plato, *Leges* 8.840e; Euripides, *Hippolytus* 1016.

62. Ignatius, *Epistula ad Polycarp* 5.

hieros
hosios
hagios
hagnos

If all the preceding analyses are correct, then when Joseph was tempted to sin by his Egyptian mistress (Gen. 39:7–12), he proved himself *hosios* by reverencing those everlasting sanctities of the marriage bond that God has founded and that one cannot violate without sinning against him: "How then can I do this great wickedness, and sin against God?" Joseph proved to be *hagios* by separating himself from any unholy fellowship with his temptress. He was *hagnos* in keeping his body pure and undefiled.

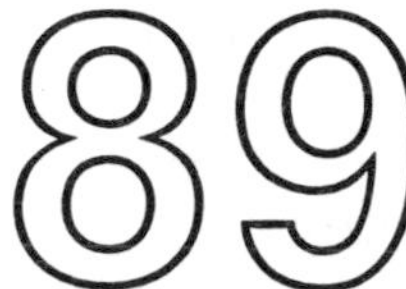

phōnē (5456)

logos (3056)

Voice
Sound
Noise
Word
Saying
Speech
Utterance

The Greek grammarians and natural philosophers wrote a great deal about *phōnē* and *logos* and their relation to one another.[1]

In the Authorized Version, *phōnē*[2] is translated as "voice" (Matt. 2:18), "sound" (John 3:8), and "noise" (Rev. 6:1). *Phōnē* is distinguished from *psophos*[3] by being the cry *of a living creature*[4] and sometimes is ascribed to God (Matt. 3:17), people (Matt. 3:3), and animals (Matt. 26:34). *Phōnē* is improperly ascribed to inanimate objects (1 Cor. 14:7), such as the trumpet (Matt. 24:31), the wind (John 3:8), and the thunder (Rev. 6:1; cf. Ps. 77:18). But *logos*, a "word" or "saying" or "rational utterance" of the mind, whether spo-

1. See Lersch, *Sprachphilosophie der Alten*, pt. 3, pp. 35, 45, and passim.
2. *Phōnē* is derived from *phaō* or "from *shine*, as *shedding light* on what is perceived by the mind" (Plutarch, *Placita philosophorum* 19).
3. L-S 2025, noise.
4. "*Hē phōnē* is some sound [*psophos*] of a living creature" (Aristotle).

phōnē

logos

ken[5] or unspoken,[6] is the correlative of reason and can only be predicated of human beings,[7] angels, and God. The *phōnē* may be merely an inarticulate cry of a person or animal. Thus the following definition of the Stoics is incorrect: "*Phōnē* of an animal is air struck by irrational impulse, of a person it is articulate air proceeding from thought."[8] The Stoics transferred to the *phōnē* what can only be consistently affirmed of the *logos*. Whenever *phōnē* and *logos* are contrasted, the particular point made is that *phōnē* is "inarticulated wind." But even in the Stoics' definition of *logos* as "a meaningful sound [*phōnē*] proceeding from thought"[9] and of *legein* (3004) as "to express a meaningful sound [*phōnē*] about something comprehended," this is not the case. Compare the Stoics' definition with Plutarch's: "*Phōnē* is something irrational and without meaning, *logos* is speech [*lexis*] in a voice [*phōnē*] indicative of thought."[10] By this unuttered "word," Plutarch affirmed that the demon of Socrates intimated his presence:

> What occurs is not an utterance, but one might liken it to a word [*logon*] of a demon, without a sound [*phōnēs*] laying hold of him who is shown what is intended. For sound [*phōnē*] is similar to an impact on the soul, receiving the word [*logon*] through the ears with force whenever they coincide. The mind of the superior one leads the well-disposed soul, needing no impact, by touching the one who has been influenced.[11]

The whole chapter has the deepest theological interest since the great theologians of the early church, especially Origen in the Greek[12] and Augustine in the Latin, loved to transfer this antithesis of *phōnē* and *logos* to John the Baptist and his Lord. John claimed only to be "the *voice* of one crying in the wilderness" (John 1:23), but Christ was emphatically declared to be the *Word* that was with God and was God (John 1:1). Augustine subtly traced the profound suitability of the "voice" and the "Word"[13] to express the relationship between John and Jesus. Augustine observed that a word is something even without a voice, for a word in the heart is as truly a word as after it is uttered. A voice, however, is nothing; it is an unmeaningful sound, an empty cry, unless it also is the vehicle of a word. When they are united, there is a sense in which the voice precedes the word, for the sound strikes the ear before the sense is conveyed to the mind. Although the voice precedes the word, the voice is not really before the word; the contrary is true. When we

5. *Prophorikos* (expressed) and thus "sound of the words [*logōn*]" in Dan. 7:11.

6. *Endiathetos* (residing in the mind).

7. "Only people participate in *logos*, all other things in *phōnē*" (Aristotle, *Problemata* 2.55).

8. Diogenes Laërtius, 7.1.38.55.

9. Ibid.

10. *De animae procreatione in Timaeo* 7. On the distinction between *logos* and *lexis* (*lexis* does not occur in the New Testament), see Petavius, *De trinitate* 6.1.6; and Lersch, *Sprachphilosophie der Alten*, pt. 3, p. 45. Plutarch's treatise *De genio Socratis* contains much information about the relations of *phōnē* and *logos* to one another and about the superior functions of the latter.

11. *De genio Socratis* 100.20.

12. *Commentarii in evangelium Joannis*, vol. 2, par. 26.

13. *Vox* and *verbum* in Latin, *phōnē* and *logos* in Greek.

speak, the word in our hearts must precede the voice on our lips. The voice is the vehicle by which the word in us is transferred to and becomes a word in another. In the act of accomplishing this, the voice passes away, but the word planted in the other person's heart and in the heart of the speaker remains. Augustine applied this argument to Jesus and John. John is nothing without Jesus, but apart from John, Jesus remains the same, though the knowledge that others have of Jesus may have come through John. Although John was the first in time, Jesus who *came* after him most truly *was* before him. John passed away as soon as he had accomplished his mission and did not have a continuing significance for the church. But Jesus, about whom John had witnessed, abides forever.

> John was a voice for a time, Christ is the eternal Word from the beginning. Remove the word, and what is a voice? Where there is no understanding, it is an empty noise. A voice without a word strikes the ear, it does not edify the heart. However in our own heart we alter the order of events by edifying. If I think of what I shall say, already the word is in my heart; but wishing to speak to you, I seek how there may be also in your heart what already is in mine. Seeking how this may reach you and how there may reside in your heart what already is in my heart, I assume a voice and with this voice I speak to you. The sound of the voice brings to you understanding of the word, and when the sound of the voice brings to you understanding of the word, the sound itself penetrates and the word which the sound brings to you now is in your heart and does not withdraw from mine.[14]

14. *Sermones* 293, par. 3. Cf. *Sermones* 288, par. 3; 289, par. 3.

90

logos (3056)

mythos (3454)

Word
Discourse
Account
Fable

Logos means *sermo* (discourse) as much as *verbum* (a connected discourse in a single word), and there has been much discussion concerning which of these words best translates the highest application of *logos* (John 1:1).[1] We will not dwell on this exceptional and purely theological employment of *logos*. In the New Testament *logos* frequently is used to refer to that word which eminently deserves the name "the word of God" (Acts 4:13) and "the word of the truth" (2 Tim. 2:15; cf. Luke 1:2; Acts 6:4; James 1:22). In this regard, we may discuss the similarities and dissimilarities between *logos* and *mythos*. Once there was only a slight difference between these two words, but the meaning of *mythos* grew so that eventually a great gulf separated it from *logos*.

Mythos passed through three distinct stages of meaning, though it never completely lost its first meaning. Initially, *mythos* did not refer at all to fables and still less to that which is false. During this period of its use, *mythos* stood on equal footing with *rhēma* (4487), *epos* (2031), and *logos*. The relationship

1. On this controversy see, Petavius, *De trinitate* 6.1.4–6.

logos

mythos

between *mythos* and *myō*,[2] *myeō* (*3453*), and *myzō*[3] shows that *mythos* originally must have signified the word within the mind or the word muttered on the lips,[4] though there are no actual examples of such a usage. Already in Homer, *mythos* was used to refer to the spoken word.[5] The tragic poets and others who were dependent on Homer continued to use *mythos* in this way,[6] even at a time in Attic prose when *mythos* almost had exchanged this meaning for another.

In the second stage of the development of *mythos*'s meaning, it was used in antithesis to *logos*, though in a respectful and often honorable sense. *Mythos* was used to refer to that which is conceived by the mind as contrasted with that which actually is true. It did not refer to a literal fact but to something that was "truer," to something that involves a higher teaching, to "an unreal account [*logos*] symbolizing the truth," as Suidas said. According to Plutarch: "*Mythos* is an image and likeness of *logou*."[7] There is "an account [*logos*] in myth [*mythō*]"[8] that may have infinitely more value than many actual facts. According to Schiller, it frequently is true that "a deeper import lurks in the legend told our infant years than lies upon the truth we live to learn." By the time of Herodotus[9] and Pindar,[10] *mythos* was being used in this sense. As we have observed, in Attic prose *mythos* rarely has any other meaning.[11]

But in a world like ours, a fable easily degenerates into a falsehood. "Tradition, time's suspected register that wears out truth's best stories into tales," always works to bring about such a result. *Story*, *tale*, and many other words attest to this fact. In the third stage of the development of *mythos*'s meaning, it came to refer to a fable in the more modern sense of that word, to a fable that is not the vehicle for some lofty truth. During this stage of its development, *mythos* refers to a lying fable with all its falsehood and pretenses. Thus Eustathius wrote: "*Mythos* in Homer is the simple account [*logos*], but in later writers it is unreal and fabricated, having an appearance of truth." This is the only sense of *mythos* in the New Testament.[12] Thus we have "profane and old wives' fables" (1 Tim. 4:7), "Jewish fables" (Titus 1:14), and "cunningly devised fables."[13] The other two occasions of the word's use (1 Tim. 1:4; 2 Tim. 4:4) are just as contemptuous. Initially, *legend* was an honorable word that referred to that which is worthy to be read, but it came to designate "a heap of

2. L-S 1157, close, shut.

3. L-S 1150, mutter.

4. See Creuzer, *Symbolik*, 4:517.

5. *Iliad* 18.254.

6. Thus Aeschylus, *Eumenides* 582; Euripides, *Phoenissae* 455.

7. *Bellum an pace* 4.

8. "A truth which lurks in the covering of a fable," noted Wyttenbach (*Annotationes in Plutarchum*, vol. 2, pt. 1, p. 406).

9. 2.45.

10. *Olympia* 1.29.

11. Plato, *Gorgias* 523a; *Phaedo* 61a; *Leges* 9.872d; Plutarch, *Septem sapientium convivium* 1.1.4.

12. It occurs only once in the Apocrypha (Ecclus. 20:19) and never in the Septuagint.

13. 2 Pet. 1:16; cf. "fabricated fables," Diodorus Siculus, 1.93.

frivolous and scandalous vanities" (Hooker). *Legend* has had much the same history as *mythos*, since similar influences were at work to degrade both. J.H.H. Schmidt said:

> *Mythos* came to denote a fictitious story because the naive faith in the ancient traditions, which had retained their transmitted titles, was gradually lost. Thus *mythos* like *logos* implies antithesis to reality, however in such a way as simultaneously pointing out the silly and improbable character of fiction.[14]

Although *logos* and *mythos* began their journey together, they gradually parted company. The antagonism between these words grew stronger and stronger until they finally stood in open opposition. This is true of words as well as of people, when one comes to belong to the kingdom of light and truth and the other to the kingdom of darkness and lies.

14. *Synonymik*, 1:100.

91

teras (5059)	*Wonder*
	Miracle
sēmeion (4592)	*Sign*
	Miracle
dynamis (1411)	*Power*
	Mighty Work
megaleion (3167)	
endoxon (1741)	*Glorious Thing*
paradoxon (3861)	*Strange Thing*
thaumasion (2297)	

All of the following words are used to characterize the supernatural works that Jesus performed during his earthly ministry: *sēmeion* (John 2:11; Acts 2:19), *teras* (Acts 2:22; John 4:48), *dynamis* (Mark 6:2; Acts 2:22), *megaleion* (Luke 1:49), *endoxon* (Luke 13:17), *paradoxon* (Luke 5:26), and *thaumasion* (Matt. 21:15). The first three words are the most common and are used to describe both the supernatural works performed in Christ's power by his apostles (2 Cor. 12:12) and the false miracles the antichrist will perform (2 Thess. 2:11). These words do not depict different kinds of miracles. Rather, they portray the miraculous from different perspectives.

teras

sēmeion

dynamis

megaleion
endoxon
paradoxon
thaumasion

Teras and *sēmeion* often are used together in the New Testament[1] and even more frequently in the Septuagint, where *teras* is the equivalent of *môpēt* (4159) and *sēmeion* of *'ôt* (226).[2] This also is the case in secular Greek—in Josephus,[3] Plutarch,[4] Polybius,[5] Philo,[6] and others. The distinction the ancients were fond of drawing between these two words, however, will not bear a moment's serious examination. This distinction was clearly expressed by Ammonius: "*Teras* differs from *sēmeion*, for *teras* occurs contrary to nature and *sēmeion* occurs contrary to custom." Theophylact said:

> *Sēmeion* and *teras* differ in that *sēmeion* is spoken of in matters according to nature, although occurring in an unusual manner, as in the immediate healing of Peter's mother-in-law when she had a fever (Matt. 8:15), while *teras* occurs in matters not according to nature, as in the healing of the man who was blind from birth (John 9:7).[7]

Upon examination, this distinction breaks down so entirely[8] that it is difficult to understand how so many (by repeating it) have given it credence. An earthquake, however rare, cannot be considered contrary to nature and therefore cannot, according to the distinction made above, be called a *teras*. Nevertheless, Herodotus[9] used *teras* to describe the earthquake that he had experienced in Delos. Neither can a serpent that has been snatched up in an eagle's talons and dropped in the midst of the Trojan army be referred to as something that is beyond and beside nature, though Homer described such an event as "a *teras* of aegis-bearing Zeus."[10] In Scripture, events that were beyond and beside nature—the healing by a word of a man who had been lame from birth, the feeding of many thousands with a few loaves, the raising of a man who had been dead for four days—are all described as *sēmeia* (John 6:14; 11:47; Acts 4:16).[11]

Therefore the distinction between *teras* and *sēmeion* must be sought elsewhere. Origen was incorrect to find a prophetic element in *sēmeion* that is not present in *teras*. According to Origen: "Those are called *sēmeia* in which, although there is something wondrous, also something of the future is indicated. *Terata*, however, are those in which only something wondrous is displayed."[12] Viewed from one perspective, a miracle is a *teras*; viewed from an-

1. John 4:48; Acts 2:22; 4:30; 2 Cor. 12:12.
2. Exod. 7:3, 9; Deut. 4:34; Neh. 9:10; Dan. 6:27.
3. *Antiquitates Judaicae* 20.8.6; *De bello Judaico* 11.
4. *Septem sapientium convivium* 3.
5. 3.112.8.
6. *De vita Mosis* 1.16.
7. *In Romanos* 15:19. Cf. Suicer, *Thesaurus*, under *sēmeion*.
8. In an excellent note on Rom. 15:19, Fritzsche clearly shows this.
9. 6.98.
10. *Iliad* 12.209. The Homeric idea of the *teras* is carefully discussed by Nägelsbach, *Homerische Theologie*, 168ff.
11. Cf. Plutarch, *Septem sapientium convivium* 3, where a monstrous birth is called both a *teras* and a *sēmeion*.
12. *Commentarii in Romanos*, under 15:19.

other, it is a *sēmeion*. These words most often refer to different qualities of a miracle, not to different classes of miracles. According to Lampe:

Wonder
Miracle
Sign
Miracle
Power
Mighty Work

Glorious Thing
Strange Thing

> The same miracles can be called *sēmeia*, insofar as they teach something either hidden or of the future, and *terata*, insofar as they present something extraordinary which arouses surprise. Hence it follows that *sēmeion* is a broader concept than *teras*. All *terata* are *sēmeia*, since they are sent by God for revealing a secret. But all *sēmeia* are not *terata*, because in pointing out heavenly things at times also common things are displayed.[13]

Teras[14] usually is understood as related to *tēreō* (5083), as something that is likely to be observed and *kept* in the memory because of its extraordinary character. *Teras* is translated "wonder" in the Authorized Version. *Teras* depicts a miracle as a startling, imposing, and amazing portent. Elsewhere, *teras* is used to refer to strange appearances in the heavens and even more frequently for monstrous births on the earth.[15] *Teras* is used with much the same meaning as the Latin *monstrum* (omen)[16] by Virgil ("Nor has Minerva given these signs with doubtful omens [*monstris*]")[17] or the Homeric *sēma*[18] ("There appeared a great omen [*sēma*], a dragon").[19] Origen[20] noted that *terata* is never used alone as a New Testament word for wonder. Instead, it always is used in conjunction with some other term for wonder, such as *sēmeia* or *dynameis* or in phrases like *terata kai sēmeia* and (more than once) *terata, sēmeia, kai dynameis*. This observation was well worth making. It is eminently characteristic of the New Testament that the title that more than any other was related to the portents of the heathen world never be used except in the company of some other title that necessarily suggested a higher meaning.

Miracles also are referred to as *sēmeia*, which Basil the Great defined this way: "*Sēmeion* is a manifest deed, having in itself an explanation of something hidden and secret."[21] Later Basil wrote: "Scripture however calls *sēmeia* what is contrary to expectation [*paradoxa*] and indicative of some mystic account." Of all the terms used to describe miracles, their ethical end and purpose are brought out most distinctively by *sēmeion* and least distinctly by *teras*. *Sēmeion* declares that the prime objective of the miracle is to lead us to some-

13. *Commentarius in Joannem*, 1:513.

14. *Teras* certainly is not derived from *treō* (L-S 1815, to fear), "the terrifying."

15. Herodotus, 7.57; Plato, *Cratylus* 393b.

16. On the similar group of synonymous words in the Latin, Augustine wrote: "Words truly supply *omens* (*monstra*) from instructing because they make known by signifying something, and *wonders* (*ostenta*) from telling of abnormal occurrences, and *portents* (*portenta*) from foretelling (that is, from telling in advance), and prophecies (*prodigia*) because they speak afar off—that is, predict the future" (*De civitate Dei* 21.8). Cf. Cicero, *Divinitate* 1.42.

17. *Aeneid* 2.171.

18. L-S 1592, omen.

19. *Iliad* 2.308.

20. *Commentarii in evangelium Joannis*, 13:60; *Commentarii in epistulam ad Romanos*, liber 10, par. 12.

21. *Ennaratio in prophetam Isaiam*, 7, par. 198.

teras

sēmeion

dynamis

megaleion
endoxon
paradoxon
thaumasion

thing beyond itself; the miracle is a kind of sign-post that points to God[22] (Isa. 7:11; 38:7). The miracle is valuable not so much for what it is as for what it indicates of the virtue and power of the one who performed it, of his immediate connection with a higher spiritual world.[23] Lampe well noted:

> *Sēmeion* designates by its very nature something not only unusual and upsetting to the senses but also such a thing which presents a *token* and a *semblance* of something else, possibly absent and in the future; hence signs of the weather (Matt. 16:3) and tokens (Matt. 12:39; Luke 11:29) and also *holy acts* as in circumcision (Rom. 4:11) are accustomed to be expressed by the same name in the New Testament. Therefore most fittingly this word is used for miracles to indicate not only that something has been performed in an unusual manner but also that it has been directed and ordained by the most wise plan of God, so that at the same time there might be displayed the *characteristics* of the Messiah by which he must be known, the *marks* of the teaching which he was presenting, and the benefits of grace offered through the Messiah, and also the *types* of God's ways and the circumstances through which such benefits are obtained.

It is unfortunate that *sēmeion* is not always translated "sign" in our Authorized Version and that in the Gospel of John[24] "sign" too often gives way to the vaguer "miracle," which sometimes results in a serious loss of meaning.[25]

But in the New Testament, miracles also are seen as "powers,"[26] as the result of the outpouring of God's mighty *power* that is inherent in Christ, the "great Power of God" after whom Simon blasphemously allowed himself to be named (Acts 8:9–10). Christ only lent these powers to those who were his witnesses and ambassadors. We should regret that the Authorized Version translates *dynameis* as "wonderful works" (Matt. 7:22), "mighty works" (Matt. 11:20; Luke 10:13), and even more frequently as "miracles" (Acts 2:22; 1 Cor. 12:10; Gal. 3:5). In some cases this produces tautologies such as "miracles and wonders" (Acts 2:22; Heb. 2:4). It always causes something of the true intention of the word to be lost. *Dynameis* always points to new and higher *forces*[27] that have entered and are working in this lower world of ours. Delitzsch wrote: "Every miracle is a display of power of the world of salvation about to enter the moribund created world." The term *megaleia*, which occurs only in Luke 1:49[28] and in Acts 2:11, is closely related to this idea. Like *dynameis*, *megaleia* portrays miracles as outpourings of the *greatness* of God's power and glory.

Miracles also are called *endoxa* (Luke 13:17), works where the *doxa* (*1391*), or glory, of God and his Son are displayed.[29] They are *paradoxa* (Luke 5:26) in

22. *Diosēmeia* (signs from Zeus) frequently occurs in later Greek.

23. Exod. 7:9–10; 1 Kings 13:3; Mark 16:20; Acts 14:3; Heb. 2:4.

24. It occurs very frequently here.

25. Thus see John 3:2; 7:31; 10:41, and above all, 6:26.

26. *Dynameis* is parallel to the Latin *virtutes*.

27. *Energeiai* (*1753*), *energēmata* (*1755*; 1 Cor. 12:6, 10), "powers of the age to come" (Heb. 6:5).

28. It is parallel to the Latin *magnalia*.

29. Luke 5:25; John 2:11; 11:40; Acts 1:13, 16.

that they are "new things" (Num. 16:30) not previously seen (Mark 2:12) and thus beside and beyond people's opinions and expectations.[30] Miracles are *thaumasia* (Matt. 21:15) in that they provoke admiration and astonishment.[31] Although never called *thaumata* (2295) in the New Testament, miracles often are referred to in this way in the writings of the Greek fathers. It took time for a word used so long by conjurers, magicians, and impostors of various kinds to be put to more noble uses.

30. Although *paradoxa* only occurs in Luke 5:26, it is used frequently in ecclesiastical Greek.
31. Matt. 8:27; 9:8, 33; 15:31; Mark 5:20; Acts 3:11.

92

kosmios (2887) — Modest; Of Good Behavior

semnos (4586) — Grace; Reverent (Worthy of Reverence)

hieroprepēs (2412)

Occasionally *kosmios* and *semnos* refer to things, though usually they refer to persons. Although they are close enough in meaning that often they are used together, they are clearly distinguishable.

Kosmios[1] occurs twice in the New Testament. Once it is translated in the Authorized Version by "modest" (1 Tim. 2:9), once by "of good behavior" (1 Tim. 3:2). *Kosmios* closely corresponds to the *compositus* (composed) of Seneca[2] and to his *compositus et ordinatus* (composed and well-ordered).[3] The Vulgate uses *ornatus* on both occasions, which is strangely incorrect, though it is easy to see how this mistake came about. *Kosmios* is a favorite word of Plato, which he (and others) frequently applied to the citizen who is quiet in the land, to the one who duly fulfills the duties incumbent on his place and order. Such a person is not *ataktos* in anything[4] but is *tetagmenos* (well or-

1. *Kosmios* is related to *kosmos* (2889) in that term's earlier sense of "ornament"; *kosmikos* (2886; Titus 2:12; Heb. 9:1) is related to its secondary sense of "world."

2. *Epistulae* 114.

3. *De vita beata* 8.

4. *813*; 1 Thess. 5:14; cf. 2 Thess. 3:6–7, 11.

dered, cf. *5021*). Both Plato and Paul associated *kosmios* with *sōphrōn*,[5] *hēmeros*,[6] *nomimos*,[7] *enkratēs*,[8] *eustalēs*,[9] *phronimos*,[10] *stasimos*,[11] *eukolos*,[12] *andreios*,[13] and *kalos*.[14] Aristotle associated *kosmios* with *eutaktos*.[15] Epictetus[16] associated it with *aidēmōn*.[17] Plutarch associated it with *gennaios*[18] and *euagōgos*.[19] Plato contrasted *kosmios* with *akolastos*.[20] Since *kosmios* is used with these terms, a definition such as "of well-ordered demeanor, decorous, courteous" (Webster) dwells too much on external concerns. This is even truer of Tyndale's translation "honestly apparelled" (1 Tim. 3:3). The *kosmios* is all this and much more. The proper order extends not only to dress and demeanor but also to the inner life, which expresses itself in outward conversation. Even Bengel has too superficial a view of the word when he said: "What *sōphrōn* is inwardly, that *kosmios* is outwardly."[21] But later, in one of his most characteristic notes, he unfolded more fully what he thought was implied in these terms:

> A new person is something solemn and shrinks from everything that is unchaste, disorderly, rude, excessive, violent, licentious, passionate, loathsome, inconsiderate, abusive, and filthy; he submits sparingly and unwillingly to the very necessity of his nature and disposition, which is driven to forcing, dissipating, and exhausting, and he keeps the vestiges of his corruptible body concealed.

Bengel came closer to the heart of the matter than did Philemon, the comic poet,[22] who defined who is *kosmios* in this way:

> *Kosmios* is the one who utters not trivialities
> And gazes not at the ground when walking;
> The one who speaks what is conducive to nature,
> Doing nothing shameful, he is *kosmios*.

5. *4998*; *Leges* 7.802e. In fact this word is its most constant companion everywhere; cf. Lysias, *Orationes* 21.163; Plutarch, *Quomodo adulator ab amico internoscatur* 36; and often.
6. L-S 771, civilized, gentle; Plato, *Republic* 410e.
7. Cf. *3545*; *Gorgias* 504d.
8. *1468*; *Phaedrus* 256b.
9. L-S 733, well-behaved; *Menexenus* 90a.
10. *5429*; *Phaedrus* 108a; Plutarch, *Mulierum virtutes*.
11. L-S 1634, steadfast, steady; Plato, *Republic* 539d.
12. L-S 718, good-natured; *Republic* 329d.
13. L-S 128, courageous; *Republic* 399e.
14. *2570*; *Republic* 403a.
15. L-S 734, orderly.
16. *Enchiridion* 40.
17. L-S 36, modest.
18. L-S 344, noble; Plutarch, *De garrulitate* 4.
19. L-S 705, easily led; Plutarch, *Maxime cum principibus philosopho esse disserendum* 2.
20. L-S 52, undisciplined; *Gorgias* 494a.
21. On 1 Tim. 3:2.
22. In four lines preserved by Stobaeus.

However much *kosmios* implies, *semnos* implies more. If the *kosmios* is well ordered in his earthly citizenship, the *semnos* has a grace and dignity not derived from earth but from his higher citizenship. He inspires not only respect but reverence and worship. In secular Greek, *semnos* often is used of the gods, especially of the Eumenides, the *semnai* goddesses. *Semnos* also is frequently used to qualify things that pertain to or that stand in any near relation with the heavenly world. This will become clearer when we list some of the terms that habitually are linked with it: *hagios*,[23] *orthos*,[24] *megas*,[25] *timios*,[26] *metrios*,[27] *basilikos*,[28] *entimos*,[29] *megaloprepēs*,[30] *theios* (*2304*), and *phoberos* (*5398*). Clearly there is something majestic and awe-inspiring about *semnos* that is not true of *kosmios*, something that does not repel but that invites and attracts. Aristotle happily defined *semnotēs* as a "a gentle and gracious arrogance."[31] Aristotle made *semnotēs* the golden mean between *areskeia* (699), or "unmanly assentation," and *authadia*, or "churlish bearishness" (pleasing itself, not caring how much it displeases others). Plutarch associated *semnos* with *philikos*,[32] *hēdys*,[33] *philanthrōpos*,[34] *epieikēs* (*1933*), and with other similar words. Josephus associated *semnos* with *prosēnēs*.[35] This does not exclude the fact that the *semnos* is one who without demanding it in words challenges and inspires reverence and worship (in our earlier use of the word).[36] It is not easy to determine the correct way to translate *semnos*. On the one occasion where it is used to qualify things rather than persons (Phil. 4:8), the Authorized Version translates it as "honest." This is an unsatisfactory translation, though we include the same concepts in *honest* as when the King James Version was translated.[37] If a change is needed, I believe that "honorable" is preferable. On the other three occasions where it is used in the New Testament, *semnos* is translated "grave" (1 Tim. 3:8, 11; Titus 2:2). Once *semnotēs* is translated "honesty" (1 Tim. 2:2) and twice "gravity" (1 Tim. 3:4; Titus 2:7); both of these translations fail to convey the full meaning of the original word. In *Twelfth Night* Malvolio is "grave," but his very gravity is ridiculous. We need a word that combines the concept of gravity with the idea of a dignity that invites reverence—a word that I fear we may look for in vain.

Modest
Of Good Behavior
Grace
Reverent (Worthy of Reverence)

23. *40*; Plato, *Sophista* 249a; *Republic* 290d; cf. Clement of Rome, *Epistula 1 ad Corinthios* par. 1, where it is used with *hagnos* (*53*) and *amōmos* (*299*).

24. *3717*; Plato, *Apologia Socratis* 412e.

25. *3173*; *Theaetetus* 203e.

26. *5093*; *Crito* 51a.

27. Cf. *3357*; Clement of Rome, *Epistula 1 ad Corinthios* par. 1.

28. *937*; Plutarch, *Quomodo adolescens poetas audire debeat* 8.

29. *1784*; *Praecepta gerendae reipublicae* 31.

30. *3169*; *De defectu oraculorum* 30.

31. *4587*; *Rhetorica* 2.19.

32. L-S 1934, friendly; *Quomodo adulator ab amico internoscatur* 26.

33. L-S 765, pleasant; *Septem sapientium convivium* 4; *Proemium*.

34. Cf. *5365*, *5364*.

35. L-S 1513, soft, gentle; *Antiquitates Judaicae* 11.6.9.

36. *Semnos* remains true to the related word *sebō* (*4576*).

37. Alford changed "honest" to "seemly."

kosmios

semnos

hieroprepēs

Hieroprepēs, which was used by Plato[38] and Xenophon,[39] belongs to the best age of the Greek language, unlike *hosioprepēs* and *hagioprepēs*, which are of later ecclesiastical formation.[40] Like *kosmios*, *hieroprepēs* belongs to the large group of noticeable words that are found only in the pastoral Epistles. The number and character of these words, the new vein of Greek that Paul opened in these later epistles,[41] constitutes a remarkable phenomenon—one that previously has not received a perfectly satisfactory explanation. In his *Prolegomena* to these epistles, Alford made a valuable contribution to such an explanation, but after all has been said, the situation still remains perplexing.

It is apparent from what has already been claimed for *semnos* that *hieroprepēs* is more closely related to it than to *kosmios*. *Hieroprepēs* expresses what is proper for a sacred person, thing, or act. On the one occasion where it is used in the New Testament (Titus 2:3), *hieroprepēs* is used with *sōphrōn*, a word that is applied to women who profess godliness, women who will be in their bearing or behavior *hieroprepeis* (professing godliness; cf. 1 Tim. 2:10). That such behavior would breed reverence and awe might reasonably be expected, but this is not implied in *hieroprepēs* as it is in *semnos*. And here we must find the distinction between these two words.

38. *Theages* 122d.

39. *Symposium* 8.40.

40. These synonyms are too late to be included in Liddell-Scott-Jones.

41. For instance, consider the adjectives that are additions to, or variations from, his ethical terminology in all his other epistles. They occur only in these letters: *hairetikos* (141), *akratēs* (193), *amachos* (269), *anepaischyntos* (422), *anepilēptos* (423), *anēmeros* (434), *anexikakos* (420), *anosios* (462), *apaideutos* (521), *artios* (739), *aphilagathos* (865), *apseudēs* (893), *didaktikos* (1317), *diabolos* (1228), *dilogos* (1351), *enkratēs* (1468), *eumetadotos* (2130), *epiorkos* (1965), *ēpios* (2261), *kalodidaskalos* (2567), *koinōnikos* (2843), *mataiologos* (3151), *nēphalios* (3524), *oikouros* (3626), *orgilos* (3711), *paroinos* (3943), *sōphrōn* (4998), *philagathos* (5358), *philandros* (5362), *philautos* (5367), *philēdonos* (5369), *philotheos* (5377), *philoxenos* (5382), *philoteknos* (5388), and *phlyaros* (5397).

93

authadēs (829) *philautos* (5367) — Self-willed, Lover of Self

The etymology of *authadēs* and *philautos* suggests that they are closer in meaning than actually is the case. Because they occasionally are used together, as in Plutarch,[1] and because the "pleaser of himself" and "the lover of himself" stand in sufficient moral proximity so that they are liable to be confused, we are justified in attempting to distinguish these words.

Authadēs[2] occurs twice in the New Testament (Titus 1:7; 2 Pet. 2:10) and three times in the Old Testament (Gen. 49:3, 7; Prov. 21:24). *Authadeia*[3] never occurs in the New Testament, and is used only once in the Old Testament (Isa. 24:8).

The *authadēs*, who etymologically is barely distinguishable from *autareskos* (5367),[4] is properly the person who is so pleased with himself and his own actions that nothing else pleases him. He is the person "who regards nothing as correct except what he himself does."[5] He so overestimates any determination of his own that he will not be moved from it.[6] Such a person obstinately

1. *De recta ratione audiendi* 6.

2. According to Aristotle (*Magna moralia* 1.29), *authadēs* is equivalent to *autoadēs* or *hautō hadōn* (pleasing oneself). It is equivalent to the Latin *sibi placens* (pleasing oneself).

3. L-S 275, stubbornness.

4. Though *authadēs* is used earlier in classical Greek.

5. Terence, *Adelphi* 4.2.18.

6. For this element of stubbornness or obstinacy so often found in *authadeia*, see the *Prometheus vinctus* of Aeschylus, 1073; Cicero translated it *pervicacia* (inflexibility).

maintains his own opinion and asserts his own rights, regardless of the rights, feelings, and interests of others. With no motive at all, he is quick to act contrary to the feelings of others, rather than to fall in with them.[7] Thus *authadēs* is associated with *idiognōmōn*,[8] *agrios*,[9] *pikros*,[10] *amathēs*,[11] *chalepos*,[12] *ameiliktos*,[13] *sklēros*,[14] *epachthēs*,[15] *authekastos*,[16] *thrasys*,[17] *akolastos*,[18] *itamos*,[19] *philoneikos*,[20] *skythrōpos*,[21] *alazōn*,[22] *propetēs*,[23] and *tolmētēs*.[24] *Authadeia* is associated with *thrasos*[25] and *tolma*.[26] The Greek grammarians list words such as *hyperēphanos* (*5244*), *thymōdēs*,[27] and *hyperoptēs*[28] as the nearest equivalents to *authadēs*. Eudemus identified the *authadēs* with the *dyskolos* (*1422*) and described him as "regulating his life with no respect to others."[29] In Latin the *authadēs* is the *praefractus* (stern), the *pertinax* (obstinate), and the *morosus* (peevish). The German *eigensinnig* (self-willed) is closer to *authadēs*'s etymological heart.[30] In their earlier senses, the English *peevish* and *humorous* represent some traits and aspects of such a person's character. The *authadēs* is the opposite of the *euprosēgoros*, "the easy of access," or "affable."[31] The *authadēs* appears in Theophrastus's unlovely portrait gallery,[32] but his rude speech, surliness, and bearishness (as we would now say) are overemphasized. This is evident from Theophrastus's superficial and inadequate definition of *authadeia* as "rudeness of communication in words."

7. This is equivalent to the German *selbstgefällig* (self-serving), *selbstsüchtig* (selfish), *anmassend* (presumptuous), *frech* (impertinent), *sich um keinen andern kümmernd* (concerned about no one), *rücksichtlos* (inconsiderate), *grausam* (cruel). Cf. Pott, *Etymologische Forschungen*, 4:315.

8. L-S 818, holding one's own opinion; Hippocrates, p. 295, 12.29.

9. 66; Euripides, *Medea* 102.

10. 4089; *Medea* 223.

11. *261*; Plato.

12. *5467*; Plato, *Leges* 950b.

13. L-S 80, harsh, cruel; Philo, *Legatio ad Gaium* 38.

14. *4642*; Polybius, 4.21; Plutarch, *Septem sapientium convivium* 7.2.1.

15. L-S 612, offensive.

16. L-S 275, self-willed; Plutarch, *Praecepta gerendae reipublicae* 31. It does not necessarily have an unfavorable meaning; thus see Aristotle, *Ethica Nicomachea* 4.7.4 and lines ascribed to the Stoic Cleanthes, found in Eusebius, *Praeparatio evangelica* 13.3.

17. L-S 804, bold; Plutarch, *Marius* 408; Prov. 21:24.

18. L-S 52, undisciplined; Plutarch, *De genio Socratis* 9.

19. L-S 844, reckless; *De laude ipsius* 16.

20. 5380; *Quomodo adulator ab amico internoscatur* 32.

21. 4659; Isocrates, see Rost and Palm.

22. Cf. *212*; Prov. 21:24.

23. *4312*; Clement of Rome, *Epistula 1 ad Corinthios*, par. 1.

24. *5113*; 2 Pet. 2:10.

25. L-S 804, courage.

26. L-S 1803, boldness; Clement of Rome, *Epistula 1 ad Corinthios*, par. 31.

27. L-S 810, hot-tempered.

28. L-S 1866, disdainful.

29. *Mēden pros heteron zōn*, Aristotle, *Ethica Eudemia* 3.7.4; cf. *Ethica Nicomachea* 4.6.9.

30. This is Luther's translation of *authadēs*.

31. Plutarch, *Praecepta gerendae reipublicae* 31.

32. *Characters*, par. 3.

Aristotle[33] contrasted *authadeia*, caring to please nobody, with *areskeia* (699), the ignoble seeking to please everybody, the endeavoring at the cost of dignity and truth to be in good standing with the whole world. These two words define the opposite extremes in Aristotle's ethical system, and *semnotēs* (4587) defines its mean. Something can be learned from the hypocoristic phrases, which are used to present an ugly thing in a better light. On the one hand, the *authadēs* is called *semnos* (4586) and *megaloprepēs*[34] by his flatterers. On the other hand, a worthy freedom of speech[35] may be misnamed *authadeia* by those who resent it or who want to induce others to do so. The sycophants of the younger Dionysius used the hateful name *authadeia* to describe Dion's manly and bold speech when they wished to ruin him with the tyrant.[36]

Bengel profoundly remarked that there are men who are "at once soft and hard," soft to themselves and hard to the rest of the world.[37] In fact these two dispositions are only two aspects and results of the same sin—the wrong love of self. If *authadēs* expresses one side of this sin, *philautos* expresses the other. In the single New Testament use of *philautos* (2 Tim. 3:2), when Paul calls bad men *philautoi*, or "lovers of themselves," the word is used abusively. The one who loves himself too much—more than God's law allows—or who loves in himself what he should not love but hate—that which constitutes his sickness and which may result in his death—is not truly a "lover of himself." Aristotle's treatment of *philautos* makes this clear. It is interesting to note Aristotle's ethical feeling for *philautos*,[38] a feeling that partially anticipates Jesus' great statement: "He that loves his life shall lose it."

Philautos is equivalent to the English *selfish*,[39] and *philautia* (cf. 5367) is equivalent to the English *selfishness*, understood as the undue sparing of one's self, as providing things easy and pleasant for one's self, rather than as harshness and rigor toward others. Thus Plutarch[40] used *philautos* with *philopsychos*,[41] which refers to one who so loves his life that he ignobly seeks to save it. Before *selfishness* existed in English,[42] an attempt was made to remedy this lacuna in our ethical terminology by using *philauty*.[43] *Philauty*, however, never took root in the language nor did *suicism*,[44] which was a second attempt to remedy this defect. A linguistic remedy was not found for this defect until the Puritan divines drew upon our native stock of words and coined the words *selfish* and *selfishness*.[45] One of these divines made a useful comparison

33. *Rhetorica* 2.19.
34. 3169; Aristotle, *Rhetorica* 1.9.3.
35. *Parrhēsia* (3954).
36. Plutarch, *Dion* 8.
37. Experience confirms the truth of this statement.
38. *Ethica Nicomachea* 9.8.
39. Plutarch, *Consolatio ad Apollonium* 19; *Quomodo adulator ab amico internoscatur* 26.
40. *Dion* 46.
41. L-S 1942, loving one's life, cowardly, faint-hearted.
42. *Selfishness* came into being in English toward the middle of the seventeenth century.
43. Thus see Beaumont's *Psyche* (passim) and similar poems.
44. From the Latin *sui* (of oneself).
45. See my *English Past and Present*, 10th ed., p. 171.

between *authadēs* and *philautos*. He likened the selfish man to the hedgehog that rolls itself up into a ball, presenting only sharp spines to those without, while at the same time keeping inside the soft, warm wool for itself. The *authadeia* of some sinful men—their ungracious bearing toward others, their being most pleased with themselves when they have most displeased others—is their leading character trait. In others the *philautia*—the undue provision of everything that ministers to their own ease and that keeps hardness away from them—is their dominant character trait. Potentially, each of these dominant traits is wrapped up in the other. But as one sinful tendency or the other predominates, a man will merit being called an *authadēs* or a *philautos*.

94

apokalypsis (602) — *Revelation*

epiphaneia (2015) — *Coming*, *Appearing*

phanerōsis (5321) — *Manifestation*

Apokalypsis is used only once in the Old Testament (1 Sam. 20:30) and then in the subordinate sense of "nakedness."[1] *Apokalypsis* occurs three times in the Apocrypha (Ecclus. 11:27; 22:22; 41:23), though without the grander meaning it has in the New Testament. In the New Testament, *apokalypsis* is predominantly, though not exclusively, a Pauline word that occurs some nineteen times. It is translated in the Authorized Version by a variety of words: "coming" (1 Cor. 1:7), "manifestation" (Rom. 8:19), "appearing" (1 Pet. 1:7), and once as "to lighten."[2] In the New Testament, *apokalypsis* always has the majestic sense of God's unveiling of himself to his creatures, an unveiling that we call by its Latin name *revelation*. In the New Testament, the verb *apokalyptein* (601) commonly has this same sense, though this is not the first time that it was so used. In the Septuagint version of Daniel, for example (Dan. 2:19, 22, 28), this sense was anticipated. *Apokalyptein* does not always mean "to reveal"; sometimes it simply means "to uncover" or "to lay bare" (Prov. 21:19; Luke 12:2).

Jerome incorrectly claimed that *apokalypsis* is not used outside of the Septuagint and New Testament:

1. This use of *apokalypsis* is equivalent to the Latin *denudatio* (nakedness).
2. *Eis apokalypsin*, Luke 2:32.

apokalypsis

epiphaneia
phanerōsis

> *Apokalypsis* is a word exclusive to the Scriptures, employed by none among the Greeks in the time of their sages. Hence they appear to me, as in other words which the Septuagint translators transferred from Hebrew to Greek, to have earnestly attempted to express the proper signification of a foreign tongue, forming new words for new things, and to give utterance when anything hidden or concealed is presented and brought to light by removing the covering.[3]

The nonexistence in Jerome's time of exhaustive lexicons or concordances of the greater writers of antiquity may well excuse his mistake. Plato used *apokalyptein* several times,[4] and in the later Greek of Plutarch, *apokalypsis* appears frequently.[5] Jerome was correct in that the religious use of *apokalypsis* was unknown in the heathen world, and the corresponding Latin word *revelatio* (revelation) was absolutely unknown in classical Latin.[6] Elsewhere,[7] Jerome made a similar mistake regarding the verb *katabrabeuein* (*2603*; Col. 2:18), which he understood as a Pauline cilicism.[8]

In its higher Christian use, Arethras explained *apokalypsis* as "the explanation of hidden mysteries, the guidance of the soul being enlightened either through divine visions or in a dream as a result of divine illumination." According to Theophylact,[9] when *apokalypsis* is used with *optasia*,[10] *optasia* refers only to what is shown or seen, possibly without being understood; *apokalypsis*, however, includes not only the thing shown and seen but its interpretation or unveiling as well. Theophylact said: "*Apokalypsis* has something more than *optasia*, for the latter grants only to see, but the former reveals also something deeper than what is seen." Thus Daniel's vision of the four beasts was seen but not understood, until the one who stood by gave Daniel the interpretation.[11] What is true of *optasia* also will be true of *horama*[12] and *horasis*.[13]

Epiphaneia[14] is used only twice in the Septuagint[15] but frequently in 2 Maccabees, where it always refers to God's supernatural apparitions in aid of his people.[16] In secular Greek, *epiphaneia* always refers to the gracious appearances of the higher powers who aided humans.[17] *Epiphainein* (*2014*) also was

3. *Commentarium in Galatas* 1:12.

4. *Protagoras* 352d; *Gorgias* 460a.

5. See *Aemilius Paullus* 14; *Cato maior* 20, where *apokalypsis* is equivalent to *gymnōsis* (L-S 363, stripping); *Quomodo adulator ab amico internoscatur* 32; and elsewhere.

6. *Revelatio* was "born" in ecclesiastical Latin.

7. *Epistulae 121 ad Algasiam*.

8. *Katabrabeuein* occurs in a document cited by Demosthenes, *In Midiam*, 544.

9. See Suicer, under this word.

10. *3701*; 2 Cor. 12:1.

11. Dan. 7:15–16, 19, 23; cf. 8:15, 19; Zech. 1:18–21. On this distinction, see Lücke's *Einleitung in die Offenbarung des Johannes*, 2d ed., 26.

12. *3705*; Matt. 17:9; Acts 7:31; 10:19.

13. *3706*; Acts 2:17. It would be impossible to draw a distinction between these words and *optasia* that would stand.

14. Tertullian translated *epiphaneia* by *apparentia* (appearance, *Adversus Marcionem* 1.19).

15. 2 Sam. 7:23, *megalōsynē* (*3172*) *kai epiphaneia*. Cf. *doxa* (*1391*) *kai epiphaneia* (Plutarch, *De tranquillitate animi* 11); Amos 5:22.

16. 2 Macc. 2:21, "appearance (*epiphaneiai*) from heaven"; 3:24; 5:4; 12:22; 15:27.

17. Dionysius of Halicarnassus, 2.68; Plutarch, *Non posse suaviter vivi secundum Epicurum* 22; *Themistocles* 30.

used in the same way,[18] though sometimes it had a much humbler meaning.[19] *Epiphaneia* is used only six times in the New Testament, always in Paul's writings. On five occasions the Authorized translators translated it as "appearing," but on the sixth (2 Thess. 2:8) they seem to have shrunk from what they thought was a tautology—"*appearance* of his coming"[20]—and instead translated *epiphaneia tēs parousias* as "*brightness* of his coming," thus giving *epiphaneia* an improper meaning. On one occasion (2 Tim. 1:10, and so *epiphainein*, Titus 2:11; 3:4), *epiphaneia* refers to our Lord's first epiphany, his "appearance [*epiphaneia*] in the flesh," but on all other occasions it refers to his second appearing in glory, the "appearance [*epiphaneia*] at his *parousia*" (2 Thess. 2:8), "the glorious appearing [*epiphaneia*] of our great God."[21]

In comparison, *apokalypsis* is the more comprehensive and grander word. It depicts the progressive and immediate unveiling of the otherwise unknown and unknowable God to his church throughout the ages. This revelation is imparted to the body that is thereby designated or constituted as his church, the object of his more immediate care that is called to spread this knowledge of him to the rest of mankind. The world may know something of God (his eternal power and Godhead) from the things that are seen, things that except for the darkening of the human heart through sin would reveal him more clearly (Rom. 1:20). But there is no *apokalypsis* except to the church. The *epiphaneiai* are contained in the *apokalypsis* as separate points or moments. If God is to be immediately known to humans, he must in some shape or other appear to those whom he has chosen for this honor. Epiphanies must be theophanies as well. The church has claimed as such not only the communications of the type recorded in Genesis 18:1 and 28:13, but also all of those instances where the angel of the Lord or of the covenant appears.[22] The church has regarded all of these as preincarnate appearances of the Son of God, the most glorious epiphany that has yet occurred, though Christ's second coming will be an even more glorious epiphany.

Phanerōsis is used only twice in the New Testament (1 Cor. 12:7; 2 Cor. 4:2). Although it is a lofty term, *phanerōsis* does not refer (as the other words do) either to the first or second appearing of our Lord Jesus Christ (though it could have done so), as does the verb *phanerousthai* (5319), which is used to refer to both.[23] The fathers often used *phanerōsis* in this way. Thus Athanasius[24] called the incarnation "the bodily manifestation [*phanerōsis*] of the Father's Logos." It is difficult to understand why *phanerōsis* was not used to depict the same glorious facts as the other words that were so closely allied with it in meaning and to understand whether this was accidental or intentional.

18. *De defectu oraculorum* 30.

19. Plutarch, *Animine an corporis affectiones sint peiores* 2; Polybius, 2.29.7.

20. This was its translation in earlier Protestant versions.

21. Titus 2:13; 1 Tim. 6:14; 2 Tim. 4:1, 8; cf. Acts 20:20.

22. Gen. 16:7; Josh. 5:13–15; Judg. 2:1; 6:11; 13:3.

23. The first coming: 1 Tim. 3:16; Heb. 9:26; 1 Pet. 1:20; 1 John 1:2; the second coming: Col. 3:4; 1 Pet. 5:4; 1 John 3:2. For other noble uses of *phanerōsis*, see John 2:11; 21:1.

24. As quoted by Suicer, under this word.

95

allos (243) / *heteros* (2087) — Another / Other

Allos[1] indicates that which is numerically distinct. Thus Christ spoke "another" parable and still "another," each succeeding parable having the same character as the previous one.[2] In each case, *allēn* is used. *Heteros*,[3] however, adds the notion of a qualitative difference. *Allos* is "divers," *heteros* is "diverse." There are many passages in the New Testament whose correct interpretation, or at least their full understanding, depends on accurately understanding this distinction. Thus Christ promised his disciples that he would send *allon* (not *heteron*) *Paraklēton*,[4] "another" Comforter similar to himself. The dogmatic force of this use of *allon* has been debated in the controversy with the various sects of *pneumatomachoi* (contenders for the Spirit). Thus Petavius argued:

> The epithet Paraclete has reference to the same thing, especially since Christ calls him *another* [*allon*] Paraclete—that is, equal [*par*] and comparable to himself. In fact the word *allos* designates that he will be truly the same and comparable in dignity and in substance, as Gregory of Nazianzus and Ambrosius advise.[5]

1. *Allos* is identical with the Latin *alius* (another).
2. Matt. 13:24, 31, 33.
3. *Heteros* is equivalent to the Latin *alter* (other) and to the German *ander* (other). On *ander*, see the instructive article in Grimm's *Wörterbuch*.
4. *3875*; John 14:16.
5. *De trinitate* 2.13.5.

allos
heteros

If *allos* negates identity, this is even truer of *heteros*, which up to a certain point negates resemblance. *Heteros* affirms not only distinctness but difference. A few examples will illustrate this. Paul said: "I see another law,"[6] a law quite different from the law of the spirit of life, even a law of sin and death, "working in my members" (Rom. 7:23). After Joseph's death, "another king arose" in Egypt,[7] one (it is generally supposed) of quite another dynasty. In any case he was of quite another spirit from the one who had invited the children of Israel into Egypt and hospitably entertained them. The *hodos* (*3598*) *hetera* and *kardia* (*2588*) *hetera* that God promises to give his people are a new way and a new heart.[8] It was not "another spirit" but a different one (*heteron pneuma* [*4151*]) that was in Caleb, as distinguished from the other spies (Num. 14:24). In the parable of the pounds, the slothful servant is *heteros* (Luke 19:18). When Iphigenia was about to die and exclaimed, "a different [*heteron*], a different [*heteron*] destiny and fate we shall live," she looked forward to a different life with quite different surroundings.[9] The spirit that had wandered through dry places seeking in vain for rest took "seven other spirits" (*hetera pneumata*) worse than himself (of a deeper malignity) to help repossess the house he had left for a while (Matt. 12:45). Those crucified with Jesus are called *heteroi duo, kakourgoi* (*2557*), "two others, criminals," as it should be punctuated.[10] It would be inconceivable and revolting to confuse Jesus and the criminals by calling them *alloi duo*. Clearly Jude spoke of "other [*hetera*] flesh" (v. 7) when he denounced what the wicked followed after (Gen. 19:5). Christ appeared to his disciples "in a different [*hetera*] form" (Mark 16:12). Here the word indicates the great change that happened at his resurrection and that was anticipated in his transfiguration (Luke 9:29). God speaks to his people in the new covenant with *cheilesin* (*5491*) *heterois*, altogether different lips (1 Cor. 14:21), just as the tongues of Pentecost are *heterai glōssai* (*1100*; Acts 2:4), languages quite different from those of the disciples. It would be easy to multiply the passages where *heteros* could not be substituted for *allos* or where it could be substituted only by diluting *allos*'s meaning (Matt. 11:3; 1 Cor. 15:40; Gal. 1:6). There are other passages where initially *allos* seems quite as appropriate (or more so) but where *heteros* retains its proper force. In Luke 22:65 the *hetera polla* are many abuses of various kinds, different blasphemous speeches. The Roman soldiers taunted Jesus from their own viewpoint as a pretender to Caesar's throne and from the Jewish viewpoint as one who claimed to be the Son of God. Certainly a qualitative difference is not intended in every case where *heteros* is used. In Hebrews 11:36, for example, it would be difficult to trace anything of the kind.

6. *Heteron nomon* (*3551*).
7. *Basileus* (*935*) *heteros*, Acts 7:18; cf. Exod. 1:8.
8. Jer. 39:39; cf. Deut. 29:22.
9. Euripides, *Iphigenia Aulidensis* 1516.
10. Luke 23:32; cf. Bornemann, *Scholia in Lucam*, 147.

What is true of *heteros* also is true of its compounds, three of which occur in the New Testament. *Heteroglōssos*[11] is used by the apostle to bring out the nonintelligibility of the tongues to many in the church.[12] *Heterodidaskalein*[13] means to teach other things, things that are alien to the faith. *Heterozygein*[14] means to yoke with partners as unsuitable as the ox and the ass (Deut. 22:10).[15] In ecclesiastical Greek, *heterodoxia* is used to refer not merely to another opinion but to one that because it is another is a worse one, is a departure from the faith. *Heterodoxia* reappears in our own "heterogeneous," something that is not merely of another kind but of a worse one. This point deserves attention and is illustrated by several of the previous examples. *Heteros* is not just "other and different"[16] but has the additional implication that whatever the difference is, it is for the worse. Thus Socrates was accused of introducing into Athens *hetera kaina daimonia* (*1140*, different new demons).[17] *Daimōn* (*1142*) *heteros*[18] is an evil or hostile deity. *Heterai thysiai*[19] are ill-omened sacrifices that result in a curse, not a blessing, on their offerer. *Dēmagōgoi heteroi*[20] are popular leaders not only of a different kind than Pericles but of a worse stamp and spirit. In the Septuagint, gods other than the true God are invariably *heteroi theoi*.[21] Aristophanes noted: "They are others [*heteroi*] to whom I pray as gods."[22] A barbarous tongue is *hetera glōssa* (Isa. 28:11).[23]

There is only one way to reproduce in English the fine distinction Paul drew between *heteron* and *allo* in Galatians 1:6–7. "I marvel," said the apostle, "that you are turning away so soon from him who called you in the grace of Christ to a *different* [*heteron*] gospel, which is not *another* [*allo*]." For the first "other" in the Authorized Version, Dean Alford substituted "different." That indeed is what Paul intended to express—his wonder that the Galatians so quickly accepted a gospel different in character and kind from the one they already had received. Such a message had no right to be called another gospel, since in fact it was not a gospel at all. There could not be two gospels that varied from one another.

First Corinthians 12:8–10; 2 Corinthians 11:4; and Acts 4:12 are the other New Testament passages that should be investigated to determine why one of these words is used instead of the other or why the words alternate.

11. *2084*; 1 Cor. 14:21.

12. It is true that we have also *alloglōssos* (L-S 69, using a strange tongue) in Ezek. 3:6.

13. *2085*; 1 Tim. 1:3.

14. *2086*; 2 Cor. 6:14.

15. Cf. *heteroklinēs* (swerving aside) in Clement of Rome, *Epistula 1 ad Corinthios*, par. 11; and *heterognōmōn* (L-S 701, of different opinion) in Clement of Rome, *Epistula 1 ad Corinthios*, par. 11, a term also applied to Lot's wife (Gen. 19:26).

16. *Allo kai diaphoron* (*1313*).

17. Xenophon, *Memorabilia* 1.1.1.

18. Pindar, *Pythia* 3.61.

19. *2378*; Aeschylus, *Agamemnon* 151.

20. Plutarch, *Pericles* 3.

21. *2316*; Deut. 5:7; Judg. 10:13; Ezek. 42:18; and often.

22. *Ranae* 889.

23. The phrase is linked with stammering lips.

96

poieō (4160)

prassō (4238)

Do
Make
Bring Forth
Work

The distinction between *poieō* and *prassō* has been the frequent subject of scholarly debates[1] that date back as far as Prodicus.[2] Prodicus correctly observed that *poiein* emphasizes the goal of an act and *prassein* the means by which the goal may be attained by removing obstacles. Unlike *poiein*,[3] *prassein*[4] also emphasizes continuity and repetition of action. *Poiein* may refer to doing something once and for all, to producing something that then has an independent existence of its own, as in *poiein paidion* (*3813*, to produce a child) for a woman, *poiein karpous* (*2591*, to produce fruits) for a tree, and *poiein eirēnēn* (*1515*, to make peace).[5] In this last example, *poiein* attains what *prassein* only hopes to attain. Demosthenes used *prattein*[6] and *poiein* together without a tautology. Concerning certain of Philip's hostile designs, Demos-

1. E.g., see the long discussion in Rost and Palm's *Lexicon* under *prassō*.

2. See Plato, *Charmides* 162d.

3. *Poiein* is equivalent to the Latin *facere* (to make) and the German *machen* (to make).

4. *Prassein* is equivalent to the Latin *agere* (to lead) or *gerere* (to carry on), the German *handeln* (to act), and the English *to practice*.

5. *Prassein eirēnēn* means to negotiate with the view to peace. See Pott, *Etymologische Forschungen*, 3:408.

6. *Prattein* is another spelling for *prassein*.

poieō

prassō

thenes assured the Athenians *hoti praxei tauta kai poiēsei*,[7] that is, that he would busy himself with bringing these things about and that he would bring them about.[8] In the words of a German scholar, *prassein* "is the busily engaged activity, while *poiein* is the productive activity."

How far can we trace this distinction in the New Testament? There are two or three passages where it is difficult not to recognize it. For example, the change of words in John 3:20–21 does not appear to be accidental, especially when the same contrast reappears in 5:29. In the first text *phaula* (*5337*) *prassein* is contrasted with *poiein tēn alētheian* (*225*) and in the second with *poiein ta agatha* (*18*), just as in Romans 7:19 we read *poiein agathon* and *prassein kakon* (*2556*). It would be foolish to assert that the *poiein* relates only to good things, since we have *poiein anomian* (*458*; Matt. 13:41), *hamartian* (*266*; 2 Cor. 5:21), and *ta kaka* (Rom. 3:8). Neither is it true that *prassein* is restricted to evil things, since the New Testament contains *prassein agathon* (Rom. 9:11). However, when the words have an ethical connotation, *poiein* often is used in a good sense and *prassein* in an evil one. This is especially true in the case of *praxis* (*4234*), which occurs six times in the New Testament.[9] In all of these instances, except Matthew 16:27, *praxis* has an evil significance that is similar to the English *practices*.[10]

Bengel correctly explained this change of words: "*Prassōn*. Evil is restless; it is something more active than truth. Hence they are designated by different words."[11] Busy activity may accompany the working of evil, but "the wicked works a deceitful work" and has nothing to show for his toil at the end; no fruit remains. Evil is manifold, but good is one. There are many *erga* (*2041*) *tēs sarkos* (*4561*; Gal. 5:22) that not only contradict the good but often one another. Good works are *karpos* (*2590*) *tou pneumatos* (*4151*; Gal. 5:19), for there is an inner consent between all the parts of good, a "consensus of the virtues," as Cicero called it, knitting them into a perfect and harmonious whole and inviting us to view them as one. The former works are of human art and device, the latter of divine nature. Concerning Galatians 5:19ff., Jerome stated: "Paul has placed works in the flesh and fruit in the spirit, because vices come to a conclusion of themselves and perish, while virtues sprout and overflow in fruits." This justifies and explains why on two occasions (John 3:20–21) John exchanged *phaula prassein* for *poiein alētheian* and *poiein ta*

7. *Orationes* 19.373.

8. In the words of Rost and Palm: "Krüger and Franke (Demosthenes, *Olynthiaca* 3.15) too distinguish between *prassein* as the *busily active* doing and *poiein* as the *productive* activity. Nevertheless it may prove to be more adequate to establish the difference as consisting in this, that in the case of *poiein* the concept of the finished product is dominant; in the case of *prassein* it is more the working toward a goal while eliminating adverse hindrances and stressing ways and means." The action in *prassein* is always more or less self-conscious and thus cannot be predicated of animals (Aristotle, *Ethica eudemia* 6.2.2); the *poiein* is more free and spontaneous. Cf. Xenophon, *Cyropaedia* 2.2.30; Aristotle, *Ethica Nicomachea* 6.5.

9. Matt. 16:27; Luke 23:51; Acts 19:18; Rom. 8:13; 12:4; Col. 3:9.

10. Cf. Polybius, 4.8.3 (*praxeis apatai* [*539*], *epiboulai* [*1917*]); 5.96.4.

11. On John 3:20.

agatha, the *practicing* of evil, for the *doing* of good. In conclusion, here are a few excellent words of Bishop Andrewes:

Do
Make
Bring Forth
Work

> There are two kinds of doers: 1. *poiētai* [*4163*], and 2. *praktikoi* [cf. *4233* and *4238*], which the Latin likewise expresseth in 1. *agere* [to lead] and 2. *facere* [to make]. *Agere*, as in music, where, when we have done singing or playing, nothing remaineth: *facere*, as in building, where, after we have done, there is a thing permanent. And *poiētai*, *factores*, they are St. James' doers. But we have both the words in the English tongue: actors, as in a play; factors, as in merchandise. When the play is done, all the actors do vanish: but of the factors' doing, there is a gain, a real thing remaining.[12]

12. On the distinction between *praxis* and *ergon*, see Wyttenbach's note on Plutarch's *Moralia*, 6:601.

97

bōmos (1041) *thysiastērion* (2379) — *Altar*

In dealing with *prophēteuō* (4395) and *manteuomai* (3132) in chapter 6, I noted several instances where the accuracy of the distinction between the sacred and the profane, between true and false religion, was preserved in the group of words that may be used with one of these terms but not with the group of words that may be used with the other term. This same precision is demonstrated in the New Testament use of *thysiastērion*[1] to refer to the altar of the true God and of *bōmos* to refer to a heathen altar.[2]

The New Testament usage of *bōmos* and *thysiastērion* is patterned after the good example of the Septuagint and maintains the distinction drawn there. Indeed, the Septuagint translators were so determined to distinguish the altars of the true God from those where abominable things were offered that they probably invented the word *thysiastērion* for this purpose. In fact, the translators of the Septuagint were more careful to maintain a linguistic distinction between true and false altars than were the Old Testament writers themselves, who used *bāmāh* (1116; Isa. 15:2; Amos 7:9) only to refer to heathen altars and *mizbēḥa* (4196) sometimes to refer to the altar of the true God (Lev. 1:9) and sometimes to heathen altars (Isa. 17:8). Because *thysiastērion*[3]

1. It occurs more than twenty times.

2. *Bōmos* is used only once in the New Testament (Acts 17:23).

3. *Thysiastērion* properly is the neuter of *thysiastērios*, as *hilastērion* (2435; Exod. 25:17; Heb. 9:5) is of *hilastērios*.

never occurs in classical Greek, Philo must have had the Septuagintal use of the word in mind when he implied that Moses invented it.[4] Nevertheless, the Septuagint does not invariably observe the distinction between *bōmos* and *thysiastērion* that is observed in the New Testament.[5] There are three occasions, one in 2 Maccabees (13:8) and two in Ecclesiasticus (50:12, 14), where *bōmos* refers to an altar of the true God[6] and several occasions where *thysiastērion* is used to designate an idol altar (Judg. 2:2; 6:25; 2 Kings 16:10). These instances are rare exceptions, and sometimes the antagonism between the words is brought out with marked emphasis. This is the case in 2 Maccabees 10:2–3, but even more remarkably in 1 Maccabees 1:59, where the historian recounted how the servants of Antiochus offered sacrifices to Olympian Jupiter on an altar that had been built over the altar of the God of Israel.[7] Here the Authorized translators, by force of expediency, translated *bōmos* as "*idol* altar" and *thysiastērion* as "altar." Concerning these same events, Josephus noted: "Having built a *bōmon* on the *thysiastēriō*, he sacrificed swine on it."[8] Even more notable (and marking the strength of their feeling) was the refusal by the Septuagint translators to call the altar of the Transjordanic tribes (Josh. 23) a *thysiastērion*, since it was erected for their own purposes, without the express command of God. Throughout Joshua 23, this altar is referred to as a *bōmos* (vv. 10–11, 16, 19, 23, 26, 34), and the legitimate, divinely ordained altar is called a *thysiastērion* (vv. 19, 28–29). The Hebrew text makes no such distinction but indiscriminately employs *mizbēḥa* to refer to both altars.

I just mentioned one occasion that proved problematic for the Authorized translators. There was no such difficulty in Latin, for at an early date the church adopted *altare* to designate her altar and reserved *ara* exclusively for heathen ones.[9] Cyprian also expressed his surprise at the profane boldness of one of the *turificati*,[10] who afterwards dared, without first obtaining the church's absolution, to continue his ministry "as though it were right, after approaching the *aras* of the devil, to approach the *altare* of God."[11] In secular Latin, *ara* is the genus, and *altare* is the specific kind of altar on which the victims were offered.[12] The distinction between *bōmos* and *thysiastērion*, which first was established in the Septuagint and later was recognized in the New Testament, was maintained in ecclesiastical Greek. In the *thysia* (*2378*) *aineseōs* (sacrifice of praise, Heb. 13:15), the *thysia anamnēseōs* (sacrifice of remembrance), and the *anamnēsis* (*364*) *thysias* (remembrance of sacrifice), the

4. *De vita Mosis* 3.10.

5. I cannot accept Num. 23:1–2 as instances of such a failure, for what altars could be more truly heathen than those reared by Balaam?

6. The Hellenizing tendencies of these two books should be noted.

7. "Sacrificing on *ton bōmon*, which was over *tou thysiastēriou*."

8. *Antiquitates Judaicae* 12.5.4.

9. Thus see the Vulgate at Judg. 6:28; 1 Macc. 1:59; 2 Macc. 10:2–3; Acts 17:23.

10. In time of persecution, these people consented to save their lives by burning incense before a heathen idol.

11. *Epistula* 63.

12. Virgil, *Eclogae* 5.65–66; cf. Tacitus, *Annales* 16.31; and Orelli thereupon.

church has the equivalent of a *thysiastērion*. There is clear testimony to this in the following passage of Chrysostom,[13] where Christ is supposed to be speaking: "So if you desire blood, do not make red the *bōmon* of idols with the slaughter of senseless creatures, but my *thysiastērion* with my blood."[14]

13. *Homilia in 1 Corinthios* 24.

14. Cf. Mede, *Works* (1672), 391; Augusti, *Christliche Archäologie*, 1:412; and Smith, *Dictionary of Christian Antiquities*, under the word *altar*.

98

laos (2992)
ethnos (1484)

dēmos (1218)
ochlos (3793)

People
Nation
Gentiles
Multitude
Crowd

Although *laos* rarely is used in Attic prose, it is used between one and two thousand times in the Septuagint, where it usually is reserved for the elect people, the Israel of God. There are, however, some exceptions. The Philistines are described as a *laos* (Gen. 26:11), as are the Egyptians (Exod. 9:16), the Moabites (Ruth 1:15), and others. Occasionally the plural *hoi laoi* is used as an equivalent for *ta ethnē*.[1] Sometimes *laoi* is used with *ethnē* as an exhaustive way to refer to the whole human race.[2] In all the passages from Revelation, the exhaustive enumeration is fourfold; *phylai* (5443) and *glōssai* (1100) are added to *laoi* and *ethnē*. On one occasion, *phylai* gives way to *basileis* (935; Rev. 10:11) and on another to *ochloi* (Rev. 17:15). The use of *laoi* and *ethnē* to refer to the whole human race in an exhaustive sense may be contrasted with a distributive use of these terms, where *laos* is used in the singular (Luke 2:32; Acts 27:17, 23). In such constructions, the two terms refer to the whole of mankind, *laos* to the chosen people of God only, and *ethnē* to all mankind

1. See Neh. 1:8; 11:30–31; Ps. 97:6; Hos. 10:10; Mic. 6:16.
2. Ps. 108:3; Wisd. of Sol. 3:8; Rev. 5:9; 7:9; 10:11; 11:9; 13:7; 14:6; 17:15.

laos
ethnos

dēmos
ochlos

outside of the covenant,[3] a distinction that generally is true when the terms are used separately. In such cases, *laos* refers to the chosen people, *ethnē*[4] to the rest of mankind.[5] In the singular, *ethnos* has no such restriction but was a name given to the Jews by others, who intended no slight by its use. Thus we read *to ethnos tōn Ioudaiōn* (*2453*; Acts 10:22). Because it was not a dishonorable title, the Jews freely applied *ethnos* to themselves in the phrases *to ethnos hēmōn* (our nation)[6] and *to ethnos touto* (this nation).[7] Sometimes, and with certain additions, *ethnos* is a title of highest honor. Thus the Jews were *ethnos hagion* (*40*, a holy nation)[8] and *ethnos ek mesou ethnōn* (a nation in the midst of Gentiles).[9] If *ethnos* is used with *ethos* (*1485*) to indicate a group of people who live according to one set of customs and rules, then no nation deserves this title more than the Jews. The lives of the citizens of Israel probably were ordered according to more distinctive and rigidly defined customs than those of any other nation in history.

Dēmos is used four times, all in Acts, in the section where Luke described the varied conditions of the heathen world (Acts 12:22; 17:5; 19:30, 33). Each of these passages exemplifies Luke's accurate and precise use of technical terms, which is characteristic of so highly educated a man. The Greek *dēmos* is equivalent to the Latin *populus* (a people), which Cicero defined this way: "*Populus* is not every assembly of people gathered in any manner, but an assembly of a large number uniting together with consent of the law and for mutual benefit."[10] Very often *dēmos* refers to an assembled group of people who are actively exercising their rights as citizens. This idea so dominates *dēmos* that *en tō dēmō* is equivalent to "in a popular assembly," which is the way Luke invariably used *dēmos*. The exact opposite to *dēmos* is *ochlos*, the disorganized or unorganized multitude.[11] In classical Greek, *ochlos* often has a certain tinge of contempt and designates those who share neither in the duties nor the privileges of free citizens. This contempt, however, is not necessarily part of *ochlos*'s meaning (Acts 1:15; Rev. 7:9), and there is no hint of it in Scripture, where a man is held worthy of honor even though the only *politeuma* (*4175*, citizenship) he can claim is that which is eternal in the heavens (Phil. 3:20).

3. Deut. 32:43; 2 Sam. 7:23; Isa. 65:1–2; Acts 15:14.

4. Sometimes *ethnē* is more fully *ta ethnē tou kosmou* "of the world," as in Luke 12:30, or *ta ethnē tēs gēs*, "of the earth" (Ezra 8:89), but always in the plural and with the article.

5. *Hoi kataloipoi* (*2645*) *tōn anthrōpōn* (*444*), Acts 15:17.

6. Luke 7:5; cf. 23:2; John 11:18.

7. Acts 24:2; cf. Exod. 33:13; Deut. 4:6; Wisd. of Sol. 17:2.

8. Exod. 19:6; cf. 1 Pet. 2:9.

9. Clement of Rome, *Epistula 1 ad Corinthios*, par. 29.

10. *De re publica* 1.25; cf. Augustine, *De civitate Dei* 2.21. In German it is *die Gemeinde* (congregation), the free commonality (Plutarch, *Mulierum virtutes* 15, at the conclusion).

11. Matt. 21:8; Luke 9:38; Acts 14:14.

99

baptismos (909) *baptisma* (908)

Washing Baptism

Baptismos and *baptisma* are exclusively ecclesiastical terms, as are *baptistēs* (910) and *baptistērion* (baptismal font). None of these terms are used in the Septuagint or in classical Greek. They occur only in the New Testament and in writings dependent on it. Each of these terms is lineally descended from *baptizein* (907),[1] which rarely occurs in classical Greek,[2] though it is used frequently in later writers such as Plutarch,[3] Lucian,[4] and others.

Before proceeding further, let us examine the relation between words of one family that are distinguished by the endings *-ma* and *-mos*, words like *kērygma* (2782) and *kērygmos*, *diōgma* and *diōgmos* (1375), *dēgma* and *dēgmos*,[5] and many others. Only infrequently are both forms of such pairs found in the New Testament. More frequently, the New Testament writers selected words that end in *-ma* over their counterparts, which end in *-mos*, for example, *apaugasma*[6] but not *apaugasmos*, *sebasma*[7] but not *sebasmos*, *bdelygma*[8] but not

1. *Baptizein* is a later form of *baptein* (911).

2. *Baptein* occurs twice in Plato (*Euthydemus* 277d; *Symposium* 176b) as *bebaptismenos*, which means "well-washed" with wine. Cf. the *uvidus* (drunken) of Horace (*Carmina* 2.19.18).

3. *De superstitione* 3; *Galba* 21.

4. *Bacchus* 7.

5. L-S 384, a bite, a sting.

6. 541; Heb. 1:3.

7. 4574; Acts 8:23.

8. 946; Matt. 24:15.

bdelygmos, *rhēgma*[9] but not *rhēgmos*, *perikatharma*[10] but not *perikatharmos*. Less frequently, the New Testament writers selected words that end in *-mos* over their counterparts, which end in *-ma*, for example, *harpagmos*[11] but not *harpagma*, *apartismos*[12] but not *apartisma*, *katartismos*[13] but not *katartisma*, *hagiasmos*[14] but not *hagiasma*. Sometimes, though rarely, both forms occur, for example, *miasma*[15] and *miasmos*,[16] and this is true of *baptisma* and *baptismos*, the words presently under discussion. Occasionally, though not in the New Testament, there is a third form. For example, *sebasma*, *sebasmos*, and *sebasis*; *apartisma*, *apartismos*, and *apartisis*; *harpagma*, *harpagmos*, and *harpasis*; and in Josephus *baptisma*, *baptismos*, and *baptisis*.[17] It is not difficult to assign each individual form its proper meaning, though in actual use the words deviate from such assignments. For example, words that end with the active termination *-mos* constantly drift into a passive sense, as is the case with *basanismos* (929), *hagiasmos*, and others. Although the converse is not as common, it occurs frequently.[18]

Baptisis is the act of baptism viewed as a baptizing. *Baptismos* is the same act viewed not only as a baptizing but as a completed act, as a baptism. And *baptisma* does not refer to the act at all but to the abiding fact that results from the act, a baptism. *Baptisis* embodies the transitive sense of the verb, *baptismos* the intransitive, and *baptisma* the result of the transitive sense. Therefore the last word is the one best suited to refer to the institution of baptism in the church as an abstract idea, or as an ever-existing fact.[19] This is only an approximation of the usage of *baptismos* in the New Testament, however, since *baptismos* is not used there to refer exclusively to the dignified concept of Christian baptism. In the New Testament, *baptismos* refers to any ceremonial washing or lustration, either ordained by God (Heb. 9:10) or invented by men (Mark 7:4, 8). In neither instance does *baptismos* possess any central significance, though *baptisma* refers to the Christian sense of *baptism*,[20] though not so strictly as to exclude the baptism of John.[21] This distinction between *baptismos* and *baptisma* primarily is preserved in the Greek ecclesiastical writers.[22] Augusti[23] incorrectly affirmed that the Greek fathers habitually used *baptismos* to refer to Christian baptism. It would be difficult to find a single

9. 4485; Luke 6:49.
10. 4027; 1 Cor. 4:13.
11. 725; Phil. 2:6.
12. 535; Luke 14:28.
13. 2677; Eph. 4:12.
14. 38; Rom. 6:19.
15. 3393; 2 Pet. 2:20.
16. 3394; 2 Pet. 2:10.
17. *Antiquitates Judaicae* 18.5.2.
18. Cf. Tholuck, *Dispectio Christi de loco Pauli Epistulae ad Philippenses* 2:6–9, 1848, p. 18.
19. Concerning these passives in *-ma*, see the exhaustive essay on *plērōma* (4138) in Lightfoot, *On the Colossians*, pp. 323–39.
20. Rom. 6:4; Eph. 4:5; 1 Pet. 3:21.
21. Luke 7:29; Acts 10:37; 11:3.
22. Josephus referred to the baptism of John as a *baptismos*, *Antiquitates Judaicae* 18.5.2.
23. *Christliche Archäologie*, 2:313.

example of this in Chrysostom or in any of the great Cappadocian fathers. In the Latin church, *baptismus* and *baptisma* were used to refer to Christian baptism,[24] but this is not the case in ecclesiastical Greek, which remained faithful to the New Testament distinction.

The distinctions between *baptismos* and *baptisma* are maintained so consistently in the New Testament that every explanation of Hebrews 6:2[25] that assumes that Christian baptism is intended breaks down. Additionally, this explanation fails to account for the use of the plural *baptismōn*. If we understand *baptismoi* in this passage in its widest sense as any type of baptism that the Christian has anything to do with—either by rejecting or by making them his own—then a "doctrine of baptisms" would refer to teaching young converts that Christ abolished Jewish ceremonial lustrations, that John's baptism was preparatory and provisional, and that the baptism of Christ is eternally valid. Because all of these acts were washings, they could be included under the one term *baptismoi*, without encroaching on the exclusive use of *baptisma* to refer to the "washing of regeneration," which is the exclusive privilege of the church of Christ.

24. Tertullian used both terms with equal frequency, though *baptismus* predominates in Augustine.
25. *Baptismōn didachēs* (*1322*, of the doctrine of baptisms).

100

skotos (4655) *gnophos* (1105) *zophos* (2217) *achlys* (887)

Darkness *Blackness* *Gloom* *Mist*

Because *skotos* is the most frequently used and most inclusive word of this group, we will not give it much attention. *Skotos* is used often in the New Testament, both in its Attic form of *skotos* and as *skotia* (4653), from the common dialect. *Skotos* is the exact opposite to *phōs* (5457), as the profoundly pathetic words of Ajax in Euripides reveals: "Alas! darkness [*skotos*] is my light [*phaos*]."[1]

Gnophos correctly is regarded as a later Doric form of *dnophos*. *Gnophos* is used only once in the New Testament (Heb. 12:18) with *zophos*, though it is used elsewhere in this same way (Exod. 10:22; Deut. 4:11; Zeph. 1:16). Early English translators apparently felt that *gnophos* included an element of tempest, as the following translations show: "mist" (Wycliffe and Tyndale), "storm" (Cranmer), "blackness" (Geneva and Authorized Version), "whirlwind" (Rheims), and the *turbo* (storm) in the Vulgate. Our ordinary lexicons indicate such a force only slightly or not at all, though it was distinctly recognized by Pott,[2] who gave as explanatory equivalents the German *Finsterniss* (darkness), *Dunkel* (absence of light), and *Wirbelwind* (tornado). Along with

1. Cf. Plato, *Republic* 518a; Job 22:11; Luke 12:3; Acts 26:18.
2. *Etymologische Forschungen*, 5:346.

the best modern scholars, Pott understood *nephos* (3509), *gnophos*, and *zophos* as a group of words that have much in common and that are, perhaps, merely different forms of what once was a single word.[3]

Zophos is used three times in the New Testament (2 Pet. 2:4, 17; Jude 6) or four, if we accept it in Hebrews 12:18 (as it seems we should). *Zophos* is not used in the Septuagint.[4] *Zophos*, which may be seen as a kind of emanation of *skotos*,[5] first refers to the twilight gloom that broods over the regions of the setting sun.[6] And usually in Homer, when *zophos* is used in this sense it occurs with *ēeroeis* (the cloudy). But *zophos* means more than this. There is an even darker darkness—the sunless underworld, the *nigra Tartara* (darkness of Tartarus) of Virgil,[7] the *opaca Tartara* (shaded Tartarus) of Ovid,[8] and the *knephaia Tartarou bathē* (dark depths of Tartarus) of Aeschylus.[9] *Zophos* also can refer to the sunless world itself, though more usually it refers to the gloom that envelops it.[10] In Egyptian mythology, Ahriman was born from the *zophos* just as Ormuzd was born from the light.[11] The appropriateness of the New Testament use of *zophos* is apparent, since it always signifies the darkness of that shadowy land where there is no light but only visible darkness.

Achlys is used only once in the New Testament (Acts 13:11) and never in the Septuagint.[12] Galen defined *achlys* as something that is more dense than *omichlē*[13] and that is less dense than *nephos*. The single New Testament use of *achlys* attests to the accuracy of Luke's choice, as so often is the case in his selection of words, especially medical terms. Luke used *achlys* to refer to the mist of darkness (*achlys kai skotos*) that fell on the sorcerer Elymas as the outward and visible sign of the inward spiritual darkness that was his temporary portion as a punishment for resisting the truth. All the translations of our English Hexapla translate *achlys* by "mist," with the exception of the Rheims, which uses "dimness." The Vulgate correctly translated *achlys* as *caligo* (mist, fog). Although Luke's use of the term in Acts is separated by nearly a thousand years from its use in Homer, the meaning of *achlys* remained unchanged.[14] In the Odyssey, when the poet describes the responsive darkness that comes over the sea when it is overshadowed by a dark cloud, he uses the

3. *Nephos* occurs frequently in the Septuagint, where it is used with *nephelē* (3507; cf. Exod. 34:12; Ps. 97:2; Joel 2:2) and with *thyella* (2366; cf. Deut. 4:11; 5:22).

4. *Zophos* is used in the version of Symmachus in Ps. 11:2.

5. Thus *ho zophos tou skotous* (the blackness of darkness) in Exod. 10:22; Jude 13.

6. This is an especially strong contrast in the Orient, where the sun may be said to be newborn each day.

7. *Aeneis* 6.134.

8. *Metamorphoses* 10.20.

9. *Prometheus vinctus* 1029.

10. Homer, *Hymnus in Cererem* 338; Euripides, *Hippolytus* 1434; cf. Job 10:21–22.

11. Plutarch, *De Iside et Osiride* 46.

12. *Achlys* occurs once in the version of Symmachus (Job 3:5).

13. L-S 1222, mist fog.

14. Words with an ethical significance, not those used to refer to the phenomena of the outward world, are the ones that change with the passage of time.

verb *achlyein*.[15] Homer used *achlys* to refer to the mist that clouds the eyes of the dying[16] or in which the gods (for one cause or another) may envelop their favorites.

15. 12.406. Cf. *inhorruit unda tenebris* [the waves bristled with the darkness], Virgil, *Aeneis* 3.195.

16. *Iliad* 16.344.

101

bebēlos (952)

koinos (2839)

Profane
Defiled
Common
Unclean

Bebēlos suggests[1] a trodden and trampled spot that is open to the casual step of every intruder or careless passer-by, or in the words of Thucydides, a *chōrion* (5564) *bebēlon* (profane place).[2] *Adyton*,[3] a spot fenced and reserved for sacred uses that is not to be approached lightly, is exactly the opposite of *bebēlos*. In the language of the Song of Solomon, an *adyton* is "a garden enclosed, a spring shut up, a fountain sealed" (Song of Sol. 4:12). Perhaps the "profaneness" of a person or thing may be described negatively as the absence of any higher consecration, rather than as the active presence of the unholy or profane. *Bebēlos* often is used with *amyntos*,[4] *anorgiastos*,[5] and as such with *arcendus a sacris*.[6] In a similar way, *artoi* (740) *bebēloi* (1 Sam. 21:4) are simply unconsecrated common loaves as contrasted with the showbread that the high priest had declared holy. The Latin *profanus* refers only to what is left

1. *Bebēlos* is derived from *bēlos* (a threshold).
2. 4.97.
3. L-S 25, a sanctuary.
4. L-S 87, uninitiated; Plutarch, *De defectu oraculorum* 16.
5. L-S 147, not celebrated with orgies.
6. Prevented from sacrifices. Cf. Plato, *Symposium* 218b, where it is used with *agroikos* (L-S 15, rustic, boorish).

bebēlos

koinos

outside of the *temenos* (sacred enclosure), to that which is *pro fano* (in front of the sanctuary) and which thus lacks the consecration of the *temenos* (sanctuary). And in English this is what we mean when we contrast sacred and profane history. The term *profane history* does not imply a positive profaneness but only that such history is not sacred; it is not a history that primarily deals with the kingdom of God and the course of that kingdom. At first this was the way *bebēlos* was used. Only later did *bebēlos* come to be contrasted with *hagios* (40; Ezek. 22:6) and with *hosios* (3741) and to be used with *anosios*,[7] *graōdēs*,[8] and *anomos*.[9] Only this later meaning allowed *bebēloi* to be used within the space of a few lines as a synonym for "defiled hands" (2 Macc. 5:16).

What is the relationship between *bebēlos* and *koinos*? Before bringing *koinos* into such questionable company, let us observe that there are many honorable New Testament uses of *koinos* and its derivatives, such as *koinōnia* (2842) and *koinōnikos* (2843).[10] In secular Greek, Dio Chrysostom characterized Socrates as *koinos kai philanthrōpos* (cf. 5363), one who did not give himself airs or withdraw from friendly conversation with others. *Koinos* also is capable of an even higher application to Christ, for some complained that he ate with publicans and sinners (Matt. 9:10–11). In this noblest sense of the term, Christ was *koinos*. Although this is interesting to note, our primary concern here is with the use of *koinos* and *koinoō* (2840) to refer to sacred things,[11] which is an exclusively Jewish Hellenistic usage. If it were not for two exceptional examples (1 Macc. 1:47, 62), one might claim that this usage was restricted to the New Testament. By comparing Acts 21:28 and 24:6, we have implicit evidence that at the time Acts was written such a use of *koinos* was unfamiliar and probably unknown to the heathen. Paul's Jewish adversaries, when addressing their fellow countrymen, made this charge: "He has defiled [*kekoinōke*] this holy place" (Acts 21:28). But in bringing this same accusation against Paul before Felix, a heathen, Paul's opponents changed their words to "he tried to profane [*bebēlōsai*] the temple" (Acts 24:6). The other language would have been out of place and perhaps even unintelligible.

Also note how in the New Testament *koinos* gradually encroached on *bebēlos*'s original meaning, so that later the two words came to share this meaning. This resulted in *koinos* gradually assuming the larger share and being used more often.[12] It is not difficult to see how *bebēlos* gradually was pushed aside after the Septuagint was written. The Jews favored *koinos*, which replaced *bebēlos*, because the former word, by virtue of its contrast with *eklogē* (1589, selection) depicted the Jewish people as a "special people" who had no fellowship with anything unclean. Since *koinos* indicated less defilement than *bebēlos*, it brought out more strongly Israel's separation from anything common. That which was ceremonially unclean more and more broke down the barrier that separated it from that which was morally unclean, thus doing away with any distinction between them.

7. 462; 1 Tim. 1:9.
8. 1126; 1 Tim. 4:7.
9. 459; Ezek. 2:25.
10. Jude 3; 2 Cor. 13:13; 1 Tim. 6:18.
11. As equivalent to *bebēlos* and *bebēloō* (953).
12. Matt. 7:2; Acts 10:14; Rom. 14:14; Heb. 10:29.

102

mochthos (3449) *ponos* (4192) *kopos* (2873)

Labor *Toil* *Travail* *Weariness*

Mochthos is used only three times in the New Testament and in each instance is closely related to *kopos* (2 Cor. 11:27; 1 Thess. 2:9; 2 Thess. 3:8). Etymologically, *mochthos* is closely related to *mogis* (3425), which Curtius suggests is a dative plural, *mogois*, that has dropped a letter and subsided into an adverb. *Mochthos*[1] is an everyday word for the type of labor that in one form or another is the lot of all of the sinful children of Adam. Some have suggested that the infinitely laborious character of labor (the varying degrees of distress that are inextricably and inescapably part of it) is not emphasized in *mochthos* to the same degree as in the other words of this group[2] and that this constitutes the difference between *mochthos* and these words. But this is hardly the case. Phrases like *polymochthos Arēs* (much-suffering Ares)[3] and numerous others do not bear this out.

Three of the four times *ponos* is used in the New Testament are in Revelation (16:10–11; 21:4). The other is in Colossians (4:13), where *ponos* is the

1. *Mochthos* does not occur in Homer or Plato.
2. This is especially the case in *ponos*.
3. Euripides, *Phoenissae* 791.

mochthos
ponos

kopos

best reading, though there are four other readings.[4] *Ponos* refers to labor that demands the greatest exertion if one is to accomplish a task. In Homer, war is always regarded as the *ponos*, not only of mortal warriors but also of immortal ones, even of Ares himself. Theognis refers to it as the *ponos andrōn* (toil of men).[5] *Ponos* is used with *dēris*[6] and *polemos*.[7] *Ponoi* is the usual word for the labors of Hercules. Less frequently they also are referred to as *mochthoi*.[8] Plato used *ponos* with *agōn eschatos*,[9] *nosos*,[10] *kindynos*,[11] and *zēmia*.[12] In the Septuagint, *ponos* is used with *odynē*,[13] *mastix*,[14] and *plēgē*.[15] The cruel bondage of the children of Israel in Egypt is their *ponos* (Exod. 2:11). Because of this meaning it is not surprising that *ponos* is expressly named as having no place in the heavenly city (Rev. 21:4).

Kopos, which occurs some twenty times in the New Testament, is the most frequently used of these three terms. *Kopos* does not refer so much to a person's actual exertion as to the lassitude or weariness[16] that results from extreme straining. *Kopos* and the verb *kopiō* (*2872*) frequently are used to designate what are (or what ought to be) the labors of the Christian ministry. When used in this way, *kopos* contains a word of warning for all who are so engaged.[17]

In conclusion, "labor," "toil" (or perhaps "travail"), and "weariness," respectively, are the three best English translations of *mochthos*, *ponos*, and *kopos*.

4. *Pothos* (L-S 1427, longing, yearning), *kopos*, *zēlos* (*2205*), and *agōn* (*73*).
5. 985.
6. L-S 388, battle; *Iliad* 17.158.
7. *4171*; *Iliad* 17.718.
8. Sophocles, *Trachiniae* 1080, 1150.
9. *2078*; *Phaedrus* 247b.
10. *3554*; *Phaedrus* 244d.
11. *2794*; *Alcibiades* 2.142b.
12. *2209*; *Republic* 365b.
13. *3601*; 1 Kings 15:23.
14. *3148*; Jer. 6:7.
15. *4127*; 2 Chron. 9:28.
16. See Pott, *Etymologische Forschungen*, 5:80.
17. John 4:38; Acts 20:35; 2 Cor. 6:5; Col. 1:29; 1 Thess. 3:5; and often.

103

amōmos (299) — *Without Blemish*, *Without Spot*, *Faultless*

amemptos (273) — *Blameless*

anenklētos (410)

anepilēptos (423) — *Unreprovable*, *Irreproachable*

Amōmos, *amemptos*, *anenklētos*, and *anepilēptos* all refer to the Christian life and to what its character should be. Words that refer individually to the absence of blemish and blame are easily confused and their distinctiveness lost, though this is not to say that a word that has one of these meanings easily acquires another. For example, the King James Version's translation of *amōmos* illustrates the frequently noted shortcoming of that version. The translators of the Authorized Version failed to translate each Greek word by a fixed and corresponding English word. Although it is true that this cannot always be done, why, in this case, did the translators use six different translations for the six different occurrences of *amōmos*? In Ephesians 1:4, *amōmos* is translated "without blame." In Colossians 1:22, *amōmos* is translated "unblamable." In Ephesians 5:27, *amōmos* is translated "without blemish." In Hebrews 9:14, *amōmos* is translated "without spot." In Jude 24, *amōmos* is translated "faultless." And in Revelation 14:15, *amōmos* is translated "with-

amōmos

amemptos
anenklētos
anepilēptos

out fault." In the first two instances, the Authorized translators failed to grasp *amōmos*'s exact force. No such criticism may be made of the other four translations, since each one is sufficiently accurate, though one may be better than another. It is inaccurate, however, to translate *amōmos* "without blame" or "unblamable," since in later Hellenistic Greek the meaning of *mōmos* (3470) changed from "blame" to that which is the subject of blame—a blot, spot, or blemish. In the same way, *amōmos*[1] became the technical term for the absence of anything amiss in a sacrifice, anything that would render it unworthy to be offered[2] or that would make the sacrificing priest unworthy to offer it (1 Macc. 4:42).

When *amōmos* is used with *aspilos* (784) in 1 Peter 1:19, *amōmos* refers to the absence of internal blemish, and *aspilos* refers to the lack of external spot. In the Septuagint, *amōmos* is used as an ethical term and consistently refers to the holy behavior of the faithful (Ps. 119:1; Prov. 11:5) and, on occasion, is even applied as a title of honor to God himself (Ps. 18:30). In the Apocrypha, *amōmos* is used with *hosios*[3] and in the New Testament with *anenklētos*[4] and *hagios*.[5] *Amōmos* depicts the complete absence of fault or blemish in whatever it describes.

If *amōmos* is the "unblemished," *amemptos* is the "unblamed." There is a difference between the two terms. Christ was *amōmos* because there was no spot or blemish in him. Thus he could ask: "Which of you convicts Me of sin?" (John 8:46). But strictly speaking, Christ was not *amemptos*, nor is this term ever applied to him in the New Testament, since he endured the persecution of sinners who slandered him and made false charges against him. No matter how the saints of God may strive to be *amemptoi*, they certainly cannot attain it, for justly or unjustly, others will find fault in them. The *amōmos* may be *amemptos*,[6] but he does not always prove so.[7] There is always a tendency to regard the *inculpatus* (blameless) as the *inculpabilis* (unblamable), so that in actual usage a breakdown occurs in the distinct and separate use of these words. The Old Testament uses of *amemptos* (as in Job 11:4) sufficiently prove this.

Like *anepilēptos*, the New Testament uses of *anenklētos* are exclusively Pauline.[8] The Authorized Version translates *anepilēptos* as "unreprovable" (Col. 1:22) and "blameless" (1 Cor. 1:8; 1 Tim. 3:10; Titus 1:6–7). Chrysostom correctly noted that *anepilēptos* implies not only acquittal but also the absence of any charge or accusation against the person under consideration. Like *amōmos*, *anepilēptos* does not refer to the subjective thoughts and estimates of

1. *Amōmos* is a rare word in classical Greek, though it is found in Herodotus (2.177) and Aeschylus (*Persae* 185).

2. Exod. 29:2; Num. 6:14; Ezek. 43:22; Philo, *De sacrificiis Abelis et Caini* 2.

3. *3741*; Wisd. of Sol. 10:15.

4. Col. 1:22.

5. 40; Eph. 1:4; 5:27.

6. Cf. Luke 1:6; Phil. 2:15.

7. 1 Pet. 2:12, 15.

8. *Anenklētos* is used five times in the Pauline epistles.

men but to the objective world of facts. Plutarch[9] accurately used *anepilēptos* with *aloidorētos*.[10] In 1 Timothy 3:10 there is an obvious allusion to a custom that still survives in our ordinations. At the opening of the ceremony, the ordaining bishop demands whether the faithful who are present know of any notable crime or charge against those who are being presented to him for holy ordination that would disqualify them. In other words, the ordaining bishop demands to know whether those who are to be ordained are *anenklētoi*, not merely unaccusable but unaccused, not merely free from any just charge[11] but free from any charge at all. The intention of this question is that if anyone present has such a charge to bring, the ordination would not go forward until this matter had been duly decided (1 Tim. 3:10).

Anepilēptos rarely is used in classical Greek[12] and never is used in the Septuagint or the Apocrypha. *Anepilēptos* is used with *katharos*,[13] *anenklētos*,[14] *teleios*,[15] and *adiablētos*.[16] The Authorized Version twice translates it as "blameless" (1 Tim. 3:2; 5:7) and once as "irreprovable" (6:14).[17] "Irreprehensible"[18] would be a more accurate translation, since it rests on the same image as the Greek—affording nothing that an adversary could use as the basis for an accusation.[19] And "unreprehended," if such a word would pass, would be an even more accurate translation.

Without Blemish
Without Spot
Faultless
Blameless

Unreprovable
Irreproachable

9. *De capienda ex inimicis utilitate* 5.
10. L-S 72, irreproachable, unreviled.
11. That question is reserved, if need be, for later investigation.
12. It is found once in Thucydides (5.17) and once in Plato (*Philebus* 43c).
13. *2513*; Lucian, *Revivescentes sive piscator* 1.8.
14. Ibid., 46.
15. *5046*; Plutarch, *Septem sapientium convivium* 9.
16. L-S 21, not listening to calumny; Plutarch, *Pericles*, cf. *De liberis educandis* 7.
17. These are its only three New Testament occurrences.
18. "Irreprehensible" is not used in the Authorized Version but is older than this version. On one occasion (1 Tim. 3:2), "irreprehensible" is used by the Rhemish Version, which derived it from the *irreprehensibilis* of the Vulgate.
19. Cf. the Scholiast on Thucydides: "not furnishing an opportunity for an accusation."

104

bradys (1021) — *Slow*
nōthros (3576) — *Sluggish*
Dull
argos (692) — *Idle*

It may be instructive to repeat Schmidt's carefully expressed conclusions about *bradys*, *nōthros*, and *argos*. According to Schmidt, *bradys* is best translated by the German *langsam* (slow), and *tachys* (5036), *ōkys*,[1] or *anchinous*[2] are its antonyms. Schmidt translated *nōthros* by the German *träge* (indolent), and understood its proper antonym as *oxys* (*3691*). Additionally, Schmidt made a moral identification between *argos* and the German *faul* (lazy) or *unthätig* (inactive) and understood *energos* (cf. *1756*) as its proper antonym.

Because *bradys* does not necessarily imply moral fault or blame, it differs from *nōthros* and *argos*. Indeed, two of the three New Testament uses of *bradys* are honorable ones. To be "slow" to evil things, rash speaking, or anger (James 1:19, twice) is a virtue. Elsewhere *bradys* also is honorably used, as when Isocrates[3] advises us to be "slow" in planning and swift in performing. Thucydides did not discredit the Spartans by describing them as slow to act

1. L-S 2032, swift; Homer, *Odyssey* 8.329.
2. L-S 17, ready of wit.
3. 1.34.

bradys
nōthros

argos

(*bradytēs*, *1022*) and the Athenians as swift. Instead, Thucydides was drawing attention to the most striking and excellent qualities of each group.[4]

Nōthros is used only twice in the New Testament, both times in Hebrews (5:11; 6:12). The etymology of *nōthros* is uncertain. Formerly, it was derived from *nē* (*3513*) and *ōthein*,[5] but this derivation no longer is favored. *Nōthros* is used in good Attic Greek, such as that of Plato,[6] where the form *nōthēs* was preferred during the language's classical period. *Nōthros* did not come into common use until the time of Koine Greek, and is used only once in the Septuagint (Prov. 22:29)[7] and twice in the Apocrypha (Ecclus. 4:34; 11:13).[8]

Nōthros refers to a deeper and more inborn sluggishness (bound up in a person's very life) than do *bradys* or *argos*. The *bradys* of today might become the *ōkys*[9] of tomorrow. The *argos* might grow to *energos* (cf. *1756*), but the very constitution of the *nōthros* makes him unfit for activities of the mind or spirit. He is *nōthros en tais epinoiais* (*1963*), "sluggish in his thoughts."[10] Dionysius of Halicarnassus used *nōthros* with *anaisthētos*,[11] *akinētos*,[12] and *apathēs*.[13] Hippocrates[14] used *nōthros* with *barys* (*926*), and Plutarch[15] used it with *dyskinētos*.[16] *Dyskinētos* clearly expresses what is only suggested by the other words—a certain awkwardness and unwieldiness of gait and demeanor, which portrays to the outer world a slowness and inaptitude for mental activities. The second use of *nōthros* (Heb. 6:12) is correctly translated in the Vulgate as *segnis* (sluggish). "Sluggish," rather than the Authorized Version's "slothful," would be a better translation for *nōthros* in this verse. Delitzsch[17] defined *nōthros* as "difficult to set in motion, sluggish, indolent, dull, feeble, idle." Pollux understood *nōthreia*[18] as a synonym for *amblytēs*.[19] In its earlier form, *nōthreia* was a common word for the ass.[20]

Argos[21] is used to refer to persons (Titus 1:12; 2 Pet. 1:8) and to things (Matt. 12:36; 20:3, 6). In 2 Peter 1:8, *argos* is used with *akarpos* (*175*) and translated "barren," which is not a very good translation. "Idle" would be a better translation, since "barren and unfruitful" constitute a tautology that

4. 8.96.
5. L-S 2031, to thrust, to push.
6. *Theaetetus* 144b.
7. *Nōthrokardios* (of a perverse heart) also occurs once (Prov. 12:8).
8. In Ecclus. 4:34 *nōthros* and "relaxed in deeds" (*pareimenos en tois ergois*) are instructively juxtaposed.
9. L-S 2032, swift.
10. Polybius, 4.8.5.
11. L-S 106, without sense or feeling.
12. L-S 50, unmoved, sluggish.
13. L-S 174, without feeling.
14. As cited by Schmidt.
15. *De defectu oraculorum*.
16. L-S 457, hard to move.
17. On Heb. 5:11.
18. L-S 1186, sluggishness, indolence.
19. L-S 79, dullness, sluggishness.
20. Homer, *Iliad* 2.559.
21. It is equivalent to *aergos*.

should be eliminated. Plato used *argos* with *amelēs*[22] and *deilos*.[23] Plutarch used *argos* with *akarpos* (as Peter already had).[24] Demosthenes used the verb *argein* (691) with *scholazein* (4980) and *aporein* (639). Xenophon[25] contrasts *argos* with *energos* (cf. *1756*), and Sophocles[26] contrasted it with *ergatis* (cf. *2040*).

"Slow" (or "tardy"), "sluggish," and "idle," respectively, represent *bradys*, *nōthros*, and *argos*.

22. Cf. *272*; *Republic* 421d.
23. *1169*; *Leges* 10.903.
24. *Publicola* 8.
25. *Cyropaedia* 3.2.19.
26. *Philoctetes* 97.

105

dēmiourgos (1217) *technitēs* (5079)

Maker *Builder* *Craftsman*

"Builder and maker" cannot be regarded as a very satisfactory translation of the *technitēs kai dēmiourgos* of Hebrews 11:10, since "maker" says little more than "builder." These translations were introduced by Tyndale and have been retained in all subsequent Protestant translations. Wycliffe used "craftyman and maker," and the Rheims Version used "artificer and builder." According to Delitzsch, God as *technitēs* laid out the scheme and blueprint of the heavenly city, and as *dēmiourgos* he embodies the divine idea or thought in actual form and shape. This distinction is the same as that made in the Vulgate[1] and in modern times by Meyer[2] Although this understanding has the advantage of naming first what *is* first[3]—the divine intention precedes the divine realization—unfortunately it assigns a meaning to *technitēs* that is difficult, if not impossible, to find examples of. It is not unworthy of God to conceive of him as the drawer of the ground plan of the heavenly city, and in the Epistle to the Hebrews[4] we might expect to find such a reference. No

1. *Artifex et conditor*, "craftsman and builder."
2. *Baukünstler und Werkmeister*, "architect and construction superintendent."
3. So far as a first and last exist in the order of the work of God.
4. With its relation to Philo and through him to Plato.

other New Testament[5] or Septuagintal[6] use of *technitēs* even hints at such a meaning. This is also true of the use of *technitēs* in nonbiblical Greek. Although I believe that *dēmiourgos* and *technitēs* may and should be distinguished, I am unable to accept the preceding distinction.

Dēmiourgos is one of those grand and (for rhetorical purposes) finely selected terms that constitute one of the remarkable and unique features of the Epistle to the Hebrews and that make it so stylistically different from the other epistles. In addition to its single occurrence in Hebrews 11:10, *dēmiourgos* is used once in the Apocrypha (2 Macc. 4:1) and not at all in the Septuagint. Initially, the proper meaning of *dēmiourgos* was "one whose works stand forth to the public gaze." Later, the public character of the works was dropped and "maker" or "author," on more or less a grand scale, is all that remained. *Dēmiourgos* is a favorite word of Plato, and he used it in different ways. Thus rhetoric is the *dēmiourgos* of persuasion.[7] By virtue of its presence or absence, the sun is the *dēmiourgos* of day or night.[8] God is the *dēmiourgos* of mortal men.[9] There is no hint in Scripture that *dēmiourgos* was adopted into the theosophical or philosophical speculations of the age, nor is there any foreboding of the prominent part this word would play in coming struggles, though some of these were close at hand.

If God as the *dēmiourgos* is recognized as the maker of all things,[10] *technitēs*, which often is used with *dēmiourgos*,[11] brings out the additional idea of the artistic side of creation. This justifies Cicero's reference to God as "artificer of the universe," one who molds and fashions in many marvelous ways the materials that by a prior act of his will[12] he called into existence. If *dēmiourgos* emphasizes the *power* of the divine Creator, then *technitēs* expresses his manifold *wisdom*, the infinite variety and beauty of his handiwork. "How manifold are Your works; in wisdom have You made them all!" All the beauty of God's world proclaims him as its Author, as the "Creator of its beauty," as a writer in the Apocrypha[13] called him. Bleek[14] was nearer the mark when he wrote: "*Technitēs* here likewise denotes the Creator but with reference to the artistic in the production of his work." He also quoted Wisdom of Solomon 13:3: "Although informed previously by his works, they did not come to know the Artificer [*technitēn*]." There is a certain difficulty in reversing the order of the words as they appear in Hebrews 11:10, that is, having *dēmiourgos* precede *technitēs*. This change in order, however, is not as great a problem as retaining the order and allowing it to dominate our interpretation.[15]

5. There are three uses of *technitēs* in the New Testament: Acts 19:24, 38; Rev. 18:22.

6. *Technitēs* is used in the Septuagint and Apocrypha thirteen times.

7. *Gorgias* 453a.

8. *Timaeus* 40a.

9. Cf. Josephus, *Antiquitates Judaicae* 1.7.1.

10. He is called *patēr* (3962) *kai poiētēs* (4163) by Plutarch (*De facie in orbe lunae* 13) and *patēr kai dēmiourgos* by Clement of Rome.

11. Thus Lucian, *Hippias* 8; Philo, *Legum allegoriarum libri* 3.32.

12. That is, prior in our conception of it.

13. I will quote further from him.

14. On Heb. 11:10.

15. It appears to me that Delitzsch has done this.

106

asteios (791) — *Fair*, *Beautiful*, *Proper*

hōraios (5611), *kalos (2570)* — *Beautiful*

Asteios is used twice in the New Testament (Acts 7:20; Heb. 11:23), and on both occasions it is applied to Moses. This use is derived from Exodus 2:2, where the Septuagint uses *asteios* as equivalent to the Hebrew *ṭôb*.[1] In Acts 7:20, *tō theō* (*2316*) is added to *asteios*, which has perplexed interpreters, as the many different translations of this verse show: *gratus Deo*, "pleasing to God" (Vulgate); "loved of God" (Wycliffe); "a proper child in the sight of God" (Tyndale); "acceptable unto God" (Cranmer, Geneva, and Rheims); and "exceeding fair" (Authorized Version). The Authorized Version's translation is probably the most accurate, since it understands *tō theō* as a heightening of the high quality it extols. For a similar idiom, note Jonah 3:3: *polis* (*4172*) *megalē tō theō*, which may be translated "an exceedingly great city." In Hebrews 11:23, many English versions translate *asteios* as "a proper child." It would not be easy to improve upon this, though "proper" here is a little out of date.

1. 2896; cf. Philo, *De vita Mosis* 1.3.

asteios

hōraios

kalos

Asty,[2] the base of *asteios*, indicates *asteios*'s starting point and explains its successive changes. First of all, one who has been born and bred (or at least reared) in the city and who therefore is urban is *asteios*. The one who is urban also may be assumed to be urbane, and this testifies to the gracious civilizing influences of the people whose contact he has enjoyed. Thus *asteios* has a certain ethical tinge that is real, though perhaps not very profound. Such a person is implicitly contrasted with the *agroikos*,[3] the churl, the boor, and the "hay-seed." In an instructive passage in Xenophon,[4] the *asteioi* are described as *eucharites*,[5] as obliging and gracious, according to the humbler uses of that word. Assuming that the higher culture that city-bred persons enjoy is manifested in their appearance, which is molded by humanizing influences, *asteios* came to be understood as fair and comely, as suggesting beauty, though not generally of a higher character. Plutarch[6] contrasted the *asteios* and the *aischros* (*150*) or positively ugly. Judith is *asteia* (Jth. 9:23).[7]

Hōraios is used frequently in the Septuagint, where it represents a large variety of Hebrew words. In the New Testament, *hōraios* is only used four times.[8] The steps by which it came to mean "the beautiful" in all of these passages are few and easy to trace. In this world everything that is subject to the laws of growth and decay has its "hour," or *hōra* (*5610*), that period when it attains its greatest grace or beauty. This *hōra*, or turning point of its existence and the time when it is at its loveliest and best, produces *hōraios*, which first referred to that which is timely. In Xenophon, *hōraios thanatos* (*2288*) is timely death because it is honorable. Next, *hōraios* came to refer to the beautiful.[9]

Asteios and *hōraios* came to mean the same thing, so that "fair" or "proper" or "beautiful" are appropriate translations of either word. But *asteios* and *hōraios* arrived at these same meanings by different paths, which began from different images. One word belongs to the realm of art, the other to the realm of nature. *Asteios* indicates neatness, symmetry, and elegance, and thus beauty. It generally refers to something small, even when proposed for our admiration. Aristotle admitted that small persons (*hoi mikroi*, *3398*) may be *asteioi* and *symmetroi*,[10] or "dapper and well-shaped," but he refused to call them *kaloi*. *Hōraios* is different. Although all things that belong to the passing world eventually perish, along with their grace, they still have their "hour," however brief, that season of their highest perfection. This last concept is part of *hōraios*.

Although the higher moral aspects and uses of *kalos* are interesting to note, especially the way the term can be used to refer to beauty and to goodness, we will not deal with this aspect of the word. Only when *kalos* refers to physical

2. L-S 263, town.
3. L-S 15, dwelling in the fields.
4. *Cyropaedia* 2.2.12.
5. L-S 738, charming, gracious.
6. *De genio Socratis* 584c.
7. Cf. *euprosōpos*, L-S 728, fair of face, which is applied to Sarah in Gen. 12:11.
8. Matt. 23:27; Acts 3:2, 10; Rom. 10:15.
9. "Standing in full development and bloom" (Schmidt).
10. L-S 1679, in due proportion.

aspects of beauty can it be compared with *hōraios*. Initially, *kalos*[11] referred to beauty, especially from the Greek viewpoint of that which is harmonious and complete, of something in which all the parts are balanced and proportionate. Basil the Great did an excellent job of distinguishing *kalos* and *hōraios*:

Fair
Beautiful
Proper

Beautiful

> *To hōraion* differs from *to kalon*; that which is developed at the suitable time to its fitting prime is called *hōraion*, as the fruit of the vine, which has fulfilled its own mission toward its fruition through the season of the year and is ready for enjoyment; *kalon* is that which is harmonious in the composition of its parts, possessing a grace blooming in it.[12]

11. It is affirmed to be of the same descent as the German *heil* (intact) and as the English *whole* (Curtius, *Grundzüge*, 130).

12. *Homilia in Psalmum* 45. Cf. Plato, *Timaeus* 365; *Republic* 10.601b; and Stallbaum's note.

Appendix

Some Synonyms Not Discussed

Useless, Worthless
achrēstos, achreios

Ignorance
agnoia, agnōsia

Eternal
aidios, aiōnios

Lamb, Sheep
amnos, arnion

Reminder, Remembrance
anamnēsis, hypomnēsis

Rest
anapausis, katapausis

Without
aneu, chōris

Folly, Foolishness
anoia, aphrosynē, mōria

Enemy, Hostile, Adversary
antidikos, echthros, hypenantios

Disobedient, Unbelieving
apeithēs, apistos

Weakness, Illness, Disease, Plague
astheneia, nosos, malakia, mastix

Weak, Ill
asthenēs, arrōstos

Weight, Burden, Millstone
baros, phortion, onkos

Establish, Fix Firmly, Found, Support
bebaioō, rhizoomai, themelioō, stērizō

Will, Wish
boulomai, thelō

Infant, Small Child
brephos, paidion

Joy, Exultation, Gladness
chara, agalliasis, euphrosynē

Devil, Demon, Accuser
diabolos, daimōn, daimonion, katēgōr

Teach, Admonish, Instruct
didaskō, noutheteō, sōphronizō

Righteous Deed, Justification, Righteousness
dikaiōma, dikaiōsis, dikaiosynē

Glory, Honor, Praiseworthy
doxa, timē, epainos

Mercy, Pity
eleos, oiktirmos

Hope, Expectation
elpis, apokaradokia

Hope, Faith
elpis, pistis

Commandment, Teaching
entalma, didaskalia

Thought, Insight, Reasoning
enthymēsis, ennoia, dialogismos

Commandment
entolē, dogma, parangelia

Steward, Manager
epitropos, oikonomos

Come
erchomai, hēkō

Quiet
ēremos, hēsychios

Strife, Contention
eris, eritheia

Praise, Give Thanks
eulogeō, eucharisteō

Generous, Liberal
eumetadotos, koinōnikos

Authority, Power, Might, Strength, Violence, Working
exousia, dynamis, kratos, ischys, bia, energeia

Treasury, Treasure Box, Storehouse
gaza, thēsauros, apothēkē

Know
ginōskō, oida, epistamai

Tongue, Language
glōssa, dialektos

Hades, Hell, Tartarus, Prison
hadēs, geenna, tartaros, phylakē

Holiness
hagiasmos, hagiotēs, hagiōsynē

Steadfast
hedraios, eumetakinētos

See, Look at, Behold, Perceive, Appear
horaō, blepō, theaomai, theōreō, hoptomai

Rain, Thunderstorm
huetos, ombros

Son of God, Servant of God
hyois theou, pais theou

Sow, Swine
hys, choiros

Heal
iaomai, therapeuō

Call, Name
kaleō, onomazō

Good
kalos, agathos

Condemn
kataginōskō, katakrinō

Restore, Complete
katartizō, teleioō

Tossed Back and Forth, Carried About, Troubled
klydōnizomai, peripherō, tarassō

Hair
komē, thrix

Labor, Strive
kopiaō, agōnizomai

Cry Out
krazō, kraugazō, boaō, anaboaō

Meat, Flesh
kreas, sarx

Property, Possessions
ktēmata, hyparxis

Craftiness, Scheming, Trickery
kybeia, methodeia, panourgia

Word
logos, rhēma

Revile, Blaspheme
loidoreō, blasphēmeō

Sorrow, Pain, Birthpain
lypē, odynē, ōdin

Redeemer, Savior
lytrōtēs, sōtēr

Sword
machaira, rhomphaia

Patience, Gentleness
makrothymia, praotēs

Partner, Companion
metochos, koinōnos

Roar
mykaomai, ōryomai

Cloud
nephos, nephelē

Lawyer, Teacher of the Law, Scribe
nomikos, nomodidaskalos, grammateus

Destruction
olethros, apōleia

Reproach, Revile, Find Fault, Curse
oneidizō, loidoreō, memphomai, kakologeō

Owe, It Is Necessary
opheilō, dei

Eye
ophthalmos, omma

Encouragement
parēgoria, paramythia, paraklēsis

Proverb, Parable
paroimia, parabolē

Send
pempō, apostellō

Dusky, Slime
pēlos, borboros

Tribute, Taxes
phoros, telos

Well, Fountain
phrear, pēgē

Be Careful, Be Anxious
phrontizō, merimnaō

Deceive
planaō, apataō, paralogizomai

Spirit, Mind
pneuma, nous

River, Brook
potamos, cheimarros

Gentle, Quiet
praus, hēsychios

Old Man
presbytēs, gerōn

Offering, Sacrifice, Gift
prosphora, thysia, dōron

Firstborn, Only Begotten
prōtotokos, monogenēs

Tale-bearer, Slanderer
psithyristēs, katalalos

Terror, Fear, Astonishment
ptoēsis, thambos, ekstasis

Split, Sect
schisma, airesis

Silent
sigaō, siōpaō

Crooked
skolios, diestrammenos

Basket
spyris, kophinos

Mark, Bruise, Blow
stigma, mōlōps, plēgē

Help
syllambanō, boētheō

Sympathize, Have Compassion
sympatheō, metriopatheō

Trouble, Stir Up
tarassō, tyrbazō

Guard
tēreō, phylassō, phroureō

Foundation, Steadfast
tethemeliōmenos, hedraios

Mortal, Dead
thnētos, nekros

Eat
trōgō, phagomai, esthiō

Type, Allegory
typos, allēgoroumenon

Type, Example, Pattern, Model
typos, hypodeigma, hypogrammos, hypotypōsis

Stranger, Foreigner, Sojourner
xenos, paroikos, parepidēmos

Tree, Cross
xylon, stauros

Index of English Concepts

Index of Greek Terms